132 DAYS

A JOURNEY
A JOURNAL AND SOME WHISKEY

132 DAYS
A JOURNEY
A JOURNAL AND SOME WHISKEY

Mike Krabal

ISBN-10: 0-615-89225-6
ISBN-13: 978-0-615-89225-2

Thank You

To everyone who supported my journey from home or from the road. To all the new friends made along the way. You all played an unforgettable part in making the adventure worthwhile. You are all family to me.

One of the gladdest moments of human life, me thinks, is the departure upon a distant journey into unknown lands. Shaking off with one mighty effort the fetters of habit, the leaden weight of routine, the cloak of many cares and the slavery of home, man feels once more happy.

Richard Burton

Contents

Travel

By nature, we humans are explorers. We are willing to go to great lengths to fulfill our curiosity and burning desire for adventure. From the ancient times, stories of travel and discovery fascinated us, from legends of Greek Argonauts to the stories of American frontiersmen to the videos and blogs of brave men and women exploring uncharted territories in our day and age. Not all the stories worth telling were recorded and passed down through generations. Thankfully, with the technology available today, more of them can be shared to entertain, enlighten, and inspire others.

Discovery of resources, which have driven many previous generations of explorers, may not be the main objective anymore, but there are still myriads of reasons people decide to take on adventure travel. Some do it to strengthen their belief in themselves, some want to prove something to the world, some want to expand their horizons by experiencing new places, and for some, it is an inner urge that they themselves have trouble rationalizing. Travel has the power to change us in ways that no book, no movie, and no wise man's advice could. Some things can only be learned by living through an experience. Life on the open road can provide more life-changing experiences in a week than a year of living life under the status quo. And no road is more open than the one traveled by motorcycle.

The motorcycle is an ultimate form of overland travel for the most daring of modern time's vagabonds. It is an exhilarating, audacious, and sometimes dangerous, open-air experience that no other mode of travel can compare to. It is a liberating experience that tests our self-reliance as we leave our material possessions behind and travel in minimal comfort, relying only on our wit, the occasional help from strangers, and a great deal of good luck.

America is a great country: vast, beautiful, and diverse. Because of its size, many of us don't take a chance to see the whole thing, preferring to search for pockets of hidden beauty nearby the place we call home. But some intrepid souls want to see everything—tread every road, explore every nook and cranny of this country, and then the rest of our wonderful planet. For them, the sky's the limit. The smaller the realm they grew up in, the stronger seems to be the urge to explore. There must be a reason why twenty-four of the US astronauts hailed from Ohio.

Explorers are strong personalities. It takes heart to leave behind the comfort of home and the warmth of the family circle, taking along only a few luggage bags worth of gear and a life's worth of good memories. However, even these tough characters are not impervious to change, and so they sooner or later give in, only to be remolded and reshaped by the beast that is the open road.

This is a story of one strong personality from West Virginia who abandoned his most prized possessions and set out to see this great country of ours in the most exhilarating way possible, taking us along with him for this wonderful humor-filled adventure, first through his blog and now through this book. If it inspires another generation of explorers to leave their safe harbor and head for the great unknown, the great chain of adventure tales will continue. By the time you finish reading this book, you may find yourself searching the local classifieds for a reliable motorcycle with a set of panniers.

Igor Scherbakov

Live in the sunshine, swim the sea, drink the wild air.

Ralph Waldo Emerson

Part 1

I'm six or seven years old and tugging and twisting at the end of an old walnut tree branch. I'm a narrow-shouldered, scrawny, little boy, and as weak as the blades of grass that I'm standing on. My strawberry blonde hair shines in the bright day, and my dark blue eyes hunt for a thin branch that looks brittle and unintimidating. My freckles, well they really don't do anything except break up the red in my flushed face. A hundred yards away, the Shenandoah River flows peacefully in its own timeless world, tirelessly hauling water to the ocean, tirelessly whittling at its muddy banks. I loved that river, and it had been the only background that I'd known, but today it was that last thing on my mind. Mom had sent me to fetch a whoopin' switch.

I can't remember what I did wrong now, but I surely had her stirred up enough to make the executive mom decision of forcing me to find the length of wood that would cause an unwelcome stinging across my hind end. I was probably running and jumping on the furniture, tormenting my little brother Shane, or talking back. Whatever I did, I was in for it, and deserved it. I snapped off the leafy end of a branch. It was flimsy and pencil thin. *Hopefully she'll settle for this*. I nervously dragged my feet up the gravel road to our trailer home.

Mom was waiting on the porch. When I reached her, her pretty face, long blonde hair, and the same dark blue eyes that she gave me, meshed together into a fierce concoction of power. She grabbed my puny little twig, tossed it aside with quarterback force, and headed off to find the right tool for the job. I cringed, knowing that running wasn't an option. She was bigger, faster, smarter, and had caught me before. She pried at the same walnut tree like a T-Rex. I could see the whoopin' device that she had found from down the road. It was impressive. She found it within seconds as if she'd had her eye on it in passing days, waiting for this moment, as if it had caught her eye like a Christmas tree ornament. It wasn't quite firewood thick, but it looked dangerous in my young eyes. She headed in my direction. Her stride erased meters of ground between the tree and me all too quickly. Always a fan of the bare-ass whoopin's, Mom pulled my pants down, I assumed position, and let adrenaline get me through it.

Our whoopin's were always brief and fair. Mom never once thought of laying a misguided hand on us. She had always been wonderful, beautiful, and strong; I could list many examples of good times and great memories. She is the only person who has been there throughout my entire life. Even my brother missed my first three and a half years. I can give no one else credit for teaching me right from wrong, how to be fair and respectful, how to love, how to be responsible, and how to appreciate consequences. The last one—the one about consequences, when applied to living a fulfilled life—is what leads me to this story. I'm just too dang aware that my time here is short and precious. I don't want to waste a minute of it.

*   *   *   *

My name's Mike, and I'm an unknown hillbilly whose life sprouted from the Appalachian mountains of West Virginia. My part of the world is ancient and long-hidden, land-locked and fortified by majestic rolling peaks. It has plentiful rivers, trickling streams, and forests full of broad leaf trees, bears, bobcats, and blue jays. Today's modern influence attempts to penetrate my home's timeworn history, but it is still there, holding on in some of the world's oldest mountains. So numerous are the ridgelines that many more years will pass before all of their secrets are revealed.

John Denver's famous folk song "Take Me Home Country Roads" described my state by saying, "life is old there." He was right. Compared to our neighboring states, we've remained rather unsettled, like an island of rough terrain in the middle of a modern, civilized sea. I've heard that a simple game of WVU Mountaineers football brings enough people to Morgantown, West Virginia, on a weekend to temporarily make that the most populated city in our state, robbing Charleston, our capital, of the title. For the most part, we are a plain group of folks just trying to get by. Coal mining's dirty, unforgiving industry toughens our people's exteriors while stealing valuable quality of life. It is the one dominating, most relevant symbol of my home state.

There are only two counties out of fifty-five in West Virginia without a significant amount of coal in their mountains. I'm from one of them, Jefferson County, a small town piece of ground where word gets around quick and it's not uncommon to run into someone you know if you go downtown. It's bordered by Maryland to the north and Virginia to the south. It's the tip of West Virginia's Eastern Panhandle. I've called it home since birth and look at it as a place getting along like a half dry sponge, absorbing only partially from our more prosperous neighbors like Virginia's Loudoun County, Baltimore, and Washington, D.C. We've yet to become full-blown city folk, ya know?

Jefferson County is rural enough to be considered country, yet it is slowly transitioning to a more contemporary American community, seeing decades of steady growth and population influx. It's positioned perfectly for folks who want to buy a cheap home away from the hustle and bustle, but still be able to commute to the city for higher-paying jobs. Even without the aid of advanced age, I remember the days where everything was closed on Sundays here, and a little snow on the road meant that we were still going to school. That's changed now. Stores are open every day of the week, and a strong thunderstorm can be enough to send the kids home. I take it that that's the price of progress. If I make it to the years of wisdom and wrinkles, I may see my home engulfed by the D.C. metro area's urban sprawl. For now, its suburbs are a few glorious Appalachian humps away.

Life wasn't always easy growing up in our mostly rural slice of West Virginia. I was born to a loving mother and a wilder-than-fire father. When I recall my earliest memories, I can't remember a time where my family's means weren't extremely meager. We weren't the type of folks who ever purchased a new car, or even had relatives who went off to college. We weren't even part of the middle class. We were good folks, lingering somewhere just beneath that. We felt fortunate to have what little we did, and took the rest on the chin. Despite a rough-and-tumble, informal rearing, somewhere along the way a sturdy desire to learn and do my best glued itself to my heart and spirit. Following right behind that, curiosity has been the only imaginary friend that I've ever known.

Through my youngest years, reality framed a picture of a ruffled family bouncing around from trailer park to trailer park and school district to school district. Mom worked multiple jobs to keep the family afloat, and Dad endlessly partied like he stopped aging at twenty-one. Both of them loved us, but my father's substance abuse overshadowed the duty of parenting bestowed upon him by the decision he and my mother made when they made me. When I neared eight or nine, Mom had had enough, ending up with a broken nose in a domestic dispute. Dad packed his things for a retreat to his native Baltimore and his more familiar way of life. Their divorce would have a tremendous effect on the way I'd interpret every aspect of life, all through life.

Now that Dad wasn't around anymore, I had no one to shadow and to teach me how things worked and how to be strong. As a result, I developed an extremely open way to absorb society and the environment around me, one that left out racism and closed mindedness, and one that let my big imagination decipher all that I saw. The downside was that my influence over Shane became regrettably destructive, and I explored negative avenues that two strong parents could have stifled. Another unbreakable trademark that developed in my turbulent younger years was unpredictability. An ounce of foresight and a smidgen of patience would have done me a whole lot of good.

My dad's absence destroyed my self-confidence. Even as a young boy, I acutely noticed that other children with stable families didn't have this problem. This was never more evident than during those school years when the occasional bully soured my day. Like the time in sixth grade when someone's dimwitted offspring, ogre in size and behind a grade, wrapped his two chubby hands around my neck and hoisted me in the air. He was almost a foot taller, had me levitating against the school's brick wall, and promised a beat down. Somehow I talked the behemoth into letting my feet reconnect with the planet without being much more than frightened.

He wasn't looking for lunch money, and if he had been, he would've picked the wrong guy. I was one who entered the cafeteria every day at lunch who got food from being on the free lunch roster. Meaning, we didn't have the money for it. Now, I can't recall what I did to light a fire under this shade-tree-sized bully's ass, but I'm glad it all went down unnoticed by anyone. I was tremendously embarrassed, too weak to do anything about it, and felt intensely vulnerable. When it happened, we were at after lunch recess, with students and faculty all around, but I felt alone. I carried the grief home, locked inside, far from Mom's ears. I had acquired the first of my closet's skeletons.

Situations like that continued for a few years, with only one being more severe. Without a dad to teach me the old one-two-three combo, the classic duck and move, or at least the last-ditch double poke in the eye, I took my fair share of bullying. I never fought back and never knew how. I just locked it inside and deeply resented the bastards for doing it. There's no question that Mom would have stood up for me, but let's face it, it just isn't the same. Besides, she had enough on her plate as she kept steadily employed and battled through a failed second marriage with a nice fellow who just wasn't Mr. Right.

Time could not have waved its graceful hand more perfectly than the day that my mom and my new stepfather met. His name was Tommy. He was a hardworking type, quiet and strong, and time would prove that he was committed to us. I was in high school by then, and thanks to him we left poverty behind for another step up the ladder toward the middle class. Under his wing, we moved into the first house, without wheels, that I'd ever lived in. It was sturdy, not temporary. I had my own room, and it felt great. Being rescued from the bottom certainly had its perks, but on a lighter note, one drawback just can't be overlooked. When Mom and Tommy finally married, I was officially a redheaded step-child, not once, but twice. Damn the luck.

In the summer of 1998, my life's greatest influence materialized. That beautiful, exciting, fulfilling, unparalleled thrill was motocross. In it, you combine a brave man or woman with an intensely powerful, well-suspended, off-road motorcycle, a dirt track littered with dangerous jumps, deep ruts, and misshapen corners that provoke a wipeout. And that's just the beginning, as it takes a group of these brave souls to make the sport happen. They're thrill-seeking, enthusiastic weekend warriors. They show up for the race and are divided into classes based on engine size, age, and skill. When it's their turn, twenty, thirty, or sometimes forty of them line up side by side behind a row of pivoting metal gates. The race begins when those gates fall simultaneously. The racers launch their bikes like dragsters toward the first turn, all hoping to take the first position right away. What ensues after the dash to the first turn is four to six two-minute laps where the riders battle one another for position, and battle gravity while flying their bikes through the air and holding on for dear life in the ruts. A checkered flag greets them at the end of the race. The winner goes back to his pit area feeling like a champion, and the rest return to their pit areas where they will verbalize the many reasons why they didn't win to their buddies, all of whom will do the same thing all day long. Motocross is camaraderie, adrenaline, and a reason for living, all in one.

Since learning about its existence from a friend, I wanted to race, needed to race, and by golly, couldn't live without it. My fascination with the sport soon turned to obsession. For the next few years, motocross consumed me. So much so that after high school graduation I chose to pursue gaining speed on the track, while hoping to turn professional one day, over going to college. Starting in July of that year, as a clueless seventeen-year-old, three-digit squirrel (an unskilled racer who has yet to earn a single digit number), in just three and a half seasons, I was racing against the best around and the occasional pro rider.

While some of my friends were out chasing girls and socializing on the weekends, I was racing, training, and dreaming about the day that I would do it for a living. My relationship with the sport taught me the importance of setting and achieving goals and finally gave this non-team player a place to fit in that school never did. My results on the track were based on the work I put in, and any failures were only carried by me, just the way I liked it. Rewards for hard work came in the form of plastic trophies, the occasional slim chunk of cash, new friends, and priceless memories.

March 9, 2003, oh what a shitty day. A brilliant white blanket of snow was covering everything at home. Shane and I headed to southern Virginia for weather warm enough to knock the dust off the race bikes. It was the first motocross race of the season. At the end of the third lap of the day's first moto (race), I was thrown a curveball in the form of a broken left femur. Things just aren't right when you can wiggle your toes but your foot is on backwards. Pain, panic, and people swarmed me. In good hands, I made it to the hospital in Charlottesville, Virginia, with no risk of amputation or permanent damage.

A six-month recovery opened the door to distraction. Through that door came late nights, heavy drinking, a new girlfriend, her son, an apartment, and a new set of priorities. Being a first-time and full-time breadwinner ultimately killed seat time on the bike. As a naive young man, I never thought I'd see the day when motocross would be lingering in third place in my daily to-do list. It's not that I wanted it to. I had simply let other things grow around me unmonitored since leaving the comfort of my folks' house. My new relationship and work ruled the days. But soon, the sweet smell of puppy love wore off in our young relationship. I was finding that I was far too immature to be a solid role model for my girlfriend's son and mentally light years away from being ready to settle down. She indeed needed someone who could be there better than I.

At work, I endlessly daydreamed about trying to make our situation better, while fighting growing debt and ceaseless bills. This was my first swing at the time-to-grow-the-hell-up ball, and I was striking out bad. Miserably punching the time clock made the weekends sweeter than a spring honeysuckle. In no time I was in full live-for-the-nightlife mode, not much different than my father, although every single day was a weekend night to him. I was already reminiscing about the days prior to apartment living when I worked to race. Now, I was working to pay debt. Job-hopping sped up to match my unbalanced hope of trying to find happiness in the workplace. Racing became something I used to do, and partying on the weekends was summoned as the new adrenaline fix. The relationship with my girlfriend evaporated, and I phased myself and my things back into the nest under my parents' wings, a bit shamefully.

Then I fell in love. Life's random, ever-changing course helped me cross paths with another force to be reckoned with. She was both a tremendously positive experience and a severely devastating one at the same time. She was my new little sweetie, and she made my days brighter than the sun. Our paths crossed via my love for motocross and her brothers' participation in the sport. From a few years of twisting the throttle and braking bikes, I had gained a decent ability to diagnose and repair motorcycles. Her brothers had a solid understanding about how to break them without yet figuring out how to fix them. So I'd show up to weld something, re-tap a stripped bolt hole, or put a new piston in. I liked them and being around the whole family. It was a combination of parents who stayed together, raised children, and kept steady employment while interacting with their community. It was completely foreign to me, and I wanted to be part of it. *This is the way it's supposed to be.*

My attraction to this gal grew like nothing I'd experienced before. She grabbed my heart and took complete and utter control of it. I was twenty-four then. Her simple action of accepting me into her life with her stable family and plentiful affection sent my self-confidence to heights previously unimaginable. I felt like a normal person. I felt like I could conquer the world.

I found myself in a position that I thought only other people enjoyed. I was involved in a family atmosphere that I've always envied, dating a girl whom I adored, working a steady job as an HVAC mechanic, exercising regularly for my return to racing, and about to take on a mammoth project—building a house— that could only be pulled off with every string attached and every cog turning smoothly. I was working two jobs, one in the booming construction industry by day and a pizza delivery driver by night. I was a mid-twenties working machine.

Welcome to the bubble: a fitting motto for the years 2005 through 2007. Like many folks during this time, I borrowed more money from a bank than should have been responsibly loaned for the purchase of a home, albeit the bank I worked with never did get caught up in all the bad mortgage deals that poisoned so many. Unlike their larger nationwide counterparts who were slinging wads of cash at perspective homebuyers like the shit grew on trees, my bank was too small, too local, too friendly, and planned to keep it that way.

I took my loan readily with a different strategy in mind. It didn't take a real estate expert to realize that tiny houses on small parcels of land were going for far more than they were worth. I wanted a house of my own with value that matched the amount of money I was borrowing, so I committed to building one, from footer to shingle. I was twenty-six. I had no contractor's license, no complete home building experience, and no idea how difficult it would really be.

After weeks of searching, I bought a set of plans for a three-bedroom, three-bathroom, three-story, three-thousand-square-foot house. It was a beauty of a place, a Tudor in shape, with large bright windows, a steep roof, and cuts, corners, and angles everywhere. It looked like a designer bird house with its three-foot-wide overhangs jutting out from each unique gable. Upon completion, it would be a perfect nest for my sweetie and me to settle down in.

So I went to work, battling my tiny plot of land's horrid drainage issues with an energizer bunny meets cocaine mentality and confidence-inspired determination. For months I juggled work with work and more work, and on the weekend nights I'd scoop up my girlfriend and party hard. I was happy and things were happening. Despite being a long, physically demanding period, in my eyes life could not have been better. Things weren't the same for my lovely little lily pad of a companion, though. She had other things in mind.

Around the time of installing utilities in my newly framed house, shit hit the fan. In one week I lost a dear friend to suicide and found out that my darling of a girlfriend developed eyes for another. Both of these things destroyed me. Suicide is hard to understand. It's not like losing someone due to an accident or natural causes. In that sense, after some investigation, the cause for loss of life can be deciphered, but losing someone to suicide leaves a dark hole tattooed right on the blood pumper. Questioning why never stops. Feeling powerless to help at the time lays the foundation for regret. Those who are successful in their suicidal attempts are always one step ahead of their unassuming loved ones. Being the second close suicide of one of my loved ones, as I lost an uncle four years before, I've had plenty of time to reflect on the matter and can admit to being tainted by the experiences.

Dealing with that alone was enough weight to carry, but my newly acquired $200,000 mortgage and the promise of a large, lonely house became the straw that broke the camel's back. Like it or not, two very special people were taken from my life in a brief moment of time. One never to be seen again and one who my eyes watched slip away. My heart was broken. I turned to late nights, alcohol, and the friends that would tolerate me. For the next few months I didn't hammer a nail. Progress on the house completely halted as I relied on whiskey to drown my sorrows.

I met Brittany when our social circles collided like two hula hoops crashing into one another. She was five foot one, eighteen, had blonde hair, blue eyes, and was about as innocent-looking as anything I'd ever seen. I was suffering from a thick state of depression, just shed thirty pounds due to it, and was teetering on the edge of loss of control.

Who knows why Brittany picked me, but she did. Maybe it was the social bug that appears sometimes when I drink, or maybe it was the potential she saw with a new house arriving soon. Whatever the case, this girl wanted to be in my life at the absolute wrong time. The last gal had taken me out at the knees, and when Brittany came along, just weeks after, she saw a guy who was half the person that he was months before. She didn't know it, though. I hid that with a curtain of alcohol. I was nowhere near over my ex yet, but as the days went by and I began to work on the house again, she showed up almost daily at the building site and expressed interest. Sometimes she'd bring food, knowing that I rarely stopped working to eat, and sometimes she just wanted to talk.

I tried and tried and tried to let her know that I wasn't looking for anything new. I shoved her off here. I shoved her off there. I made her cry thunderstorms of tears. I would use any excuse in the book to make her go away the same way a grumpy old man deals with solicitors. Plainly, she wasn't what I was looking for—if I had been looking for anything at all—and secretly, her figure was awfully similar to my unfavorable ex's, making it hard not to think about the past. I wanted time to heal and frankly needed it. It was obvious that she was trying hard, so I entertained her visits by being civil most of the time.

Weeks passed, and we remained verbally connected. Then months passed, and I started to cave but not heal. She held on with a Velcro-like open heart, and I hoped that she would just get the point. Eventually, after months of denial, I accepted her. She was my new other half. Her persistence had paid off. It had won her a broken prize full of regret, pain, and indifference and she didn't seem to care. Soon, I was semi-back on track, had a good gal behind me, and a house that was nearing completion. All was looking up.

Up and up it went, until the real estate bubble erupted in an explosion of corruption and greed. I was left without a job. It was January, 2008, and I was a fella who completely relied on the HVAC trade to get by. My income from HVAC had paid handsomely during most of my new home's construction, but a sudden lack of construction in the marketplace left me with a shiny new mortgage on an unfinished house and no way to pay for it. In an attempt to find work and make yet another career change, I applied for a position at the County Assessor's Office. A few months passed, and I briefly took one more shot at the HVAC trade before receiving a call from the Assessor for an interview. *Finally, I'll use my mind to make money and not my back.*

Nineteen months had passed since breaking ground on the house. A project was finally completed that seemed as though it would never end. Brittany and I moved in, taking the load off of my parents. Our relationship normalized as we played the role of any young couple working in America—tending to debt, cleaning a house, and entertaining friends on the weekend. We even got a dog. From the outside looking in, it looked like I was doing well, like I had everything a middle-class man could want. The Assessor called me back with news that I hoped to hear. The office confirmed their desire to hire me and I took the job.

My office co-workers were great; however, this job was a test that I had not predicted. It was an against-the-grain, into-the-wind, uphill-both-ways, nose-to-the-grindstone sort of test. Selfishly, I knew that I had lucked out by being chosen over the other applicants, and I knew that some folks would've given their first born to get stable, county government employment in a down market. But there I was, with benefits from day one, a company car, a five-mile drive to work at a job that was impossible to break a sweat at, and I still found the same lack of satisfaction I had felt in every job before.

In the beginning I was testing, training, and using my thinker to learn the many requirements of the position. I was leaving town to go to the state capital for classes, and my mind had no choice but to be mentally stimulated. Then the reality set in. This position was a rinse-and-repeat, repetitious, non-evolving, uncreative, thirty-year task of attrition, if I chose to keep it. Half of my work year would be spent knocking on surprised and suspicious taxpayers' doors outside of the office, and the other half would be spent in a 5' x 7' cubicle forcing myself to be a productive data-entry type. The job might have been the peanut butter, but I wasn't born the jelly. As the daily eight hours of soul-sucking dissolved my creative mind, hence turning me into a disgruntled monster, I began to dream.

How can I break this cycle? Why do I work forty hours a week and lack two pennies to rub together? Why am I only thirty years old and working my twenty-third unsatisfying job? Five fast-food joints, four motorcycle dealerships, three HVAC companies, two house-framing crews, a sawmill, a meat distributor, fiberglass insulation factory, grocery store, vending-machine-stocking company, telemarketing firm, a friend's window company, Circuit City, and an Assessor's office would soon be left in my wake. None of them even closely grabbed my interest long enough to keep me around for any length of time. *If I have to trudge through endless days of supremely uninteresting work for the rest of my life, then I'll never be happy.* Something was vitally wrong. Happiness was gone. I was punishing Brittany at home with my poor attitude developed during the work day. My drinking increased. I didn't know what to do.

Living like that kept my brain in overdrive. Not one day passed where I didn't strain the grey matter for a way out, or at least a way to combine work with interest and happiness. From basic observation, there is a system in play that people just seem to settle with, like the proverbial herd of sheep. I think of it as a three-tier strategy to make it to a coffin relatively unscathed and I start it with school, the only part of it that I truly respect. I can't say enough about education. It is the key to solving most issues of our day. Educated people provide better paths for their children, take better care of their health, and from their many years of hard work, they bring us conveniences like hospitals with competent surgeons and reliable automobiles.

Tier two is the working years. In America, it seems as though these are the years to buy a house, stuff your wallet full of credit cards, buy as much plastic junk and electronics as possible to fill that house, have children, and starting with their first birthday, load them down with a bunch of plastic toys that they play with for five minutes before trying to climb into the toy's box, show up to work every day wishing it was Friday, finally relax for two days after that, start stressing about work again on Sunday night, and show up for thirty years of Mondays. Same job or not, all Mondays suck after a weekend of being yourself.

The effects of tier two are dangerous, with weight gain leading the way. Tier two is tiring and stressful. So what do a lot of us do? We indulge ourselves in America's overabundance of food and stimulants as a quick, self-medicating remedy. If I may add, I'm not proud that West Virginia is one of the fattest states in the nation. This is my current tier, as I have not yet invented a perpetual motion machine, cured cancer, discovered a clean and easily renewable energy source, found a 100-pound gold nugget, or anything else that would lift me into the top one percentile with early retirees. And worst of all, I'm usually promised a puny one or two week vacation that I have to wait a whole year to enjoy. Two grey hairs just sprang from my scalp while thinking about it.

Tier three is retirement, the last tier before six feet of dirt hides your decomposition and nutrient transfer back to the soil. Sadly, not everyone makes it to the third tier. The luckiest individuals have a bit of money in the bank and can avoid part-time work and enjoy years of leisure. Finally, after spending their whole youth, they can focus on their interests and hobbies, full time.

I observe folks, talk to folks, and listen to folks, especially older folks. They are wise. They've been there and done that, but generally, they are no longer in perfect health. A lot of folks who make it to tier three are alarmingly overweight. I'm thirty now and already full of back pain. I have two eighteen-inch metal rods in my legs (one in my left femur and the other in my right tibia) and can't walk to the bathroom first thing in the morning without looking like that chart where you see the evolution of man, starting with a hunched-over ape, and step by step becoming ever more erect.

I've always been thin and relatively fit, but how in the world am I going to hike a steep mountain at retirement age or trek long distances on a multi-day camping trip? Will I be able to kayak, bicycle, ride motocross? Why should I wait for my most physically vulnerable adult years to do the things I enjoy when I can do them now and want to do them now? Like a big, juicy Florida orange, I want to squeeze every last drop out of life that I can, while I still can. The three-tier system is like a drug—everybody's doing it—but I'm just going to say no.

One morning, an unassuming eighty-one-year-old woman planted a seed of change in my head without her knowing it. I was doing field work for the Assessor when I pulled up to the next property to review. Two solid knocks on the door interrupted her chores. She answered the door with a friendly "How can I help you?" She was thin, tall, and moved about with the grace of someone two decades younger. I gave her my mind-numbing spiel, developed through hundreds of awkward encounters on unsuspecting strangers' doorsteps. As I began asking her my standard questions, she spoke up and said that she was not the homeowner. She was visiting from Arizona and here for a wedding. She was the grandmother of the bride. Normally I'd finish the review visually, record a code stating that I had not spoken to the homeowner, and continue to the next parcel of ground, but something made me inquire about her home in Arizona.

At the time, I knew that Arizona was mostly dry and rugged, was home to the Grand Canyon, and that it made up a huge portion of the Southwest. Other than that, I knew very little. She described her home in Arizona, the weather, the desert, and the people of the area. Then she described the ten other states where she had lived and the multiple countries that she had visited. For the next half hour, I spoke very little and listened acutely. She smiled as she painted a picture of her life, and I was naturally envious. She had my full attention.

When she finished, she asked me one simple, but powerful question and said one stern, but wise sentence. She asked, "Where have you lived?" I replied, "Right here in Jefferson County, my whole life." Then her eyebrows lowered and her voice deepened to a more serious tone as she said, "Son, you need to get out more!" And she meant it! I vividly remember a feeling of commitment rush over me. I was going to do it. I trusted her judgment when she gave me that advice like it came directly from God.

My brain developed a plan before I even pulled out of the driveway. I was going to ride a bicycle across the United States! *That's perfect.* Well, it would have been if I had been in a position to pack up and leave the next day. I was a new homeowner, and to walk away, cold turkey, from my responsibility wasn't an option. Momma had raised me better 'n that.

After leaving that moment of enlightenment behind, with the mystery woman from Arizona, another year passed. In that year, things began to manifest in my favor toward the goal of traveling the country. Like the day when my co-worker Matt came into work carrying a nearly two-pound object of interest. Matt had brought in a book titled *1000 Places To See Before You Die*. The author, Patricia Shultz, had traveled to 1000 great destinations across our planet and delivered perfectly on paper a brief description of each, noting the right time of year to travel, where to eat, and where to stay.

Matt was closest in age to me in the office, had bushels of travel knowledge, and could see how I desired to pick apart that book. He let me borrow it long enough to thoroughly examine every page. He was one of only two co-workers that I could talk with about my escape. With the help of the book (using it as a field guide/trip planner), I hung a map on the wall in my kitchen, pegged the living daylights out of it with thumbtacks, began to let the cat out of the bag to my family about my plan, and watched the evolution of the journey unfold.

Also in that year, I received a phone call from Baltimore. It was September 19, 2010, and the call came from my Uncle Joe, my dad's brother. Uncle Joe is a man of few words. Those words have always been on the bright side, followed by a short and sharp laugh. The tone in his voice over the phone this time was urgent and serious. He said that my dad had been in Intensive Care for a number of days at Franklin Square Hospital and that it wasn't looking good. Dad had been on a few days' binge and had wound up in a coma-like state. Shane and I discussed how we would go see him. It was decided that I would go and report back his condition. Shane and I expected a full recovery despite my uncle's warning.

A few years before, a nearly identical situation faced us. My dad had ended up in the very same ICU, and the phone call came from my grandmother with urgency and concern. Dad had been on a drinking binge until his body collapsed and went into a coma-like state. My mom, Shane, and I arrived at Franklin Square where my dad had been motionless and unresponsive for eight days. It had been a while since any of us had seen him. His hair had thinned considerably. His frame seemed to have been whittled down to a smaller size, and he looked like he had aged fifteen years, instead of three or four. We hardly recognized him. Seeing him in such a state was scary.

We grabbed his hand, said his name, cried a little, and for a while nothing happened. Then, out of nowhere, his eyes opened, wide and confused. He started saying our names in a light and wispy voice. It was a voice that labored to overcome a set of vocal cords that hadn't moved in a week. He was instantly happy to have us around. This moment was hands down the closest thing to a miracle that I have ever seen. The doctor said that no amount of movement or elevated voices had stirred him in the slightest during his stay, but our caring whispers over his still body somehow brought him out of it.

Now, I was back, standing in the ICU of Franklin Square in one of those white rooms full of pumps, beeps, and other equipment too complicated for my understanding. Dad was lying motionless and clearly in bad shape. He had aged considerably, again. To the uninformed, a man of seventy-five could have been lying out in front of them, but Dad was nowhere near that. I was concerned on a whole new level this time. His frame seemed even smaller, yet his abdomen was abnormally large.

Uncle Joe soon arrived, and we were ushered into a room where a surgeon gently laid out the options, saying, "He'll never survive surgery." It was his liver. It was failing fast. Years of alcoholism had caught up to him. Uncle Joe did what any loving brother would do and instructed the surgeon to take any measure possible. I had no idea about what angle to take, but I trusted the surgeon. Secretly and sincerely, I thought that Dad would snap out of it again, like he did a few years before, and I held on to that thought with every ounce of my being, hoping, wishing, praying.

Uncle Joe and I finished our meeting with the surgeon and went back into the ICU room. We stood for quite a while in hopeful, yet somber conversation. He thought that Dad might pull through as well, saying, "If anyone can pull through, it's Brian." After an hour or so of consistent vitals, Uncle Joe left to take care of something, promising to come back around four o'clock that afternoon. I notified my mom and brother and sat down beside my dad under the curtain of those beeps, wondering if he was going to pull through, praying that he would.

A half an hour passed. The beeps hastened. At first I took this as a good sign, thinking that he was about to come out of it, like stirring to life. Then they shuffled up and down for minutes at a time. Finally, they began a slow descent.

All day, I could tell that the only thing Dad was doing was breathing, with a little aid from a machine. That was his only activity. When I noticed he was having some trouble breathing, I looked around for help. The only other people I saw in the ICU were other patients in critical condition. I returned to his room. The machines that Dad was hooked to were emitting warning signals. The inevitable was coming. Not knowing what to do, and panicking, I instinctively stayed with my dad. I grabbed his hand and tried to transfer all the love in my body to him. It wasn't enough. My dad passed as I held his hand tighter than I ever had, the first time since I was a boy. I loved him no matter how hard things were sometimes.

Shane and I picked a wonderfully pretty spot along the Shenandoah River to release our father's ashes. It was an early Saturday morning when we hiked along the water's edge. Geese and songbirds broke the heavy silence. Not a soul was in sight. When we found the spot we wanted, I told Shane to do the honors since Dad had passed before Shane could make it to the hospital that day. As the ashes dissipated like smoke in the breeze, so did any chance of ever having a normal relationship with my dad. I'll miss him forever. He was only fifty-six.

Life just keeps ticking along, inescapably piling one second on top of the next. And time is the greatest healer. Things were subtly and steadily changing at the office. On the bright side, I secretly knew that I was getting out. Like a prisoner who etched, scraped, and clawed his way through concrete block, I could finally see the light at the end of the tunnel. On the other hand, the days became long, really long. The cubicle seemed more confining, growing smaller and smaller each day. The thought of it devouring me whole, like some ferocious cubi-gator, chilled my bones. Motivation to begin my daily tasks became nonexistent. Only after huge doses of caffeine would I feel up to walking the plank toward the next taxpayer's front door. My distaste for the job turned to full-on illness. Home life dove dramatically for the worse. I would try to determine more immediate ways to find daily happiness, oftentimes through drinking heavily, and Brittany—again—had to be tough. Our relationship up until that point still had not encountered a smooth moment. Constant tension from my fruitless job and lack of answers strained my soul. Still, she held on.

Some positives came in those final months. On April 15, 2011, I bought a motorcycle. It was a 2003 Yamaha FZ1 and was my first street bike. This bike would become the weapon of choice for my ever-evolving, cross-country journey, erasing any plans to ride coast to coast on a bicycle. Within a week it became my new best friend. I had discovered the wind-in-the-hair effect. Since friends have names, this friend politely accepted "the Goose" as its title. Starting out as "the Grey Goose," due to its shimmery metal flake paint job and the popular alcoholic beverage, I shortened the name for simplicity's sake. An overly dorky, touring windscreen was mounted to the bike on the day of the purchase which helped contribute to the passive name. The bike itself was a 140-horsepower brute, reaching speeds of seventy-five mph in first gear, followed by warp drive, light speed, and on the top end, butt pucker. Without question, the Goose was fast.

From April to July, I only drove my little Nissan truck twice, and in mid-July, I became a motorcycle-only commuter. At the time, things were so tight financially that the sale of the truck was the only way to make the mortgage payment. I was working daily while the financial struggle continued.

That left three months until I took off, but I wasn't yet aware of it. The task of selling my house still remained. In August, I placed a homemade wooden For Sale sign in the yard and ordered some business cards to hand out, advertising the sale of the house, promising $1,000 after closing to anyone who found me a buyer. A few weeks passed before the tiny sign lured in some prospective buyers. On a quick Friday morning, just before leaving for work, a couple from Philadelphia, who were visiting friends in Harpers Ferry, took twenty minutes out of their day to put the final piece of my journey's puzzle in place. They walked through my house and confidently expressed interest in beginning the purchasing process. I was stunned by their speedy decision making.

September proved to be another month of attrition. Brittany and I called it quits, much to her dismay. I had desperately needed time alone after the other break-up with my ex-girlfriend, but that time never came. Like grass that has been covered with a sheet of plywood, my relationship with Brittany was alive but never really healthy. In our three years together, I didn't grow an ounce as a person. I remained locked in constant mental strife, thinking, "With great effort, I can bear this, but I'm not into it at all," while she prayed that I would just get over it.

The break-up was ugly, real ugly. She just didn't want to split up. She fought hard to keep the relationship intact. I knew the trip was coming after closing day on the house, and I'd finally have the time I needed to sort myself out. Ultimately, that was more important. If only one of us was happy, it would never work.

Closing day arrived on October 1, 2011. All of my energy, hard work, and time to build the place became a memory. My house was now owned by folks who were much better off financially than I was. My pride took a shot that day, but on October 7, 2011, I was free. That's the day when I put the last long minute of obligation into my job at the Assessor's Office. I said goodbye to Matt and the rest of the staff and walked out when the courthouse bell struck five. At the end of that day, I lacked a mortgage, a girlfriend, and a job. On the fourteenth I would leave.

During the last week at home, I stayed with Shane and his wife, Kayla, at their place in Gerrardstown, West Virginia, in the next county over. While they spent their days at work, my days were spent handling paperwork and shopping for supplies. On the edge of leaving it all behind, I became aware of how entangled the web of life can become as we spend years creating our adult identities. Paperwork and address changes seemed to go on forever. Nights were juggled between last-minute visits with friends and family, and prepping the Goose. I mounted new tires, new sprockets, a chain, and changed the motor oil and coolant. My friend Steve T. worked well into the small hours of the morning, helping me build homemade racks out of square three-quarter and one-inch steel tubing for the storage boxes that I wanted to use. With his welding skills and my imagination, we pulled off some fine hillbilly engineering.

A friend of mine, Igor, and a friend of his, Vivek, wanted to tag along with their motorcycles on the first two days of the journey. I agreed and looked forward to having their company. They'd help ease me out into the world. Igor has been a good friend for the past five years or so. I met him like I met Brittany, through long nights of drinking, shared friends, and house parties. He's a Ukrainian/American fella who spent a long portion of his young life in North Carolina. He has an English vocabulary that trumps mine and is one of the most sincere and outgoing people I've ever met. Here in West Virginia, two of his cousins and an aunt have called my home state home for some time now. One of those cousins became a dear friend of mine; this was the friend I mentioned earlier who took his life. Since then, I've grown much closer to Igor's family. They've made my life enormously richer.

In preparation for the ride, Igor had willingly set up and urged me to record the trip via a blog. Without a tech-savvy bone in my body, I said that I'd give recording the trip a shot, while thinking that there was no way I'd have the time or patience to put it together on the road. Brittany and I worked out a plan to meet on day two in southern West Virginia, as friends. After that, I'd be alone.

The adventure was set to begin. I was heading out into America to heal and find myself . . . to fight off a one-dimensional lifestyle . . . to touch and experience . . . to get out more . . . to embrace life . . . to loosen up . . . to think . . . to reset.

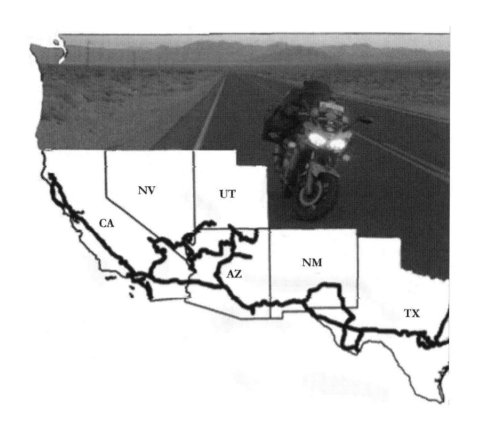

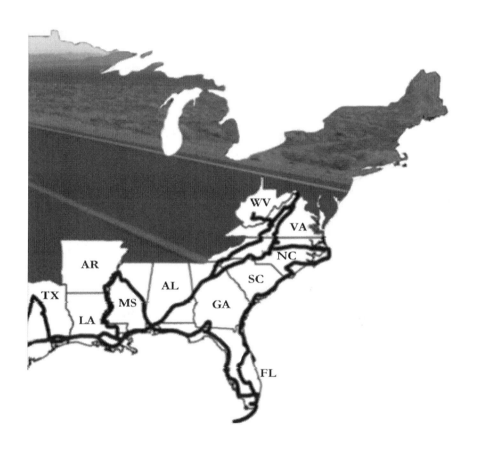

The World is a book, and those who do not travel read only a page.

St. Augustine

Part 2

The Mighty Day 1
October 14, 2011

Being born again usually parallels a religious thought. Day one marked my rebirth. A motorcycle, a map, pavement, and wanderlust were all that mattered. Properly living life with the herd contributed little to how I'd exist starting today. Countless hours of on-the-job training, mixed with a mediocre education, a hint of advice from friends and family, sprinkled with a dash of unstable childhood, and topped off with every other form of normality that faces us along the way, made for a tasteless nine-to-five soup. Everything that life had shown me until now, all of it, was suddenly obsolete. For the very first time in my thirty years, money did not limit me. The weight was lifted and worry gone. . . .

At 7:00am the raspy beeps of an alarm clock filtered through the air in Shane's spare bedroom. I opened my eyes to see the Eastern Panhandle of West Virginia for the last time in a long time. I split the curtains and looked outside to see light rain falling and fog. The trees with smooth bark were shiny, and the ones with rough bark were just shy of black. Their canopies were beginning to give way to the autumn color change. Inside, Shane's woodstove had his small chalet warm and toasty. I closed the curtains, thinking how I didn't like the cold, mid-October rain invading my momentous day.

Shane and Kayla were wide awake, already dressed for work and stirring in the kitchen before I walked in. Shane offered to help with anything I needed, but I just asked for coffee. Our words were that of well wishes and good lucks. When it came time for them to leave, our goodbye had just a hair of emotion in it. I was focused on the task at hand, and they were heading off to fulfill another day's worth of paperwork and responsibility, as both of them were supervisors in their respective fields. When they left, the door closed and silence filled the kitchen. I inhaled and exhaled a deep breath, finished that coffee, took a hot shower, and began feverishly packing. I had to meet Igor and Vivek around 1:00pm in Front Royal, Virginia, and had yet to test load my gear on the bike.

The gear was scattered widely on the kitchen floor, making it easy to see and grab each piece as needed. I picked the larger items first, like the tent and the air mattr, and stuffed them in the side boxes. Medium-sized things like tools and hygienics went in next. Food and my folded road atlas topped off the panniers. In the trunk, I wedged in as many changes of clothes as possible and returned the rest to a storage container. I stuck the tank bag full of snacks and paperwork on the fuel tank. Then I fired up the Goose. It was parked on Shane's deck under a portable canopy. The rear tire broke loose a few times as I rode off of the slippery old deck boards and into the cul-de-sac.

I paused for a minute, glancing back and forth from the safety and sanity of my brother's house to the endless road in front of me. *It would be so easy not to go. I could start fresh with money to spare. Life would be easy for a good while.* I looked down at the road. *The dirt and gravel of Sunrise Lane will link to a slightly larger road, followed by another slightly larger road, and on and on until my comfort zone is a distant memory.* Choosing the road over any other option, there was nothing left to do except let out on the clutch lever and ride.

Brittany's new apartment in Martinsburg, West Virginia, was the first stop of the day. I was after a quick goodbye. Our encounter was short and to the point. She knew that she would be seeing me one last time at Bridge Day tomorrow before cutting the cord permanently.

I left and headed to my mom's house for the same thing, a quick farewell to avoid a stream of tears. I was mentally prepared to start the journey, but fully expected it to be difficult to tell Mom goodbye. I showed up with wet raingear and a smile. Mom wasn't crying, but she wasn't smiling either. She told me, "I thought about this a lot, and I'm ready now." Then she added, "You know you don't have to go." We talked for just a few minutes outside, standing by the bike. When it came time to leave, she stayed strong. As I rode away, I kept my eyes on her until she was out of sight. I was proud of her. The moment couldn't have been smoother.

Before leaving Jefferson County behind for good, I stopped at a decal company downtown. I was hoping to get some stickers with my blog name made for the bike. I didn't know that I should've ordered them in advance. The pretty gal behind the counter listened to me babble on for a second about leaving today to cross the country. She took an interest, generously hooking me up with the website stickers on a rushed, walk-in basis, veering away from their standard procedure. I thanked her sincerely. Their company's sticker took up the first bit of painted real estate on the Goose. I put the glittery silver and black logo right on top of the fuel tank. Once I passed the southern county line, the trip was on!

Igor and Vivek braved the early morning rain and the long, cold ride from Washington, D.C. to meet me in Front Royal. As they approached, I could see that Igor was geared up well for the weather. He was wearing a heavy riding jacket and riding pants capable of blocking the wind. Vivek, on the other hand, had to be freezing under his modest leather jacket and thin pants. I had not met Vivek before, but silently gave him a few tough guy points for not even making a complaining squeak about the chill in the dreary weather. We shook hands and exchanged a few words over smiles. Upon first hearing him, it took me a second to process what he was saying. He spoke English well, but with a heavy Hindi accent and very fast. West Virginians aren't known for communicating rapidly, if ya know what I mean? Nonetheless, throughout the day I started catching on.

Lunch in town at the rustic Knotty Pine restaurant became our first three musketeer mission. The Knotty Pine's interior was cozy and lined with dark wood panels making for a superbly country feel. A few dumbfounded and slightly unfriendly looks drifted toward us from the bar at the other side of the room. I imagined that people didn't know what to make of us. I'm sure it's not every day that a trio of two wet foreigners and an equally wet hillbilly lumber in, squishing with every step, carrying helmets, and giggling like children. As we ate, we met a lady named Joy who described the Blue Ridge Parkway as 469 miles of bliss. Joy talking about bliss was a good omen for the coming day's adventures, I hoped.

From Front Royal, Virginia, we ascended to Skyline Drive, eager and itching to lean. For 109 miles, this paved wonder way snakes along the apex of a section of the Blue Ridge Mountains in Shenandoah National Park. It's a phenomenally pretty ride. Overlooks, often marked with huge boulders, showcase the gently rolling farmland below. Looking out, I imagined that I'd stumbled into a postcard scene from Ireland. Autumn's magic was working hard here. The natural color spectrum displayed in these glorious mountains has given them a reputation for beauty that's second to none. The weather changed to fit our happy mood, and now sky blue accompanied the greens, oranges, yellows, and reds of the forest. We rode Skyline Drive in short sections, stopping at nearly every lookout we came to.

Igor, being our tech guy and somewhat of a director, would find a perfect corner and motion for us to stop. He'd go for his tripod and with Ukrainian seriousness command us to ride down the road. He'd have us turn around out of sight and ride back through the corner past his lens. Vivek and I would do it each time with smiles blazing under our helmets. Igor was responsible for most of the first day's pictures, and I was happy for it. Those pictures will undoubtedly add to the few memories I have from childhood when the family and I managed a couple weekend car rides to Skyline Drive. Comparing then to now— and seeing it on the back of a motorcycle—the lack of a roof and limiting windows opened up the terrain around us, making Skyline Drive better than I'd remembered, hands down.

Our sights were set on Waynesboro, Virginia. If we had made it, we would've finished all 109 miles of Skyline Drive, but instead we reached the first snag of the trip. Months of planning flew right out the window, along with the rubber on Igor's rear tire. It was as bald as a baby's bottom. The ride from D.C. was enough to expose a strip of cords. Seeing a different color than black surfacing in the center of his rear wheel meant that we were gambling with distance. The pegged map in my kitchen that I diligently updated before leaving became obsolete in that very instant. The bad news forced us to modify the plan. Igor, Vivek, and I jetted off—away from the perfect mountain curves of the national park—through Luray, and eventually to Harrisonburg, Virginia, with our fingers crossed. We hoped to find a dealership open and willing to mount a new tire the next morning in time for Bridge Day.

We were in Harrisonburg hunting for lodging. Neither of them had packed tents or planned to camp. While looking for a place to shack up for the night, Igor handed me the phone and told me to talk to the motel receptionist. He said, "You have the *local* accent." His Ukrainian accent had failed him in the past while trying to make reservations, and at the time we completely wrote off Vivek's Hindi-influenced English. Perhaps motel owners fear folks who sound like Russian mobsters. Who knows?

After two solid rings an Indian feller at the Harrisonburg Budget Inn answered the phone. I almost couldn't speak for laughing. I told the guys what had happened, and a hearty chuckle ensued. I suppose *local* can mean a lot of things these days.

Once arriving at the bombastic Budget Inn, Vivek palled up with the owner, who we learned could have been his uncle, and we scored a bit of a break on the rate. Actually, Vivek said that denoting older folks as uncles—whether they are or not—is common practice in Indian culture. He said that practically anyone can be referred to as uncle, so Igor and I agreed that we were traveling with Uncle Vivek. In the hotel room we cracked open a large vessel of Jack Daniels and celebrated the completion of day one. Whiskey stirred and blurred the next few hours. Still, I recall bar hopping until the fat lady sang, a cab ride, and destroying a few Papa John's pizzas around the crack of 3:00am. Day one started with a gravel road wet with rain and uncertainty and ended perfectly among the comfort and company of friends.

Day 2 – October 15, 2011

A word so vicious, so insidious and positively terrible, had bit me right on the head on day two. It is, in fact, my most feared word. No, it is not spider, although spider is a close second. The word I'm talking about falls just shy of demonic possession in the way that it takes over the body and makes you pay for indulgence. It's the great unwelcome equalizer in my life. The word I'm speaking of is *hangover.* I shudder at the very mention of it.

Without its intense, wretched blessing, I'd likely fall into the cycle of waking up and drinking more to ease the pain, thus taking the first concrete step toward alcoholism. Thankfully, the mere thought of a warm shot of whiskey the morning after has always been enough to send me darting through a spell of dry heaves toward the nearest commode. When I'm in its nauseating grasp, I feel as though I'm sitting on a spinning merry-go-round beside a man holding out a spade shovel. On each revolution my head smacks the man's shovel, causing a full day's worth of thumping, nausea, and concentration loss.

So far, I've managed to wait this feeling out each time I poison myself for fun, but I find myself wishing that I could trade the war going on in my head for the pain of a smashed finger from a closing car door or a good ol' kick in the nards. Both are intense, but subside more quickly. Robust hangovers have been a regular part of my life since I was old enough to drink. So what do they have to do with riding a motorcycle? Well, nothing is sweeter than wearing your new, super-tight helmet for four hours while your brain feels as though it's going to escape your skull by means of explosion. This was just the beginning of one of the most absent-minded days I've ever had.

I left the guys in Harrisonburg for a solo ride to Fayetteville, West Virginia, in the south central part of the state. They managed to find a bike shop that could change Igor's tire right away and promised to meet me in a few hours to celebrate all the Bridge Day that we could handle. Bridge Day is the one and only day of the year that folks are legally permitted to walk across the New River Gorge Bridge. It's a fantastic piece of engineering that allows southern West Virginians the ability to cross the gorge in less than a minute, when before they would have to navigate winding roads to the bottom and back up again, making a simple traverse of the gorge a journey in itself. Upon completion of the 876-foot-high behemoth, it became the world's largest single-arch bridge. For this, a huge annual festival was spawned—West Virginia's largest—featuring death-defying base jumps, repelling, music, food, and family fun.

Unfortunately, Brittany was the only one of us to get a full share of the festivities, as she arrived well before we did. Igor and Vivek completely missed Bridge Day due to Igor's tire issues and his not so awesome choice to take the slow, scenic route through rural West Virginia from Harrisonburg to Beckley. He even topped that off with a ticket from some coal mining municipality's friendly police officer for not having his motorcycle inspected. "Maybe I should consider leaving the Ukrainian at home next time," I lightly entertained.

As for me, I barely made it to Bridge Day. For three and a half hours, I fought a ferocious headwind on Interstates 81 S and 64 W. Riding south, it pounded me. Riding west, it pounded me. Without fail, the wind changed direction as if to rub it in a little as I plowed through Virginia and West Virginia's dense mountainous terrain. I arrived around 1:30, sporting a sore neck, and began a patented version of the blurred-brained Olympics.

First, there was my favorite, the old lose-your-keys-in-seconds competition. I won that hands down. The trophy awarded for that event was an increased level of confusion adorned with tiny hammers pounding my temples. A half hour of searching passed before I realized that I had locked them in the right side storage box while in a hurry to get to the bridge. With time slipping away and blood pressure rising, I pried the box open on one end, stuck my arm in, simultaneously cracking the other end, and snagged the keys. It was day two, and I already had a broken storage box. Hooray!

Next, I was off for the speed walking competition from the parking area to the bridge. I again won that handily as I passed folks who had been there all day and were in no hurry. Then at 2:00pm, the third event started when I made it to the entry gate for the bridge. It was called the you-can't-bring-that-here-dumbass competition. An officer sharply sent me back to the parking area citing, "No backpacks allowed." I could have belted out the ol' F bomb in seven unique tones right then, but instead I quickly jogged back to the bike to stash the backpack, all the while building up a sense of panic about missing the base jumping since the whole thing was over in an hour.

So now the backpack was stashed, and I was on my way back to the gate when I realized that I just left my camera lying on the ground right beside the bike, open for anyone to snatch. Thank you, Hangover Fairy! And thus, the final event, the supersonic sprint, took place. Again, I won uncontested. Folks looked at me like I was running from hot lava. I raced to the Goose and was relieved to find the camera still waiting behind the rear tire. Now, damn near seeing red, I grabbed the camera and ran back to the entry gate to meet Brittany.

At 2:30 I saw a man leap from the New River Gorge Bridge, utterly depending on his parachute to save his life. How spectacular and how eerie! Like Hollywood stuntmen, one after the other would raise both hands in the air (one hand holding a parachute) and confidently jump off the platform. Nearly nine hundred feet below, the river's surface waited to absorb a mistake. Some jumpers began with Olympic-diving-style acrobatics and some wound the windows up as they fell, flapping like fish out of water.

The jump combination that took my breath away was one when two fellas jumped together. As they left the platform, the crazies were embracing one another, face to face. Halfway down, one of them, who was holding onto the other, let go and continued to fall at full speed while his buddy pulled the first chute. From above, it looked as though the guy still falling wasn't going to make it, but his chute opened to the relief of thousands of onlookers. I smiled and sighed at the same time. Four to five seconds of free fall were all they had to pull off moves like that. Every last jump was priceless, yet disturbingly suicidal-looking. At 3:00pm the police kicked us off the bridge and off we went. In that short time, I had reached full satisfaction.

Since Igor and Vivek never made it, I set about creating a plan to track them down. Brittany left to retrieve her car on the north side of the bridge, and while waiting for her to return I realized that my phone was dead. There was no way to find the guys with a dead phone, and she didn't know where my bike was parked among the thousands of cars scattered about, so I backtracked to a Dairy Queen that I had noticed just down the road a few hours earlier.

I plugged my phone charger into DQ's outside receptacle, turned it on, and called her. Perhaps it was the hangover talking, or an ultra-conservative moment of conscience, but thieving power from an outside receptacle without buying an ice cream felt criminal. Foolishly, I imagined the manager swinging around a corner and barking, "Hey you! You can't do that here," in which case, I'd grab the charger and run for the bike. This was my first taste of finding resources on the road, albeit a small taste. I reflected on how I had always taken the simple act of charging a phone for granted.

Brittany found the Dairy Queen, and we headed south to Chili's in Beckley for some grub. The dubious duo of Igor and Vivek met us there at 6:30pm. They were full of adventure stories through the mountain state's interior. *That probably isn't the safest place for two foreign fellas with such pretty mouths to be lost.* We laughed about their shenanigans and caught up over dinner. Again, the topic of finding reasonable shelter arose. This time Igor handed the phone to Brittany, noticing that she had the *local* accent down pat. We made a joke right before she called the Budget Inn about an Indian answering the phone. Without fail, one did. Brittany lost it. She laughed like a hyena while she held the phone out stiff-arm style. She couldn't even talk to the poor guy. We had Vivek call back since he was fluent in Budget Inn-glish. After clarifying with the motel owner that he was just Indian Vivek, not Vivek from California, we were set; Budget Inn came through again. A ground rule stating that Vivek, by default, shall call for lodging arrangements was never mentioned; however, I made a mental note for next time. We all took some much-needed showers and shots, relaxed in one another's good company, and stayed in. We called it a day around midnight.

Day 3 – October 16, 2011

Brittany and I beat the sunrise. Waking well before first light allowed us another chance to see Igor and Vivek before they made tracks back to Igor's place in Washington, D.C. I think anxiety for the upcoming day's splits ruined any hope for a good night's rest. As planned, the guys were almost finished packing by the time we knocked on their door. Igor wished me luck in his usual steady and optimistic fashion, and Vivek bid farewell knowing that he could count on me as a new lifelong friend. As I watched them round the corner I had a sense that the journey was finally in full swing. There is a huge amount of comfort in having your friends with you. Although Brittany was still with me, I would learn later on in the day what being alone really feels like.

Packing the bike with all the gear I brought into the room the night before commenced shortly after my two buddies were out of sight. The Goose was sitting elevated on the sidewalk right outside of our room, and I was strapping something down when a friendly older gentleman approached and started to inquire about my trip, while educating me about some of the bikes he had owned. His name was Rick and he carried that serious, yet open understanding that motorcyclists have in the presence of one another. It's a state where we become immediate great friends because of our shared hobby but still have to talk bikes like manly men, chests out and ready at any moment for a pissing contest if one guy says that his bike is faster, has more horsepower, or is shinier.

Rick and I kept it cool, though. He was a native of Ohio and traveling through with his wife. He told me that he'd owned a couple of bikes with over 140,000 miles on them (approximately 120,000 more miles than the Goose). One was a Moto Guzzi that he said "just wouldn't break down." I listened, quite impressed, while holding back the urge to blurt out, "Oh yeah, well my bike is awesome man!" Rick was just too nice for that. He went on to tell me that he's been everywhere but the northwestern United States. I told him that I hoped to make it that far, take some pictures, and put them on the web to get him inspired to go. He said he'd make it there someday. We shook hands, he and his wife finished stuffing their last bag in the trunk, and they were off as quickly as they had arrived. I continued to pack, turned my key in, and Brittany and I took our turn to leave Beckley in the dust.

Along the way, we decided to visit the town rated "America's coolest small town" in 2011, Lewisburg, West Virginia. We rode through charming Lewisburg rather quickly, stopping only once to snag an I've-been-there picture with the welcome sign. Being a native of the state, I was sure that I would get a more complete taste of Lewisburg later in life.

We continued on, following 64 E to the Greenbrier Hotel in White Sulphur Springs, West Virginia. The Greenbrier is a five-star hotel that blocks any chance of seeing the horizon beyond its brilliant white façade and broad-as-a-barn-door front entry. For West Virginia, it's a big deal, a crown jewel, and maybe the fanciest thing in our state. If not, I'm sure that it has but few rivals. We rode through the Greenbrier's perfectly manicured grounds, passed tennis courts, and folks dressed in golf attire. I had seen the Greenbrier Hotel a few times before, but this quick visit was for Brittany. She was able to check the Greenbrier Hotel off her bucket list. Our upper-class excursion was over in a flash. We reconnected our tires to 64 E and headed for Lexington, Virginia.

In Lexington, Brittany followed me to another Dairy Queen, where I secretly wished that some ice cream would soften the mood as we prepared to part ways. All of the creamy cold sweetness in the world could not have stopped that moment from being difficult. It was easy to say so long to the guys with Brittany still by my side, but when it was time to go completely solo, that became a whole different story. I'm going to admit that I truly believe that the girl loved me as I let her go. *Who else wants to hang on to me so badly?* Right then, it dawned on me that I'd have something serious to think about on the road. *Am I throwing away the one?* A few rogue tears trespassed onto my cheeks. Even though I stood a foot taller than Brittany, as we hugged for the final time, I felt dwarfed emotionally. She was hurting bad. It was the kind of hurt that squeezes your chest at funerals. Her big blue eyes said please change your mind, while her lips fought to hold back those words. I questioned why I was leaving the last person that I was really comfortable with in order to take this long, soul-searching trip.

Her little white Camry faded into the Virginia hills with Interstate 81 on the horizon. She had a three-hour drive ahead of her before she reached her new apartment in a shabby section of Martinsburg, a destination that she was fearful of and that would promise to lock in months of loneliness.

I took a deep breath and circled the bike once or twice. Singularity took hold for a few minutes. The feeling was heavy and discouraging. When I looked around, I recognized no one. I felt like a stranger here. I thought about what comes next. Staying in the parking lot at Dairy Queen wasn't an option, so I made tracks toward the Blue Ridge Parkway. Once I took off for parts unknown, the spirit of adventure and the need to pay attention to my surroundings took over. My emotions settled.

Buena Vista, Virginia, sits between the Blue Ridge Parkway and Lexington. At a fuel station I got word from a fella that the nearest parkway campground was closed for the winter, so in Buena Vista I found a campground at Glen Maury Park. The park reminded me of an equal mix schoolyard and KOA. For $26, a teenager handed me a pass, granting me permission to pitch my tent at the tent sites up the hill and away from most of the park's facilities. The price for camping came as a shock as I had never paid to camp anywhere before. Twenty-six dollars was an eye-opening number, and one that I hoped would not turn into a trend.

I piloted the Goose up the hill to the tent sites. Three other people were there. Two of them were set up as if trying to put as much space between one another as possible. I set up camp in the rapidly fading light. Leaves covered the ground like a crunchy blanket. I felt unsettled. The darkening sky amplified the loneliness. I didn't have a drop of alcohol packed on the bike to take the edge off. This was my first time camping solo, ever.

Since childhood, camping had always been a family outing done with a few select friends. My dad would take us camping. He and his cohorts would set the tents up, start campfires, turn the music up, party like it was 1999 (really 1986), and not see the inside of the tent again until passing out in the wee hours of the morning. This learned approach to camping has followed me into adulthood, and I'm not going to sugarcoat it. It's fun. To camp without drinking is almost unfathomable. Because of this, our tenting excursions had always been short and leaned toward an outside party rather than an escape into nature. Nonetheless, I always have appreciated every aspect of the simplicity of it all, but hadn't had a real (sober) camping experience. My nights would be spent draining bottles, often searching for the cooler using a lighter for light, listening to music, and searching for the tent in a drunken daze like someone had moved it.

So here I was at Glen Maury Park, dry as a bone, thirsty for a drop to ease the uneasiness, and slightly apprehensive about being alone. And to be rightfully honest, here is a good spot to mention that I'm pathetically, although not tremendously, afraid of the dark. I relate the dark to the feeling one gets in really deep water far from shore. It all has to do with vulnerability, and a smidgen of overactive imagination. That night of solo camping proved to be more of a learning experience rather than something to fear. All was well as I switched the tent light off.

Day 4 – October 17, 2011

Day four started out just like any other day—dull, boring, and in need of a good cubicle. I'm kidding. I was on my trip and rising to a beautiful day in a new place. Best of all, every rustle of the leaves in the night and every snapped twig or mammalian snort in the dark left me alone.

Just after dusk yesterday, a man pulled into the campground on an older touring bike loaded up in a similar fashion to mine. He parked three tent sites up the hill from me. Trees were blocking the last bit of light as he pitched his tent. I felt like I wanted to go say something since both of us were obviously packed for long distance trips, but my default response is to mind my own business, so I didn't say anything. I was apprehensive as well and hate to admit that negative thoughts about the sort of character he could be stirred my imagination. The fella was tall and thin, sporting shoulder-length hair and glasses. From a hundred feet away he looked like that wacky cult guy from Waco, Texas, David Koresh, and why the memory of that crazy incident in central Texas still sticks with me, I may never know. Nonetheless, I was unnerved and shouldn't have been.

We were both loaded up and ready to take off when he walked down the hill to chat. The bright morning sun eased any tension that I had felt the night before. He said his name was Jack and that he was riding from Connecticut. His plan was to wander the East Coast for two weeks and end up in Asheville, North Carolina. Both of us were planning to ride the Blue Ridge Parkway from Virginia to Asheville. Jack and I exchanged info, wished each other luck, and parted ways. He went straight for the parkway, but I detoured south for a site to see. He was so genuine. I shouldn't have judged a book by its cover.

While Jack was no doubt riding along on the parkway in a state of true peace, I headed a few miles south for the Natural Bridge. It's located in none other than Natural Bridge, Virginia. Eighteen dollars sounded steep just for a quick walk and gawk self-guided tour of the facilities, but who am I to judge?

A paved walkway descended sharply through seemingly unlogged, old eastern forest toward the base of the ancient rock formation. When the path led me through a blind right hand turn and dumped me out in front of the formation, I traded walking for a stiff stare.

At 215 feet tall and nearly forty feet thick, the Natural Bridge is a monolith hiding out in a mountain valley. Standing below—eyes pointed skyward and feeling quite small—I quickly forgot about the ticket price. Mother Nature had provided the value. As I lingered, small droplets filtered through the rock overhead, gained momentum on their descent, and clapped the water's surface, creating a slight echo. Folks slowly strolled under the beautiful arch, hoping that it would stay aloft for another day. Trees grew on even the thinnest section, happily unaware of gravity's long term plan. The forest seemed to be the only thing using the bridge as a byway these days, and I imagined raccoons and possums using it as a shortcut in their night's wanderings. The Natural Bridge was a great opening act that left me excited to see more of America's rare oddities.

Once a year, when Autumn and the Appalachians team up to display their festival of colors, their broadleaf bonanza, or their final hoorah before hibernating for the winter, the Blue Ridge Parkway bests all mountain rides, even Skyline Drive, as the ultimate way to achieve a front and center view of the show. I planned to spend a few days surfing my motorcycle through every snaking corner from Natural Bridge to Asheville.

Besides the green, red, and yellow leafy eye candy, the parkway is also dotted with small points of interest. You'll notice them if you can take your eyes off the trees long enough to look at the roadside. I came across a tiny cabin where a woman once lived who reached 102 years old. This I find incredible as the cabin was right on top of a mountain and about the size of one of those drop off sheds from your local home improvement warehouse. She was a midwife who had delivered more than one thousand babies, but ironically, out of her own twenty-four children, not one survived childhood.

Later on and further south, I stopped for a quick leg stretch at a ranger station and had the pleasure of chatting with a fascinating young park ranger named Natasha. At twenty-nine she had already lived the kind of life that I dream about—a life full of travel, full of culture, and full of energy—a life that I was out on the road searching for. Before I left the station she was sure to hook me up with some great recommendations for the western portion of the country, suggesting with tremendous enthusiasm just which stretch of road or coastal highway I just had to ride.

Nearly 150 gloriously twisty miles had passed beneath my Michelins when I veered off the parkway at Fancy Gap, Virginia. At one of Fancy Gap's intersections I looked right and left and noticed nothing more than two or three lonely motels. They didn't fit my mood. I wanted to feel a slight bit of civilization. Still sitting in the intersection, Goose patiently waiting on me to make up my mind, I looked down to notice that I was practically on top of the state line and the quaint town of Mt. Airy, North Carolina. The hometown of Andy Griffith was just a hop, skip, and a jump away.

Crossing into North Carolina at sunset felt strangely adventurous. It wasn't my first time in the state. Through the years, I had gone there to visit friends, ride motocross, and pass through on my way to South Carolina's Myrtle Beach for vacation. Regardless of the reason, every time I left the Virginias for something slightly more southern, I experienced a feeling of freedom that can only be obtained through a spot of travel. Here, along with the abundance of deciduous trees, narrow pines grow in the increasingly red soil. In some places the dirt looks as though it has been mixed with rust in a tumbler, and any old fuel stop reveals a thicker twang in voices, showing that more has changed through the passing miles than just your latitude.

Mt. Airy's Main Street greeted me with a replica police cruiser piloted by an old feller and his Andy Griffith cardboard cutout. This caught me off guard as I whipped my helmet sideways twice to solidify what I just saw. The feel of Mt. Airy's Main Street is one where time has stopped, like it said enough is enough and made a law against new development. Take a quick second to create an image of an idealistic small town Main Street in your mind. You probably just pictured Mt. Airy's Main Street. I would've explored it a little more, but darkness was falling and shops were closing. Two first gear drifts along the short straight stretch was the best I would do.

I backtracked through town in search of a place to crash that didn't involve a zipper. A clean-looking, roadside motel called the Hollows Inn caught my eye. The owner of the place, a friendly and helpful older gentleman, had a map in his office with little colored cushion pins showing where he has been and plans to go. I studied it with as much intrigue as if it were my own travels highlighted there on the wall. His visited locations far outnumbered his locations remaining to see. I was envious. The idea that a motel owner could be so well-traveled never crossed my mind. I thought they were practically glued to the position, always there to check someone in 24/7, doing endless paperwork, cleaning rooms destroyed by partying youth, or just sitting around mindlessly watching something uninspiring on the lobby television. But no, this man's map was outright porcupine-ish. In fact, the only place that I recall seeing still unpegged was Siberia. He said that he planned to go.

He handed me the key to Room 112—my favorite number and my mx racing number. Each room was charmed up with a white rocking chair just outside the door. I planted my ass there, made the cap on a glass bottle of beer snap and spit as I twisted it, and watched the traffic go by like I was retired. North Carolina was starting out on the right foot.

Day 5 – October 18, 2011

Five days in. That would sound so hard-core if it were a hundred days in. I was just a little baby traveler who hadn't seen nothin' yet. Yet somehow, at only five days, it was already the biggest adventure of my life. To my surprise and assuredly to the surprise of my family and a few friends back home, I was still on the road. And to tell the truth, I wanted to be. I was doing fine with concrete and pavement below me—crossing bridges, carving corners, twisting the throttle, and hauling ass—but some things just shouldn't mingle with the road. I began to loosely tally up the unluckiest of asphalt's visitors. The East Coast's lack or loss of large predators has surely been replaced by a skilled hunter, otherwise known as the automobile. With only five days under my belt, I saw a million flat, tire-wrangling squirrels, dead deer by the dozens, three expired black snakes, and one road kill raccoon. Speaking of animals, the Goose and I were barely south of Virginia and had already covered more than 600 miles.

I packed an extremely light and compact Primus butane stove for the ride and had yet to see if it was of any count. Right outside the motel room door, on the cold October concrete walkway, my tiny stove handily conquered a pot of oatmeal. Once again, I sat in the rocking chair ('cause how often does anyone my age take time to enjoy a real rocking chair?) and warmed up a little more with each bite. My stove made me proud. It's not often that I spend money wisely, but I'll brag about purchasing that stove for life.

Sliding through town the evening before, I noticed Mt. Airy Yamaha. I was in need of chain lube and curious to see what sort of new bikes were hitting the showroom floor for the new model year. I walked in, bought the lube, and never left the parts counter. Chris and J.R., the parts guys, welcomed me to their shop with nothing but southern kindness. Talking with those guys brought back good memories of my days as a parts picker at the local bike shops. Then somehow our conversation turned to the other dreaded *H* word, not hangover but Harley. Being a die-hard Japanese motorcycle fan, I've been exposed to the looks and jeers from my fellow two-wheelers on the heavy American motorcycles. Without thinking too much, I proceeded to rag on the American made machines. J.R. jumped right in. After all, we were in a Yamaha dealership. The Harley jokes were running along smoother than an in-line four when Chris filled me in that he owned a Harley. *Shit!* I didn't want to insult the guy. He took it lightly, but when he finally had his turn to speak, I received a detailed schooling about the HD brand, with his biggest point being, "They became good reliable bikes in 1992." I countered with a perfectly timed wise crack, "So is yours a 91?" He just shoved it off with a smile. Those guys were great.

When it came time to tell the guys about my trip, I did it like an overly enthusiastic motormouth. They listened politely and were more than responsive with all sorts of recommendations for riding in North Carolina. They posed for a few pictures and gave me some stickers to slap on the Goose. I left Mt. Airy Yamaha happy.

Day two of the one-man, two-wheeled party on the parkway began next, although with a hiccup. A section of the parkway was closed, so I was detoured to Route 18 S, which could arguably be renamed the Christmas tree farm capital of the world. That stretch of two-lane had an annoying way of remaining beautiful while not promising to, unlike the parkway, which is going to be amazing the whole time and therefore your camera is always on standby. On 18 S I never went for my camera, but I kept passing perfect farms and an unending patchwork of Christmas trees clinging to steep green hillsides. There were no warning signs saying, "For your next ten miles your neck will swing wildly and your shutter finger will begin to itch." There were no Santa-Crossing signs either. If there ever was a place that the jolly fat man would vacation, this would be it. The detour was a pleasant surprise.

Freeborne's Eatery and Lodge appeared on the right at the end of the detour. It was a modest building that kind of looked like a two-story house converted into a business. I walked in looking for a bite to eat. The place had a small bar and a pretty little bartender. Naturally, I had no choice but to gravitate in her direction. I ordered some grub and a couple New Castle Brown Ales, which later helped to dull the sting of one of my most embarrassing bathroom visits ever.

I don't think that it was any of Freeborne's food that got to me, but I had to go blow up the men's room. It's already bad enough cleaning out the pipes at any public throne, but to have company while performing is just unpleasant.

Freeborne's restroom was sized for one at a time. The slight buzz from the beer must have hindered my door locking skills. This became starkly clear as a large man in black leather riding apparel with a long grey ponytail, probably a proud HD motorcyclist, lumbered in while I was pulling north on my trousers. Fortunately, I was quick enough to cover the blind snake. He shot out of there like a big leather bullet. I wasn't quick enough when I blurted, "Guess I've been caught with my pants down." The only response I heard was the backfire-like sound of the door slamming shut. Normally this would make me feel incredibly bashful, but I was having one of those days where you couldn't wipe that stupid grin off my face.

I paid my two-brew tab and walked onto the covered porch outside. There were some other bikers standing around having a couple cold ones. They were undoubtedly drawn to Freeborne's after the detour, just as I had been. Like bike guys do, we started talking about our trips. I just finished spewing out my best long version of my trip to those guys when a new guy walked up and asked where I was headed. The other guys and I just laughed. The new guy got the express version. I had to make time if I was going to make it to Asheville before dark. One of the guys told me that if my trip was long enough, I should write a book about it. He confidently said, "I'd buy one." And thus the idea to put all these words together in between two slabs of cardboard was born.

I hopped back on the parkway for a ride through a land of Fruity Pebbles. The delicious and crispy breakfast treat of a cereal kept forcing itself into my thoughts high atop the mountains. Here, just north of Asheville, the Blue Ridge Parkway flaunted outrageous seasonal colors, like the view was influenced by a handful of magic mushrooms. It must be that one day of the year the tree's colors have to peak. Today was that day. The trees were intensely red, yellow, and green—just like a giant bowl of Fruity Pebbles without the milk—or maybe I was the milk. Hell, I'm whiter than milk. Years back, some cool guys yelled *Milk* at me from their car as I was pedaling a bicycle, shirtless, at the beach. Since then I pedal in sweaters. Anyway, a ride along the BRP during the autumn leaf change is a must if you own a motorcycle.

I whizzed by Mt. Mitchell, the highest peak east of the Mississippi. Its big, semi-bald dome looked cold and uninviting. I thought that it would be just another rolling, heavily vegetated hump in the endless Appalachians. Dense clouds lingered just over its summit. Wind whipped through the trees growing near the top, making them bend and sway. I rode along in a minor state of awe. On one overlook a small brown sign confirmed that I had crossed the mile-high mark for the first time in my life, making me the newest member of a mile-high, something-or-other club that has nothing to do with me being cool or even gaining anything to brag about. I was finding that the best part about traveling without every last mind-numbing detail figured out is the constant stimulation brought by not knowing what's around the next corner.

The sun set on the muscle-shaped hills of western North Carolina, and I found myself still scampering to Asheville in a heavy downpour. It was just before 8:00pm when I checked into the first place I found, the Downtown Inn and Suites. Camping was the furthest thing from my mind. Soaked to the bone and looking like a drowned rat, I unloaded any gear that could be easily snatched by a sticky-fingered parking lot parasite and retired to my room, still sporting that stupid grin.

An hour and a half after midnight, I finally let my eyes rest from the deep, mesmerizing gaze that they'd been locked in for hours. The fifteen-inch laptop screen had held my attention like a bug at a street lamp as I worked late into the night, catching up on email and a slight bit of online reality that I had been avoiding. Nonstop travel left very little time to do anything else. Every so often I would break from the bright glow coming from the electric rectangle in front of me to take a lap around the darkened room. Right before I called it quits, I took a few minutes to research Asheville's attractions. There were quite a few, so I planned to sleep on the options, hoping to be able to decide what to do with a fresh mind in the morning.

Day 6 – October 19, 2011

Seven fifteen came as quick as a blink. I was awake entirely too early. It was one of those mornings, like the ones before a workday where your belligerent alarm rudely blasts signals announcing, "Time for work lazy ass," while the bed feels better than it ever has. What woke me was an absolutely silent biological clock. Since the sun was already pushing rays into my room, I couldn't get back to sleep. It was time to make a decision, get breakfast, and go explore Asheville.

Rain was lightly falling as I heaved a load of clothes into the hotel's laundry. It had been two days solid with the same britches on. In the spirit of grimy adventure, I could've picked the cleanest dirty pair and kept trucking or could've trudged around Asheville in oh-no-commando style. And I know what you're thinking, "Sexy-sexy!" Or maybe you weren't thinking that at all. Anyway, time had come for my first road load. With the clothes in the tumbler my stomach began to rumble.

I've accepted breakfast as the most important meal of the day, and I think that sometimes it's so important and delicious that it should be enjoyed twice daily. Who hasn't tried pancakes and eggs for dinner? The Downtown Inn's continental breakfast featured an item of legend, an item that my taste buds seek with the ferocity of hungry wolves. It was the almighty Big Texas Cinnamon Roll. Never mind the wrapper says "baked in Chicago." A pile of those vending machine inhabiting suckers lured me to their large clear plastic container, swirls of icing calling my name. I'd never seen a free one outside of a locked Plexiglas and steel contraption, but there they were, sitting as tall as the pyramids and going nowhere. I destroyed one immediately and packed away three for the road. That first cinnamon roll didn't stand a chance, while the other three begged for mercy.

While walking back to the room with the rest of my breakfast, I noticed police everywhere and a camera guy standing directly below my balcony. I shouted to him, "What's up with the police?" He replied, "Wells Fargo is expanding into the Asheville area and they are bringing their carriage through town"—as they do with select, newly acquired territories and marketing events. He also said sarcastically, "It's just another thing to get me up out of bed at eight in the morning." I laughed and turned my attention to the matchbox-sized commotion in motion coming down Patton Street. The carriage was preceded by what I would like to describe as a parade where everyone forgot to show up. There were about eighty people involved in the whole thing, all working hard to look enthused. I think the camera guy was on to something.

Somewhere between breakfast and checkout time, I committed to seeing Asheville's largest house. Scratch that and insert America's largest house, the Biltmore Estate. I knew that it was an attraction lurking somewhere around the moist mountainous city, but due to the steep entrance fee, I was wary of forking out the money. In the end, I *had* to buy a tour ticket for the Biltmore Estate or go without the experience. The decision was made based on one small bit of reasoning. This was a once in a lifetime (I hate that expression) trip, and to pass up the opportunity to squeeze in our nation's largest private residence seemed illogical.

I packed up right at checkout time, threw the rain gear on, and made tracks to the Biltmore, clean underwear in tow. After all, one should be rather spic and span for a pinky-raised visit to the grounds. The $49 ticket price buckled my knees a little at the entry gate. No amount of eye fluttering or light flirting helped me sway the gal in charge of tour tickets. Forty-nine dollars was the asking price plain and simple. *I guess she's not into the dashing, young, motorcycle adventurer standing in front of her.*

Like the Natural Bridge, your first glimpse of this cousin-of-a-castle estate will leave you with a mild case of ticket-booth amnesia. It was as if a slice of Europe had been catapulted to the hills of North Carolina. I grabbed my camera faster than the lady at the ticket booth could deny a discount and headed right for it. I ran this way and that, up a hill and around the back, snapping pictures as I went, with energy far from spent, to the lawns and through the gardens, passing folks with subtle pardons, seeing endless stone packed with mortar, windows aligned in perfect order. I was out to capture every view. I didn't know what else to do. I was a tourist at the Biltmore, looking forward to what lay in store.

One can best describe the gargantuan Biltmore Estate by simply noting its specifications. It has forty-three bathrooms and thirty-five bedrooms, comprises 178,926 square feet of living space, and has 250 rooms. It is five stories tall, counting the finished basement level; however, the main dining hall peaks out at around seventy feet. The entire building weighs . . . I'm kidding. Construction began in 1889 and lasted until 1895. Outside, it is surrounded by an 8,000-acre farm.

Inside, my favorite room was the two-story library that housed more than 23,000 books. It was the kind of room that could make a cigar smoker out of me. Deep, dark wooden shelves carried the weight of all of those hardbacks. I wanted to walk along a row of those books with my pointer finger out, slightly brushing the spines of each one as I went, waiting for the right title to grab my eye. It was almost too much to bear. Rooms went on and on like a maze of perfectly decorated confusion, each one spotless and as grand as a sunset. Through the five floors, not one single step made a squeak, proving that the place was solid. Even the servant quarters were head and shoulders better than any room that I'd ever called my own. George Vanderbilt must have been filthy, stinky rich and well read.

A portion of the estate is owned by the government, as the taxes are quite a burden on the heirs. In the end, the place was amazing, and I wouldn't mind volunteering there for a while simply to see some stuff kept off-limits to the public. Taking nothing away from the Biltmore, I wonder if any of those forty-three old toilets can flush a five-gallon bucket of golf balls. Living in our day and age has its advantages, ya know? I loved the tour and finished up with a trip to the winery.

Walking back to the Goose, I had the good fortune of meeting an older couple from Louisiana named John and Jerri. Jerri asked me if I wanted to join them in a little tailgating. I said sure and walked over to the back of their minivan where they were sitting in the shade of its big square rear door. She also asked if I was hungry. I said, "I'm starving. Can I have one of your cookies?" She eagerly handed me one. My Big Texas breakfast had worn off during the tour. I hung around for a short spell. We talked about work, the weather and the Tabasco factory near their home. They were fine folks, just out enjoying life.

A while back, the Travel Channel featured a McDonald's of Asheville that was known for being Biltmore-esque. I knew that it had to be nearby. I found it camouflaged among the Biltmore District's other upper-class businesses. The exterior appearance matched the surrounding buildings, and the interior set new standards for fast food. A fireplace, piano, and chandeliers adorned the dining area. That sentence is worth a second read. As I sat there chomping on a number one, the piano keys were fluttering as if an invisible man was playing his heart out. It was almost enough to persuade me to chew with my mouth closed. Honestly, I felt that McDonald's could have, tastefully, left this part of Asheville alone. Nonetheless, experiencing a place that you've seen on the tube is neat.

After lunch, I was off to find some gasoline. I pulled into a fuel station and nailed the damn concrete post by the gas pump with my left side box. I hadn't yet gained a feel for the width of the bike with the luggage boxes attached. It was a hell of a whack. I nearly toppled over. A lady wearing a dark brown hood ie stood nearby. She came over to see if I was okay. I told her I was. She seemed only slightly alarmed over the cool move that I just pulled off and much less impressed. Her name was Tara, and she was a friendly, helpful Ashevillian. We exchanged contact info, and she pointed me in the direction of the nearest Blue Ridge Parkway intersection. I waved goodbye in the dreary October weather and was off, making those two wheels turn.

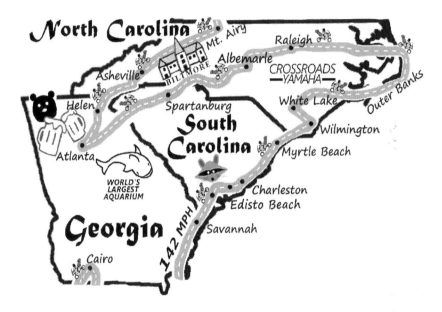

On the road again, literally, this was the third day on the good ol' parkway. It is a beautiful place with its endless curves, hollowed-out tunnels, and mile-high overlooks. It would be hard to find a visit to the parkway in mid-October regrettable. My goal for the night was Mt. Pisgah campground. Goal reached. A goal that I hoped to avoid was busting my ass on a wet railroad tie. At the campground each 12' x 12' tent pad was lined by four railroad ties and filled with crushed gravel. I was headed to the right side of my tent to smash in an-other peg when my left foot made a millisecond's worth of contact with the tie. It was like stepping on a banana peel that was splayed on a hockey rink. My arms went skyward as my ass kissed the ground. The whole thing was caught on camera, as I had it set up on the site's picnic table on the time-lapse setting. I was too happy to do anything but laugh.

An hour's worth of light still hung in the sky. I walked up the hill to a res-taurant overlooking a spectacular valley. In an instant a thick and aggressive fog rolled in. It consumed the absolutely heavenly view like a giant unstoppable ghost. Within minutes, my twenty or thirty-mile view was down to just seventy-five feet and the sun said bye-bye. The temperature dropped, and I made haste back to the warmth of my sleeping bag. Before I fell asleep that night, the clouds over Mt. Pisgah released a dusting of snow.

Day 7 – October 20, 2011

The park ranger had told me that I shouldn't have to worry about bears in Mt. Pisgah's campground. She said, "We haven't seen one in about a month. They've most likely moved to a lower elevation already." That made staying in my little tent slightly better. The potential for furry havoc was replaced by forty-mph winds from a coughing Mother Nature. Strong gusts accompanied dropping temperatures all night.

I awoke to ridiculous wind, snow flurries, and a thick brown carpet of agitated leaves. Shivering, I told myself, "Right now it would be nice not to have a set of balls, so it would be impossible to freeze 'em off." I wasn't feeling nearly motivated enough to ride the bike eighty miles or more to Helen, Georgia. For twenty minutes before takeoff, I bathed in the heat of the sturdy bathhouse. Its vaulted and beamed wood ceiling and thick concrete walls would make a nice place to escape a bear lurking in the campground. Just outside those walls, a temperature in the low thirties dared me to come out.

I must have cursed my journey's itinerary somehow before leaving home. After months of planning, not one day thus far had I been able to stick to the painstakingly charted route. The morning's plan was to inevitably bid farewell to the BRP and replace its park roads for Route 23 S, straight into Georgia. As fate would have it, I shouldn't have planned anything. I was only nine miles from Richland Balsam, the BRP's highest road surface elevation, when snow and black ice threw me off course far sooner than I expected.

A man heading in the opposite direction on a Honda cruiser flagged me down to warn of the road's treachery ahead. I never actually saw black ice. I just relied on the honesty and concern in his dark brown eyes as he peered through a balaclava cloaking his head under his helmet. I had no choice but to find a detour. The snow was changing from pea-sized flakes to heavy-looking, nickel-sized ones. As I hightailed it out of there, the yellow center lines began to change to one wide white line with road shoulders to match. Route 215 was the closest artery off the mountain and came just in the nick of time. The conditions were almost white-out.

Detouring turned out for the best. Route 215's awesome corners escorted the Goose and me right back into the land of bright autumn colors. It seemed as quick of a shot as any to drop elevation fast. The detour continued through small rustic towns along Route 64. They seemed like hidden villages with their countless supply of wood-framed shops and homes. I stopped in a town named Cashiers and bought some coffee at the Ingles Grocery Store. The temperature was thirty-four degrees. Inside, I met three ladies who were on their lunch break from the local county health department. We talked about work, relationships, and why I wasn't married with children yet. I obliged their curiosities with friendly answers like, "I'm just not ready to settle down yet." I basked in their refreshing southern kindness and admired every word of their North

Carolina drawl. Inevitably, their lunch break had to end. We bid adieu to one another as I realized that my fingers were warm enough to feel again.

From Cashiers to Helen I stayed in a tight tuck behind my windscreen and alternated the left and right glove on the Goose's cylinder head covers. Somewhere near fifteen miles out from Helen there is a road sign at a T-shaped intersection that says "Helen 15" and points the direction. I turned that way, and after three miles I looked up to see another sign that read "Helen 15." Either some unseen force was playing a cruel joke on me, or somebody was drinking when they measured the distance between that T-intersection and Helen. I was freezing and had no idea if there were still fifteen miles to cover or twelve.

When I arrived in Helen, or "Alpine Helen" as the town describes itself, I was captivated by its fairy tale Bavarian theme. It looked as though Disney had released its Imagineers on a small, unsuspecting mountain village, or as if the dolls in a coo-coo clock came to life and constructed their ideal town. Words that end in schnitzel and tag wanted to creep from my lips. It's hard to believe that places so neat actually exist.

Before hunting down an authentic carbonated German beverage, I had to find a room. Being Oktoberfest, I knew that the town would have slim pickin's. Thick droves of tourists had already gobbled up the majority of the town's vacancies. The Haufbrau Motel was perfectly perched next to the town's trickling creek. I stopped there and was lucky enough to secure one of their last rooms. Finally, it was time to track down a brewski. Hell yeah!

I went to Spontain's Bar and Grill. It was a second-floor joint, housed in a building themed with a yellow Bavarian exterior and a dark rock-n-roll interior. The place was nearly empty, but that didn't stop me from sliding on a barstool and asking for the most German beer available. The bartender handed me an Erdinger. I sat there alone for a spell, like a wannabe Bavarian bump on a log, until the owner of the joint came over to chat. He introduced himself as Bug Spray, his biker name. It should be said that he was wearing black, had facial hair, tattoos, and could probably have twisted my arm into a pretzel. I told him, "I could use some bug spray for camping." I didn't get much of a reaction. He was in a biker club called the Black Pistons, which according to him was one of our nation's oldest biker clubs.

Despite his menacing outward appearance, he was a pretty good dude and even a family man. He showed me a couple of pictures on his phone. They were of his house, with snow in the yard, and his kids. The snow in the picture may have been an inch deep, yet he seemed shocked to see so much of it. I thought about the amount of snow that we sometimes get back home. His reaction to the snow told me that the southern Appalachians must not see much snow at all. It was kind of an eye opener. I shared a brief version of my ride and told him where I was headed. Like the fellas at Mt. Airy Yamaha, Bug Spray suggested that I see a few places that he liked on the Eastern Seaboard, places like Savannah and Tybee Island if I was passing by.

Bug Spray had to tend to some other things, so I sat there by myself until a couple from Ringo County, Georgia, showed up and took the seats right beside me. A dozen seats on either side of us were empty. I was glad to have the company. Their names were Neil and Donna, and we struck up a friendly conversation. Shortly after that, these two cats from Pike County, Georgia, Ray and Trey, joined in. They were both big country boys, as tall as me and carrying around fifty or sixty extra pounds. Ray had short brown hair, and Trey had even shorter blonde hair. The details aren't as important as the fun, though. I didn't know it at the time, but all five of us were wound tight like coiled springs and ready to party. The stage was set for a wild night at Oktoberfest.

Our encounter started with beer. Then Ray, who will tell you loud and proud that "Women don't get old; they get seasoned," had the bright idea to order some Kamikazes, and I had to add a shot of Jack Daniels—because I make really intelligent decisions while drinking. It was on after that. We were off to our next bar like a bunch of drunken hoodlums. We all piled in Trey's big Chevy truck (he was light years behind us in the drink count) and headed for the Hay Loft Bar. Trey was a guy of few words, so finding a blonde wig in the back seat of his truck was strange, yet very amusing. I grabbed the wig and held it as high as I could, bringing attention to it like I had just discovered buried treasure. Within seconds it made a lap around the truck. No heads were safe. We were grabbing it and installing it like it was a king's crown. I laughed 'til tears and was thankful that nobody had a healthy case of lice.

I'll never know the fate of that wig. I wore it for the first hour in the Hay Loft until this group of young folks just had to know if it was a wig or not. They were college students who thought that I was some sort of actor or something. They said, "We've never seen a head of hair so full in our lives." I hated to let 'em down when I pulled the wig off, displaying my dwindling supply of natural hair.

Ray, Trey, Neil, Donna, and I all partook in slurred karaoke until the moment the bar closed. We took turns on the mic and shook a leg on the dance floor for as long as I can remember, and then some. I'm not sure how I made it back to the room, but I surely made it.

Day 8 – October 21, 2011

Morning started with another visit from the Hangover Fairy. Piercing my ears with a deer antler would have felt better than the pounding in my dome. Why couldn't the Tooth Fairy have visited me instead? I'd take a black hole in my smile any day if I could find a foolproof way to drink and avoid hangovers. Checkout time at the Haufbrau snuck up on my nauseous ass faster than I downed one of last night's shots. I had to go secure a place to stay before I went to town and tied one on again, as this was Oktoberfest, and drinking is what you do here.

The weekend's festivities left little in the way of in-town options for finding a room. Nearby, Unicoi State Park offered camping and sounded like the best option. I rode over there only to find that they were booked solid. How could a fairly large state park not have enough room for a tent that's only 4' x 7'? I mean, my tent was so little that it could have fit in a handicap stall. Hell, I've seen people who have hogged up more space just by standing up. How could there not be enough room? If only the park could limit RV usage there would be more spots for people who really want to camp in the outdoors. Is it really camping if you have a stinking microwave with you? Anyway, gotta love over-regulation. I silently protested by telling myself that I would pitch my tent somewhere around Helen that night and I was not going to pay to do it, after I would have gladly paid the park to borrow a tiny morsel of land.

On my way out of the park, a black bear cub turned my world upside down. Upon seeing it, I went from fuming to fascinated. The little guy was darting through the woods barely forty feet away. This was my first time seeing a wild bear. I kept my eyes locked on it like those crazy Midwesterners who watch tornadoes too long and get whacked by a piece of lumber instead of taking shelter early. There beside me was a creature that has long inhabited the woods of my home county without me ever seeing one.

When I was a child, two black bears climbed onto our porch to snag some leftovers that my mom had planned to throw away. Dad called the police while Mom rushed us to the bedroom farthest away from the porch in case the bears broke through our flimsy trailer door. Even though they were on our front porch, my eyes didn't actually see the bears.

This one at the park was small, maybe the size of a cocker spaniel. I captured it on film with one eye, while keeping the Goose out of the ditch with the other. Knowing that mama bear had to be near, I never took the bike out of first gear. My senses were elevated. If mama bear wanted to scrap, she would have to catch me first. It seemed that the cub was all alone, though. For five minutes I watched it watch me. It would run from tree to tree, stopping to peek its head in my direction before taking off again. The encounter proved to be fulfilling, and I remember telling myself that if I had not taken off a week ago, I would have missed the bear sighting. It put me in a state of peace.

I wandered around Helen aimlessly all day, trying not to think about my sleeping situation. I reassured myself by saying, "Something will work out. Just have fun." I forced it to the back of my mind and decided to go grab a beer. I trekked on over to the Old Heidelberg Bar and met the bartender. She was blocked in by the bar during working hours with nowhere to run, and I was thirsty, leaving her no choice but to meet me. Her name was Martina. She was a tall, thin gal with bleached blonde hair and slightly more than average piercings. She was also authentically German. She was a strong minded sort of character and obviously a well-traveled person. To top that off, she used to race moto-cross in Germany. *Was I still in Helen, or Heaven?* It's not often that I cross paths with a female that has anything in common with me.

Sitting there in her presence during Oktoberfest, in that culturally decorated drinking hole—with no worries of bills to pay, or a work week approaching, or a boss who could hold me to the minute at the start of the work day—was the first time that I felt peace at a level never before experienced in my life. It was a monumental moment, maybe a trip-changing moment. I was happy, and it didn't feel temporary. It felt robust. It was the first time in years that I could confidently use happy to describe myself. And I knew it.

Nighttime was coming, so I walked down the street to where the Goose was parked to grab a jacket. A woman walked by me, and I thought nothing of it, but I did do the mandatory head turn, butt glance thing that guys can't help but do. Then about two minutes later she came back and asked if I was alone. I said, "Yeah" and thought, "This shit never happens to me." She said that she was too and I said, "Let's hang out" and thought, "Did I just say the right thing."

She was an attractive woman, probably fifteen years my elder, blonde hair, blue eyes, and talkative. Her name was Priscilla, and she and I would spend the next four hours at Oktoberfest having some drinks (mine beer and hers water), talking about anything and everything under the sun. She just went through a divorce and really needed to vent. I just happened to have nothing but time.

Her world had been rocked. For the first time since her early twenties, she was single and lonely and out in the world as a newbie. I could tell that her family's split hit her hard as she described how scary it was to have to start all over again and find things to do without her long-time partner. A heavily concealed secret that her husband held for many, many, years ruined her hopes for a happily ever after marriage. He had recently come out of the closet. Priscilla was left to reflect upon all of those years she spent dedicated to a dishonest man. She was heartbroken knowing that she couldn't get those years back. A bit of honesty in the beginning of their relationship could have saved a shipload of grief. It was my time to be a shoulder to lean on. There have been plenty of times when I surely have needed a shoulder.

Priscilla's night ended much sooner than mine as she left Helen at 10:00pm. I hoped that she would have stayed long enough to at least drown some sorrows with a few pints, but it was not to be. We made plans to go to the Georgia Aquarium together the next day. In hindsight, I thought that she was pretty brave for coming up to me like that earlier in the evening. I could've been a weirdo or a serial killer on the run or something. Hell, she could've been a serial killer who preyed on poor, traveling, two-wheeling gingers. But I was safe, and she was safe. I'm just a heavy-drinking, throttle-twistin', confused, crazy guy— nothing to worry about here.

It really hit me when she left that I didn't have a place to stay, so instead of caving in and riding out of town to buy a room, I sucked it up and partied hard, reckless and wild. The night flew into warp drive. I met a bunch of people that I stand absolutely no chance of remembering. A fuzzy, late-night trip to the Bavarian-themed Wendy's, with a group of young cats who gave me a ride, vaguely holds space in my brain. It was well into the small hours when I made it back to the Goose. With nowhere to stay and only my trusty FZ1 to hang out with, I pulled the tarp out of the side box, unleashed my fortress of a sleeping bag, covered up the Goose, and wormed my way up against the tires. *Now I'm living!*

Day 9 – October 22, 2011

"How'd you sleep?" a deep voice asked as I was crawling out of my sleeping bag, still pretty tuned in. Before responding, I whispered, "Shit! They're gonna run me outta here." The voice had come from the parking lot attendant standing no more than five or six feet behind me. I took his question to be suspicious and sarcastic at first, but I was mistaken. The thin, old man was also the owner of the lot, and as we spoke he displayed nothing short of a welcoming nature. I began to think that he was quite pleased to be an unsuspecting parking lot host for my overnight escapade. He told me at one point, "If I knew ya was gonna sleep on the ground then I'd a left my ticket shed open for ya." Before I left he reminded me to track him down on my next trip to Helen so that he could leave it open. I said thanks and rode away. At that point, everything was smooth.

In order to keep my plans with Priscilla to visit the aquarium in Atlanta, I would have to show Helen my rear tire. I had a splendid time there, and as I left I vowed to return. Another lady, who I met at the town liquor store, told me about a small Indian mound on the outskirts of town. From her description, it wasn't the biggest or most impressive thing around, and I could have easily just pushed on to Atlanta without seeing it, but curiosity got the best of me, and besides, it would be the first Indian mound that I ever saw, so I rode out to it.

When I pulled off the shoulder beside a fenced-in meadow where the mound sat centered and bulging from the surrounding ground, I realized that I had seen it on my way into town a couple of days ago. It was about ten feet high, plateau-like and circular, maybe fifty feet across. On top of it sat a small white gazebo. When I passed it before, I chalked it up as a neat elevated place to hold a wedding ceremony or something. A background of rolling green mountains made for a serene postcard scene. The mound was covered in thick, green grass and probably would've blended right into the pasture if not for the gazebo. I snapped a couple pictures from the road, not wanting to breach the fence.

While standing roadside thinking about the "why's" of the mound, folks passing in their warm vehicles kept stopping to ask if I was broke down. It was frequent and unexpected. It seemed as though every driver that passed did this. I guess they weren't noticing my camera in hand. When they'd slow and begin cranking down the window, I'd turn and wave and say that everything's alright and thank them for stopping. Most of the folks were in their advanced years. I found it amusing and appreciated the good nature of the people here. My head was feeling fine since the buzz was still lingering from last night. From there, there was nothing to do but ride.

It wasn't long before coffee's addictive clutch began to tug on my weakened thought process. I stopped at a little country store and bought a large coffee to try to sober up. The cashier greeted me like a family member; then we talked like we had known one another forever. It was just her and me there. She was busy cleaning shelves, and I sat at one of four round tables. An ancient man entered the store, breaking our conversational stride. He was wearing suspenders over a set of clothes that only an old man can pull off without looking ridiculous. He had to be eighty-five. He was on the hunt for biscuits and gravy.

When he noticed me, and probably determined that I wasn't from around there, he hobbled over and asked where I was from. I replied, "West Virginia" followed by a big smile. He said fondly, "Ahh, West Virginia," and wasted no time announcing his favorite fiddler, like his mission of the day was to share that knowledge. The late West Virginian Senator Robert Byrd was the fiddler who tickled his fancy the most. His proclamation was loud enough to grab my full attention. Then he got down to business. He turned in the direction of the clerk and semi-demanded biscuits.

I watched a sad scene unfold. The poor guy left there dejected. There were no biscuits that morning. The clerk told him that they were out. I'll never forget the way his jaw dropped when the cashier broke the news. If there ever was a time to see a man's heart break, this was it. One moment he was flying high, pronouncing his passion for Robert Byrd's fiddling, and in the next he was blindsided and distraught by a simple lack of biscuits. On his way out the door he labored out a wheezy, "No biscuits?" As I rode away from that store, I thought *I gotta get me some of these damn biscuits.* Then I became distraught. The **H** word was knocking at my door.

I rode for a couple hours and arrived in Norcross, Georgia. By then the dreaded hangover was in full force. I couldn't even twist the throttle without dry heaving. The wind at sixty mph felt like hurricane force. The coffee did nothing to save me. Between that and Priscilla canceling on the aquarium, I decided to get a room and recover from the weekend's madness. Once I checked into my room, which also made me dry heave, I plopped down on the bed and initiated operation pillow drool. For five hours, drips of goo lubed up those freshly washed pillows, evidenced by the cold wet spot that my cheek swam in upon waking.

After coming back to life, I went to get some pizza. If you ever happen to be in Norcross, by golly, stop by Manhattan NY Pizza and have a few slices. They take pizza almost too seriously. The owner was a thirty-one-year-old guy who wore an incredibly tall chef's hat while making each slice by hand. To taste a pie that had some thought put into it and that was not lacking in the toppings department was a nice change of pizza pace. For a couple kind words about their pizza, the guys behind the counter hooked me up with some stickers for the Goose. I joined hundreds of other folks who had signed the walls with a sharpie and rode back to the room, patiently waiting for the next day.

Day 10 – October 23, 2011

Day ten started with a bang, literally. Although I didn't hear it, the drunken assholes, who thought it necessary to push the Goose over on its side, heard the bang. I was in Norcross, Georgia, at the GuestHouse Inn. I had made a final check on my bike around 11:45pm, and it was still standing solid on the center stand where it had been for hours. The parking lot was perfectly level with no wind to speak of. When I awoke at 8:30am and looked out my room window, I was horrified to see the Goose lying on its side. Instantly, a fire went through me, and I stormed out of Room 138 like I was shot out of a cannon. I was a skinny white man twice as pissed off as the big green hulk. Marching toward the fallen bike, I grumbled, "I'm gonna kill somebody."

I wanted to pick the bike up off the ground, but then I realized the opportunity to capture an incredibly real part of this cross-country adventure. I had to film the incident. I ran back to the room and then back to the Goose. I turned the camera on and angrily said my piece while pointing the camera at my fallen friend. In the heat of the moment I didn't notice that my camera's memory card was full. After recording, I strained to pick the bike up and then checked the camera for the footage, but there was a problem. When I found that it didn't record, I had a choice: lay the bike right back over to depict the actual moment or just keep it up and begin to try to find out what exactly happened. I kept it standing. The Goose did not come out of the fall unscathed. The right side storage box had a huge hole in it with my long john pants hanging out, and the tongue on my Saddleman trunk was broken off. The replacement cost would be about $180.

I made my way to the front office where I was still hotter than fire. The front desk attendant, Jose, patiently put up with my attitude and gave me the number to the local police department. I called without hesitation. Within fifteen minutes an officer arrived. We walked around and looked for explanations. There was a brownish Chevrolet Denali from Tennessee parked ridiculously close to where my bike had been. Jose said that the SUV, and its occupants, didn't arrive at the hotel until after 2:00am. I told the officer, "According to Jose, the incident should be on the surveillance camera." The officer then told me rudely, "I don't have time to sit and watch all that film." *It wouldn't take that long since the fast forward feature was invented decades ago, you dumb bastard.* I didn't tell him that though. It's no fun having the police against you when you need their help. He wrote a case number down on a card and told me to turn it in to my insurance company. *Thanks a lot, Officer Lazy Ass.* His figure gave away the fact that he had made plenty of time for donuts, though. And I bet if it were a donut delivery truck that was tipped, he would go to the ends of the Earth to find the culprit.

The storage boxes bolted to the side of the Goose were actually plastic, waterproof Stanley toolboxes. I bought them for $30 at a Lowe's Home Improvement Warehouse. Before leaving home, I had an account full of money and could have bought any top-of-the-line panniers on the market, ones that could have shrugged off any parking lot tumble. But that would have set me back about $1,200. My choice to use cheap plastic boxes now bit me in the rear. Fortunately, a Lowe's was a mile away from the GuestHouse Inn. And guess what? They had dozens of Stanley toolboxes for the taking. I rearranged the contents of the broken box, so that no small stuff would fall out as I rode over, and left the hotel behind.

My Lowe's receipt had a new Stanley toolbox, some nuts and bolts, and a hatchet on it (for the next time some asshole knocks my bike over). Just kidding. The hatchet will be for firewood and driving tent stakes into the ground. It took me about an hour and a half to mount up the new box in the

Lowe's parking lot. In between stares of curious onlookers, I used my pocket-knife to whittle some bolt holes and had shit scattered everywhere.

I made for Atlanta and the Georgia Aquarium, the world's largest aquarium, and the lone reason I was in that part of the world in the first place. As a child, I absolutely loved visiting the National Aquarium in Baltimore's Inner Harbor. Animals of the deep blue waters, that should be thousands of miles away, were right there in front of me. Oddly enough, the rainforest exhibit was always my favorite part, as I hunted for a hidden monkey in the branches or some reptile scurrying around. Most of my visits to the National Aquarium were shared with my father, since he lived in Baltimore. He expressed a sense of wonder about the animals that had permanently rubbed off on me; like a brainwashed cult member, I couldn't help but share the feeling. Now, nervously, and against the advice of a couple of Lowe's employees, as they feared that I would be flattened by the city drivers, I headed into the big city of Atlanta for another taste of the oceans. Sometimes you have to make choices that you can live with, and I chose not to be afraid to take the Goose into the city.

Against the Lowe's employee predictions, I made it to the aquarium. The traffic had been light. I parked my bike in a small side lot run by two natives of Atlanta. I locked everything up solid, except my big hiking pack, and went on in hoping that it would still be there when I returned. I felt incredibly uneasy knowing that there was no way to chain down my pack, and that my expensive sleeping bag could be so easily stolen. The morning's incident with the Goose being pushed over, and dealing with the worthless police officer, reinforced that if I were to see the aquarium then I'd have to take a chance that my pack wouldn't be there when I returned, and if that was the case, calling the cops would render no help whatsoever. What a damn shame.

Tickets were $27. The Georgia Aquarium was known for having two of the world's largest fish, the undisputed size king of the non-mammalian ocean, the almighty whale shark. I raced around for a little bit, trying to find what had to be the largest enclosed tank in the building. Finally, there they were: two submarine-sized beauties, spotted and looking slightly blue from the deep water, circling in a thick school of fish a tenth their size. The gentle giants sailed through the tank, unaware of their effect on me or their place in the animal kingdom. I watched them in complete awe.

One industrious little fish impressed me with a skill that I had never related to an aquatic animal. It was a Yellowhead Jawfish, and it acted like the prairie dog of the ocean. It may have been five inches long and about as thick as a tube of toothpaste. It sat like a horseshoe peg floating halfway out of its volcano-shaped mound. Every few seconds, it would do a one-eighty, disappear into its mound, and come back out with a mouthful of rocks that it spat out on the sides of its mound. I didn't know that such a fish existed. It surely enhanced my appreciation for the ocean's diversity. What a fascinating creature.

As much as I hate to admit it, I did rush through a few exhibits. I love nothing more than to experience new things, but having my pack so exposed to the public while trying to enjoy myself, dampened my visit. Other than really soaking in the whale shark exhibit, I went through the building haunted by the thought of my pack getting stolen. I couldn't force it away.

After the aquarium, I quickly rode by the Occupy Atlanta movement, where I briefly entertained the idea of popping my tent up with the other folks just for the experience, but I opted out. I really had no idea what they were up to, but one of the parking attendants recommended it. From there my travels took me to Interstate 85 E where I decided to put the hammer down and let the Goose fly. I needed to make miles.

Somewhere in South Carolina, on my way northeast, a rather large man sitting in the rear middle spot of a white king cab truck gave me the bird. *What the heck did I do to him?* I threw my hand up in protest and tried to let it go. *Nope, I'm not going to be able to let it go. I didn't do anything to this idiot.* In an effort to live with my choices, I nailed the throttle to catch back up to them and extended the ol' center digit as far as it would go. Relief washed over me as I sped past. After the day I was having, there was no need to take any more shit.

Miles passed and the sun took its daily nap. I was shooting for Morrow Mountain State Park, near Albemarle, North Carolina. It was 10:00pm and pitch black at Morrow Mountain's gate. A sign read, "Park closes at eight." *Schweet!* After hours of riding and hoping to just collapse on my air mattress, I was left with the awareness that I had to backtrack to Albemarle to find another damn motel room. Exhausted and in no mood to hunt for the best deal in town, I checked in at the first place I came to. Parting words for day ten are "still better than a day at the office."

Day 11 – October 24, 2011

My morning routine was getting faster and more efficient each day. When it came time to load up the bike, bits of gear were finding their places and packing became easier: clothes in the rear trunk, any brochures or papers in the tank bag, right side box for tools and camping gear, left side box for food, camera gear, hygiene articles and cooking equipment, and then there was my midget-sized passenger of a hiking pack—containing a sleeping bag, more food, solar shower, and more clothes—that rested high on the passenger seat. I had everything out of the room and on the bike in no time. Last night I noticed a Yamaha dealership as I was riding through Albemarle in search of a hotel room. Since I only packed one tire iron on the bike before I left home, I thought that a quick stop at the local bike shop would be just the ticket to add another one to the gear.

After checking out of my room in record time, I rode over to Crossroads Yamaha, unprepared for what was about to happen. The store was a clean rectangle with a large blue rim at roof level holding big white letters that spelled Crossroads. It seemed as typical as any shop that I'd seen, with its broad glass front and company vehicles parked around the side. I walked in just like any Joe off the street, expecting to wander around for two or three minutes before anyone noticed me, but instead I was greeted by enthusiastic, friendly smiles from three folks behind the counter: Jason, Carmen, and Jed. I told them of my need for a tire iron, and that broke the ice for more than an hour's worth of unreal hospitality.

Jason and Carmen were the married owners and a fit-looking, mid-thirties couple who seemed happy and eager to help. Jed was a twenty-year-old guy and an aspiring pro motocross racer. While talking to him, I saw myself ten years before: tall, thin as a paper clip, and downright obsessed with motocross. This guy bled motocross, and I was no stranger to the feeling. He, like me, was supporting his own racing effort without the help of strong financial backing. As I listened to him, I hoped that he'd reach every goal, but I knew the burden of trying to become a professional racer with limited funds all too well. All four of us discussed the ins and outs of what needed to happen to take his racing to the next level. The best advice was to step back, develop a plan, and get some better equipment. He had been riding older bikes and having the hardest time keeping them in good running condition. I wished him the best on his journey to his highest level of racing and secretly wished that I was twenty-one again.

The need for a tire iron became a distant memory as we started talking about my trip. I busted out a decent long version of the last ten days and shared my plans for crossing the country. The events that happened next still have my mind boggled. Jason said sharply, "He's gonna need a sweatshirt." I thought that was very generous of him, but he had bigger plans, and they snowballed until I was left speechless. Carmen came out of the back with a new Crossroads Yamaha hoodie and T-shirt. *Wow!* Then they started asking about my bike, and we walked outside. I rather followed them, as they were now in full control. I told them that I hadn't had a chance to wash the Goose yet, and almost immediately Jason said to take the bike back to the shop and they would take care of that. *Awesome!* So I rode the bike to the back, where they not only scrubbed and hand washed it (I mean really going hog wild with a set of wet and soapy shop brushes), but also filled it up with fuel, checked the tire pressure, gave me some food, and slapped on a bunch of free stickers! Man I was blown away.

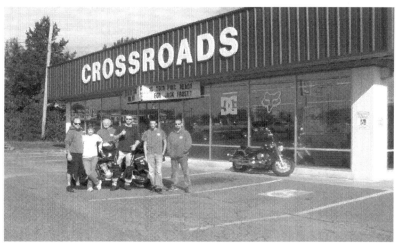

Jason, Carmen, John, me, Jed, and Jeff

[49]

Jason was a spiritual man who practiced what he preached. He told me of his belief in the Lord and how he incorporated it into his business. Like any great leader, he genuinely looked out for others while setting a good example. I admired him deeply. Before I left, we all stood in a circle, heads bowed, as Jason lead us in prayer. I appreciated every word of it. He gave thanks so sincerely, as if my arrival there was a gift when in reality meeting those folks was a gift to me. Carmen and I whipped out some cameras and snapped a few farewell pictures. I left there so stunned that I forgot to buy the tire iron and went the wrong way out of the parking lot. *Did that really just happen?*

On the complete opposite end of the spectrum, my next stop would involve a rendezvous with the Devil. Igor had recommended a paranormal site to see called the Devil's Tramping Ground. This area of mystery is in Siler City, North Carolina, way out in the country on Devil's Tramping Ground Road. I searched for some directions on the Internet and headed that way, as my map wasn't nearly specific enough to guide me into the realm of the unknown.

So what is the Devil's Tramping Ground, you ask? Well, the legend states that if an object is placed in this little plot of land at night, sometime, presumably when no one is looking, a force will remove the object from the circle, placing it just on the edge. Legend also claims that the Devil dances in these spots. I have always enjoyed a clutter free dance floor myself, so I don't really disagree with the tidiness. Through the years, I've heard of these spots and read just a bit about them. I've heard of more than one being located in the USA and a few others scattered abroad. The common denominator for each barren circle is the shape—a circle—and the obvious lack of plant life. What really goes down there? I can't say, but I did have to go have a looksee.

Once there on DTG road, I found what I believed to be the spot. I followed the online directions verbatim but was still unsure. I hopped off the bike and had a quick look around and decided to backtrack four miles to a service station to ask someone. A young fella working there claimed to know nothing about the legend but did inform me of a party spot where locals drank on the weekend. His directions were the same as the ones I had, so I thanked him and set off again, back to where I just left. This time I thought I should hike around in the woods a little bit. I had read that it was almost visible from the road. I left the Goose on the shoulder, to keep look out, and stood facing a patch of North Carolinian woods with a cattle pasture to my back. A slight trail poked into the woods. I followed it and sure enough, roughly 150 feet away, there was a clearing, a more or less circular clearing.

The spot had been overrun by people camping or partying. Broken bottles mixed with the soil. A huge log was blackened in the center of a fire pit, undoubtedly placed there by four or five drunken country boys. I doubt that even the Devil would have been able to budge that thing. A sign saying "Devil's Tramping Ground" would have been nice to announce that I was where I thought I was.

As I stood there, hidden from any passing car on the road, butterflies fluttered in my stomach. I quickly snapped a few pictures while feeling like I was being watched. It's safe to say that I walked much quicker in the direction of the Goose than I did in the direction of the circle. Still though, without any solid evidence that I was in the absolute correct spot, I searched a nearby pull-in and found a small pile of bones encircled by standing bottles and a freshly deceased calf. What the calf was doing out of the pasture and in the woods was beyond me. That creeped me out enough to want to get back to civilization.

I left Siler City and continued due east toward Raleigh, stopping only once at a biker bar called the Iron Horse. I received absolutely no welcome by the Harley riders sitting around the bar. Perhaps they saw my bonehead move as I swerved off the highway, down through a grassy culvert, and into the parking lot, standing up the whole time. Igor had recommended the Iron Horse, and I just caught a glimpse of it as I was passing by, forcing me to pull off said maneuver (some of my old motocross skills came to use there). In the whole of the trip, the Iron Horse took the cake for most dirty looks given to the guy on the Japanese bike.

And so, for the third time today, Igor played a role in how my day would go. Igor's name could be changed to Igor Gotcherbak Scherbakov; it would fit him perfectly. He had a friend in Raleigh named Bryan who owed him a favor. Bryan agreed to host me for a night since Igor hosted one of his French buddies in Washington, D.C. a while back. I arrived in Raleigh around 7:30pm at a townhouse being overrun by the smell of a manly, stainless steel pot full of beef stew. Bryan—a tall, thin guy with long, straight brown hair—asked if I wanted to take turns sautéing the onions. If I helped, I'd add another person to the rotation to the relief of Bryan's roommates, who were also sautéing. I'd only just met them, and already we were in tears. I had no idea they'd like me so much.

Getting back to reality, we all sat around and got to know each other for a few hours, ate dinner, and headed over to Bryan's mad scientist lab, as it became apparent that we shared the chronic tinkerer bug. His lab was a 30' x 30' insulated storage unit that he rented in order to have room for his many hobbies. The guy was a genius and could build anything. He had electronics, mechanics, and design mastered in his respective hobbies. We hung out there for a bit and headed back to his place where my body just said "no more." I politely told them that I had to crash and that was that for an absolutely wonderful day.

Day 12 – October 25, 2011

Another night passed with little more than a few hours of sleep. A long night with friends in Harrisonburg, a couple nights of tent camping, a long weekend at Oktoberfest, and trying to sleep in unfamiliar motel rooms started to catch up with me. Day after day of sleep deprivation was taking its toll. I started day twelve pretty early at Bryan's place, just after the sun pierced the horizon. The night before, Bryan told me to knock on his door upstairs before I took off in the morning. I didn't remember which door that he said to knock on, and there were three occupied bedrooms up there, so I planned to quietly pack my things and leave a thank you note like a drifter who knows no other way.

While loading the bike, Bryan came downstairs to meet me. He must have heard me moving about. He made breakfast and a steaming pot of coffee and handed me a mason jar full of last night's beef stew. Outside, and just minutes from leaving, my new friend and I posed for a picture. I told him that my door was always open in West Virginia if he ever needed a place to stay. Then I took off for another day of adventure.

Alternate 64 E was the appetizer, main course, and dessert for the day's travels. It encompassed a pretty ride from Raleigh to the Outer Banks. Lots of small towns, with few traffic lights, dotted the countryside. Brown and utterly flat cotton fields welcomed me to the Eastern Seaboard. I stopped to snag a rogue piece of cotton as it was caught in some grass near a guardrail. I stuffed it away in my tank bag to send to my mom. She had never seen a cotton field or cotton that wasn't perfectly white and formed in neat little circles. North Carolina's mountains had become yesterday's memory as well. The terrain was changing with my plans, and I had no idea how long it would be before I saw another mountain. For the foreseeable future I would be hugging the coast all the way to Texas. Being from the mountain state, the coast has always felt like another world, a place that I liked but wasn't in tune with.

Before leaving home, my Aunt Linda said that her dream vacation would be Nashville. Well, I found a Nashville, but it wasn't the one she was talking about. The Nashville that I passed through was a quiet little town in northeastern North Carolina and had nothing to do with the huge country music scene. Instead, large cotton fields defined the area. I don't know if it is my lack of experience with them or some sort of strange fondness for the South, but the cotton fields just fascinated me as I rode by. They were simply foreign to me.

Honestly, there wasn't much going on along the road. I had a relatively easy goal of making it to the beach. The weather was nice, ocean breezes were ahead, and the Goose was running smooth, almost seeming to enjoy the sun and flat roads that hardly put a load on its engine. I liked the change of pace and didn't have any problem finding the little things fascinating. At times, simplicity is all I need for entertainment.

As I was riding, my camera battery died and the cell phone camera was all I had. Knowing I needed to stop somewhere and charge up, I decided to find a liquor store, buy some whiskey, and ask if they would let me charge my camera. The young lady behind the counter said it was okay with the sweetest of southern twangs. She wasn't too hard on the eyes either.

A muscular fella, fresh out of the military, and purchasing a bottle, questioned me up and down while in the liquor store. He had noticed the bike all packed up and wondered about my travels. He had thought of making a similar trip. I told him to go for it. He wondered how it was possible for me to take off like that and asked, "Are you a millionaire or something?" I laughed and said, "No" and told him how I had to sacrifice my house to take the trip. He seemed to respect that. I'm sure that he had made some tough sacrifices as well. That was in Williamston, North Carolina. I still had about seventy miles in between me and the beach.

I pushed on, arriving in Nags Head with about an hour of daylight to spare. I stopped by a McDonald's, grabbed a bite to eat, wrote some stuff down, and headed for the dunes. As a seventh grader, I tagged along on a friend's family vacation to Nags Head. I remember seeing the dunes for the first time then and wishing that his dad would pull over so that we could go play in them. In fact, I wanted to shout, "Pull over!" as his dad passed them by with barely a look. As an adult, still holding onto that memory, I finally had my chance. Man, I ran around on the dunes like a crazy person. I took flying leaps, took pictures of my tracks, and took time to soak it all in. A big orange setting sun was the only thing that chased me away. Waiting for that last bit of light to expire, I found myself riding to the Outer Bank's Camp Hatteras campground, forty miles south, in the dark.

Day 13 – October 26, 2011

Day thirteen would take me from Camp Hatteras in Rodanthe, North Carolina, to Morehead City, North Carolina. The past three nights, I had arrived at my destination behind the beam of headlights. A night or two of that is tolerable, but every night is not so amusing. Riding a motorcycle at night adds another huge and dangerous obstacle to the endless list of difficulties to be overcome by riding these wonderful machines. For a start, motorcycles do not want to stand up. They're heavy, and have a teeter-tottering fulcrum point at the center of their two wheels. A wee bit of metal on a hinge called a kickstand only supports an upright position if placed exactly right. Basically, they want to fall over, or more so practically beg to fall over. The human placed in the saddle is the balancing extension or necessary equipment needed to give the motorcycle its logical function.

Then there is a world full of obstacles that need navigating: patches of ice, family pets, deer, large potholes, debris, and spine-chilling, two-ton-four-wheeled boxes being operated by texting teenagers. These test the rider's ability to keep the bike's rubber side down. Not to mention the lack of familiarity with local roads. These night rides were tripling the threat of each obstacle and adding a harmless side effect. Lonely, dark roads were making me homesick. When the sun was shining, I was fine.

I awoke to sunshine at Camp Hatteras's flat patchwork of campsites. Picnic tables—where I sat last night listening to waves brush the shore, star gazing and sipping whiskey—broke the two-dimensional look of the campground's terrain. Coarse grass and sand filled the gaps between my toes. I packed my bike up and walked to the beach to see with my eyes what my nose was telling me was right there all along—the big, cold Atlantic. I snapped off a bunch of pictures and was about to take a picture of my camera on the tripod with my cell phone camera when three very nice ladies, tanned and in appropriate beach attire, came over and filled me in on the recent devastation of Hurricane Irene.

Irene had smashed through the Hatteras area a few months before. Two of the ladies experienced substantial property loss from the storm. They've vacationed in the Outer Banks for twenty years or more and claimed to have never seen anything like Irene's destruction. The storm had veered farther north than average. They told me about rubble piles that would take months to clean up. Like folks had along the way, they also told me of great can't-miss spots for my future travels. We exchanged info, and I reluctantly had to cut our friendly morning meeting short if I was to make the ferry back to the mainland later on.

I continued south on Route 12 to the Cape Hatteras Lighthouse. Again, in an effort to make time, I shortened my visit at the perfectly preserved seaside attraction. I spent most of the visit staring at the candy cane spiraled, Godzilla-sized flashlight while idly chatting with a newlywed couple. In the back of my mind, I romanticized about the days when lighthouses were critical and navigation more crude. Some footage and snapshots of the lighthouse and grounds would have to suffice for now. *It's close enough to home that I'll surely see it again and more than likely, more than once.* I needed to make the Hatteras to Ocracoke Island Ferry. That one was free and required nearly forty-five minutes to cross.

I was ushered on first as the only motorcycle of the ferry ride. A dozen cars followed suit. I sat on the bike to keep it steady. It wanted to fall over. A gentle breeze pushed against my face. I was close enough to the front to see only the ferry's safety net and the water ahead. For a second, I let myself fantasize of being on a long adventure to a foreign shore, crossing dangerous waters, and having no clue what the natives were saying. Then I took a look around to see older folks leaning against the handrail or standing beside their cars, stretching their legs, and looking awfully bored.

Once again ashore, Ocracoke Island looked as though my fantasy was real. We were dropped off on the end of the island that would be featureless if not for the blowing sand. I let every car pass on its way to the next ferry so that I could get a picture of the absolute empty landscape. A tall dune on my left blocked the view of the ocean, and a line of power poles paralleled it on my right. Both were perfectly straight into the horizon's vanishing point. It felt more desert than coastal island. It was my first piece of alien terrain on the trip.

After indulging in a few desolate, sand-filled pictures, I rode south for fifteen miles until the island dead ended at the next ferry. That one would take me to Cedar Island and the mainland. While waiting on the delayed ferry ride, I had a few Coronas and a burger at a place called SmacNally's. It was right on the marina and had open-air seating and a beautiful view of dozens of capable, seaworthy vessels. The food wasn't bad either. I met a German family, on vacation from their current home in Sterling, Virginia. We all took turns taking pictures and passing cameras. No doubt, their photos will end up in a cherished family album to be enjoyed for a lifetime. I appreciated the opportunity to get a picture without setting up a tripod and a timer.

The second ferry began to load passengers. This one was ship-like and large enough to hold full-size RVs. Free coffee was available in the inner waiting room. The ride would take about two hours and twenty minutes. While traveling across the sound, I met a fellow from Michigan named Dave. He was in his late fifties and the proud owner of a 1988 Honda Goldwing. We got along great, like we were old riding buddies. Dave was into my journey, so much so, that he went as far as asking his wife if I could pitch my tent at their daughter's place in Jacksonville, North Carolina, after the ferry ride. I told him of my plan to hit the mainland and ride into the nearest town to shack up. Unfortunately, our plan was foiled when his daughter voted against it. Ultimately, it was her decision and her comfort that had to be respected.

Dave broke the news with a smile, like one of those that says, "Oh man, we almost pulled that off." He understood the bond that motorcyclists share on the road and had an appreciation for a guy out there on a soul-searching journey. Motorcyclists won't even pass one another on the road without throwing a hand out as to say, "Ride safe brother." Too bad all aspects of society aren't like this. The wave does get a bit repetitive in heavily populated areas, but nonetheless I still give it a go every time. Dave promised me that if I made it anywhere close to Detroit, he would at least let me camp in his yard. Dave understood what I was doing. His daughter, on the other hand, probably wasn't a motorcycle fan. She may have been one of those you're-gonna-break-your-neck-on-that-thing folks.

The sunlight was fading fast. We were ushered off the ferry, and I was again headed to parts unknown. I was jetting down some dead-straight and really dark roads toward Morehead City, North Carolina. I arrived around 8:30pm, found another room, and had the most uncomfortable conversation with an extremely feminine man working the front desk at the motel. I honestly believe that he was trying to come on to me. He was short, probably in his mid-forties, dressed well, and full of rings on his fingers. Ten minutes into me trying to get the paperwork completed, he left the counter for a seat in the lobby, where he sat with his dainty little lisp, legs crossed, and described every person that he had ever known. I did not understand the point of this as I fought off eye contact. The dude just would not stop talking and I didn't want to be rude. A half hour later, I had to say, "Look man, I have been riding for ten hours today, and I'm completely exhausted. All I want is a room, a shower, and some sleep." His talking silenced as he pranced back to the proper side of the front desk, like I had offended him. He quietly handed me my key. That night, my body shut down long enough to finally get eight hours of sleep.

Day 14 – October 27, 2011

I awoke feeling like a new man. Eight hours of sleep was like traveling back to my teens again. The night before, I was a bit depressed, exhausted, and lonely, but not lonely enough to hang out with the front desk clerk. Now, I was as bright as the sun. The world was perfect again. For the first time in two weeks, I planned to really slow down on the day's ride. There was no need to rush the meandering country roads on the way to my friend Keith's house in White Lake, North Carolina. He lived about sixty-five miles away.

I didn't actually know if he'd be home or not. Before I left Morehead City, I shot him a voicemail across those sixty-five miles, explaining my plan, and I took off in his direction. It was a bit of a gamble, I guess. Keith and I had not spoken in over five years. I trusted that the time span hadn't damaged our friendship.

I would love to say it was an awesome ride to White Lake, but unless you're in search of the long lost birthplace of billboards, you'd be disappointed. Signs the size of movie theatre screens urgently pulled my eyes off of the road for the better part of the ride. Pine-filled woodlands surrounded shopping plazas and developments along the way and were a slight reminder that I was taking a detour from the coast. A ridiculous-looking Honda ATV sitting in a fuel station parking lot caught my eye at a red light. It was bright yellow and had large car tires mounted in place of ATV tires. I think people of the cool persuasion call them dubs or something. Massive chrome rims filled the gap between the rubber. To me, it looked like the biggest waste of an income tax check possible, unless you consider the opportunity to spend the money on the midget strippers that occasionally frequent the Eastern Panhandle of West Virginia.

Still cruising along leisurely, I stopped at a Burger King in Wallace to hunt down some food and Wi-Fi. While eating, Keith got back to me, and it was set in stone: I'd have my second host of the trip. I call that balancing the budget. I don't want to come across greedy, and I wouldn't have minded camping every day, but it was hard to beat staying at a friend's/host's house. Before I left home, I researched quite a few KOAs across the nation and couldn't find one that charged less than $25 a night for a primitive tent spot, a spot lacking a water spigot and an electric hookup. Some friends recommended couchsurfing.com as an option, so I signed up online there at Burger King with hopes of taking advantage of open couches later on in the journey. I ended up stretching that lunch out for nearly two and a half hours while trying to get caught up on emails and a couple more address changes in between a handful of fries and sloppy bites-o-whopper.

White Lake is thirty-five miles from Wallace. I made it there with time to spare and sent Keith a text message asking him what type of beer he liked. My cell phone beeped right back his reply. It was, "All." I made a mental note and jetted over to nearby Elizabethtown to get some beer and to burn up even more time. Upon arriving in E-town, I was greeted on the right hand side of the road by a place called The Tree House Bar and Grill. I made the Goose hang a hard right like it was on rails.

When I was a kid, a few friends and I built a huge three-story tree house that had two zip-lines and was thirty-five feet high. I kept a picture of what was left of that tree house on my laptop as my background. Today it's a skeleton of its former self. Each floor still has a handful of boards nailed to an old maple tree along the Shenandoah River. In its heyday, I was about fourteen and running around with a scrappy crew of kids. We collected material from everywhere and everyone, sometimes on borrowing terms not discussed with the owner, I admit shamefully. Despite that, it was a fort to end all forts, a refuge from the parents, and a beauty to behold through intoxicated eyes. I learned a lot in those days, a lot about certain chemicals and a lot about shoddy construction practices. I'll always be very fond of it.

The Tree House Bar and Grill sits off the ground on wooden piers and was nice and clean inside, nothing like the tree house from our teenage years. I met some friendly locals. One offered to let me stay in a barn. As hindsight would prove, these offers only came when I already had a place to stay lined up. Whether he liked it or not, like the dork that I am, I had to show the owner of the bar my laptop's background picture, the picture of the tree house that I'm so proud of. He looked with polite interest and returned to doing more important things.

I had a brewski while keeping an eye on the TV screen and an eye on the smoking hot bartender and an eye on anyone watching me keep an eye on the hot bartender. Gotta watch your back, ya know? My short stay at the Tree House Bar was traded for dinner at a place called Cape Fear BBQ and Chicken. There, they gave me a free fried chicken gizzard. The texture was interesting. The fries and BBQ sandwich were great, though. Keith wasn't home yet, so I left there, full of soul food, and went to the local BP station to pick up a twelve pack. The cashier looked out the window, keeping one eye on me and one on the counter, as she took tremendous delight in watching me look for a place to stash the big square box-o-beer on my bike. I smiled back at her through the sturdy pane of glass, confident that I wouldn't leave a bottle behind.

Time came to leave Elizabethtown and start heading back to White Lake. On the way, I stopped by a motocross track that I had seen on my way to Elizabethtown earlier. Cape Fear MX was the name, and it was the sandiest track that these eyes had ever seen. Deep, dune-like and dry sand defined the track. And surprisingly, one of the ingredients I found in the motocross track soil was not only sand, but full cans of Natural Light. I found four of them lying, half exposed, in the middle of the track, waiting to blacken someone's eye after being roosted off of a wildly spinning rear tire.

I explored the grounds on the Goose. When I was riding through the pits in the deep sand, I took a right and face planted! The Goose went down and I tumbled off like a practicing stuntman. Again, I didn't get the picture. Panic set in when the bike was over, and in the rush to pick it up, I forgot to get the camera. Since night was approaching, I left the empty track and rode to Keith's.

Keith and I met close to a decade ago when he moved from St. Clairsville, Ohio, to my neck of the woods in West Virginia's Eastern Panhandle. He may not have been born in West Virginia or like to admit it, but he is practically a native. St. Clairsville is about a dozen miles from the Ohio River and our border. So close in fact, that a bit of our sister-loving, sheep-startling, hillbilly ways may have rubbed off on him, although you wouldn't guess it.

Keith was the unofficial adopted son to the family of one of my ex's, and he raced motocross. His cool as an ice cube in a snow storm mentality and sarcastic comebacks made him an instant hit with our clique. I have never seen the guy get upset. At a track some years ago, during a morning practice, Keith tried to wad himself into a pretzel, and was mostly successful. It was an incident so severe that he died twice and was luckily revived in the operating room. Still though, in between deep groans like those of a person who's had the wind knocked out of them, he managed a thumbs-up as they slid his battered body into the back of the ambulance. That crash left him with an unsightly abdominal scar, that instead of hiding, he readily jokes about. I like the guy.

It had been a long day waiting for my buddy to get off of work. I made it to his place just before he did. His wife, Cory, greeted me at the door. Being our first meeting, I was relieved that she was so nice a gal. Cory and I got along smoothly, which really helped melt away the minutes until Keith arrived. When Keith popped through the door, it was awesome to see him and to close the multi-year gap of disconnection. We would go on to have a great evening eating pizza, having some cold ones, and watching Beavis and Butthead until I almost made a beer fountain come out of my nose. Seeing those simple bastards back on the television transported me back to better years, years when all I cared about was motocross, and years when Keith still lived in West Virginia.

Day 15 – October 28, 2011
Keith was working some serious hours at his new job just outside of White Lake. He came downstairs around 6:00am, and I happened to wake up at about

the same time. I had another good night's sleep. So good, in fact, that somehow my lips stuck to my teeth. Mere mouth movements wouldn't free them up. I used my fingers to pry them loose. Maybe laughing so much did it; maybe the beer did it; maybe snoring did it. I'm not sure, but it felt like they were glued together. As I activated my salivary glands, Keith headed off for work. I followed him out a few minutes later. After traveling at such a hectic pace for two weeks, it was awfully weird to think about having a whole day of inactivity and the potential for boredom. Unlike the couple of days spent in Helen, Georgia, nothing was going on.

I started the day back in Elizabethtown searching for coffee and some black plastic buckets. The plan was to cut those buckets in half and attach the halves to the front of my side boxes to slightly improve the bike's aerodynamics. The Goose was as aerodynamic as a Lego block, a clear disadvantage of homemade storage containers. I stopped at a Dollar General and found the perfect pails for the job. They were $1.50 each. Then I was off to the Elizabethtown's hardware store for some screws and silicon to hold the whole contraption together. Back at Keith's, I had the place to myself. Cory had left for work in Wilmington.

It was butcher time, and butchering I did. I whipped out my knife and made the plastic fly, ripping off the metal handles and quickly halving the buckets. The design wasn't pretty at all, but neither was the rest of my setup. Other than the solid engine, my bike was kind of a jalopy. Fully packed, it resembled a covered wagon more than a motorcycle. It had been wrecked once before by the previous owner in the rain, smashing in the fuel cap, cracking a fairing, and adding an assortment of character raising scratches. I've never been one to treat a motorcycle, or a car for that matter, as an ornament. That's for the weekend-only, fair-weather phonies who spend more time behind a polishing rag than behind the handlebars. My philosophy has always been "function before fashion, and I'm here to ride!" My buckets solidly mounted, the project was over.

Having so much time on my hands allowed me to catch up on some things like taking inventory of my gear and making a few phone calls to people I hadn't conversed with in a while back home. On the first day of the trip, I randomly stuffed things on the bike that I thought I'd need. Now, with a few weeks in, I could organize the lot and begin to think about things to send home. I laid out every last item of gear on Keith's front steps, taking up more than five of them and a bit of the concrete below. Strewn out fully, it was hard to imagine everything fitting on the bike.

When Keith and Cory got home that night, we decided to head to Elizabethtown for dinner and drinks. The only bar in the whole area was the Tree House Bar. We ordered some burgers and got pretty blurry with the help of two of my best friends, Mr. Jack and Mr. Coke. Cory was our designated driver and witness to our ever-increasing, shit-eating grins. Perhaps it was the alcohol, or perhaps it was the right time, but Keith spilled the beans that Cory had a bun in the oven (pregnant). My friend was about to encounter an extreme lifestyle change. I was happy for them and happy to be with them and happy to be the first to know. We made it back to their place safely and finished the night off with another Beavis and Butthead induced abdominal workout.

Day 16 – October 29, 2011

It was great staying with Keith and Cory, but I was getting antsy. Somehow, in just a couple of weeks, I became accustomed to the high-pace, on-the-go travel that had defined the trip. Staying in White Lake for just two days made me feel like I was settling down a bit. I was longing to get on the road again, even if it meant that I wouldn't know where I would stay that night and that I'd have to encounter road after unfamiliar road. Keith planned to sleep in that morning, and I didn't blame him. Drinks and late nights sound fun in the evening but always collect payment in the morning.

I was up early, as usual. They were still sawing logs when I left for my morning meeting with Juan Valdez and his coffee-bean-sack-carrying donkey. I had a hankering for a country breakfast. Elizabethtown had a place called the Corner Café. It was a small diner packed with every sort of character from grandpas to little ones still in their first year. It was the kind of place where the same folks sit in the same chairs every week, and the waitresses already know what you want. Every town has one. I snagged a booth and a menu, searching for any dish including a lot of pancakes. Generous portions soon filled the table top. I kept the coffee coming to counteract any food coma that might set in.

Satisfied more than usual, I lazily throttled back to Keith's house. It was time to tell my good buddy goodbye for who knew how long. I sure hoped that it wasn't going to be another half-dozen years. They were stirring when I arrived. We walked outside, snapped a blurry farewell picture, and I was on my way to Myrtle Beach, South Carolina, via Wilmington.

Igor, my tech support guy and right hand man, highly recommended Flaming Amy's burrito joint in Wilmington. He attended college in North Carolina a few years back and may have dined at every cool nook, cranny, or obscure restaurant in the state. He is an encyclopedia of everything hip. When he approaches the appropriate age, or the guy from the Dos Equis commercials kicks the bucket, Igor may become the most interesting man in the world. I can hear it now, "I don't always eat in Wilmington, but when I do, I chose Flaming Amy's"—complete with Ukrainian accent. He told me that Flaming Amy's is known for their large burritos without a large price. They lived up to their reputation, and I might add would be a wonderful complement to any hammered night of drinking where you ingest food by the alligator-sized mouthful and swallow whole. I ordered a po-boy burrito that lasted for lunch and dinner.

While visiting any new town, I'd try to see as much of its oldest section as possible before moving on. Wilmington's Riverwalk was the can't-miss spot on the way through. I stopped just long enough to snap some pictures. I would have stayed longer if the streets weren't blocked off and littered with tons of folks racing in the Beach to Battleship Triathlon. Rather than stick around and get in the way, I decided to scurry off to Myrtle Beach, where I wanted to camp out and save some loot.

Like a secret agency tapping into my thoughts, my plan was foiled by Myrtle Beach's KOA. They eagerly pushed to sell me a primitive tent spot for $49.95 a night. That was outrageous. I stiffly refused the offer with a sarcastic laugh and heard the click as the KOA employee on the other end hung up, ending any chance of future negotiation. I was left to look for a room and decided to look for a Budget Inn for two reasons: first, to see if it was owned by an Indian or one of Vivek's uncles, and second, to see if they had any cheap rooms. While searching online I came across the Sandcastle Hotel with oceanfront rooms for $41.95. Take that, KOA! I checked in victoriously. Budget Inn would have to wait.

For the evening, I wanted to relax and see what the bar scene could throw at me on Halloween weekend. I had been to Myrtle Beach before a handful of times and was always impressed with the nightlife. In 2002, I went there with three of my best friends, and at Mother Fletcher's a spunky little blonde pulled me onto the dance floor, instantly illuminating me. Before then I had only crossed a dance floor to grab another drink or hold up a wall. That gal introduced me to shakin' a leg, cuttin' a rug, getting jiggy wit' it, boogying down, and generally gyrating in a hypnotic trance near other folks who have rhythm and style. I loved it. I loved her for picking me. I was very naive back then, as I thought that she wanted to not only dance but hang out afterwards. But as I would learn throughout the years, girls love dancing twice as much as men, or more, and if they don't have anyone to pair up with they'll often pick someone at random. It is just a simple act of having fun.

That night, she and I danced on and off for a few songs. I felt like I was flying, and she was obviously a tried-and-true veteran of the hip hop and hardwood. My drink gushed from my spastic pulses, getting her wet and irritated. Finally, the glass escaped my grip and shattered on the dance floor, ending any contact with the lovely little blonde. She picked a new person to excite, and I haven't stopped dancing since. My friends have seen the patented sideways, arms out, zombie-ish swaying, and the crowd clearing bouncing. My dancing is not dissimilar to an inflated balloon, left untied, and released to eject its air and fly around in every direction. One time I even broke my foot on a cruise ship when overtaken by techno music. I swear to this day that I was floating over the dance floor. It had all started in Myrtle Beach, and I was back, ready to relive the past.

The evening began with me optimistically roaming from the Beach House Bar to the Parrot Bar to the Bowery. All three, put together, lacked enough patrons for a big shebang. At first, I tried to drink in the fun as I happily found the bottom of several containers of liquid courage, but I still found myself uninspired. Where was everybody? This was Halloween! Back home, this was a big day. We celebrated Halloween with a fierceness at my brother's house, with parties often reaching forty or more costumed hooligans. Myrtle Beach was letting me down. I spotted maybe five or six enthusiastic barflies dressed for the occasion all evening. Not feeling the scene, I turned in early and prayed that the Hangover Fairy would skip my room.

Day 17 – October 30, 2011

The Hangover Fairy must have heat-seeking radar with an extra sensitive setting for gingers. I woke up feeling great, if great meant sticking your head in a vice and spinning in circles. Even so, I had bungee jumping on the mind.

On our visit in 2002, my buddies and I were roaming around near Myrtle Beach's tiny amusement park when we saw a bungee tower. My friend Nelson and I bucked up and handed the two chilled-out tower workers $25 for the opportunity to tie us to their three-inch-thick rubber band and allow us to leap off their eighty-foot tower. Nelson went first, like a torpedo, right off of the plank, fully committed and fearless. That was Nelson, though. He was always ready for anything.

I, on the other hand, started to quiver on the painfully long walk to the plank. Eighty feet looked like child's play from the pavement; from the top, it looked like an accident waiting to happen. I trembled like a quake, with butterflies the size of eagles in my stomach. One of those relaxed tower workers strapped me up and told me to count to three. On three, I left the plank with the utmost of uncertain feelings. I wound the windows up and fell with the grace of a wounded pigeon. But on the rebound, heading north again, the experience became glorious. I didn't die! Instead, I was blanketed in adrenaline and fun, so much so that I jumped three or four more times. Each time after that first leap, the cool-headed tower workers let me jump for $15. I was stoked!

I was looking for that thrill again, and the butterflies were already beginning to stir wildly. The Goose and I roamed around block after block, looking for the tower, but just couldn't find it. I don't know if it was the hangover fogging up my navigation, or if the tower had been removed, but it was nowhere in sight. My gut told me that it had been removed. I had hoped to live it up on the trip, but considering the way I was feeling, bungee jumping might not have been for me. I rode out of town with my head feeling like it was two sizes too big for my helmet.

Charleston is about eighty-five miles south of Myrtle Beach. I hugged the Atlantic on Route 17 all the way to South Carolina's gem of a city. It's an amazing little patch of the world. From the north, the city is introduced by the Arthur Ravenel Jr. Bridge. It was an unexpected treat, as I had pictured arriving in such an historic city by way of something a little flatter and a little older. Its heft of concrete and its steel suspension wires made the bridge the tallest hill that I'd seen in days. I navigated into the city and parked in front of a beautiful Presbyterian Church, large, well kept, and dated 1761. Its over-the-top splendor stood guard over the Goose as I lost myself in a walk of historic perfection.

First off, if Charleston had one more drop of character it would self-destruct. My miniscule Samsung camcorder nearly overheated from the shutter clicking. I should've looked into a liquid-cooled version before buying this one. Undeterred, I wandered aimlessly on cobbled streets, strolling along worn brick walls, hand out to feel the texture whenever possible. Plentiful details on every building made each one utterly unique yet at home and in sync with all other neighboring structures. The bases of window frames supported pots full of draping plants. Strange, skin-colored crape myrtles invaded Charleston's worn sidewalks. Their smooth pinkish bark made the trees seem animalian as they pushed and cracked their way into the soil below. Steps covered in a carpet of leafy vines marked the front entrance to a fortunate family's home. Alleyways beckoned me around each new corner, provoking my curiosity. An elevated stone seawall was wrapped around the city like a ribbon on a giant present. Folks looked happy as they strutted across the top of it. I found a shaded park bench under some wiggly armed trees and spent some time in a thankful gaze. All this was but a fraction of the unending charm of Charleston's historic district.

Leaving Charleston for the road felt too soon. I had to make an executive decision to speed up my pace a bit and cut out some of the stops along the East Coast. For instance, Myrtle Beach is an eight-hour drive from home in the Eastern Panhandle of West Virginia, but somehow I managed to take sixteen days to get there. If I were to continue at this pace, I'd be out of money by Louisiana. The call of the West began to creep up inside of me. West of the Mississippi is much more vast, and if I was going to slow down I planned to do it out there. Soon I would be moving west. I couldn't wait. For now, I was still headed south, stimulated and in a wonderful mood.

With that, I needed to find a spot to camp after Charleston. My sight was set on Edisto Beach State Park, some thirty miles south of Charleston as the crow flies. The countryside along the way was full of trees covered in Spanish moss and vast tracts of marshland. I imagined alligators mucking around through the reeds, while reminding myself that I was too far north for that. The landscape differed drastically from the Appalachian region that I called home. Experiencing this change of scenery, and escaping the fresh blanket of snow that my native part of West Virginia was currently covered in, was refreshing.

Miles passed, and I made it to the park about an hour before dark, set up camp, and headed off in search of a pillow. I had camped three times now without a pillow. The seaside village of Edisto Beach had nothing to offer, so my Crossroads Yamaha hoodie would have to do.

Seventeen days had also passed without a campfire. I was about to change that. I gathered up some palm husks and thin branches from the campsite and filled the air with campfire scent for the shortest of moments. To my dismay, I simply needed real chunks of wood. Firewood was for sale at the park's entrance for $5 a bundle, but I wasn't too fond of taking that route.

With my fire out and nothing but the stars to stare at, I climbed onto the site's picnic table. I relaxed to the comfortable sound of ocean waves pounding the shore in the distance and the dark South Carolina night overhead. A few minutes of raw peace had passed when suddenly I heard about six or seven little thumps on the picnic table. I raised my head to investigate the noise. I had company! Right down by my knee a raccoon and his two buddies were curiously perched on the benches and sniffing my legs. I nearly soiled myself! They had me surrounded. With nowhere to escape, I wheezed out an unconfident yelp. It was just loud enough to scare off the troublesome little fur balls. Once they vanished, I climbed off of the picnic table and quickly made for the safety of my tent. *That was close!*

Day 18 – October 31, 2011

I woke feeling rejuvenated and raccoon-free. I was back in my element, the daytime, and those varmints were back in their mysterious hideouts where they would wait patiently to do it all again when the sun went down. Edisto Beach State Park was full of top-notch facilities, like sturdy bathhouses and clean campsites with electric and water. After the morning's hygienic ritual and a steaming pot of oatmeal, I walked to the beach for some pictures.

Edisto Beach State Park's shoreline seemed primitive. Walking onto a beach that hasn't been overly commercialized takes you back to a time before Europeans stepped upon these shores. Here the sand was dark and coarse, with a lasting supply of seashells to investigate. I found it easy to imagine a pirate ship in the distance, with a tall mast and a rugged deck hand with long matted hair yelling "Land ho!" from his crow's nest perch.

To me, the beach used to symbolize a place where I would show up to party—period. Stretches of shoreline at the party spots never had character, unless you were talking about some character that looked like a lobster scalded by the summer sun. Those types of beaches have sterile-looking sand and seashells that have been picked up more than once. I enjoyed the rugged change of ocean shore at Edisto Beach.

Beaufort, South Carolina, had been in my radar since reading about it in *1000 Places To See Before You Die*. In case you're not familiar with good ol' Beaufort, it's the place where a good chunk of *Forrest Gump* was filmed. That was my sole reason for going there. I don't want to take anything away from the rich history of the place, but I am a huge fan of the movie, and that was enough for me. Beaufort is about thirty minutes southwest of Edisto Beach, so the ride over was pretty pleasant and right on course for getting me to Savannah, Georgia, with a bit of time to spare.

When I arrived in "Gumpville," I searched for and found the odd-looking visitor center with the goal in mind of asking for directions to a few places that would be familiar from the movie. Inside the yellow fort/mini-castle-looking visitor center, the receptionist told me of a candy store down the street called the Chocolate Tree. She said that Forrest Gump bought his chocolates there. At the time, I took her word for it. Later on, after a bit of research, I realized that the label on the box of chocolates in the movie did not belong to the Chocolate Tree candy store. On a positive note, the crew filming the movie did frequent the Chocolate Tree for candy while in town. She also made mention of a bridge in the movie that Forrest ran across. She said that an Alabama sign was placed at the bridge for the movie. I attempted to find the bridge with her directions but was unsuccessful. Still, I was happy to visit Beaufort. I rode away with a huge slab of white chocolate with Oreo bits from the Chocolate Tree.

Moon River Brewing Company in Savannah, Georgia, was next on the accelerated agenda. Savannah is a lot like Charleston in the respect that it greets you with a massive, shimmering, modern bridge. Plus, you could go there with nothing but a camera, snap pictures all day, and still need a week to see all of the good stuff. I could almost insert the description of Charleston here to suffice for Savannah, but each city is indeed unique. They do, however, share a similar richness in Old-South beauty. Since I went camera crazy in Charleston, I decided to entertain a more personal interest here. That's where Moon River Brewing Company comes in. And no, I didn't just go there to get drunk.

I had watched the *Ghost Adventures* show on the Travel Channel for years, and those guys investigated the brewery's basement and came up with some pretty decent paranormal results—if you believe in all of that. Zak, Nick, and Aaron were the paranormal investigators on the show. Out of every wacky paranormal investigation show on the tube, I liked them and believed them the most. A lot of it was due to how Zak, the ring leader, spoke. His way of expressing interest in what he was doing was extremely similar to mine. He spoke with sincerity and was extremely focused on the task at hand. He could be loud and demanding if he was onto something, and that's the trait I share. If I'm into something, I take it seriously when I could just lighten up and smile a little more and savor the moment. Also, you never saw the guys running away from anything in the dark, shrieking and hands flailing, only to return after they've properly calmed down. They just seemed like the real deal.

Like the unique McDonald's in Asheville that I had seen on the Travel Channel, the Moon River Brewing Company was a must see for me since I'd seen that episode of *Ghost Adventures* three times. When I arrived, I ordered lunch and a house-brewed beverage and worked on the blog for a bit. While stuffing my face, I asked a waiter if I could go in the basement and take some pictures. "No prob," he said, surprising me with the quickness of his answer. I finished chowing down and nervously made my way down into the dark, brick-walled basement alone.

Shallow ceilings loomed overhead. Three or four arched doorways led to other empty rooms where, as I approached them, I expected to stir up something. It was pretty creepy, especially since the bartender was just talking about how she always felt like she was being watched when she'd go down there. After a minute or two of touring the brewery underworld, I lightened up and it wasn't so bad. However, every time I snapped a picture, I expected there to be some sort of pasty white face showing up in the background that didn't belong to me. I was not disappointed to come up, paranormally speaking, empty-handed. The day was getting shorter, and I needed time to make tracks out of Savannah.

With Moon River behind me and nothing but road ahead, the Goose and I scrambled for the Florida border like a pair of runaway outlaws. *Let's shoot for Jacksonville.* I was sure that I could make it before dark and I almost did. A few other motorists and I created a chain on 95 S and kept the pace just under 100 mph. Here and there they tailgated my bike just a bit too closely. I needed to get out of the pack but wanted to keep the pace. One car, in particular, had a male driver who drove like he was God's gift to the road and like his BMW was a one of a kind. He was the primary tailgating offender, all decked out with big sunglasses and slicked-back, greasy hair. With empty road ahead and no curves in sight, or police for that matter, I wicked open the throttle until the speedometer touched 142 mph, leaving the pack behind. *Not bad for a bike that's cinder block sleek, hauling a hillbilly and a hundred pounds of gear.* Florida's border came soon enough and I crossed it standing up with one fist in the air. It felt good.

Florida was just the change I needed to fight off the slow-moving pace I was keeping in the Carolinas and Georgia. Florida had that new state smell. Now, the Keys were only a few days away! Since it was dark, and I was in a new city, I checked into a room. The front desk clerk kindly gave me the Harley rider's discount. She made my day.

Day 19 – November 1, 2011

Day nineteen began in a laundry room amongst the dullest of appliances. White washers and dryers were lined against the wall like pack mules capable of taking on a heavy load, but not much else. I looked around for the least stubborn-looking unit to toss my laundry and box of soap into. It wasn't all fun and games out on the road, folks. Inevitably, those ripe underwear and musky socks were going to need to wrestle some bubbly water. I later heard some flak from friends and family back home about not camping more. In response, the amount of money that I slapped down for a tent and sleeping bag certainly announced my intentions, but it was ever so hard to beat a shower, continental breakfast, and laundry facilities. Traveling on a motorcycle lends one to being sweaty, as you are constantly outdoors, and any amount of sunshine could heat up my thick, black riding gear. You get wind on a two-wheeler, but you don't get air conditioning. I was in Florida now, the perpetually warm state.

I scarfed down one of those wonderfully varied continental breakfasts, folded the laundry, packed up, and rode to Wal-Mart to buy a pillow. On the way, I spotted a bumper sticker that read, "I live in my own little world, but it's okay, they know me there." *Finally, someone made one about me.* I tried like hell to get the camera out at the intersection and take a picture of it glued to the back of a big SUV, but the green light was too quick on the draw. I rode on to Wal-Mart. At the end of an aisle, a flimsy wire-framed display was stuffed to the gills with pillows. I coughed up $2.50 for one and walked outside.

What happened next disturbed me for hours. And no, it wasn't a run-in with a Cyclops Wal-Mart greeter. I was carrying my goods to the Goose when an old, white-haired, biker type jumped out of his truck, ran to the vehicle behind his, and started screaming at an elderly woman who was in her Honda Pilot waiting for him to choose a spot. He sharply directed her to another spot and warned her, "Back off my ass or I'm going to ram you."

Let me set the scene a little. He knew that I was leaving and wanted my spot, which was the second spot closest to the store. The old lady wasn't waiting for any spot in particular since after six parking spots from the front doors the whole parking lot was nothing but pavement and lines. At worst, he would've had to park a dreadful *seven* spots away from the front door of Wal-Mart. I couldn't believe what I was seeing, and it was by far the worst case of public harassment that I'd ever witnessed. After he gave in and parked six spots away from the Wal-Mart entrance, he climbed out of his truck—knowing that I had witnessed the whole thing—and coldly stared at me with a say-something-punk vibe. I stared back the whole time thinking, "Your old ass should be ashamed of yourself." Back in his day he probably would've wore me out—since he was a big boy—but now he was much older, and I would've easily handled his ignorant ass. A few of my friends back home would've used this as a perfect opportunity to knock the dust off of their knuckles, asking questions only after, but I'm not exactly that way. I've always weighed the consequences, even if for a brief second.

I left that parking lot pretty pissed at myself that I didn't at least say something, and really angry about his disrespect for his fellow man. The good thing about riding for hours on end with a helmet on is undistracted thought. While riding, I asked myself, "Why was he so angry?" I thought of a few things that could make a person lose it so easily. Perhaps he was a veteran and had been through severe mental trauma. In that case, I would've felt bad for choking him out. Maybe he just lost a child, brother, or parent. Maybe he forgot to take his meds, or he could've been intoxicated. I just don't know. Those thoughts took away my anger, and the day was bright again.

Pacified and peaceful, I rode to St. Augustine, Florida, our country's oldest permanent European settlement. Route 1 South led me right into town. Right away, I noticed a bike shop and planned to stop there for the elusive tire iron. The place was First Coast Honda. I parked my beast of a Yamaha outside and strolled on in with thoughts of great conversation and new friends in mind like I had experienced in North Carolina.

I was greeted with staff who ignored me for three or four minutes until my lost face, which I'm very good at, pried a "Can I help you?" out of a gal behind the parts counter. I asked for a tire iron, and she directed me to a fellow on the sales floor. He then walked me over to the parts counter where we scanned over a small section of maintenance products and apparel. First Coast was out of tire irons. The search would have to go on. I walked out thinking that their service left something to be desired. Luckily for First Coast, they employed Alex. I met him outside with only a few steps left to the Goose. He noticed me leaving and followed up with a "Can I help you?" And help he did. Alex changed my opinion of the whole operation. After fifteen minutes of friendly assistance, I headed for old town St. Augustine, completely in the know. Alex had been a tour guide there in years past, and if he couldn't sell me a tire iron, then he could help me with the sights. He even gave me some stickers.

I was waterside and downtown a few minutes later. A parking spot had a scooter and a Harley in it, and looked as though it was long enough for the Goose to squeeze in there, too. The Harley rider, a large man with long brown hair and appropriate apparel, was standing by his bike. My first impression was that he was intimidating. I second guessed sharing the spot with him. Nonetheless, I gave it a whirl. His name was Chris, and we sparked up a long conversation about road tripping and BMW motorcycles, which neither of us owned. At the time, his enthusiasm led me to believe that he was on the verge of taking off across the country, too. Like me, he had yet to visit the West. We both talked of how exciting it must be riding out there. Chris recommended a spot where I could grab some pizza, and I was off.

I walked around St. Augustine just under the speed of a Segway and slightly faster than the horse and buggy tours, snapping pictures and absorbing the Atlantic's cool, salty breeze. The place was absolutely pristine. Like Charleston and Savannah, it lacked nothing in character. Colorful homes occupied brick-paved streets. Palm trees lifted me up and reminded me that I was in Florida. Cannons sat heavily in formation at Ft. Marion, overlooking a stretch of water filled with light boats that carried vacationers instead of soldiers. It was history beautified.

I planned for Daytona that day as well, so I headed back to the bike. The Goose had been parked beside Trade Winds Tropical Lounge for a few hours. Trade Winds had a feel that was perfect for a cold beer and was dark enough inside that your eyes could rest from constantly squinting. I am like metal to a magnet when it comes to a relaxed drinking hole. I chatted with the bartender over a helping of free popcorn. Unknowingly, I was also sharing the parking spot with his scooter. He shared some advice with me about my stay in Daytona. It was a slow day for him behind the bar, so in between washing glasses he kept on recommending things to do in the area. My stay on the bar stool was barely long enough to warm it up. I thanked him and walked outside.

When I got to the Goose, I noticed a business card placed between the seat and gas tank with some writing on it. My first thought was, "It's probably just an advertisement," but I was wrong. Chris, the Harley rider, left me a small donation to help on my journey. That marked the first random donation and a new friendship. I was blown away! I'll never forget his generosity.

St. Augustine was good to me, but Daytona still called from the south. On the way down Route 1, I was distracted by Pax Trax Motocross Park. Not to be redundant, but I am like metal to a magnet when it comes to motocross tracks. I'd read about Pax Trax for years in all sorts of motocross magazines, which I collect like comic books. After a U-turn, I rode back the lane, past Thunder Gulch Campground, and to the track.

There were a few riders practicing. I noticed that they were abnormally fast, a speed that one rarely sees outside of a big national race, a speed where the rider is one with the machine. A kid riding a Kawasaki KX100 wearing number 92 was making tabletops look flat and corners look like straightaways. I turned to a guy standing beside me on one of the blue, two-story lookout platforms and asked, "Who am I looking at on number 92?" He said, "Zac Commans on the 125 and my son on the smaller bike," which was number 92. "What's your son's name?" I asked. "Adam Cianciarulo," he replied. I was blown away again! What an outstanding day this was turning out to be.

This kid was one of the top rising motocross racers in the country. Watching him practice was comparable to watching a rider like Travis Pastrana right before he turned pro. Allen, Adam's dad, and I talked for a while as Zac and Adam continued to own every last black grain of sand on the track. When they finished up another practice session, Allen called me over to meet his son. Fighting off being star struck, I went over.

I tossed my jacket and gloves on the ground in order to shake hands and take a picture. Adam stooped down, picked my belongings up for me and said, "You don't have to put them on the ground." Little did he know that I'd been roughing it for a few weeks and I didn't mind if they were on the ground. My gear was sweaty and well worn. His parents had clearly raised a respectful and humble young man. He already displayed a professional demeanor without yet making a dollar from the sport. I left those guys with a deep sense of gratitude and awe. The quick chance encounter reminded me of my deeply cherished motocross side, and that I'd been letting it slip away.

I backtracked about five hundred feet to the Thunder Gulch campground. Everything I needed was there: tent sites, a restaurant for dinner, and the track, just in case I wanted to wander over and reminisce later on. I found it too perfect not to stay a night. I paid for a campsite, set up my tent against an assault from Florida's mosquitoes (my first encounter with the sunshine state's blood-sucking devils), and made my way to the restaurant for dinner and a drink.

I sat alone at the bar for quite some time sipping on soda infused with whiskey after a dinner of liver and onions. A waitress sent an older guy named Charlie over to talk to me. I must've looked lonely in her eyes. She knew Charlie well and had briefly spoken to me. Her instinct told her that he and I would get along. Charlie had been injecting wine into his bloodstream one light swaller at a time before he came over. He looked like Lieutenant Dan from *Forrest Gump*, with a short white beard and white hair, clean-cut, and aged about sixty-five. He was born and raised in the Florida Keys and had lived on a boat for twenty-two years straight when he was a younger man.

We talked like old buddies, him giving me advice now that he was able to reflect on almost a full life lived. He was intelligent and interesting and kind, like the way I hope to be at his age. Our time at the bar reminded me of that country song by Billy Currington, "People are Crazy." In it, the singer describes a young man and old man sitting at a bar, and connecting over a few beers. He helped me plan my route for the next few days before our conversation turned more philosophical—like they do when drinking. Our views of the world and humanity's built-in characteristics were incredibly similar. He confidently assured me that the trip would be something I'd never regret. Like the old lady who gave me the idea to get out more, I trusted that Charlie was right. It was a day of chance encounters, good company, beautiful weather, peace, and thankfulness. How can you top that?

Day 20 – November 2, 2011

I awoke at Thunder Gulch Campground to one of Florida's warm November mornings. Back home, we just didn't have warm November mornings. Oh, how I welcomed the change, even if it threw my sense of the seasons off. Daytona, a racer's paradise, sat roughly thirty miles south. If I had camped on a mountain, I could have seen it.

After packing my things and fighting off a calorie-laden breakfast with coffee, I raced to Daytona. It was still morning as I lurched off Route 1 and onto Main Street. The bartender from Trade Winds Tropical Lounge highly recommended Froggy's Saloon while in Daytona. In the spirit of living with no particular route, I took his advice, parking the Goose on the brick sidewalk between two Harley cruisers, and walked on in.

Like the semi-nerd that I am, I entered Froggy's with my laptop in hand and held tight against my ribcage like a school book, and stumbled upon a crime scene covered in caution tape. The place was dark and cavernous with high ceilings. The bartender looked my way and welcomed me. As my eyes adjusted, I looked her way and about shit my pants. All she had on was caution tape, yellow, *thin*, flexible, caution tape. It was criminal for her to do that to me, welcoming me like that. I didn't know what to say and couldn't stop my eyes from bouncing up and down her torso—breasts, thighs, ass, breasts, thighs, ass, breasts, thighs, face, ass, left tit, right tit, ass, ass—you get the picture. She was probably five foot eight, maybe 110 pounds, blonde as a Swede, and had a face that could sharpen a knife. I prayed for that knot to come loose as her breasts had stretched the word *caution* on the caution tape into a wide font. What I would have done for a pair of scissors, oh my. I guess teeth would've worked just fine, too.

Shame on me for noticing, but she was also as friendly as a three-month-old puppy. Right then, I realized that love at first sight was real. So, what did I do? I ordered a Jack and Coke to cool off with and pretended to do something on my laptop as the screen hid my glances. Every man in the place was having the same issue. The damn Jack and Coke just made me a little less slick and a little more tickled. I drank my first three as quickly as possible just so she would have to come over with a refill. (I have maybe two regrets from the entire trip, and one of them was not getting a picture of that gal. I planned to get one when I came back from the hotel room and the beach later on, but she wasn't working anymore. Damn the luck.)

Getting back on track . . . By then it was getting late. Hours of grinning and feeling lucky had passed. Our star was setting, so I left to snap some pictures around town and at the beach before the wild and wonderful night began. Outside, clouds and colors collided to make a scene not unlike a bomb just detonated. The Atlantic's waves patted the shore like smooth, wet licks. As I've done before, I stood there, staring out, thinking about the piece of land you'd meet if you tried to swim straight across. An ocean's volume never ceases to amaze me.

To clear up something that had me concerned at the time, I didn't plan to spend every day partying and blowing a bunch of money, but there were going to be a few spots along the way that required a person to party hard. A couple of examples are Bourbon Street in New Orleans, Vegas baby, a night or two with my buddy Adam in Houston, and the Duval Crawl in Key West.

With that said, this journey was the first time in my life where I had ample money to enjoy myself and freedom to go as I pleased. I gotta say, it's hard to save money, when it finally comes along, after you've been a poor sucker your whole life. So here I was in Daytona, with some catching up to do. My night's shenanigans took place in the midst of many other bikers who were there enjoying a bike night. I barhopped like a kangaroo. My mission: head to the first joint, then to the next, and to the next, and so on until I forgot where I started. Mission accomplished.

Day 21 – November 3, 2011

Morning came at me ferociously. I must have sleep walked right into a whole nest of hangover fairies. I can see it now: each one bitch-slapping me while yelling something like "I told you so! I told you so! I told you so!" directly in my ear in a high-pitched fairy voice. The poisoned grey matter in my head, which I call a brain, felt like a railroad spike had been freshly pounded in. It was wonderful! I woke up wearing my full party outfit, fully clothed, shoes still on, sideways on the bed, and a note written on my hand so big that it could have been spray painted on. The note had a smiley face and said, "Love Ashley." *Who the heck is Ashley?* I didn't know, but apparently she liked me. Day twenty-one was gonna be hard.

I knew I that I couldn't leave Daytona without checking out the speedway and at least getting the Goose on the beach. First, I went toward the water. A friendly older gentleman was working the ticket booth. With a sideways grin and a bit of foggy persuasion, I told him that I just wanted to quickly snap some pictures of the bike on the sand. I told him that I wouldn't be more than five or ten minutes. I hoped to avoid paying for a full day's pass. He was cool with that and said, "People do that all the time." I jumped on the bike and cautiously inched forward off the pavement and onto the sand, remembering my wipeout at Cape Fear MX a week ago. To my surprise, Daytona's shore was packed as hard as concrete from years of traffic, and traction was good. I had imagined getting rapidly stuck and throttling a rut in the sand. I kept the Goose back just far enough to avoid the really wet sand. A few camera shots, with arms spread wide as in accomplishment, and I was out of there. As I left, I gave the old feller a thankful wave and sped off to the speedway.

Navigating with a hangover is horrible. Every five seconds, I'd look down at my map for directions, and upon returning my eyes to the road, I'd forget what I just read. The memory portion of my brain had clearly suffered some sort of damage from last night's mischief. I was no better than a little orange goldfish and getting worse. In a mental fog, and after a dozen U-turns, I made it to the speedway.

The facility looked top-notch for all I could tell, as I wasn't able to get any pictures of the track since it had a fence all the way around it; paying for a tour wasn't quite in the budget. I went inside the visitor area to see if there were any spots to see the track. Again, no go. I walked out, rode my bike to the shade of a nearby palm tree growing on the edge of the vast emptiness that is Daytona Speedway's parking lot on a weekday, and spread out on the ground like a chalk outlined figure, using my riding jacket as a pillow and a sun block. I needed a power nap.

It wasn't to be, though. Within minutes, a rascally bunch of hungry crows were in the palm directly above me, and some scavenging vultures were circling me a hundred feet up, wondering if I was a goner. Since I had to deal with those pesky raccoons a couple of nights back, I wasn't exactly thrilled with the thought of more intimate critter-company. It was time to find a place to sleep it off.

Wekiwa Springs State Park was on the way from Daytona to Haines City, one of my next stops. I pointed the Goose in the right direction and cruised toward the state park. There's no helmet law in Florida. That was the only thing that contributed to successfully making it to the state park without a volcano of vomit gushing out of my helmet. If forced to wear my helmet feeling that bad, I wouldn't have made it out of the speedway parking lot. I knew it was highly dangerous, but it was kind of fun riding with no helmet. Visibility was second to none, and the cool breeze on my face was just what the doctor ordered.

I made it to Wekiwa, set up camp, squashed a ton of mozzies, and turned the coma switch on for a few hours. Just before dark, still feeling horrible, I got up and pitifully tried to make a fire with the damp wood that the park ranger sold me. Upon entering the park earlier, I paid for my night's stay and for a $5 bundle of firewood. I wanted a real campfire. When a ranger dropped off a huge black plastic bag full of quartered logs, I smiled with anticipation. Nowhere, before the trip or during, did I see so many hunks of firewood for only $5. Looking back, that could have been some sort of deranged strategy where the same bundle of wet wood was sold over and over to other poor saps wanting a campfire. I knew that I stood no chance of igniting the useless logs. It was like the giant bag was meant to hold water in instead of keeping it out. With no fire and no desire to hang out with the hungry, blood-sucking, winged vampires, I retired to my estate (tent) and went into a deep, replenishing sleep. Today, my brother turned twenty-seven.

Day 22 – November 4, 2011

What kind of bird is making that god-awful noise? I was summoned to consciousness by what sounded like a sick crow choking on a hairball. From listening to it, I could tell that it was right over my tent. Before unzipping, I made sure that I had my camera ready so that I could film the thing before it flew off. I grabbed the zipper and stealthily unzipped the door of the tent. I looked up to find a branch growing at a forty-five-degree angle roughly nine feet above my tent, and attached to it was a skinny little squirrel with its mouth agape, teeth clamping onto some sort of nut. I had been fooled. When the long, raspy chirp escaped the small pocket of open mouth around the nut, his chest caved in making him about an inch wide. I'm not sure if the noise he was making was normal or not, but he seemed to be doing fine. He sat there for a few more minutes while I captured some hilarious footage. When I attempted to review the clip later, my camera conveniently said "card read error." Somehow the footage had been wiped clean. Damn it! It was tremendously funny.

I grabbed a shower at the Wekiwa Springs park facilities and quickly packed up camp to avoid the rain that had just started falling. When you pack away wet gear it develops a *fancy* smell. The blue tarp that I was carrying already had this pleasant aroma. It smelled like a basement in a fifty-year-old house mixed with a few slices of mushroom. Throughout the trip I would lay the tarp on the ground and put my tent on it to protect the tent liner from damage. The drawback was that moisture collected under the tarp at night, and even though I shook it off and laid it out in the sun for a bit, it had yet to fully dry out since the first time I used it on day two. My race with the rain was quick enough to get most of the gear packed away while it was still dry. I was off for central Florida after that, feeling ten times better than yesterday.

Haines City is by no means a lucrative travel destination. It's more of a mid-sized town full of people who work all year to leave Haines City for vacation elsewhere. Orange groves border the town limits. It looked as though it could have been anywhere America, but just a slight bit warmer. I noticed a white sign with large red letters announcing "Budget Inn of Haines City." If not for having a goal of inching closer to the Florida Keys, perhaps I would have relished in their accommodations for a night. Maybe the owner was one of Vivek's uncles. Who knows? It was all too exciting.

I had but one personal reason for coming to Haines City, and that was to ride by James Bubba Stewart's house and motocross track to see what I could see, from the road, while hoping that some travel magic would happen and I'd have a chance encounter with him or his dad at a gas pump or something. I envisioned topping off the Goose and having a bright yellow Lamborghini roll up for some petrol. Out would step Bubba and his dad, Big James, and they would give me a friendly, "Hey Mike, have you ever driven a Lamborghini?" At which point I'd say, "Hmmm, let me see. No. No, I don't think I have." And they'd reply with, "Well, why don't you take ours for a spin? In fact, we should just trade even up for that clapped-out Goose that you have sitting there." Pink slips would change hands, yadda, yadda, yadda, and I'd be crossing the country in a bright yellow Lamborghini.

Snapping back to reality, I came to Haines City with no real plan. I just wanted to see what an area was like that produced one of my all-time favorite athletes. Bubba is, arguably (although I don't know who would argue this point), the fastest professional racer to ever throw a leg over a motocross bike. In years past, while he was still racing a 125, he was often the fastest rider on the track all day: fastest lap times, highest corner speed, best starts, and of course he could jump a motocross bike better than anyone, even the high-paid professionals on bikes with engines twice the size of his.

He revolutionized motocross with a move called the Bubba Scrub. To pull it off, the rider approaches a jump at higher speed than needed to clear it. The rider then leans the bike and turns the front wheel simultaneously while launching from the face of a jump. This keeps the rider lower to the ground, allowing his rear tire to get back on the surface of the track sooner, thus shortening the time in the air and lengthening the amount of time accelerating. And what do you want to do most in racing? Accelerate as much as possible on every inch of the track. He also has had his own television show and, like me, he started from the bottom. I respect that to no end. All of that made the extra miles inland worth it. I'd see the ocean again soon enough.

In Haines City, I came upon Maryland Fried Chicken. It was a small red and white building sitting at a T-shaped intersection and was the second MFC franchise I'd ever seen. Due to my home state's proximity to Maryland, I wanted to stop in and see what all the fuss was about. The owner of the place was a San Jose, California, transplant. I was the lone customer, and he didn't seem busy, so I questioned him about the franchise for a few minutes while his cook prepared the food. I wanted MFC's back story and he gave me the lowdown on how the restaurant began. In his words, it all started in Georgia when a group of guys from Baltimore moved south. Things happened, a recipe was carried with them, and voila, the restaurant began. That's the extremely short version.

I suppose naming a restaurant for any far-off place gives it a touch of the exotic. Maryland Fried Chicken may not have the same ring in Maryland, ya know? The owner comped my plate of fried chicken, coleslaw, and fried rice. To his credit, the coleslaw was phenomenal, and the chicken exceeded expectations—greasy and crispy to perfection. After eating, he sat down with me and I found out that he was also a bike guy, so I hung around for a bit longer to talk with him about motorcycles and everything else from real estate, to air planes, to life in general. He was a very motivated character and like me, thirty years old. I left there appreciative, with a full belly, some advice, and a new friend.

I made tracks to Bubba's house. Word on the street was that it was located on a country road a few miles from town. The locals warned me not to attempt to go to the house directly because the Stewart family had an armed guard on the property. I heeded the warning and assured them that I was just going to discreetly ride by. The locals kind of kept it a secret, a town secret that everyone was in on, and wanted me to respect the Stewarts' privacy. I had no intentions otherwise.

All I can say from my visit is that there is very little worth seeing without actually being on the property. A few cattle grazed in a nearby field, the top of a huge takeoff ramp was visible, a pavilion's roof broke the tree line, their mailbox was moto'd out with half an mx tire sticking out of a brick mailbox enclosure, and a fancy little "S" marked the front gate. I really didn't push the issue and spent about two minutes there on the country road, wondering how much greener the grass was on the other side.

Dusk was approaching. I aimed to get as close to Miami as possible. Earlier, the owner of Maryland Fried Chicken recommended taking Route 27 S, due to it being *silver season* (older folk season) in Florida, and I'd have less traffic to deal with going to Miami. I took his advice and headed out of town. The sun's unblinking stare turned deep orange as it left to have a look at another part of the planet. I changed my goal from reaching Miami to finding a cheap room in Clewiston. The ride along 27 S, although incredibly straight, and rather silverless, was full of beautiful farmland that at times reminded me of Africa's Serengeti. A few firsts made the ride even sweeter: orange groves, sugar cane fields, and cows in pastures full of palm trees. It was just so different from West Virginia.

Thoughts gang up on you after hours in a helmet. My protective bucket started to fill with them when I looked at my surroundings, recognizing that I wasn't in any well-known destination and yet, it was great. Traveling for weeks on end, on the road, covering every inch of pavement along the way, skipping any urge to fly, allows a person to see a more real side of the world in which they live. It's a world that's not all bad and not all good. It's varied and stimulating and surprisingly beautiful. I imagine that truckers know this feeling better than most. It seemed increasingly clear to me, as I rode, that by working all year to take a week or two off for a rushed vacation, a person would be shorting themselves of so much. When you only allow yourself a limited amount of time to experience a new place, you tend to be drawn to the tourist traps (speaking from experience), which are the fakest places in the world.

What if you work your whole life and take thirty or forty vacations? Is that enough? What if every vacation taken is to a tourist trap and you haven't seen a real thing in your whole life? And why do some people vacation at the same beach, lodge, or park each year? I don't understand it. The world is jam packed with great things to experience and life is short. Are we collectively working too many hours for too many unnecessary, materialistic reasons? I felt better than I had in years because of this break, and I was only three weeks in. The gain, possess, and acquire style of living was a fast-fading memory, and I didn't want it back.

In Clewiston, I found a skeevy room at the West Express Inn, then hit up the local Wal-Mart for sun block to fight off Florida's attack on the palest skin in the South.

Day 23 – November 5, 2011

The Sun began another long vigil over the Western Hemisphere. It was a warm and breezy morning in Clewiston, Florida. I packed and made for the road. There wasn't much going on in Clewiston. It held the distinction of having the last McDonald's for about ninety miles, considering that you were heading south on 27 out of town. *Oh no, a stretch of the open road that's not littered with golden arches! What shall I do? Someone call somebody!*

Oh yeah, there is one thing about Clewiston worth mentioning. It just so happens to sit on the southwestern shore of Lake Okeechobee, America's next largest lake after the Great Lakes. Before leaving, a stop at Lake O was required. I didn't originally plan to travel near the lake, but due to my lack of a concrete itinerary, I was able to experience something that I probably would've never taken time to visit.

I motored up to Lake O, expecting to see a giant expanse of endless water, like an inland ocean. Not so. From what I could tell, a ring of open water met the shore line. The ring was maybe seventy feet wide. Inside of the ring looked like marsh land. It was so large, however, that I couldn't see the opposite shore. I was looking for something to stand on to get a better view, but all I could find was a guardrail, which I'm pretty sure is the tallest thing in fantastically flat Florida. From my high perch, it looked like there could be open water out there somewhere in the distance. Without the help of a large tree or helicopter, I just assumed that the lake was filled with reeds. At three or four pull-offs on the way out of town, I checked out the lake shore again only to find the same ring of water against the shore and the same plain of marsh in the center.

Route 27 S, just below Clewiston, displays an awfully remote portion of Florida. There are no gas stations, no fast-food joints, no Wal-Marts; just open, straight road with forty miles of sugar cane on the left and various agricultural land on the right. That is it. A word of advice before traversing this stretch of road is to fill your tank. I pulled over several times to snap pictures, and no one even slowed down to investigate my situation. Had I been out of fuel, I would've been out of luck. It was an intriguing East Coast no-man's land. The song "America the Beautiful" came to mind. The part where you sing "amber waves of grain" could be substituted for "army green waves of cane" here. While riding, I stood up several times to glance left. Power line poles jutted out from the cane fields in ever-shrinking vertical lines. The dense, dark leaves resembled a choppy green ocean. The fields were massive, larger than any corn field I'd ever seen. Unfortunately, all good things come to an end, and even those fields, as large as they were, had boundaries. Soon, I was back in Urbanville.

Since I survived Atlanta rather unscathed, I approached Miami with confidence in my big city motoring skills. I was naive. My goal was to leave 27, on the western side of the city, and navigate east to South Beach where Joe's Stone Crab was. I had a hankering for some seafood. I read about Joe's Stone Crab in *1000 Places To See Before You Die*. With my road atlas and a slight bit of help from Google Maps, I thought I'd drive right up to the front door of the place with no issues.

Boy was I wrong. Between the blind-spot-eliminating swerves and the apparent misleading map that I was carrying, I almost gave up on looking. People in Miami drive like they wash down their cocaine with Redbull. I would not recommend taking a motorcycle there unless you know the streets like the back of your hand and possess a higher riding ability. Cities tend to make me perform a bunch of U-turns. On more than one occasion, I needed to turn left and head back up a street while a never-ending stream of cars were flying by well over the posted speed limit. I could've sat there forever waiting on a break, but I jumped out in the rushing stream of traffic and accelerated so hard, to keep up, that the bike wheelied. That was okay with me. I'm used to that and pulled wheelies almost daily, but I couldn't imagine being a novice on a motorcycle in Miami. You'd be asking for it.

I was doing what I could to avoid the toll roads on my way to South Beach. My pockets were nearly empty of anything worth trading, but somehow I rode right into the mouth of the toll troll, two pennies short of the toll, and the toll booth worker didn't plan to let me pass. I sat there, cars piling up behind me, in stiff negotiations with the lady, saying, "Ma'am it's only two cents." She would respond robotically, "But chu need one twenty-fibe." I couldn't believe that there was no way to look past two measly pennies. After what felt like a lifetime, she must have realized how incredibly pointless it was to inconvenience all of those folks behind me over two cents. Reluctantly, she let me pass.

I knew that I didn't have the cash for a toll and planned a route accordingly, but there's a phenomenon in the way some roads are marked that drives non-natives nuts. It goes like this. Maps often mark either the road number (like Route 41) or the alphabetical name (like Sunset Blvd). Both will be the correct designation. I entered the city with all of the numerical road names that I would need, leaving out any alphabetical road names unless the street only had one designation. When I found myself headed for the toll road, the road I needed was right there, but was posted by the alphabetical name, which I did not know. My map only displayed its numerical designation. A much better strategy would have been to jot down both the numerical road name and the alphabetical road name for every road to Joe's Stone Crab. I learned something, and learning is half the battle.

It's also worth mentioning that my map led me onto Miami's shipyard loading docks, where customs and border patrol officers chased me down and motivated me to get out of there quickly. It was interesting to say the least.

Finally, I made it to Joe's Stone Crab and sat down to a meal of stone crab claws and shrimp. I felt severely underdressed and outclassed. Folks were in business attire, with ties, suits, and fancy skirts being the norm. Even so, I'm not really sure why the place got such great reviews. The claws were good, but I still preferred the good ol' Maryland blue crab by miles. The shrimp was tasty, but not earth-shattering. Thirty-seven dollars later, I wondered why I didn't do something else in Miami.

I strolled to the beach looking to raise my spirits with a round of babe watching. Blue jeans and black riding boots didn't exactly fit in on South Beach's sand. Everyone's attire matched the warm weather. Again, I was dressed inappropriately. I felt like a two-headed creeper. The water was that great tropical turquoise. Waves pounded the shore aggressively. People were beautiful, as I thought they would be. None like the bartender at Froggy's, though.

On my way back to the bike, I heavily scuffed through the sand past a family of four. The children were bouncing around normally, flinging sand as they went. Dad was wearing a Speedo, I tried look away, but mom—beautiful busty mom—brought my eyes back to their direction. She was topless! Hallelujah! She had had some work done, and those puppies were blazing. *What a great day this has been!*

Getting out of Miami was refreshing. I took Route 1 S and State Route 9336 toward Everglades National Park. The only thing more numerous than saw grass in the Everglades is mosquitoes. I pulled up to the park just before feeding time, or dark, and made my way to Long Pine Campground. All of the camping spots seemed to be taken, at first. There was another vehicle doing loops around the campground with me, looking for a spot. Vehicular musical chairs was in full effect. Eventually, I crossed the last open camp spot. The guy in the car, whom I had just stuffed out of a spot (hey, it's survival out here, man), saw his fate and drove over and asked if we could share the spot. Without any hesitation, I said, "Absolutely."

His coming to ask to share the spot is an act that I am positively incapable of performing myself. If he had found and taken the last spot, I would have returned to town to find a room before asking to share the spot. I have the utmost trouble with asking for help, charity, or in this case assuming that someone wants to share something with me. I just don't do it. Almost nothing in this world makes me more uncomfortable. It's weakness, I suppose. A lifetime of something that I can't explain has turned off my ability to reach out to others in this rather light social situation. Because of this, though, I've become a more capable person, as I'm often forced to figure things out on my own. I love relying on my own mind to sort out life's hardships. At any rate, in this case I was the one who got to help someone, which I'm always happy to do.

My camping buddy's name was Will, and he had been on the road for three and a half months, traveling to all of America's national parks in his green Honda Civic. That Civic was Will's home, stuffed like a Thanksgiving turkey with supplies. He was about twenty-eight, had been a restaurant employee, had messy long hair, and a that's-cool-with-me-dude attitude, like a surfer. Will was chill.

Before long we became the main course for the park's bazillion winged varmints. The setting sun had released the biting permits. We had to dress like a blizzard was coming—despite temperatures in the eighties—just to pop our tents up. If it was long sleeved, I had it on. Will had the drawstring pulled so tight on his hooded jacket that his nose was the only thing poking through. I wondered how he could see. The bug spray I had didn't work, and cursing the little bastards wasn't getting us anywhere. Will and I jumped into our tents and settled in for an abnormally early night.

Day 24 – November 6, 2011

I came out of the tent ready for battle. The tubed-tongued mozzy squad would bite me no more. Will, on the other hand, did not heed the warning they gave him last night. Poor Will unzipped his tent and walked to the restroom in nothing but a pair of basketball shorts. *Bad move, buddy.* He came back from the restroom punching and clawing at the air. He was fully awake and fully aware! It wasn't long before he too was dressed in his best Eskimo outfit.

Our campground was flat, hot, beautiful, and quite prehistoric-looking. Huge leafy plants in the shape of green sunrays encircled each tent site. Trees were thin, tall, and plentiful and poked like spikes out of an impenetrable jungle of low lying plants. We were surrounded by a sea of chirps, clicks, and whistles. The forest felt alive. I thought of the movie *Jurassic Park*, without the mountains. I loved it, but perhaps January would have been a better time of year to avoid the bites. The damn mosquitoes were relentless. I packed up fast and got out of there feeling like I didn't get the full experience of the Everglades. I saw no alligators, no invasive Burmese pythons, and no air boats. *Maybe next time.* Meanwhile, Will set off for parts unknown. I'm sure that he was just happy to be outside.

Time was on my side for the rest of the day. Key West was waiting a cool 125 miles south. I planned for a slow, easy-on-the-throttle cruise in the sunshine. My last stop on the mainland was Florida City for breakfast and fuel. The day was looking bright. I crossed into Key Largo with excitement. I stopped by the local Chamber of Commerce and visitor center to get some info on Key West's campgrounds. There were only two; I called them both before leaving Key Largo and received no answer. The lady at the visitor center hooked me up with one of those advertisement/generic maps and reassured me that there should be no problem pitching a tent in one of the two campgrounds. She did say, however, that finding a room would be nearly impossible, especially one with a reasonable rate, as it was prime season in the Keys.

I walked outside and noticed a guy hovering over my bike. His name was Blair, and the Goose's setup had caught his eye. He wanted to know about my travels. I gave him the spiel, trying to sound humble. I think that Blair was homeless. He was wearing black shorts, a really heavy black coat, and carrying a case that looked as though some woodwind instrument might be inside. He was friendly enough, and we had a nice chat. Blair had recently read a book titled *What Color Is Your Parachute?* In it, as explained by Blair, your life's purpose is discussed. He went on, describing how you can never be happy unless you're doing the thing that fits you best (which I utterly agreed with), and he gave me solid advice about reaching goals. Whether Blair was homeless or not, he seemed happy in that moment. And so was I. It started raining, and our brief meeting was adjourned.

I took off without rain gear on and didn't really worry about getting wet. I just thought about what a friend told me when I bought the Goose, "You'll dry out fast while you're moving." Sure enough, forty miles later and ten more Keys or so down, I was dry again and the weather was great. As I island hopped south, on the right and left, smaller uninhabited islands floated like clouds in the sky blue water. Long, low bridges linked each pocket of civilization. One island had a single house on it and no road to get there. Arriving by boat was the only way for them to get around. I thought about the stark contrast between island life and the mainland. Then I saw a green iguana that had recently lost a game of chicken with a car. It had never occurred to me that I'd ever see iguana road kill. It disturbed me immensely. For twelve years, starting in seventh grade, I had an iguana as a pet. It would roam freely around my room and sometimes the whole house. The cats got along with it. It felt like your average household pet. The flat one in the road was like seeing the family dog in the same situation. Again, island life is different. An hour later, I rolled into Key West.

Home, during my visit to Key West, was Boyd's campground. I picked it over the other option due to much better reviews. Both campgrounds were expensive. Boyd's tent sites were $60 per night. The other place was $10 less, but Boyd's was a piece of paradise. My site was surrounded by palms and ultra clean facilities. For a tent guy, I couldn't ask for more. After setting up camp, I really just wanted to go downtown to Duval Street and get my drink on, but I was starting to smell like cat fish bait. It had been two days in Florida's heat since my last shower. I calmed down and let a few hours pass, caught up on some things, and finally hit the streets via the community bus.

The bus ran nearly once an hour and cost $2 per ride. I stood under a street lamp outside of Boyd's for an hour waiting for the bus. It arrived and hissed to a halt. I climbed in and handed the driver $20. The driver said, "You need exact change." Damn! Florida was getting the best of my inexperience. He took pity on my out-of-towner ass and let me ride for free. He dropped me off at the best spot for sightseeing downtown and my night began.

Duval Street is the happening place. I found that, after roaming from bar to bar, I wasn't feeling the scene and I did *not* want another Daytona-esque hangover, so I kept the drinks at a minimum. I found my amusement of the night when a fellow with a dinosaur-sized iguana on his shoulder asked if I wanted to take a picture with it. I said, "Hell yeah." I asked how much. He said, "I usually charge people on vacation five bucks." I told him that I wasn't on vacation; I was a homeless guy traveling the country on my bike. He let me take a picture for free; then he and I walked up the street a few blocks, talking about his iguana named Elvis. He asked me to tie Elvis's hat back together while he hustled some pictures. Elvis's get up was a straw hat, a set of beads, and big shades. I enjoyed the time spent talking to the guy, who looked a lot like Brett Michaels, but I had to go do my own thing.

I bar hopped hoping to get revved up, but in a record-breaking, newsworthy, unimaginable fashion, I just couldn't get loose. Another hour passed as I ducked into this door or that, downed another drink, stepped out onto the street, watched an old black man pedal an incredibly loud three-wheeled boom box down Duval, talked to an Asian woman with a Burmese python around her neck, and generally people watched. Soon I found myself in Bobalus's Restaurant and Bar, soaking a piece of heavy porcelain on a wall with a firm yellow stream of urine from the night's earlier drinks. I walked out of the restroom and noticed that the restaurant portion of Bobalus's was closing up, but they had just made a fresh pizza. I asked if they would sell me a slice. They did and I pulled up a seat.

I ate and nonchalantly watched them clean the place. One of the closing duties was to fold pizza boxes, and they picked the wrong guy for the job. The guy assigned to the task was an incredibly short Hispanic man. He was trying to fold the boxes on a rather tall counter. First, if you're going to fold a pizza box, you hold it against your abdomen at about a forty-five-degree angle toward the floor, then begin folding the tabs. I ate and observed. The guy had horrible technique. Jokingly I said, "Let me show you how to do it, man." He took me seriously. He looked square at me and silently gave me a stack of boxes. Within seconds, I was folding three boxes to his one (some of those old job skills coming into play). I folded about forty boxes for them, and for the effort they gave me another slice of pepperoni. The whole thing made me reflect on my job as a pizza delivery guy. That may have been the only line of work that I remotely enjoyed, due to the freedom of delivering at your own pace, in your own car, and being around young energetic people while at work who didn't take the job too seriously.

I left Bobalus's and tried to do the bar scene one more time. I was getting pretty bored, so I called it a night and took a taxi back to camp. On a side note, my shyness was killing me. I was finding it incredibly difficult to start a conversation with anyone who wasn't hustling on the street. I've always been the observer, never the speaker, unless highly intoxicated. *I guess I'll always be who I am no matter where I go.*

Day 25 – November 7, 2011

Boyd's Campground was a painfully pretty place. The campsites were top-notch; every palm's leaves seemed to be combed into the perfect position. Waking up against salty breezes and climbing out of my tent knowing that I didn't have to rush away was splendid. I could've easily stayed there for a month.

My morning and afternoon were rather uneventful. I wandered around downtown like a robo-tourist. I went through the motions of seeming interested in exploring the area while feeling indifferent on the inside. Those hours melted away and I headed back to camp to prepare for the evening by wiping off the day's sweat and packing away electronics that I had been dragging around all day. When I arrived back at camp, I had neighbors.

Previously, my tent was all alone in one corner of the campground. My new neighbors were a friendly couple from Gainesville, Florida. They were in their mid-thirties, seemed to be the family type, and had set up a mansion of a tent. We were located really close to one another—practically zipped together—so I went over and introduced myself, knowing that I'd be leaving some of my more valuable belongings at the site while I was out on the town. They were great; we got along instantly. They offered me a Modelo, and we chatted until I had to run off to the sunset. I had nothing to worry about.

Several folks that I'd met on the way to Key West said that a Mallory Square sunset is a can't-miss. I almost did miss it. I arrived just in time to see the top curve of the sun sink into the ocean. Mallory Square sunsets bring visitors to the spot daily. It's a wonderfully free attraction. Two hundred people stood with me, heads all turned in the same direction. Couples held one another. Older folks gazed with thankfulness and the red bricks of a nearby building could not have looked warmer in any light. I grabbed my camera and waited for the perfect opportunity to catch a drifting sailboat silhouetting itself against the last bit of sunshine. The sun disappeared. I changed my camera's settings to black and white to better capture the unchoreographed gathering of enthusiastic sunsetters—knowing that it will happen every sunny day from here on out as long as people vacation and Mallory Square exists.

The sky grew darker and I thought of what to do next. My feet carried me unknowingly to the nightly Sunset Celebration at Mallory Square Dock. Street performers were eagerly engaging and entertaining tourists. Like many folks, I became quickly entranced by the performers. Some juggled fire. Others told jokes while balancing on top of strange metal contraptions, and some pedaled and swayed high atop their twelve-foot-tall unicycles. The dark cool night only added to their mysterious nature. For the children around, it was a dreamland.

I continued on to Captain Tony's Bar. The gals I met along the beach at Camp Hatteras had recommended the place. At the entrance of Captain Tony's, some folks were standing backwards and tossing quarters into a fish's mouth. The fish was projecting out of the building, fifteen feet above them. My competitive side was building up steam and I was ready to toss next, but a guy with a thick New York accent, who looked exactly like Paul Sr. from Orange County Choppers, asked for a quarter. I gave him one and he made it on his first attempt. That wasn't and easy feat. I decided not to toss a coin and felt good just to be a part of his success. He made a few more perfect shots.

Live music lured me inside. A man who looked like he came from somewhere else to visit Key West, then put on a tropical button-up and never left, was playing an acoustic guitar. I ordered a drink and looked around. Bras hung from the ceiling, reminders of many, many good times. A shirt on the wall said, "All you need in life is a tremendous sex drive and a great ego. Brains don't mean shit." I reevaluated my life for a second in light of this message. I like knowing things and love learning. I have a damaged ego and a great sex drive. The guy who has both is probably a cocky asshole, and we wouldn't get along. Eventually I succumbed to the night and took a bus back to the tent.

Day 26 – November 8, 2011

Day twenty-six started out great. No hangover, a bit of sleep, and another day in paradise. There were a couple things that I finally had time to do. The first was to patch my leaky air mattress; somehow a hole had magically appeared in it. I inflated the air mattress and carried it to the campground pool where I hoped to submerge it and find the air leak. Two young girls were swimming when I arrived. I bet that they thought that I had just brought the ugliest pool raft ever. One side was lime green, and the other, pine needle green. The fact that I looked like I was trying to drown the thing probably unnerved them, as they scattered a few minutes later. It turned out to be a puncture, small enough to barely make bubbles, but large enough to be flat at 3:37am, every morning. The camp store just so happened to have the exact nylon repair kit I needed and the right glue for the job. Boyd's had everything.

My stomach started growling as I wrapped up the patch. I stopped at a Denny's Restaurant downtown. While paying for my order, I took a shot in the dark and asked the waitress if there were any weird or quirky things that I just couldn't pass up while visiting Key West, and boy did she deliver. Very sternly, she mentioned Robert. I was taken aback by her conviction when telling me the story. Robert was a blame doll that a local artist owned his whole life. At the ripe old age of four, the artist began blaming every misfortune he encountered on Robert the Doll. The legend states that Robert received so much negativity that he absorbed a sort of strikingly powerful malicious energy. She said that Robert was located in the museum on the Route A1A side of the island. The waitress warned me not to say anything negative about Robert. She said that I would suffer ill consequences if I wasn't polite to him. I left her a generous tip and took off for the museum.

Seven dollars got me in. It was a brick building, once serving as a fort where cannons bombarded ships. Its halls were wide but shallow and segmented with brick arches. It was as quiet as you'd imagine an immensely solid building being. Footsteps made echoes. It seemed the perfect place to house something sinister, a place where you wouldn't want something to escape. Between the waitress's cautions and the front desk assistant's warning about Robert not liking pictures, I was kind of worked up. Alone, I walked past cannons and displays of Key West's history, past Native American artifacts and local art.

Then Robert came into view. Hundreds of apology letters hung from the walls around him. Almost all of them were from people who had visited the museum and taken pictures of Robert. All of the letters that I read included apologies for taking pictures of Robert and asked for Robert to stop the acts of misfortune that they encountered since leaving the museum. I decided to heed all warnings and asked permission first before taking a picture. Robert seemed to understand my respectfulness, and granted permission.

He was about the size of a three-year-old child, and displayed lots of time-worn character. He had the most intense eyes. They were like piercing black holes that led into an unknown realm. I did not like looking into them. I was standing there by myself, having a little one on one, and began to feel short-winded, kind of like being in the presence of a super predator, like a shark at the aquarium—you know that it's not capable of empathy and just wants to harm you, that sort of feeling. Would a great misfortune come my way for taking a picture? I had no idea, but it was worth the gamble.

I checked out a few more displays and then rode back downtown to see the Southernmost Point of the continental United States. During the day, the marker has a line, and I wasn't too interested in waiting, so I walked around town until my feet started to hurt. Most of it was coming from my toes being smashed together in my shoes. Fortunately, Key West had a shop that sold Vibram Five Finger toe shoes. I bought my third pair; the other two pairs were packed away at my brother's house.

It was getting late, and I attempted to make another Mallory Square sunset. I came up shy by about five minutes. People were still lingering and there was fun in the air. All felt good in the world. I was in a really great mood and began the night with a nice solid brewski.

For a few hours I checked out some more of the Duval Crawl scene, but that became boring, so I got the idea to go visit the Southernmost Point at night. No lines! For about twenty-five minutes I was further south than any other American in the continental US. My legs dangled over the sea wall, the gentle waves submitted to the concrete below, and the stillness of night soothed my thoughts. It was one of those there's-no-place-I'd-rather-be moments. I then ventured back to the bat cave (tent) for a night of snoozing on a freshly patched mattress.

Day 27 – November 9, 2011

Key West has a special geographic location and beauty by the shipload. Mosquitoes don't live there. Key West's people are friendly and eccentric. It's known for a lot of things and one of those is the adventurous writer, Ernest Hemingway. A fair portion of his life's work was written on the island.

Igor admired Hemingway as a traveler and told me that he had a picture of Hemingway on a wall in his room as a child. Mr. Hemingway seemed interesting, so I laid my money down and took a tour of his house. A spunky, redheaded tour guide blurted out facts while a dozen other folks and I came within inches of the writer's possessions. The house was left complete, as if Hemingway was about to return any minute. A six-foot-high brick wall surrounds the grounds and a micro jungle finishes off any chance of seeing anything but the front of the house from the road. Mild green shutters were open, allowing the famous six-toed cats to sleep on the master bed in the sunshine. The house was old and airy, and not too big. For an island home, it was a comfortable size. The tour was worth it, the grounds spectacular, and the tour guide filled me in on things that I would've never thought to search for on my own. I was a new fan.

One of the last things before heading north that I wanted to do was finish my loop around the island and head back to Smathers Beach for some pictures. At that point, Smathers Beach was the prettiest beach I'd ever put my peekers on. What made it even better was the dozen or so folks hanging out on the long stretch of sand. Even I could run around with my reflective white skin, like a catfish's belly, and not feel overpowered by looks from the bronze people nearby. Sadly, time to leave Key West had arrived. In three short days of stability, the place felt like home, and I really didn't want to leave. As I rode away, I experienced the exact same level of uncertainty about the road ahead as I felt on day one. Again, I just clicked the Goose into first and rolled forward.

My mood lightened at mile marker seventeen, the location of a sky diving joint. I woke up that morning with the thought of just going ahead and sky diving and getting it over with while here. I had the nerve and money for once. The day before, I found a coupon in an ad and the price wasn't so bad. I exited off of the pavement for a sandy road that led to a small, vacant shed where two planes were tied down. The door was locked, but there was a sign saying to call the number if you wanted to sky dive. I called and called, but they never answered. Oh well, I was only in Florida. There would be a lot of other places to do it along the way. Then north I went, enjoying the beautiful ride.

I had a loose notion to make it to the mainland, but in Key Largo I met a man named Pat, and my day turned in a direction that I couldn't have guessed in a million years. I was wiped out and in need of some caffeine and a snack. At a Shell service station, I was sitting on the curb, drinking my coffee and chewing on a Slim Jim when a fellow pulled up and said, "I like those boxes." He was hanging out the window of his tan Chevy truck and looked enthused. He parked his truck and walked over, taking a seat on the curb beside me.

He was about fifty years young with a polite way about him. We talked bikes for a solid half hour. He owned a Suzuki V-Strom Adventure bike, and believe it or not, had the exact same idea about using the exact same toolboxes for his bike. He said, "When I saw those boxes I just had to talk to you." I'm glad he did. The timing was perfect. As we rambled on, I mentioned that the Goose needed an oil change. He offered me a place to do that at his house.

He had just returned from a two-month trip from Key Largo to Maine and back and understood how helpful it was to lend a hand to a fellow traveler and rider. We left the curb and drove back to his house where I met his wife Sharon. We finished up the oil change, and I felt obliged to head out, but we just clicked so well that we never really stopped talking. Talking to Pat was like talking to my future self. It was bizarre yet promising.

He and Sharon ended up offering me a delicious home cooked meal and a place to crash, even entertaining the idea of letting me spend a night on their house boat, docked in a canal just steps from their front door. I couldn't believe it. They eventually settled on letting me stay in an upstairs apartment. I was humbled to no end. The best part of the whole deal was sitting at their kitchen table, sharing some beer, and feeling like I have never been in better company. How lucky was I? These folks had come out of nowhere, were like-minded, intelligent, kind, and well-traveled. Their company was highly refreshing. Pat had been into motorcycling forever, and his wife had traveled to all of the places that I've dreamt about. That night, life could not have been better. I knew then that I made a couple more lifelong friends.

Day 28 – November 10, 2011

I managed a solid eight hours of sleep. Perhaps just feeling so good inside is the only sleeping pill you need. I got moving, packed my things up, and met Pat downstairs. I thought that we'd just shake hands and say our farewells, but he and I started right where we left off the night before, like two motorcycling chatterboxes. Talking bikes with him wasn't an ego-infused pissing contest; it was simple, intelligent conversing. If we wanted to talk technical specs, we could. If we wanted to talk about bikes of the past, that was no problem. We honestly respected one another and didn't have to work at it. Before we knew it, a few hours of rambling on about motorcycles passed again, and we decided to grab some breakfast.

A little place called Evelyn's came highly recommended. We jumped on our bikes and crossed all but a mile's worth of pavement to get there. Pat and I sat in the abundant outside dining area, taking in the warm morning air. The food was great and inexpensive, as promised, but the company was better. I literally could've palled around with Pat all day. In the spirit of the journey, I vowed to get rolling. We stopped back at his place one more time so that I could get a business card and he could get my contact info. He told me about a trip to Oregon that he was planning for the following summer. I said thanks for everything and took off, feeling great.

I was shooting for Clearwater, Florida, to stay with my friend's mom, but first I needed to take care of some of yesterday's business. At a pull-over not far south of Key Largo, I stopped for a picture and to fish something out of my backpack, the place where I kept my laptop. I had the camera sitting on the tank bag and the laptop sitting on the front part of the seat. I picked up the camera and walked across the road to take a picture, not planning to take much time there. With my back turned away from the bike, I heard a heavy plastic crunch. My laptop had slid off of the Goose's seat. I bolted back to the bike as if there was something I could do, picked up the laptop, did a visual inspection, and turned it on. Lights on the laptop's base blinked on, but the monitor was busted. Without that, I couldn't write, and without writing, I'd lose a new piece of myself. I thought that perhaps Radio Shack could help me out since I just bought the thing there two months before.

I stopped at the Radio Shack in Key Largo, and we hooked the laptop up to a separate monitor. Sure enough, the laptop was fine, but the screen was dead. Radio Shack could only offer to have the manufacturer repair it, but that would take two weeks. My laptop was covered under a one-year warranty; however, I couldn't hang around Key Largo and had no idea where I'd be in two weeks, so I decided to try Comp USA, back on the mainland. I was determined to find a solution that would keep me writing without a hiccup.

The repair guys at Comp USA hooked my laptop to one of their monitors. Once they realized what I already knew, they gave me a quote on a new screen and installation. I was looking at $290 for everything. That was the price of a cheap, new laptop, so I phoned my tech-guru, Igor, and took his advice to buy a new one. I planned to send the old one home for use as a desktop unit later on. While on the phone, Igor also suggested purchasing the new laptop from Best Buy, citing the stores generous warranties. I located a Best Buy on Route 1 near Miami and headed that way.

I purchased a small, grey Toshiba laptop designed for children. It was water resistant, had green corner bumpers, and was built to take a minor hit. It put a huge dent in my budget, but there was a lesson to be learned in there somewhere. With new laptop in hand, or in backpack, it was time to fight Miami's drivers once again to get north of the city. I battled, scraped, and clawed my way through that terrible traffic again, only this time it was in the dark. I stopped in Fort Lauderdale and found a room. The Goose's odometer had added 3,934.1 new miles since leaving home.

Day 29 – November 11, 2011

My day started with the sun's arrival through the giant windows of my Fort Lauderdale hotel room. I was seven stories up in one of the thousands of random hotels that speckle Florida's beach towns. As far as I could see, the view was flat, green, and commercialized. I ran downstairs for an assault on the continental breakfast. I stuffed my face like a hamster with cereal, eggs, sausage, orange juice, and apple juice in order to recoup some of the costs of the room. It was more than $70 per night and was against my budget's religion. Full of coffee and grub, I waddled back to the room to take an extra-long hot shower and wring out the last bit of Wi-Fi possible before checkout.

Leaving the room, I was loaded with the backpack, tank bag, hiking pack, helmet, loose hygienics, and a handful of random gear, making one trip from the room to the bike. Normally I'd take two or three. I looked like an over packed camel and took up three spots in the elevator, which happened to be jam packed full of people and nearly a thousand degrees. One guy in the elevator made a joke that wasn't at all funny and afterward said, "Relax. It's Friday. You people can laugh." It made me realize that I kept losing track of what day it was since I no longer kept a work schedule. We all filed out of the elevator and I carried my load to the bike.

Outside of the lobby a group of nearly twenty silvers had gathered; they moved slowly like the tides and were all clean and dressed well. They were waiting for buses to take them to the cruise ships. I was the stand-alone oddball of the group as I loaded the Goose with all my belongings. Their curious stares gave clear notice that they were itching to find out what I was up to. One older gentleman—with those gigantic blacked-out sunglasses, the ones that seem to do a complete lap around a person's head—creaked over to comment on my tattered road map. He smiled while making the suggestion that I should buy a new one. *This one works just fine, sir.* I shot a smile his way, agreed with him in order to be civil, and continued loading my bike up like the studly adventurer that I was. In fact, the attention kind of made me feel like a bit of a badass as I loaded up my manly and unrefined monster of a bike. Yep, I was cool, until . . . until I put the Goose in first gear and lurched forward. I initiated a hard right U-turn away from the lobby door only to eat shit and hit the pavement when my rear brake disc lock smacked the brake caliper.

No one in the world at that moment could have been less cool than me. All of the silvers had already suspected that something was wrong with me, and by me forgetting to unlock the disc lock before takeoff, I confirmed their suspicions. One lady stepped toward me to help pick the Goose up, like a mother concerned for a fallen child, but my embarrassed and adrenaline-filled body easily hoisted it back to the upright position. After that I struggled to unlock the slightly bent master lock, but there was a benefit to my delay. The lady who was going to help me lift the bike started to talk about travel, mentioning her travels to places full of Civil War history. I told her about my hometown of Harpers Ferry and its role in the war. She had been there and was quite familiar with its historical past. Sometimes it did seem like such a small world.

The Sunshine State's west coast was calling. Originally, I wanted to ride a more southern route west along Route 41 to Clearwater, but since yesterday's electronic woes landed me in Fort Lauderdale, my path was redirected a bit further north to Route 75 across Alligator Alley. Crikey! The scary nickname leaves out the real details of this portion of road. It was numbingly straight and surrounded on both sides by the Everglades—by water, sawgrass, reeds, egrets, guardrail, and fence. It was like swampy plains, featureless and paper flat if not for the elevated road splitting the glades. A large section is designated to the elusive Florida Panther as a wildlife refuge. The Miccosukee Indian Tribe owns a service station on their reservation along the Alley, and I stopped there to fuel up. That was my first experience with an Indian reservation. I didn't see much; the service station was indecipherable from any other service station, and travelers like me were the only ones lingering around. I was happy to be there, nonetheless, even if it left out any chance to gain a cultural experience. I took off again across Alligator Alley toward Clearwater with a micro bit more of travel knowledge under my helmet.

At about mile marker fifty-four, the Goose broke four thousand miles for the ride. Those straight Florida roads were beginning to wear an annoying flat spot in the center of my rear tire. I missed cornering. Perhaps the only corners in Florida are located smack-dab in the middle of intersections. Just a thought.

The plan for shelter for the evening had been evolving over a few weeks. Some motocross friends from West Virginia, Paul and Jeff, talked to their mom Carolyn a while back and told her that I'd be traveling through. She agreed to put me up for a night after short notice, and it was set. I'd have a place to stay with someone I knew again. Carolyn didn't get off work until 9:00pm, and I arrived in Clearwater at 7:45pm. Earlier that day, Paul told me about a place called Gator's, just outside of Clearwater. It was a bar and restaurant that sat beautifully on the edge of an inlet. I decided to wait there until it was time to meet Carolyn.

Gator's was large, painted light grey, and had a bright aqua roof. Architecturally, it boasted a seaside demeanor common among buildings along America's East Coast. Inside, a fun atmosphere that was surprisingly country-like, made me wish that I could stay and drink all night, shake a leg, and camp on the beach, if it was legal. It was early and folks were already dancing and having a good ol' time. For being so close to the beach, I thought it odd to have such a down-home flare, but maybe that's how it is there on Fridays. Not wanting to be rude, I left to meet up with my generous hostess.

We met at a Citgo just before ten. Carolyn pulled up in a small maroon car under the light of the service station. It was nice to see her again. She used to live in West Virginia but had been in Florida for a few years. She liked the weather, had a job that she enjoyed, and appreciated all of the amenities of the Sunshine State. I didn't blame her. West Virginia is slowly catching up but is still far behind Florida for things to do. I followed her to her apartment. We talked for a bit, catching up on the years that had flown by. Then she showed me where I'd be sleeping, and before long I was out like a light.

Day 30 – November 12, 2011

Morning arrived at Carolyn's apartment. She asked me where I'd like to have breakfast. I said, "Anywhere but a fast-food place. A country-style diner would be nice." I followed her to the Country Skillet. It was exactly what I was in the mood for. We finished eating, and she decided to give me the quick tour of Clearwater. I followed on the Goose as she drove on, sometimes making a pointing gesture out the window with her left hand and telling me about it after we stopped. When on our way to the beach, we stopped by the original Hooters restaurant, one of man's holiest places. For Hooters, it all began in Clearwater in 1983. Being morning, it was too early to go in, so I snapped a few pictures for evidence that I'd seen the Promised Land, and we ventured to the beach.

The sand in Clearwater is extremely white and fine, so fine that it has made the beach world famous. It will flow through your fingers like the thinnest of fluids. People liken it to baby powder. Its reflective properties keep it nice and cool, even on the hottest of days. While we were there, sinking slowly with every step across the tiny grains, some Marines were doing drills in the ocean surf. They ran back and forth along the beach in what looked like a vicious workout. *Better them than me.* I was out of shape then. My daily workouts consisted of lifting twelve-ounce cans one at a time. Their shouting and camaraderie reminded me of just how much of a loner I am. I heard "Hoorah Gallagher! Hoorah Jones!" and so on in between clapping and back patting. Being a team player has never been one of my strong points, and even though the military may add rich experiences to one's life, it just wasn't for me.

Last on the list of Carolyn's whirlwind tour of Clearwater was Bubba Gump Shrimp Factory. The successful restaurant chain opened its first location in 1996 and was indeed inspired by the movie *Forrest Gump*. I jumped at the chance to add another Gumpified notch to my travel belt. The restaurant sat right on the water. Its interior was littered with scenes from the movie hanging from the walls, like the one where Forrest's simple ass leaps off of his shrimpin' boat, leaving it to smash into a pier. I laughed and bought a "Run Forrest Run" sticker in the gift shop for the Goose. It was red, white and blue and shaped like a license plate. Carolyn and I held off eating and walked back to our vehicles. I placed the sticker on my trunk above the real license plate, thanked her for her kindness, and we said our goodbyes. It was time to put some miles in.

I pointed a finger at Chiefland, Florida, on my map. There, Manatee Springs State Park was just outside of town. I rode in the general direction, fighting endless traffic lights and cars packed tight like sardines on 19 N. Shopping centers provided the only view when I was able to take my eyes off the congested road. I arrived just before dark. While setting my tent up, I looked around at all my fellow campers and was discouraged by the thought of sitting there and boringly watching it get darker and darker. There's only so much one can do at a picnic table. I had a notion to head to town to meet some new people. I left the tent and park behind for a quick ride to civilization.

In Chiefland, I stopped at BubbaQue's for an appetizer. It was a rather large BBQ joint tucked into a plaza a few hundred feet off the road and utterly empty. Its walls were covered in old tools, license plates, animal heads, and beer advertisements. The men's room was marked with big white crooked letters that spelled "OUTHOUSE." I liked the theme. The waitress hooked me up with some redneck nachos, which are French fries topped with pulled pork, cheddar cheese, and barbeque sauce. On the menu "tractor grease" denoted the BBQ sauce. The fries came in a heavy portion, piled high enough to need a caffeinated beverage afterwards to fight off a siesta. The waitress told me that if I wanted to have a good time in Chiefland, I should swing over to Club 19 to check out a band called Steel Bridge. With that bit of info, I paid my bill and took off north on Route 19 to Club 19.

I walked in and perched my hind end at the last open barstool while asking the strikingly pretty girl beside me if it was taken. She replied, "No," with a smile. In rare form, I was able to talk to her like a normal person after that. Normally, I clam up and go into mute mode around attractive women. I have an undisputed, God-given talent for turning even the most benign situations into full-blown events of awkwardness, so awkward that some have scarred me for life. Also, like an electronic disconnect, words get lost and distorted when traveling from my brain to my mouth. It's not quite stuttering, but more of a loss for words altogether. This happens so much that I just prefer to stay quiet in the presence of most female strangers. Thank God, that night my awkward switch was left back at the tent.

The pretty little gal beside me was visiting from England. Her pretty little name was Carly. She was twenty-five, thin, had long light-brown hair, a face of an angel, and was waiting on a guy to show up from Orlando. She had been there patiently waiting on him for more than an hour and was certain that he had ditched her. I could not imagine what could be more important than meeting up with her, after she had crossed the Atlantic to see him. Cupid had already zapped me, and when I got over the initial shock of *I may have a shot here,* I told her, "I'm also from a far-off, exotic land. You may have heard of it; it's called West Virginia." She laughed and said that she'd heard of it. A few years back she took a three-month journey around the United States aboard a Greyhound bus. Once I found that out, we had plenty to talk about. She made me feel like I should have taken off on a journey a little earlier in life, but oh well, what can you do? The bug strikes us at different times. Carly and I were getting along great. I looked forward to the next few hours.

There was a lady to my left named Red from Staten Island, New York, and a fellow named Scott sitting beside her, who was the local of the group. I found it completely amusing, conversing with those English-speaking folks with their wildly contrasting accents. I was sportin' my good-ol'-hillbilly, West Virginia accent that favors the letter *R*. Red spewed out her super-thick, New Yawk accent that did not include the letter *R*. Scott had the classic wide southern drawl that took full minutes to get a letter out, and Carly was speaking in her very proper British tone.

Steel Bridge kicked off around 10:30pm, and the conversation died down when the volume went up. It was incredibly loud inside Club 19. At one point, I left to drain the lizard and came back to find the band taking an intermission and the lead singer sitting in my seat talking to Carly. *You can't win them all.* My existence has been littered with cooler guys always getting the girl. This has resulted in desensitization to the situation, meaning that I don't even put up a fight. In some ways, I know myself too dang well.

Carly ended up hanging out beside the stage and chatting with the lead singer after every set. I ended up getting thrown the scraps. A rather aggressive, and let's say "healthy" redhead with bad teeth took a serious fancy to me. I was leaning against a different end of the bar when she came at me with an offer to dance. Scared shitless, I replied, "No thanks, I don't know how." She said, "I don't mind" and kept trying to break down my defenses. That was round one. Later she came back with a little piece of blue paper with her phone number on it. Under the number she wrote, "Sin." Her name was Cynthia, and she was a bad girl in every sense of the word. I politely took the paper and held her off again. I'd receive one more attack from Sin that night, and again, I blocked her advances, wishing that Carly was into me like that.

I roamed around, met various people, and watched Club 19 turn into a mad house. Guys were going in the ladies room. Ladies were pulling up their skirts while exiting the men's room. Shady characters piled in by the carload. The music stayed loud and hectic, and Carly stayed by the stage. Just when I thought that I should get out of there before someone's drug deal went horribly wrong,

I met a gal from Naples, Florida. She had been into motorcycling with her family for years, both on-road and off-road. Unfortunately, she lost her thirteen-year-old son in a car accident a year before and was having a rough time grieving with her husband. They were on the outs, and I imagined that that was what brought her to the bar scene. I could feel the strength she used to hold back tears while she was telling me about it. I didn't mind being a set of ears and a solid shoulder for someone who needed help moving on. My night was a little busted already anyway. Like any good mother, she couldn't stop thinking about her son. *We all live on as long as we are not forgotten.*

Day 31 – November 13, 2011

I headed north to fulfill a curiosity. Cairo, in southern Georgia, holds a slice of motocross perfection known as Millsap's Training Facility. I had wanted to visit it for years. For those not familiar, it is a motocross training camp run by the mother of one of our nation's fastest racers, Davi Millsaps. I wanted to spend a day there. I started late in the morning at Manatee Springs State Park with plenty of miles to cover from Chiefland to Cairo. I stopped at Chiefland's McDonald's for my morning Wi-Fi session before resuming travels on 19 N. Like a third hand, McDonald's was always there, ready with a reliable Internet connection and all the coffee I could handle. It was hard not to use the place, though each time I walked through its doors, I felt like a traveling sellout.

The route for the day was pretty easy, 19 N to 84 W. That was it, two roads, wide and well-marked. Somehow along the way, near Capps, Florida, I was daydreaming and jumped onto 27 W. I rode that for about fifteen miles straight into Tallahassee. "How in the world did I get here," I mumbled, the way one with amnesia does when they snap out of it. Looking back, I'm still not sure where the 19 N and 27 W intersection was. I backtracked eight miles to 59 N and took that and a few other country roads at a nice leisurely pace all the way to 84 W. It all looked good on the road atlas. Spanish moss appeared once again, hanging like a tree's version of a wedding dress. I found it rejuvenating to get off the four-lane highway and ride some back roads.

As you're traveling on 19 N toward Georgia, the last county before the state line is good ol' Jefferson County, Florida. I thought it ironic to cross into Jefferson County since I was so desperately trying to get away from it back home. My first time crossing into Jefferson County, Florida, that day was right before the daydream-influenced visit to Tallahassee. When I did a U-turn onto 27 E near Tallahassee, to correct my mistake, I crossed into it again. The third time I arrived in Jefferson County, Florida, that day was on a back road just off of Route 59 where you go from Jefferson to Leon County and back to Jefferson before the Georgia state line. Man, I couldn't get away from it!

Finally, I left the twilight zone and arrived in the peach state, my third time visiting Georgia on this trip. Twenty miles later, I arrived in Cairo, just before dark. By then it was too late to go to Millsap's Training Facility, so I chilled out in a fast-food joint parking lot and leached a Wi-Fi connection. The night air was warm and the manicured grass, soft. As I sat on the ground between two green shrubs, in the golden glow of an *M*, I successfully finished my couchsurfing.com account verification. *Bring on the couches!* Then I searched for an open couch in Cairo and came up empty-handed.

My friend Keith, from White Lake, North Carolina, had emailed me a short list of songs he wrote and sang in a wonderfully deep and monotone voice. Most of them were inspired by his life's experiences. One was titled "Facebook Bully" in which Keith sang of his first use of the social network, often picking on people through sarcastic comments (he still does this to me). His lyrics were funny, but even funnier than that was the effort he was putting in to project them. Like a wacky old man, I sat in the grass and listened to each song, laughing hysterically. The folks that had been slowly creeping through the drive-thru lane often noticed me chuckling, shoulders bouncing, and wiping tears from my eyes, not knowing that I was listening to music on my laptop (it was hidden behind my backpack). When I was finished being a parking lot parasite, I tracked down a local motel and shacked up for the night. There was no way that the next day would be so dull. On the bright side, I didn't have a hangover.

Day 32 – November 14, 2011

My journey reached a month. Before I left home, some what-ifs were discussed. What if the trip doesn't last too long? What if I come back after my first week, like a scared little boy? What if I run into trouble on the road and don't come back at all? These were all issues that weighed heavily on my mind then. I didn't want to fail, if failure meant not crossing the USA. I was afraid that my label would be the smack-talking quitter who couldn't hang out on the road.

Well, my view changed dramatically since day one. I still had no clue as to what sort of career to pursue, and I had yet to really slow down long enough to ponder my future and explore the options. Failure, on the other hand, reached impossibility. Here's why. One can estimate that they will live to be somewhere around eighty years old, if they're lucky. That's approximately 960 months to be born, live, reproduce, and die. This one amazing month was so diverse, so filled with moments of joy and humbleness, so full of uncertainty, and so entertaining, that just living through the wonderful experiences of the last four weeks erased any chance of failure. Out of an estimated 960 months of life, I was fully aware that few would be as good as this one. I could've made a beeline for home right then and taken with me a dozen new friends and memories that would be forever engraved in my mind. No amount of money could take that away. I was alive. . . .

Everyone's favorite star, the sun, made another appearance over Cairo, Georgia, and the very Indian-owned America's Best Value Inn. Since I bought those Vibram Five Finger shoes in Key West, I thought that it was time to put them to work. They are designed to be running shoes, so that was the plan: a morning run to fine-tune my Hasselhoff-like frame. Months before, I ran in those things and overdid it, locking my lower calves up for a week. Learning from the past, I decided to jog for just twenty minutes to see what happened. Out on the sidewalk, I was okay for about the first seven minutes. My stamina was still there, but I could hear my lower calves telling me to stop. The twenty-minute run turned into a fourteen-minute break-in period. Back in the room, I busted out some of my favorite moves that I learned from doing the P90x and Insanity workouts. It felt good to break a sweat again, and I planned to incorporate more exercise into the days on the road.

In retrospect, I'm glad I arrived in Cairo too late the day before. By getting to see Millsap's Training Facility first thing in the morning, I had plenty of time to stroll around all of the tracks without the usual speed walking. MTF was located on Bold Springs Road about four miles outside of Cairo. A slew of flags hanging off a black, four-rail fence, representing various countries of the world, greeted all visitors. The whole feel, upon entry, was very welcoming. I was expecting to be stopped at a gate and charged a spectator fee since MTF is one of the more exclusive practice tracks in the country. Instead I rode right in, hopped off the bike, and started taking pictures. No one said a thing.

The park had five practice tracks. Two of them were tiny and set up for cornering practice only. A lengthy, sweeping, outdoor-style motocross track ribboned around the property and around MTF's two supercross tracks. Parents and trainers zipped around the tracks' edges on golf carts, undoubtedly thinking of ways to help their racers gain speed and keep the dream of becoming a professional racer alive. Real starting gates and electronic lap time monitors were on-site to help their progress. Near the entrance to the park, an office with free Redbull and stickers was open and ready to handle any new arrivals. Rental cabins and a turquoise pond with a bike ramp and a rope swing topped off the view. *Is this moto heaven?* All of the riders practicing that day were extremely fast, not quite Adam Cianciarulo fast, but respectably talented. I wish that I could've had one of my motocross bikes with me. In the company of the riders who were practicing, I'd look like an old squid for sure.

Adjacent to MTF was the Georgia Practice Facility. I'm not sure if the two training facilities were in cahoots or not, but GPF's sign did say that it was a private club. In the spirit of adventure, I walked on in. GPF had a few less tracks with no less quality. Their outdoor-style motocross track had huge sandy berms and reminded me of the Southwick, Massachusetts, professional track. It weaved its way in and out of tall, skinny pines. I sat down for a moment and took it in. I realized that I was living the dream. I've always said that I want to be in charge of my day, every day. Sitting at the track, watching the riders pound out lap after lap, thinking about how fortunate I was to be there, I couldn't help but feel like I was where I belonged. There are some moments that you wish you could hang onto forever, and this was one, but the journey had to continue.

Riding south along County Road 12, I stopped at a mom-and-pop country store for a snack and asked if I could charge my camera. The owner's southern hospitality wouldn't let her turn me down. While the camera soaked up electrons, I listened while the cashier gave directions to another gal who was traveling through. More than a few times I had asked for directions on the trip and was left with the impression that the general population had not yet latched onto the north, south, east, west thing. The two employees of the store tried landmarking the young lady to her destination. She seemed confused. I had just traveled the way she was headed, so I spoke up and gave her the route using road names and geographical directions (ex. 84 east). The young lady understood me and was off right away. The store owner and cashier turned and looked at me like I had pulled a rabbit out of a hat, like "How did you do that?"

When you're not a local, landmarks help very little. As an outsider, you haven't seen what those landmarks look like. When you're told to take a left at the chicken coop, and a right past Aunt Betty's brick house, and stay straight when you see the big oak tree, you don't know if that chicken coop is five feet tall or warehouse size. You don't know if Aunt Betty's house is the only brick house or among others. And will that big oak tree look so big through your eyes? Who knows? But a road sign is a road sign is a road sign. I left the store feeling slightly better for helping someone, and my camera was charged again and ready to go.

Panama City filled the horizon. My atlas vaguely illustrated the area, as it does with smaller cities. I rode to where I thought the state park would be according to the map. No go, again. Plan B was to find some locals or a place with Wi-Fi. As I was roaming near the water's edge, I found a bar (surprise, surprise) named Time Out and they just happened to have locals there. They didn't have Wi-Fi, though, which led to bombarding the bartender with questions. She jotted down some directions and for her kindness, I ordered a few brews, tipping well. Time came for her to clock out of her daytime shift and hand over her duties to the evening bartender.

Then those brews done went and snuck up on me. I had been bit by the social bug. When I had the chance to speak to a gal waiting tables, I asked her if I could pitch my tent at her place. How the question was born, I cannot begin to remember. When she stopped laughing and realized that I was serious, she surprisingly agreed. It was official. I had my first yard camp of the trip. Her name was Tina. She was an attractive brunette, right at my age, and dating someone. After talking to her boyfriend Nick on the phone, to make sure he was cool with it and that I wouldn't become a punching bag for a jealous boyfriend, we were off. I quickly set my tent up in her backyard. She planned to go to Nick's house when I finished. I was along for the ride.

With the Goose parked, Tina, her daughter, and I headed across town. I didn't know it at the time, but Nick was staying with his parents. When we arrived, his parents didn't know me from a hole in the ground. The old saying, "look what the cat dragged in," couldn't have fit me better. I was that weird half-eaten shit that the cat dragged in. Was it a mole? Was it a mouse? Was it a bird? You can never tell. Talk about awkward. His parents looked at me, and I peered at them. I rode over there with a stranger, only to meet more strangers, and by golly, it left me feeling strange.

The feeling was short-lived. Nick was more than cool, and his dad and I had a good ol' man-to-man drinking talk. We sat three stories high on the rear deck of his house. Everyone else was inside working on hanging new curtains. The air felt crisp and clean. Moonlight revealed a long pier behind the house. The deck rails, although permeable, seemed to lock in our words like at Catholic Confessional. He spilled the beans to me about some heavy stuff that I'll no doubt take to the grave. He instinctively trusted me. He was a motorcycle enthusiast, and perhaps it was the way I listened respectfully that led him to confiding. We were fellow countrymen who needed nothing more than a few beers and a cool breeze to get along. The night turned out great, and I walked out of there with another group of friends.

Back at Tina's, I crawled in the tent, completely wiped out. Just as I was falling asleep, the damn sprinklers came on, and every twenty seconds, for about an hour, it sounded like my tent was in the middle of a monsoon. The randomness was perfect.

Day 33 – November 15, 2011

Now that I'd made it as far south as I could ride and back north to Georgia again, it was time to head west, and for me that's the great unknown. Every day promised to inch me a little farther across the country to California. I'd been waiting for this. Everything on the East Coast is loaded with some shade of green. That's not a bad thing. Green is a wonderful color, but I'd never seen a desert, and I couldn't wait to experience the remoteness of that parched land. It would still be a few weeks before I got close, though. In the meantime, I just had to take it one mile at a time until those miles got me there.

The sun sets in the west, and I was learning quickly that I'd be blinded by it almost every evening while sluggishly riding on. My eyes have always been super sensitive to light and in a constant battle with the big yellow fireball. The winter's low-hanging evening sun was killing me.

I awoke in Tina's backyard to an overwhelmingly musky smell. The thought crossed my mind, before I unzipped and climbed out, that someone took a leak on my tent while I was sleeping. The smell was downright pungent. I felt the floor of the tent, looking for extra wetness, and found nothing. Relief struck when I climbed out and realized that something was in the air and that my tent had not received a golden shower. I've always been a really early riser, so I took advantage of the apartment complex's laundry room. Waiting for the laundry to finish would allow Tina and Nick time to wake up.

The night before, I stashed a bunch of gear inside their place so that it couldn't be stolen without thinking that I'd have to wait to get it in the morning. The dryer finished its thing about the same time that Nick unlocked the back door. We chatted a bit and I was off, headed to the beach to get a bath/go swimming. I hoped to at least smell like seawater for the day, instead of sweat.

I found a public beach access point behind the United States' largest nightclub, Club LaVela. The nightclub was closed, and the beach nearly empty, so I decided to indulge in a bit of swimming while safely unleashing the extreme white sheen that is my shirtless body on the public. I kid not when I declare that I'm so white that simply removing my shirt in a crowd can be considered an act of terrorism. The Milky Way contains stars envious of my shine, and there are viruses safer than my full birthday suit. Like fish of the deep, I too am bioluminescent. Concern for other folks' retinas overwhelmed me as I stood in the sand yanking off my pants, socks, riding jacket, and shirt. Still, I stuck to the plan.

Waves smashed the shore in washing machine fashion. The Gulf of Mexico's water was that pretty blue, reminiscent of the tropics. I was looking forward to getting clean. Excitedly, I ran in there like a lifeguard trying to save someone, only to lose my breath like I'd just been punched in the gut. It was cold as shit. My lungs tried to rapidly inhale as each cold drop stuck to my skin. I helplessly splashed around, diving under and gasping for air each time I surfaced. A more out of place sight would be hard to find. My fingers were turning an arctic purple by the time I finished up. Nonetheless, I came out cleaner than I went in. Mission complete.

The night before, among the brews and social bug, I met a guy at the Time Out Bar who recommended that I stop by McGuire's in Destin, Florida, on my way to Pensacola. It was located halfway from Panama City to Pensacola.

McGuire's was your typical dark, rustic brew pub and had wooden charm for days. It was the perfect lunchtime break from the saddle. I ordered an Irish Scotch ale and made small talk with the bartender who was hovering near a pair of beer taps that sprouted from the nipples of a sculptured woman. When I had to drain the main vein, I walked downstairs to the facilities and took a healthy leak in the ladies room, yep, the ladies room. McGuire's had these clever signs that were meant to fool the new guys on the scene. They said something like *MEN* (in real big letters) don't go in here because it's the *ladies* (in really small letters) room. All I read when I rounded the corner was *MEN* in the large letters. As I was taking a leak, I thought to myself that this was the first public men's room that I'd whizzed in that didn't have at least one urinal. Upon exit, I almost ran some poor woman over as she gave me the evil eye. *Honest mistake lady.*

Pensacola promised a meeting with some extended family. My brother's wife's mom, Pam, and stepdad, Joe, live there, and they agreed to shack me up for a couple of days. I spoke with them about the trip a few months prior when they came to West Virginia to visit. I motored into town at dusk and was met by Pam, Joe, and their four huge Mastiff/Great Danes. Pam and Joe one-upped the Gulf of Mexico by letting me properly wash off the stink. Then we headed off to Waffle House for dinner and a round of how've you been.

We caught up and laughed. We tore up a few Waffle House delights and talked about the next few days. We were back at their house by 8:30. I fell asleep on the couch, wiped out from last night's sprinkler ambush. It felt great to be the one who traveled to see them instead of the other way around, as it's always been.

Day 34 – November 16, 2011

I woke up on Pam and Joe's couch to a Pensacola sunrise plagued with gloominess and clouds. Like normal folks, they had to work, and I didn't want to hinder their plans. I was headed for downtown as a Goose-riding tourist. Pam stirred first that morning, fixing me a welcomed cappuccino. Joe lumbered downstairs as I was about to hit the streets.

Despite the dreary weather, I rode to Pensacola's welcome center in search of things to see and do, knowing that my rain gear was in my plastic pannier. The nice lady behind the desk drew up all the routes needed on a complimentary map of the city. She was proud of Pensacola's history and its attractions. She was happy that I had come to see her town. Before the sightseeing, my first stop was going to be Cordova Mall to get my cell phone screen fixed. It had been severely cracked since dropping it in the Outer Banks, and now the touchscreen would only respond some of the time. Joe had called a place in the mall and got a quote for me. Just as I was about to take off from the welcome center, I realized that I left my money back at their place. I hurried back in hopes that Joe had not left for work yet and locked the gate.

Fortunately, he was still there loading his trusty van full of tomatoes for the day's deliveries. While there, a thought hit me that I should ask to ride around with him as he made his deliveries. I felt that I'd get to know Joe and Pensacola better that way. He agreed to let me tag along. The rain was approaching anyway, and I'd probably spend the day walking from place to place in that bulky rain gear, looking really hip.

Joe is a pretty well-known fella to Pensacola restaurateurs and grocers. His business consists of buying the best quality regional tomatoes, hand sorting the absolute best tomatoes from that group, and delivering them to Pensacola's nicer dining establishments and grocery stores. He's known to the grocers and the restaurateurs in the area simply as Tomato Joe. He has a basic white cargo van displaying no advertisements. All of his business is strictly word of mouth, and his track record of being in business for over twenty years speaks for itself. His motto is "Only the best quality," and if you've eaten at an upscale restaurant in Pensacola, chances are you've had one of his tomatoes in your salad, on your burger, or in a sauce. A better tasting tomato would be hard to find anywhere. With that, we were off to make some rounds.

We stopped by a few places to fill orders. Tomato Joe's delivery routine involved parking the van and walking in the back door with a box of tomatoes. At each establishment he was kindly greeted and returned the gesture. He addressed folks by their first name and gave them a big ol' smile. This went on all around town. At one grocery store, he was placing tomatoes on a display, facing them all perfectly for the desired effect. We needed a price gun and couldn't find one. Joe wandered the store searching for one. Soon two or three other people were in on the hunt. All of them knew Joe and wanted to help. It gave me the impression of a small town. Folks in Pensacola seemed top-notch. We found a price gun and finished up. Then he mentioned that he could take me to the mall to turn my cell phone in for repair. We dropped it off. They said it will be a few hours. Back to work we went. I was getting a kick out of watching a sole proprietor in action. *One day I'd like to be in business like Tomato Joe.*

Back at Cordova Mall, a few hours later, we stopped to check on the progress of my cell phone. "Fifteen minutes," they said. Joe and I decided to hit up the food court for some free lunch. The mall had about seven food vendors, arranged in a circular fashion, and all giving away free samples. As we walked by, teenage employees bombarded us with some sort of meat or bread on a stick. Being the nice guys that we are, we didn't refuse their offers. At the seventh stop I was full, so we made our way back to the cell phone repair store.

"Fifteen minutes," they repeated. This time we just sat on a bench and waited them out, chatting, and gazing in their direction. Fifteen minutes passed, and we went back in to discover that the repair guy tried three screens that were not made for my phone, and when he put the original screen back on, my phone wouldn't work. As a mechanic, I know never to use the wrong part on whatever you're working on. If you have a Ford truck, don't try to put Chevy pistons in it. It won't work. How the guy became a repair man, I have no idea.

Joe, realizing that I was phoneless, offered to take me to the local Sprint store to find a solution. Well, the fix turned out to be a new phone, new phone number, and $150 down the drain. The repair shop was going to charge $130 to put a new screen on, so all was not lost.

Our work day wrapped up and we headed home. Joe whipped up a huge pot of jambalaya. I cleaned up and prepared for a night out on the town after dinner. My brother had told me about Seville Quarter, a sizeable drinking establishment that he and Kayla visited on their trips to Pensacola. It wasn't just a bar or nightclub. It was seven large rooms under one roof, with a slightly different theme in each. My duty as a bar fly is to find as many opportunities to drink in dark rooms, in the presence of fine-looking women, as possible. I wouldn't have missed it for the world.

I meandered through a billiards room, karaoke room, techno dance club, dueling piano bar, blues bar, and an upscale lounge. I had a great time checking the place out, although it would've been nice to have some of my rowdy West Virginian buddies with me. I met just a few people, including a pretty hot one-armed chick, who was way outta my league. She and I talked for a spell, but my lack of game sentenced me to nothing more than a relaxing time.

Earlier in the day, Pam and Joe informed me that they'd be in Las Vegas on January 16, 2012, with Shane and Kayla. *Could I pull off the timing?* Once again the fluid-like plan was modified.

Day 35 – November 17, 2011

The time to say so long to my gracious hosts and extended family, Pam and Tomato Joe, came early on Thursday morning. Before making Pensacola a memory, there were a few things I wanted to see. Pensacola's Naval Air Station was one of them, and it was right down the street. I was after a visit to its lighthouse and free air museum. This was my first time stepping foot on an actual military base and could have possibly been a serious lapse in judgment.

Two menacing soldiers stopped me at the gate to check my ID. I nervously handed them my driver's license. With my bike packed up the way it was, I was concerned that they would want me to unpack all of my gear to make sure I was safe to enter. If that would've happened, they could have discovered my pistol, which might have snowballed into a whole heap of trouble.

I was carrying a pistol for protection obviously, but not necessarily from humans. I wanted it for any sort of predator that may have wanted to turn me into a future pile of poo, like a mountain lion or bear. Although not there yet, I wanted to go hiking out West or possibly camp alone somewhere remote. A cell phone call to the local authorities will only get you so far when a bear is munching on your hind end. Some nights, like on Mt. Pisgah, I kept the pistol in the tent with me as I slept as a last line of defense.

As sad as it is to admit, talk of mountain lions and bears is kind of cheap. Statistics show an incredibly low amount of attacks on humans. Deep down, I carried a thought that one night a group of ill-intentioned folks could quickly overtake me or drag me out of my tent. Or one deranged, armed individual could overtake me and leave me for dead. In that circumstance, I wouldn't have regretted being armed at all. As I traveled, the body of the weapon would be in a large Ziploc bag in my rear trunk. The magazine was emptied and stored in my left side box and the bullets kept in the right. Against advice from several people, I brought the pistol with me. It's always those who think it can't happen to them that, sure enough, end up putting lotion on their skin in a hole in someone's cellar. The pistol was always in the back of my mind, and I approached carrying it with the utmost responsibility.

I sighed with relief when the guards returned my ID and sent me on my way, although not without being instructed to wear gloves. One is not allowed to ride a motorcycle on a military base without gloves. *Learn somethin' new every day*. While cruising over to the museum, I couldn't help but notice how the base looked a bit like a resort. It had beach front, a golf course, and running trails. I thought it would be all fence, camo, and barbed wire.

The National Museum of Naval Aviation is about a mile from the gate. It houses close to eighty military aircraft ranging from newer jets to old, home-made-looking aircraft. I spent about an hour and a half wandering around, oohing and aahhing at all of the airplane eye candy. Sensory overload soon kicked in. I couldn't handle any more facts, any more scale models, or any more shiny pieces of awesomeness. Kudos to those in charge of preserving the military show pieces; they were wonderful. I sat down at the museum's cafeteria for lunch, staring out a window and wondering if the military would've ever made a good fit for me, but clearly knowing the answer.

Now for a real highlight. I was off to visit the lighthouse. A small, mandatory donation of $5 allowed access to the lamp room at the top. "The price you pay for climbing 177 steep-ass stairs ought to be enough," I whispered on the way to the staircase. My burning calves, from the run a few days ago, hoisted me one spiraled step at a time until I had reached the 150-foot overlook. A vantage point of twenty-seven miles extended all around. On one side, blue water shimmered endlessly and on the other, the base faded into Pensacola's sprawl. What a reward.

I was the lone visitor. A small lady in her mid-sixties, named Georganne, worked the observation deck. She was an encyclopedia of the lighthouse's history. I was still stuffed with facts from the aviation museum, so instead we talked about a piece of driftwood lying on the beach. She had had her eye on it for quite some time and wanted it as a yard decoration. I suppose there wasn't much else to do up there all day, and maybe the altitude had gotten to her. I whipped out my camera and zoomed in on the piece of wood. It didn't look so big on my tiny LCD screen, so I told her that I'd go fetch it for her as long as it wasn't too large to move. Honestly, from the lighthouse, it looked doable. I thought it would be nice to help someone else out since so many had been helping me. Spread the love, ya know?

Down the steps I went, en route to the driftwood. When I got to that sucker, it turned out to be a large tree, and water logged at that. A supremely funky smell hung in the air around it. Flies swarmed the wood, and it had thousands of holes bored into it from some unknown insect. I could see about the first twenty-five feet of it and the rest was buried in the sand. I peered up at the lighthouse and could see Georganne checking my progress. With no way to verbally tell her that it was way too big, I opened my arms up as wide as I could in her direction in hopes that she'd understand that it was so big that you would need a tractor to move it. Four large soldiers couldn't have budged this thing. My mission was incomplete. As I walked under the lighthouse on the way back to the Goose, I looked up at her, waved, and left there hoping she understood my signal. Florida was fun, but I had to push on.

It seemed like only minutes, and I was in Alabama. Poor ol' Alabama. I went right through it without even stopping for anything more than a picture. It really didn't feel right to not get some sort of experience from a state. Entering Mobile on Interstate 10 W was rather unflattering. Oil refineries gave me my first impression. They looked harsh and unwelcoming, like I was entering a city focused on nothing but industry. A few snapshots of Mobile would be all I'd have to remember it by. On the bright side, I did have the pleasure of listening to *Sweet Home Alabama* while riding through. It randomly popped up on Pandora Radio a few minutes after I crossed the state line. That's about all I can say about that.

Mississippi's bright blue and red sign, "Birthplace of America's Music," welcomed me well after dark. It had a neon glow about it that gave me a little charge. The heat of Florida had vanished. Mississippi's air was crisp and cold. I stopped at a place called Krazy K's Convenience Store for some coffee and warmth. Inside, it took three seconds to realize that I would have a hard time understanding this new dialect. I did not know that a place existed with a backwoods accent so strong that a hillbilly from West Virginia couldn't decipher it. The beginning and ending of words blended into one another in each sentence. It was like they were talking fast and slow at the same time.

While warming up at a booth, both hands on the coffee cup, I noticed that a police officer had someone pulled over in front of the store. This sent the employees and customers into a frenzy. The whole place, minus me, went bananas when they officially arrested the poor guy. It was like I had unknowingly stumbled upon an episode of Jerry Springer. I was the only one in the building who took pity on the poor sap. Civility was lost in these folks and replaced by brutish ignorance. It left me to conclude that not much happened in southeast Mississippi when the sun went down.

I finished my cup of coffee and headed for the Goose. Outside, I ran into some old drunk who eagerly made me an offer that I *could* refuse. He said he would sign the titles over from his old Ford truck and ratty-looking Dodge Neon for my bike. I replied, "No thanks, buddy, but I appreciate the offer." There was something in the water in those parts, I'm telling you. Those folks were missing a chromosome or had been fed plastic for breakfast as children. I felt proud to be a West Virginian. *At least we have one state beat.* From there, I pushed on to Waynesboro, Mississippi, where I found a room at the Budget Inn.

Day 36 – November 18, 2011

It's hard to make a day sound interesting when all you do is lay down the miles. I was in Waynesboro with my sights set on a northwesterly dart across Mississippi to Clarksdale. As I was gearing up for the marathon run, the Budget Inn owner and I talked travel. He was an Indian man in his mid to late forties who had been sweeping the concrete walkway near me, and wearing a Redskins beanie to fight off the cold Mississippi morning. He was quiet, polite, and intrigued that I was traveling across the country on a motorcycle. He said that he planned to do a three-month trip around the United States when his son went off to college. I wished him luck and encouraged him to go for it, then finished packing and hit the road Jack. The ride to Clarksdale would take all day.

I never really welcomed the punishment that my ass endured on a big mileage day. If I were on a Goldwing, I'm sure it would have been a breeze. Hell, you could probably ride through two states just for fun on a 'Wing, before lunch. Riding on the Goose's stock seat was brutal. Its ergonomics worked with the forward slant of the seat and gravity to leave one with smashed nards by the end of the day, no matter what I tried. I concluded, "I'll surely be sterile by the end of this trip." Anyway, I kept my eyes open for photo ops all day and ol' Miss just wasn't producing. Gentle rolling hills in the center of the state broke the elevation freeze that I'd been in—giving me a momentary whirl—while white dotted lines threatened hypnosis. The Goose's four-cylinder hum added to the effect. A wide median full of wildflowers or a geriatric barn would have been nice. Contrary to my subtle bitching, I felt wonderfully far from any cubicle and was on a cross-country motorcycle adventure. Life was good.

When I was lurking around central Mississippi, still favoring the east, I found a Honda motorcycle dealership. I needed to get some thinner riding gloves. I left my Fox gloves in a gas station restroom in Key Largo. My only backup was my set of oversized winter gloves, and it was way too warm for those gigantic finger jackets. The Honda delearship stocked a small supply of Joe Rocket street gloves, but no motocross gloves as I was accustomed to. The Joe Rockets would have to do. My experience at the dealership was lacking. I hoped for good conversation and a bit of camaraderie from the guys behind the counter, and walked out with no such luck. They never once asked if they could help me find something. My lost face and hurried pacing didn't even spark a reaction. I longed for the service from the folks at Crossroads Yamaha.

For the next few hours, very little happened. The basic route from Meridian to Clarksdale was 19 W, to 55 N, to 82 W, to Route 49, straight into town. Approaching Clarksdale, I was blessed with a spectacular cotton candy sunset against a completely flat Mississippi Delta farmland backdrop. The clouds were wispy thin, almost like fading letters. The sun's warm glow turned the rich green crops all but neon. The white dotted lines of the highway were replaced by two yellow highlighter marks, splitting the rural roads evenly down the center. I glanced right at my perfectly formed, hundred-foot-long shadow and pretended that I had a buddy riding with me. It was wonderful.

Night draped its dark cape on me before I could make it into town. That was an uneasy feeling that I never really got used to. Every new town was full of mystery waiting to be unlocked. With no campgrounds in my radar and not being fully operating on couchsurfing.com yet, I found yet another Budget Inn. The Indian feller behind the desk was the most helpful Budget Inn employee I'd met. He was proud of Clarksdale, spitting out facts and upcoming events like he was the mayor, and would not let me check into my room without first having me hear all of it. I appreciated his enthusiasm. It pumped me up for the night.

With a head full of local knowledge, I prepared for a night out in Clarksdale, the place where all this blues stuff began. Muddy Waters, Robert Johnson, Sam Cooke, and Ike Turner all hailed from this tough little part of America. I have loved the blues since hearing a lyric by Robert Johnson that goes "A woman's like a dresser. Someone's always going through her drawers." Actually, I liked the blues before that. The blues are about struggle, and I've known no other way to get through life. Until that day comes, I'll recharge every once in a while in a dark room, by myself, listening to the blues and feeling them sink deep into my skin.

The Ground Zero Blues Club was where I planned to get my fix. For those not in the know, the actor Morgan Freeman co-owns the place. I was in search of an authentic blues atmosphere; I'd say the building couldn't have fit the bill any better. It's a rejuvenated cotton warehouse with a distressed brick veneer and a sloppy ol' front porch. A few beatup couches on that porch near the entrance seem to say "Ain't never gonna be a dress code here." Inside, a stage dead ends at the opposite wall. The rest of Ground Zero is one large, dark room with a bar on the right and tables filling the rest of the space. As I walked in, some young folks were playing beer pong near the pool tables. *Really?* I was let down. I had hoped to get an authentic, as possible, blues experience.

Despite the infiltration of college culture, I took a seat and slowly sipped on whiskey, keeping my mouth wet, but not overdoing it. The place packed up nicely as the band took the stage. They were the TCB Blues Band. Unfortunately, they only played a couple of old blues songs. Their playlist was more modern and way faster than I was hoping to hear. Still, I had fun and fought the urge to shake a leg. For me, it wasn't one of those nights, even if it was a weekend. According to the townsfolk, Red's is the place to hear the most consistent old blues. If I ever swing by there again, I'm going to Red's. My night ended early. I was wiped out from the long day of riding.

Day 37 – November 19, 2011

Day thirty-seven began really early. So early, in fact, that the action started at about 1:00am at the Budget Inn in Clarksdale, Mississippi. All eyes were on me. These were eyes that I wish were pointed elsewhere. I made it back to my room from Ground Zero and did my usual handlebar lock, disc lock, and tarp cover routine. All three had kept the Goose with me thus far. When I arrived at the U-shaped Budget Inn yesterday evening, two shady characters perversely stared at me from their motel room across the way, and being aware of that, I wanted to take a little extra precaution with how I secured the bike. I went a few steps further by setting a motion-sensitive alarm on the rear wheel. When I went in the room and shut the door, I had a feeling that those steps were not enough, so for fun I decided to leave the curtain cracked and my camcorder facing the covered bike. In order to sleep better, I hoped to get a few hours of time-lapse. That would be the lengthiest setting to record on. If the bike got stolen, then at least I'd have a face on film to show the cops.

I turned the lights off feeling like I did all that I could to make sure the Goose would still be mine in the morning, short of pushing it in the room with me. It was still there when I woke up. I smiled. Immediately, I reviewed the time-lapse film. Sure enough, about five minutes after I turned my light off and lay down, one of those shady bastards uncovered the front of my bike and quickly covered it back up. I think the guy noticed the camera in the window. I'm just glad he changed his mind. Since I was time-lapse filming, I didn't get the clearest image of the guy. All I really captured was a dark brown arm with two big pimp-like gold bracelets. After reviewing the footage, I opened my room door to notice a fella from a room across from mine already looking in my direction, like he had taken the night watch. He continued to stare for the entire half hour it took to pack the bike up and take off. A sense of relief washed over me when I pulled out of there.

Even though all that went down, I still liked Clarksdale for its blues scene and planned to see one more thing. Its unrefined edges weren't going to get the best of me. Clarksdale has its rough spots, and that's no BS. Of all the places I went in the Southeast, Clarksdale had the most tattered houses. One street had shacks so beaten that I thought the street was abandoned, but people were out and sitting on crooked porches as if they'd never noticed what I was seeing. A few buckets of paint, a truck load of lumber, and a level would have made a world of difference.

The Cat Head music store is a must if you find yourself in the top left corner of Mississippi. I read about it in *1000 Places To See Before You Die*. Like the rest of Clarksdale, it has a veneer of busted stucco and exposed weathered brick. Inside, it's filled with music selections and local art. An unframed picture hanging from the brick interior wall held me still for a moment. It was of a man squatting by a tombstone and holding a guitar. Engraved on the tombstone was "Give me beefsteak when I'm hungry. Whiskey when I'm dry. Pretty women when I'm living. Heaven when I die." *Ain't nothin' wrong with that*. I bought a Cat Head sticker and rode on.

I fought a ferocious headwind for ten rounds down 61 S until I threw in the white towel at a small restaurant called the Blue Levee. Upon entry I noticed that every guy in the place was wearing full camo gear. "Guess who the stranger is?" came to mind. A spot was open at the bar, so I sat down and ordered a catfish po-boy and fries while spreading the atlas out and planning my next move. The po-boy came and went, leaving me nice and full. I took a look behind me to see a few people using their laptops. The area outside was rural and sparsely populated. Here was the last place I would expect to find Wi-Fi. A few people came over to inquire about my travels. They'd seen the bike waiting for me in the cracked concrete parking lot.

I was happy to have someone to talk to. My last two conversations came while people were on the clock. Everyone who came by to say hello smiled big like they had known me and missed me. I smiled back contagiously. I've always loved smiling. Sometimes I smile and don't even know why, like it's an involuntary reaction. If I could have a nickel for every time someone asked me what's so funny when nothing was going on in my head, I'd be rich. I just can't help it. The folks at the Blue Levee really went the extra mile to make me feel welcome. One lady dropped a twenty-dollar bill while talking to me. I brought it to her attention. She picked it up, smiled, and never missed a beat. She seemed so happy.

The Blue Levee closed at 2:00pm on Saturdays, so the locals filed out; I remained, with permission, to finish up a bit of writing. The staff didn't seem to mind, and for the favor I played some music on my laptop that the waitress requested while she was sweeping the floor around me. She made it clear that she wasn't feeling the blues that were playing on the restaurant's stereo. She was all blues'ed out from being around the scene for many years. I finished up, gathered my things, and walked outside with a large handful of gear and electronics. Two things happened immediately that left me feeling extremely perplexed. The first was dropping my brand spanking new phone and cracking its screen. I wanted to shoot fire from my eyes, but then I noticed an envelope stuffed behind my bungee cord. *Oh wow. What's this?* As fate would have it, someone who had talked with me in the restaurant had taken an interest in my journey and wanted to help out with a donation of $30 (I now wanted to shoot ice cream out of my eyes). It made me feel terrific inside. The best part was that all I had to do was be myself and just be happy to have someone to talk to.

I left the Blue Levee behind to hunt for the Mississippi River. On the way down Route 1 S, I came across the Winterville Indian Mounds. Those manmade goliaths were an unexpected treat. They were easily the tallest things around. I thought of them as being the Mississippi Delta's Monument Valley. The largest one was thirty feet high and shaped like a flat-topped volcano. Each mound was almost unimaginably piled by hand with primitive tools, hundreds of years before the diesel-powered earth movers of today. I walked a few hundred yards past the closed visitor center, following a mowed-grass path, to the first mound. I ran up eighty-seven steps to the top to get the same view that the natives would have shared.

I cannot begin to speculate the exact reason for that much labor, but if it was in order to gain high ground during a Mississippi River flood, then it would have been worth it. Some cattle bones were found in the mound sometime in the early nineteen hundreds. It is known that cattle weren't introduced to this part of the Americas until long after these mounds were created by the native Indians. One can only assume, according to the facts at the location, that the cattle used the mounds as safe ground when the Mississippi flooded in 1927. I investigated the 360-degree view of farmland until the urge to move took over.

Earlier, while eating at the Blue Levee, I reviewed the atlas and decided to pay a visit to the southeastern corner of Arkansas. It was to be my first visit to Bill Clinton's homeland. I meandered south on Highway 1 again, roughly curving with the Mississippi on the way to Greenville and Route 82 W. Another one of those sleek, concrete suspension bridges—like the ones in Charleston and Savannah—stood between me and my crossing the Mississippi River for the first time. This moment, thirty years in the making, was surprisingly monumental for me. I had seen the Mississippi before, years ago while visiting New Orleans. Not once did I cross it, though. Now I had my chance to see if the grass was greener on the other side.

I approached the Arkansas line with anticipation. The bridge's concrete supports looked as if they had been dyed to a warm autumn shade of yellow by the big orange setting sun. Arkansas' blue and white square welcome sign was impossible to read until I hopped off the bike. The sun had masterfully silhouetted it. I soaked in that peculiar thrill of being somewhere new.

Through the clear plastic map holder of my tankbag, I spotted a nearby state park and headed that way. Fortunately, Pecan Grove RV Park intercepted my travels not more than a handful of miles from the river. I pulled in. The park was all but empty. A few RVs packed up the right side. Autumn leaves speckled Arkansas' dark green grass. It was growing without hindrance from the surplus of vacant tent sites. A small white house doubled as the office. I rode up to it and walked in. Dusk was in full control.

The park owner, a large man in denim coveralls, seemed happy to see me as he greeted me with a joke. When he held out his hand, I did what I always do when I meet somebody new; I latched on for a friendly shake. He shook and quickly pulled back, hand still out, and said, "No son. I need $20 for camping." Like I said before, I can turn anything into an awkward situation. His hand fisted my twenty and stuffed it away as I listened to a brief set of campground instructions. I left and set up camp, never seeing the owner again. Staying at Pecan Grove saved me $10 on a camping fee and had every utility that a state park would offer. Score!

I pitched the tent in the dark and headed to a restaurant called the Lakefront Café, along Lake Chicot. I was hunting for a Wi-Fi connection and a chance meeting with an interesting person or two. I didn't happen to meet any native Arkansans, other than Pecan Grove's odd owner, but I did hang out with the whole staff after closing. We threw back a bucket of cold ones as I listened to them crack on Arkansans like they were still dragging their women around by the hair or haven't discovered the wheel. I found it amusing that all of the employees hailed from Greenville, Mississippi, just a stone's throw across the river from where we were sitting. The hours passed quickly, through bouts of clean and dirty jokes, and when it came time for me to settle up, the bartender said, "Don't worry about it." With that, I thanked them and gratefully moseyed on over to my tent and fell asleep to a peaceful night in rural Arkansas.

Day 38 – November 20, 2011

Laundry was the word of the morning, and oh how exciting that always is. Sitting at Pecan Grove were four or five rustic shacks, all the color of dried blood and all looking a century old. Each one sat off the ground by a foot or two and may have been used as cabin rentals. One was converted into a shower room and laundry area. That's where I spent the morning refreshing my wardrobe. Again, I was outta socks and clean britches; the stink goblin was beginning to stir.

The campground had two washers and two dryers. One fella, who started earlier than I did, decided to use both washers for his load. I had hoped to get an early start that morning but had to wait on the laundry room hoarder to finally get around to putting his clothes in the dryer. *Can anything be more annoying than someone who hogs the washers and takes his merry old time to return?* I must have looked in those washing machines ten times in an hour, waiting for his ass to move his clothes. One of my pet peeves is people who exist who act like others don't exist. We all might as well get used to sharing. I may not be the best at the practice, but I'll surely participate if it means that someone else can benefit. I can't foresee a world where only one redneck is left and will always have an open washer when he needs it. There's a point about the golden rule in here somewhere. When he finally tossed his load in the dryer, both washer loads miraculously fit into one dryer. *Interesting.*

As with anything, you take the good and the bad. On the bright side, I had some time to check out Lake Chicot. As my clothes were swishing, I walked across the street to a rickety pier jutting into the lake. The Mississippi River has changed course naturally many times in the past. As it did this, several lakes formed. They mimic a portion of river when you stand beside them and seem to share a distinct and thin, half-moon shape. Lake Chicot was no different. The weather was gloomy and the water's surface reflected that.

I looked out, back and forth, but nothing was happening. Two athletic turtles had managed to climb a few feet up an exposed branch of a sunken tree. As they began to dry out, some sort of fishing bird attempted to share their space. Startled, both turtles performed evasive leaps into the water. They fell heavily like two sinkers. It was the fastest I'd seen a shelled reptile move since the last *Teenage Mutant Ninja Turtles* movie. The day was plum full of excitement.

At last, my clothes were dry. I had the Goose's trunk popped and was jamming folded items into every space possible when an old man working as park maintenance stopped at my site with his golf cart. He was weathered and perhaps older than the campground's shacks. Hell, he may have built a few of them. As he snagged my site's trash can and extracted the half-full bag from it, he began speaking to me. I had a hard time understanding him through his drawl and lack of teeth.

He was as nice as they come and I'd say twice as tough. This man was wearing heavy black insulated coveralls, a thick winter toboggan, sturdy boots, and was way overdressed for just changing trash bags. The weather was dreary, but not all that cold. He was shorter than me, with hands the size of Bigfoot's that were cracked and calloused and looked as though they could've been made of hickory. He continued to make small talk when he was finished with my can. I told him that I was headed across the USA, and he said, "Well, don't forget to stop here on your way back." I didn't plan to see Arkansas twice, so I just nodded in agreement to be polite. From talking to him, I got the impression that he had never ventured much farther than the state line, which is fine if you've found happiness where you are. I never got his name, but as I left I thought of how delicate he made men of today look and how unmistakably real he was. The guy will probably outlive me.

I was heading south toward the Big Easy with a goal of splitting the miles between Lake Chicot and New Orleans. I followed Route 65 in Arkansas, through the extreme northeastern part of Louisiana, back into Mississippi via Vicksburg, then down scenic Route 61 south to the Natchez Trace Parkway and to Natchez State Park. Along the way, I passed through slow and easy towns like Lake Providence, with its chaotically pointing wooden corner sign, showing distances throughout the region, and Transylvania, where a Mississippi River flood could be the only thing remotely scary going on. Long, flat, and straight paved roads guided the way. Here and there, intersections gave an option of driving deeper into endless farmland. The side roads, if paved, were derelict and crumbling to pieces. For a while, a broken set of train tracks paralleled Route 65. They were wavy and warped, like a train too heavy bent 'em all up. I took a few pictures, just inches off the ground, for that perfect tracks-into-the-horizon shot.

Soon I found myself in a forest among broad leaves. If not for the Spanish moss and lack of overlooks, I could have laid money down that I was on the Blue Ridge Parkway. A few sections looked just like the Appalachians. I was on the Natchez Trace Parkway and in southwestern Mississippi. The speed limit was forty-five; a strobe light of sunshine pierced through the branches as I coasted along in anything but a hurry. I came across a historic house that was bordered by a split rail fence stacked four feet high. It looked so much like the Civil War battlefield fences around my hometown of Harpers Ferry that I felt slightly homesick. For a split second, I was transported back to West Virginia.

Feeling a bit blue, I had to crank up the Goose and get the heck outta there. I was five miles from Natchez State Park and nighttime was clocking in. A helpful park ranger took extra care while pointing me in the direction of tent spot eighteen. He told me the last folks who camped there had left a big pile of firewood. Finally, on day thirty-eight, I got to sit down and lose myself in my thoughts as I gazed at a perfect campfire.

Day 39 – November 21, 2011

It wasn't yet daylight when I started day thirty-nine. I woke up refreshed at 5:20am at tent site eighteen in Natchez State Park. I wanted to make it to New Orleans with enough daylight to find a place to stay and make it to the French Quarter before dark. The sun sluggishly began to rise, giving me the chance that I'd been waiting for to get a few pictures of camp. Between a shower and generally moving slowly, I didn't officially hit the road until 8:00am.

I rode two miles down the Natchez Trace Parkway and crossed Emerald Mound. It's the United States' second largest Indian mound; Monk's Mound in Cahokia, Illinois, is the largest. The Emerald Mound's eight-acre girth made my imagination run wild. The Winterville Mounds of day thirty-seven were but a squirt compared to this grassy heap. I climbed the steep, dewy side—trying not to slip and roll back down—toward the soccer-field-sized top where temples once stood. The Mississippians, ancestors of the Natchez Indians, erected and used the mound from about the fourteenth to the seventeenth century. Ceremonies and burials of religious leaders were its main use. While slowly progressing from one end to the other, I tried to imagine the years, the generations, and the amount of hands involved in piling that much dirt. The mound is shaped like a plateau and stands seventy feet high. Two more mounds, raised at either end of the main mound, keep it from being perfectly flat. One of the end mounds was as big, or bigger, than the average Winterville Mound.

I left feeling mound-tastic and continued south to the city of Natchez, a place that I planned to chug on through. Advice from a fella at the state park that morning changed my plans. He said that half of the United States' millionaires lived in Natchez before the Civil War. He told me that Natchez was littered with wonderfully aged antebellum homes, and I shouldn't skip it while in the area. The parkway led right into town. He was correct about Natchez's magnificence.

Natchez sits along the Mississippi River on an exaggerated bluff. It's an oddly formed location: on one side of the Mississippi River, the ground is barely above water level, and on the other side the city of Natchez sits high above the river's surface. Just to add a bit of geographical insight, a bluff is generally created when top soil is blown by the wind over many years until it forms a giant hill full of really deep topsoil. Natchez is a perfect example of this. A concrete wall is now in place, holding back the topsoil, and making for an edge-of-town cliff. I wandered to the visitor center for a map and decided to do a quick, Gooseback tour of the town.

Richly restored homes filled the blocks as reminders of the city's wealthy past. Brick was the dominating veneer, and stately front entrances were graced with thick concrete pillars. Many of Natchez's homes were far above ordinary. The town center was decorated with a large Christmas tree, enclosed at the base by a larger-than-life toy drum. The seasons were changing.

From Natchez, New Orleans was still two hours and forty-five minutes south. I was itching to get there. I traded Mississippi for a "Welcome to Louisiana Beinvenue en Louisiane" sign. Solid land gave way to swamps and bridges. Water was everywhere until the awfully inimitable city of *Nawlins* interrupted the flatness. It was four o'clock. I rode around and oriented myself with the French Quarter, then went off in search of a nearby room. Only folks who are down on their luck do any sort of camping in New Orleans. I planned to keep the tent sacked up and stored away. The Comfort Inn was positioned just a few blocks from the action I wanted and was more than good enough for me.

Two hours later, I footed it to the infamous Bourbon Street, the land of balconies, beer, and boobs. It's a narrow street with old French Quarter homes lurking tall and straight on either side, blocking any crowd from becoming too wide. Businesses of all sorts operate at street level, while the other two or three floors remain a mystery to me. One time, however, at Mardi Gras—the year after Hurricane Katrina—my buddy and I made it to a second-floor Bacardi Girl Party with help from a midget, but that's another story.

I'm sure the French Quarter has its peaceful and clean side, but it sure doesn't share any ground with Bourbon Street. Trash, and the smell of trash juice, emits from the street curbs. Strip joints, where girls actually try to pull you in the door, dot either side. Souvenir shops abound, and food joints are always littered with blurry-eyed zombies (which I've been more than once). It's a wild, young man's paradise. Back in 2005 and 2006 when I visited for Mardi Gras, I went ape shit.

First things first, I was on the hunt for cold ones and music. At the Famous Door, the music was loud, the beers were plenty, and a few gals were looking shweet! I plowed through a Jack and Coke and three Coronas. The first sip of Jack in the presence of loud music never fails to bring a smirk to my face. The Coronas were for maintaining the budget. Soon, I left there in search of music a bit more jazzy and a crowd a bit more snazzy. From one door to the next, I darted in like a wannabe player, drank at least three, and took off again. I was having fun, but not the kind of fun that I had with my buddies here with me.

On a corner, I was crowd watching when a friendly young girl named Lisa approached me. She was African American, about five foot three, wore glasses, and might have been 160 pounds. Her story was that she had been in New Orleans for nearly two weeks from her home state of Arizona, and she was waiting for her cousin, the stripper, to get off work at the Little Darlings nudie club. I got along with Lisa just fine—like any young man would in the presence of a female while intoxicated. We grabbed a few slices of pizza and walked the length of Bourbon Street about three times. About an hour and a half passed when she mentioned that we should go to Armstrong Park, somewhere around two blocks from the party scene, and check out the spot where the city just did a huge ribbon-cutting ceremony for some respected black lady. I said "Cool," and in the spirit of adventure and not being stuck in the touristy areas, I walked over with her.

At the park, the crowd was gone, the lights were gone, and the busy sounds of a cityscape filled the air. We looked at the spot where she said the ceremony was held and moved on. Nothing was happening there. I assumed that the park was closed after dark. Inside the tall park fence, fountains shot a story or two high over bright orange ground lights making them look like fire. I made mention of that and Lisa agreed. We strolled on about a half a block further and turned left, away from the direction of Bourbon Street. We found a spot to sit down. It was a square inlet about 20' x 20' where that tall, metal fence bumped in toward the center of the park. A concrete stoop lined the area, and we sat on it facing the street. Our conversation turned to the subjects of life, relationships, and travel for about fifteen more minutes. It was plain casual; however, I did keep an eye out for the few stragglers slowly walking by. Most of them had their hoods up on their jackets and paid us no mind as far as I could tell.

Then Lisa mentioned that the mosquitoes were tearing her up. She asked if I minded waiting for her while she ran to her cousin's to get a jacket. I asked how long it would take. She said, "Five minutes." I said, "Do you want me to walk with you?" and she replied, "No. My cousin's an asshole and I don't want you around him." Going against my gut instinct, I stayed put for about two minutes, watching shady characters lurk nearby.

Then wham! The butterflies were already frantically flapping in my stomach when two young black males came up to me with a gun and pressed it firmly into the left side of my neck! They did not stroll up slyly. Instead, they rounded the corner of the inlet and blitzed to meet me face to face. I barely had time to stand up. I noticed that they had walked by about five minutes before when Lisa was still with me.

Their first demand was my cell phone. Then they ordered me to put my hands down. Next they wanted my wallet. I told them that I don't carry one. Then they demanded that I empty my pockets. Without question, I did. When a gun is stuck to your neck, you'll do what they say. Trust me on that one. I handed them my keys last and they refused them. The tall one said, "Man, we don't want your car." I didn't tell them that I was on a motorcycle or perhaps they would've kept my keys. They didn't reach into my pockets. If they would've, they would have found my knife. Unfortunately, it was useless in this circumstance. The tall and scrawny perpetrators walked away, but they didn't forget to tell me, "Stay there or I'll shoot you."

I watched them round a corner, and just before they were out of sight they took off running. I got the hell outta Dodge right after that. It's pretty apparent that I got rolled, as the officer described it. On my way back to the safety of Bourbon Street (an oxymoron), a group of French kids were headed in the direction that I came from. I told them about what just happened to me and they didn't hesitate to do a U-turn and follow me.

I found an officer right away, and he called a detective over to pick me up. The detective and I rode by the scene, he seemingly unafraid, and me slightly hunched down in the seat and highly concerned about the possibility of being struck by a stray bullet. The detective needed a better feel for what happened. I described it to him in detail. After that, we took care of paperwork at the station. We did the normal interview the victim thing, and he did a little investigating. He directed me to the lobby where I was to wait to be cross examined.

In the lobby, three officers were engaged in a heated conversation about relationships in the office. One of them said something so ridiculous that I had to speak up and ask him if he was serious. It was on after that. Now, it was officially a four-way conversation, and just to set the scene, it was me, two black male officers, and one black female officer. Through all of the jaw slapping and BS I could handle, a few hours passed, and the female officer didn't realize that I was sitting there waiting for her to cross examine me. About the time she started to question why I was sitting there, the detective came out of his office and told me that he traced my cell phone back to the Comfort Inn. *Shit!* Since they stole my room card also, I thought they were in my room stealing the rest of my stuff while I was sitting at the police station.

Then the detective started questioning my story again. He thought that I had Lisa in my room and that I was soliciting her for sex. He thought something fishy was going on. Generally, when a male tourist gets rolled by a chick in New Orleans, the guy won't tell the police the whole story, and usually the girl that sets him up is a prostitute. Let me tell you that if Lisa was a prostitute, she'd be broke. Insert the joke about falling out of the ugly tree here. Ol' Lisa was a walrus-faced buffarilla. Sure, I would've hit on her, but only after my second five-gallon bucket of moonshine.

Anyway, I became extremely frustrated that they were questioning me, and I spoke my mind. I angrily spat out, "How the hell am I going to get out of this damn city. My bike is almost out of gas. I have no money and no debit card." Then the female officer offered me a ten-dollar bill for gas, surprisingly taking my side. I took it because I was giving them the truth from the bottom of my heart. But they just . . . kept . . . pressing . . . me into confessing that I had her in my room. I was fuming. I was there for their help, and all they wanted to do was hang me out to dry. I stood up, balled up the ten-dollar bill, and tossed it back at the officer saying, "I don't want help from people like you. Keep your money." When I walked out of the police station, it was 5:00am.

Their thing was that they have a formula for that type of crime, and my story was not fitting *their* formula. It's not every day that a guy and a girl, who meet on Bourbon Street, just talk. That's all that happened, and they just did not want to believe it. I'm not your everyday person either, and besides, I have never, nor plan on ever fornicating with a buffarilla. I was out on the road for an incredible experience without trying to get myself killed. I was out to experience America and Americans. I would've talked to anyone. When all was said and done, Lisa must've known the gunman because she returned my cell phone, driver's license, and debit card to Comfort Inn's front desk. All they walked away with was about $60 in cash, which I would've happily spent on alcohol. The bandits probably saved me from having a visit with the Hangover Fairy. I had to look on the bright side.

Perhaps I'll never know Lisa's motivation for returning my things, but I'm so glad she did. Lisa could have thrown my belongings in the Mississippi River, never to be seen again. Instead, she returned them, and I don't feel bad when I say that I think the detective could have been indirectly in on it, or could have known exactly who Lisa was or if her real name was even Lisa. My visit to New Orleans left an immensely bad taste in my mouth. If you can't trust the police, then who can you trust?

Day 40 – November 22, 2011

Morning was filled with a sense of urgency to get the hell out of the Big Easy. It wasn't brought about by fear; it was a sense of urgency to seek the road, my place of peace. That was my third visit to the French Quarter in a decade, and I felt eager to see some new landscape. I couldn't wait to see the desert. Sometimes I just wanted to fast forward to that part.

Right before I checked out of my room, the calls started coming in. First, my friend Adam from Houston—who I was planning to see the very next day—called, followed by Tomato Joe. They had already read the blog post and just wanted to make sure that I was okay. I checked out of my room and carried my huge bundle of gear to the Goose. It was in a parking garage a few blocks away. Again, the looks from the well-dressed office types that I absorbed while carrying all of that camping gear through the big city were splendid. I imagined that they thought of me as the king of the homeless, well supplied and completely disorganized. Bags and gear draped from me like elephant trunks.

With the bike all loaded up, I got directions to the closest gas station from the parking valet and was off. A mile down St. Charles Avenue, I fueled up and called my mom about my debit card situation. She had been a bank teller and knew exactly how to handle it. Since the thugs briefly had my card number, she mentioned that they could still use it to buy stuff online. I had not thought about that angle, so I called my bank and they took care of it.

I set off from New Orleans with nothing more than a day of riding planned in southern Louisiana. The doable goal was Houston, but it wasn't necessary to be that productive. I just wanted to relax and click off some miles. Lake Charles, Louisiana, seemed like a fine stopping point. It was a dot on the map about 200 miles west. To get there, I bridge hopped my way along 90 W out of the city, out of the swamp, through suburbia and towns full of McDonald's and shopping centers. Interesting scenery of any kind was absent.

It became inarguably obvious when I made it to Lafayette that it was going to rain and rain hard. I got a wild hair, and instead of pulling over early for a room, I just decided that it would be a proper time for a rain gear test. I picked up Interstate 10 W and plowed on. *The 10,* as it's known, is an anaconda of a highway, stretching from Florida to California. It's not the world's longest road, but it is one hell of a paved track in the southern United States. There are ways to avoid its lure and convenience. You can go north or south of it. There are options, but I found from time to time that Interstate 10 could be my friend. Like today, where I needed speed, distance, and rain to really give the ol' gear a whoopin'. I wanted to find leaks, baby!

In Lafayette, the clouds began to piss on me. It was no ordinary piss. It was one of those drunken pisses, where you're shooting away and your stream couldn't be any stronger and you actually say aloud, "Damn! When izziisshit gonna stop?" Man, it rained for fifty miles, thick the whole time. There were a few miles where I couldn't see at all. I just kept the handlebars straight and the speed low. My visor fogged, and I spent most of the time riding one-handed, wiping the visor with my glove. My jacket worked fine. The pants did well also, but they were a bit too short, and when my feet were on the pegs, everything from mid-shin down took on water. My Alpinestar riding boots were waterproof, but my long black socks were not. Since the pants were short, the socks got soaked, and all the water funneled into my boots. After ten minutes in the hard rain, I developed a delightful case of swamp foot. My new gloves weren't waterproof, but even while wet I still had a better feel on the controls than with the gigantic, waterproof winter gloves. I couldn't stand to ride with those bulky bastards unless it was freezing outside. All in all, the gear fared well. The storm passed, and right before dark I found a room in Iowa, Louisiana, a tiny town about ten miles east of Lake Charles.

I squished into the lobby of a Howard Johnson. Once checked in, I headed to the room and thought about a shower. I could hear a faint scratching in the bathroom. It was coming from the bathtub. I entered the bathroom and flung open the curtain, feeling every nerve on my skin's surface ignite at the same time. There before me, was a two-inch-long roach trying to escape. I squirmed and thrashed the curtain shut. My neck muscles tightened. This thing was so big that I could've put a saddle on it and charged for rides. Gravity pulled hard against each of the roach's failed attempts at scaling the bathtub walls. The roach could climb five or six inches high before sliding back to the tub's base. When that happened, the slight scrape that its six legs made hit me like fingernails on a chalkboard.

I went to the front desk for assistance. The clerk said that maintenance wasn't available. I told her that I could capture it and asked about a discount. She didn't come off the price. I was whooped from riding all day and felt no need to argue.

Back at the room, I collected myself, grabbed a bleached white bath towel, and headed to the bathroom. This time I opened the curtain slowly. The beast was still there, still trying to escape, still scratching, and still falling back. I aimed and threw the towel on the roach. It made a hump in the towel, but at least it stopped moving. I folded the towel over it, teeth clinched and ready to run for my life. I had it captured. *Now what do I do with it?* There was the smash option, but that would make a terrible mess, and I'm sure that the popping sensation would give me nightmares. I settled on the mercy option. I've never been one to kill large animals, so I released it outside. When I returned to my room and looked out the window, I could see the damn thing under the street light, running across the parking lot in that jittery, jerky gait that roaches have.

I needed a drink bad after that. I asked the front desk clerk if there was a place to grab a beer nearby. She said the truck stop next door had a lounge. *Perfect.* I walked over there, seeking relief. Since I had been enjoying the encounters with my fellow Americans from other states (not counting the ones in New Orleans), I hoped to meet someone to talk to. Perhaps a little conversation could clear out any six-legged images. In simple observation, folks that I'd met along the way were surprisingly similar, and almost always friendly. People just seemed nice, unless you remember how some Mississippians think that Arkansans are from the third world. Hell, I'd always thought that West Virginia was nearly third world until a couple of nights ago at Krazy K's in Mississippi. With that, I was beginning to realize that every state has a cornucopia of good and bad neighborhoods, and wholesome and seedy folks. America is diverse.

I ended up meeting the bartender of the lounge. Who didn't see that coming? Her name was Sarah, and she was a twenty-nine-year-old native of the Louisiana Delta. She was a tall, thin brunette, easy to talk to and soft on the eyes. I was the only patron, so she had a choice. She could've hidden from me or talked to me. Fortunately, she chose the latter. I made two Coronas last an hour and a half, breaking some sort of personal record, while she told me about herself and her two children. I enjoyed her company. She asked me what my favorite place was so far, and it took quite a bit of time to think of an answer. I had to give her two places. Key West was number one for location and atmosphere, and northern Georgia to central North Carolina for the friendliest people. I thought it would be interesting to see how the answer to that question would evolve as the trip continued. Before I left the lounge, I gave Sarah my info in hopes that she'd stay in touch. She never did.

Day 41 – November 23, 2011

I set sail, wind to the back of the Goose, on an awfully nice morning in Iowa, Louisiana. This marked the end of the journey's first chapter. It was the eastern chapter and the end of the most familiar chapter I'd experience. That was okay with me. I had anticipated heading west and crossing into the giant state of Texas for a long time. Texas had deserts, cacti, open plain, cowgirls, and a country and western music scene that I couldn't wait to get lost in.

The ride from Iowa to Texas's state line on Interstate 10 was almost too easy. Within a half hour of hitting the road, I was there. Texas's welcoming station greeted me with one lone star—semi-submerged in the ground—that was as big as everything else in Texas. Overwhelmed with excitement, I whipped the Goose into the parking lot, snatched the camera, and got a picture with the giant star, super-tourist style. While standing still, waiting for the picture to take, I was greeted by my first native Texan. It was a giant tiger mosquito that bit me square on the cheek. As I remained posed for the ten seconds to count down, I fought the urge to scratch, while thinking that I had left those guys behind in Florida. My new, winged Texan friends motivated me to get back on the road. I was off to Houston to stay with my buddy Adam.

Having friends spread across the country is great while traveling. You can pop in on them, mooch for a couple days, and get back on the road before any hard feelings develop. You save money on lodging (that ends up getting spent on drinks) and do your now-it's-your-turn-to-come-visit-me part. I had already proven this once. On the opposite end of the spectrum, it's not so great when you settle down and plant roots somewhere. Work, family life, and bills nail you to the board of responsibility. Questions like "Who knows when I'll see them again?" or "Will they have grey hair the next time we meet?" or the morbid one, "Will they be in a pine box, eyes glued shut, aged beyond recognition, and giving the afterlife hell?" fill your thoughts.

Adam and I had known one another for years. We met through motocross, my friend-finding social network. Off the track, Adam rode like hell on wheels, often pulling wheelies and hanging turns on his Honda CR250R like he had a death wish. As long as the road was smooth, he was hauling ass. On the track, life was different for my buddy. As my brother and I were fighting for positions in the expert classes, Adam was fighting for his life in the 250C novice class. Bumps, ruts, and jumps had a way of taming the beast inside of him.

I remember one race in Pennsylvania, perhaps Adam's first race ever, where he was holding on tight to last place. He was on his last lap, yet still moving forward. The speed at which he was moving was reminiscent of a tortoise pulling a cinder block. Sometimes at motocross races, the folks running the show do staggered starts, which means, as one class is wrapping up its final lap, they send off the next class to save time. At this race, the class after 250C novice was the 50cc seven-to-eight-year-old division.

Adam had about a quarter of a lap to cover before he reached the checkered flag. In that time, a talented 50cc rider gained so much time on him that we became concerned that he would overtake Adam, thus making Adam look like the slowest rider in the history of motocross. Foot by foot, Adam and the 50cc rider raced toward the finish line. Adam hurriedly singled the jumps, while the 50cc rider gained heaps of time by doubling the jumps. Soon the checkers were in sight. Like a shark on a wounded fish, the little guy was coming! With no more than a five-foot lead, my buddy punched the gas and barely, I mean barely squeaked across the line ahead of the tiny racer. His effort earned him the right to hold onto what was left of his testicular fortitude. He almost became a moto legend for all the wrong reasons.

Now, it was almost a decade later. The 50cc rider grew up to be a local professional racer, and Adam was living in Texas with the same trusty CR250R, still giving it hell through the neighborhood when he had the chance. Since leaving West Virginia, he'd moved around the southern United States chasing surveying jobs for the pipeline industry, and I hadn't been south to see him. Adam was to be a father for the first time in less than a month, and I wanted to see him at this special time in his life.

We spoke a few hours before I arrived. He wasn't going to get off of work until later in the day, so I had to kill some time on my way there. I decided to get off I-10 and take 90 W to slow down a bit. Little places like the town of

China (population 300 and a herd of cattle) and genuine Texas ranches introduced me to a new, drier landscape. In the town of Liberty, Texas, I passed my first Jack in the Box restaurant. Years ago, Jack in the Box sponsored former motocross champion, Mike LaRocco, and since then I've wanted to eat there. I knew it was only a burger joint, but it was a first for me. As far as I know, the franchise has yet to penetrate the hills of West Virginia. The burger I ordered was pretty good, and for a fast-food place the meat wasn't nearly as bland as most of the other places that run rampant along America's highways. I'd eat there again.

Leaving Liberty, I stayed on 90 W all the way to Houston. Heading west felt great. I knew that the scenery would soon change into something completely alien to me. My first experience with the Texan countryside came to an end, and like a fleet of concrete transformers, the buildings of the huge, industrious city of Houston took over the horizon. As it turned out, I had not lollygagged enough and arrived at Adam's place about an hour before he did. Adam's girlfriend's son, Zack, was there and he let me park my bike in the garage. An hour quickly passed as I moved my things into my temporary room. Adam and his girlfriend, Cindy, popped through the door. It was refreshing to see my friend again and to finally meet the gal who he had told me so much about. He went on to slap huge slabs of barbeque chicken on the grill as we talked about work, his unborn son's new bedroom, and generally caught up on the past few years.

After dinner, we jumped in his Toyota Tundra for a whirlwind, nighttime tour of Houston. He took me uptown, downtown, and to what I'm going to call oil town. Houston is kind of defined by these three areas. Uptown and downtown are separated by a few miles, and both have a cluster of skyscrapers right in the center, like two competing cities in one. For the most part, those two areas look similar to any large city. What really got my imagination working was oil town. When I asked where we were, Adam said, "Pasadena, Texas."

Pasadena was littered with oil refineries, thousands of acres of them. Seeing the area at night for the first time drove my imagination wild. It was a cross between a cold, industrial complex of massive proportions and a hellish, fire-breathing, sinister underworld. Huge stacks—shooting flames thirty feet into the darkness—rose above the thousands of thin, dimly lit towers. Giant, sentry-like cylinders containing the refined black gold stood watch at the edges of this oil city. Here and there, small signs indicated which massive oil company owned which refinery. As we crossed over a bridge that allowed us a bird's eye view of the oil city, I felt a sense of amazement at the sheer scale of man's capabilities and an equal sense of alarm that came from thinking about the tremendous amount of pollution that those refineries help create. Our tour of Houston ended, and so did evening number one at Adam's place.

Day 42 – November 24, 2011

Breakfast's aroma filled the air as I walked downstairs. I followed the scent trail to the kitchen where Cindy was cooking up a storm. It brought me to life like those sleepy-looking people in the Folgers commercials when they catch the first whiff. Her knack for combining just the right morning foods matched an equal ability to prepare them. My knack for smelling the sizzling food matched an equal ability to eat it. I have yet to find a breakfast that I don't like. On my deathbed I could say, "Well, ya know, breakfast was always good to me."

We sat down for the first helping of a day full of good eatin'. It was Thanksgiving, the day when many American families gather for food and football games. In our family, it was the one day of the year when the kitchen table reached maximum load capacity. Dishes, jam packed with more food than the family sees in a week, promised to inflict an incurable case of food coma. I've seen the strongest men in my family get knocked out cold by a sofa cushion after a turkey and stuffing ass kicking at the kitchen table. Even as a light sleeper, I've fallen victim once or twice.

This was my first major holiday away from home, and I'd love to say that all I wanted was to be back in West Virginia, and I'd love to write a tear jerker about unbearably missing my folks, but those feelings never surfaced. Being on the road in the company of friends was enough. I was content knowing we would all sit down to a big meal later. I was happy to be in Texas and looking forward to a day where mileage didn't matter. In fact, the most complicated thing I did was watch Adam Skype four of his family members at once. The laptop screen shared four faces, all smiling, and all with similar facial features. He was in Houston, making a video call to family members in West Virginia, North Carolina, and California. Everyone could see and hear one another as they shared "Happy Thanksgiving's" and "I love you's." Everyone took turns talking to the little tikes, while spinning and angling the laptops for more views of family gathered around in the background. Adam's smile couldn't have been surgically removed.

After he finished, I did the same thing on a much smaller scale by Skyping my family. They were all gathered at Mom's house. It was the first time in forty-two days that I'd seen my brother, as I'd Skyped Mom once or twice along the way. Skype created an instant bridge across all of those miles that had taken six weeks to cover.

Hours of normality passed before we headed off toward our Thanksgiving dinner. We arrived at Elena's house, Cindy's sister, a few miles away in another part of Houston. Elena had prepared a meal fit for a king. We combined food with football, which comes close to religion in Texas.

The Texas Longhorns were set to battle the Texas A&M Aggies for the last time, as the Aggies were moving to the Southeastern Conference. The rivalry was legendary. They had met 118 times in the past and this game had to be one of the closest games they'd ever played. For four quarters, they went at it like warriors. Pride, infinite bragging rights, and history were on the line. Someone had to win. Someone had to lose. As the last seconds of the fourth quarter fell away, the perfect storm of football had arrived.

It all came down to two seconds left on the clock with the Longhorns' kicker carrying the weight of the world—or better yet, the weight of the universe—on his shoulders. The world may have been just too light to describe the anxiety he faced and that thousands of others watching the game endured. We were sitting on sofa cushions, leaning forward, and glued to the action on the screen. If I were in the kicker's position, Thanksgiving dinner would have flown out of me like a rocket. If he missed, he would forever be known as the guy who blew the Longhorns' last shot at rivalry success. Making it would turn him into a god for that night and unforgettable for years to come. As the ball was snapped and set in front of him, he approached and kicked with the force of the Big Bang, straight into fate. The football seemed to soar for minutes. The giant yellow goal posts accepted his kick. It was good! The young kicker turned legend, and the Longhorns tasted the final victory. That was the best football game I had ever seen. It was a special moment in time. Adam was pumped!

With the game over and bellies still full, we headed back to Adam's house. The night wasn't quite over. Adam, Zack, and I made a short journey past the huge lines at Best Buy and over to the local Wal-Mart. Black Friday madness was in full force and it wasn't yet midnight. Adam, lacking proper clarity, wanted to purchase a football. We walked into the belly of the discount beast. Crowds wrestled through aisles, shoulder to shoulder, after the best deal on some plastic contraption, or some electronic doohickey, or some widget that would end up wrapped in a pretty box under a Christmas tree. I felt like I was in an ant farm. People moved chaotically, all seemingly doing the same thing, yet heading in different directions. Lines were as thick as tree trunks and as long as rivers. Forty-inch flat screens filled the horizon. We realized that no football was worth the time, unless it was that game-winning ball kicked earlier. That was my first and last Black Friday shopping experience. I promise you that!

Day 43 – November 25, 2011

Cindy repeated another fine breakfast. Again, I planned for a day of relaxation. The Goose planned for a day of center stand garage life. Before lunch, Adam suggested another easy tour of Houston since my nighttime pictures came out grainy and distorted two nights before. We piled in his truck and headed to the land of tall buildings, colorful people, and grassy parks with water features. We passed Reliant Stadium, where a round of Supercross is hosted once a year. We swung through uptown and back through downtown and past the oil refineries again. He stopped at a few sites that he'd worked at in the pipeline surveying industry, proudly showing off some of his handiwork. Once seeing Houston, my perception of its size completely changed. I had already thought of it as a large city, but never as one of America's largest. That changed when I made the connection with the oil industry and the city's proximity to the Gulf and shipping industries. Nor did I realize how many skyscrapers it has. I was impressed and overwhelmed.

Houston is also home to one of NASA's space centers. The control room famous for the line "Houston, we have a problem" is housed at Houston's Space Center. Adam and I tracked the place down for a tour. The entry fee almost sent us running back to the truck. It was indeed pricey, especially compared to the free National Naval Aviation Museum in Pensacola, Florida.

Inside, heaps of interactive displays made up for it. Both Adam and I climbed on a simulator that measured an astronaut's efficiency and dexterity at small tasks, like operating multiple buttons while in motion. The simulator chair floated like a puck on an air hockey table. A small joystick, operated with one hand, controlled direction with bursts of air while the other hand and your eyes were focused upward on the task. Mock-ups and real portions of spacecraft sat around, inviting folks to climb on in.

The Space Center comprises a campus full of buildings and offers a trolley tour of the facility. Adam and I hopped on. We were led to Christopher C. Kraft Jr. Mission Control Center, then on to an auditorium where a scientist gave us the lowdown on space center activities and recent missions. Finally, we went to a long, white, metal pole building where the Saturn V rocket lives. I'd seen large pole buildings before, and the building's size didn't really make much of an impression—until I saw the rocket inside. The Saturn V rocket was lying horizontal, ready for a blast across the landscape. Somehow it seemed larger than the building it was in. I felt tiny.

Before then, I could only guess at the size of one of those rockets as it hoisted a load of important equipment skyward. My only impression had been from the television screen, where they are always four or five inches tall. What an impressive feat of engineering. I was also impressed to learn that the giant cloud of exhaust that comes from a huge rocket launch is from spent hydrogen. I had always thought that it was some form of super expensive, highly toxic rocket fuel. I'm glad that the launches are relatively eco-friendly. *Why don't we power other forms of transportation with hydrogen? After all, it's all around us. The big oil companies would fight that to the death.* The Houston Space Center is a place where the most intelligent brains get exercise by making incredibly difficult decisions. I loved it. The money that we spent in the beginning seemed trivial when we left.

Back at the house, Adam fixed up a couple racks of BBQ ribs and turned in pretty early. I found *Forrest Gump* playing on the tube and couldn't help but watch it for the gumpteenth time. The part where Forrest says, "I miss you Jeeunny" to her headstone, under the big tree, still pulls at me. The scene where he's running out of the jungle and screams, "Something bit me!" as he's shot in the ass, never fails to crack me up. I will always love that movie! *Forrest Gump* ended and *Shawshank Redemption* followed as the next program on air. Morgan Freeman stars in it. I had never watched it but felt somewhat obliged to keep my eyes open during the entire movie since I just went to Mr. Freeman's bar in Clarksdale, Mississippi. During the movie, I made mental notes pertaining to prison escape techniques for future reference and then bowed to the Sandman.

Day 44 – November 26, 2011

It was Adam's birthday. It rained most of the day. Adam made it clear that I didn't have to move on for another day or two. With that, I just wanted him to have a good day. He's the type who doesn't miss a beat, the anti-couch-potato type, so I found it as no surprise when he made a few plans for the day. First, he wanted to swing by a bike shop so that I could get a new shield for my helmet. I was riding with a Scorpion EXO-550. It had nice styling, and the price was right. Unfortunately, a few screws and a lever for my tinted inner sun shield vibrated out about two weeks into the trip, and I'd been using a bright green earplug as a wedge to hold the inner shield up. Adam took me to Cycle Gear, a place in Houston that only dealt in motorcycle gear and parts.

We leaped out of the truck in the pouring rain and ran inside the store, making an eye-catching entrance. There were two fellows working the counter. Before we left for the shop that morning, I drank two large cups of strong coffee, and I guess some sort of mental short circuit may have been activated by the high dose of caffeine. While in the shop, I stuttered endlessly while describing the parts I needed for my helmet. I couldn't keep track of my thoughts, and kept forgetting to grab my things. On most days, without any sort of external stimulant, I'm naturally high-strung like a tight banjo string. All I wanted was to make a good impression on the guys, as a fellow rider, which surely created a bit of anxiety. I felt an awkward moment brewing.

One of the guys told me of a long motorcycle trip that he took where he did a bit of blogging. I wanted to check it out at my next convenience, so we wrote our info on two small sheets of paper. When I walked out, I took with me the paper that I just wrote my info on, that I was supposed to hand to him. He just looked at me funny. I'm not sure why I did that, and didn't even catch myself doing it. Whether it was the coffee or not, for fifteen minutes that morning, I had lost it. I was sure that the guys were thinking, "I'm surprised that flake made it this far on two wheels." Still, they helped me find the correct shield, and after they patiently listened to my stories about helmet woes, they went the extra mile and comped the parts I needed. I left thankful yet utterly embarrassed.

Whatever was ailing my thinker soon wore off. Adam wanted to do something fun to celebrate his newest full rotation around the sun. He and I purchased tickets to a comedy show starring Donnell Rawlings, A.K.A. Ashy Larry from the Chappelle Show. Ashy Larry is the short, bald fellow who seems to be rolling dice in every episode. On the show, he grabs the dice tight with both hands, shakes them while wishing for luck, gives them a good luck blow—unleashing a plume of dry ashy skin—and rolls a losing hand every time. He was one of a perfect lineup of characters that made the Chappelle Show perhaps the funniest show to ever grace the TV. Donnell's show started at 10:00pm.

The lazy afternoon soon turned to night. Adam and I headed to town for dinner. While eating, I knocked back a few while he took the responsible route. We headed to the show and were seated a few rows back from the stage. The room was dark and filled with seats big enough to have some elbow room. The floor gently ascended from the stage to the rear. Everyone had a view.

Donnell joked about white people, black people, and these cool (or so they thought) people who wandered in late with big sunglasses on and gelled hair. *Who wears sunglasses in a room this dark?* As the cool people tried to find seats, he busted them out for interrupting the show. When they tried to say something back, his quick wit put a stop to that. The face cramp I earned from laughing hyena-style lasted for hours.

We walked to the lobby where folks were gathering for drinks. Donnell joined everyone at the bar for autographs. Adam and I put back a small pond's worth of whiskey at the show, and now my buddy was turning into a big social lug. He managed to coax Donnell into a picture, while others did the same. I wanted to get one too, but the crowd wasn't really giving him any breathing room. I just snapped a mental picture and went about my business. I met a fellow from Fairfax, Virginia, who was there with his family. He and I talked for a while. His question about why I was all the way in Texas led to a quick version of my trip. He really liked the idea of getting away on a journey like mine, as his employment left him deeply unsatisfied and far from happy. He was exceptionally clean-cut. I imagined him to be an office type and a high earner. I continued to make small talk with him and his family while Adam really started to limber up. Our night was about to take a drastic turn for the worse.

Adam and I both have a wild side a country mile wide. That night mine was in remission. Adam's, on the other hand, was building up steam with every glass of whiskey he downed. Adam and I aren't angels. We will never receive awards for stern responsibility, and we have always embraced risk for the sake of a good time. On our way home, he decided to show me just how lawless Houston's underbelly is.

From the Improv, we meandered to a strip club and lingered until it closed. Then we hit the streets again. We paid a blurry visit to a few "massage parlors," to say it nicely. He knew that I'd been on the road for a while and that I was newly single. Being his birthday, and being tuned in, I didn't want to be disagreeable, so we checked one out, then another, and then another. Each time when he and I would stroll into the dark and shady buildings, a group of gals in lingerie would appear, give us their best hundred-dollar smile, and each time I just backed out. There were white gals, black gals, Latina gals, and a disproportionate amount of Asian gals.

At one whorehouse, the gals came out on cue and lined up in a **V** with the two closest to me farthest apart from one another. It looked like such a practiced maneuver that I imagined that they had done it a hundred times that night. Some of them were pretty fine-looking, but an overwhelming thought kept me in check. I could not ignore the possibility that these gals could have just crawled right out from under somebody five minutes ago. Don't get me wrong, I had the money and time, but some things are just too easy greasy to be explored. I decided that if that was what I was after, then I'd find it at a bit less skeevy of an establishment. The lesson here is that Houston is out of control. Who knew? Not this hillbilly. Everyone has heard about those types of places in Las Vegas and other party hotspots. Needless to say, my eyes were opened a bit wider to the world around me.

With the comedy show over and the massage parlors behind us, we ventured home, where Cindy was patiently waiting. We had thought that she was fast asleep. As a couple they had a rule: if Adam drank, he was to avoid coming home and he was supposed to get a room somewhere. Past disputes between the two made this rule necessary. Man, I wish we would have gotten a room. Both of us had a few hours to sober up and really thought nothing of returning home. I can't say that we could've walked a perfectly straight line at that point, but we were doing alright. Cindy, on the other hand, was livid. We walked into the front door, right into a trap. Cindy let my buddy have it and Adam wasn't backing down. He was never the type to back down.

I recall an episode in Ocean City, Maryland, where Adam and I were wasted and heading back to the room after a fun night out on the town. His beer goggles led him to cat call four college dudes walking on the opposite side of the street. He yelled to them, "Hey ladies!" thinking they were girls. The smallest of the four took the most offense and yelled, "Fuck you man." Adam's drunk-switch flipped. He marched across six lanes of traffic towards them. I followed, trying to dissuade him the whole time like the good angel on the shoulder. We were outnumbered by two to one. Even so, he was set on kicking some ass, and I wanted nothing to do with those odds.

We approached the group. The small guy stood face to chest with Adam. Adam cruises around at six foot four and was bigger than any of them. The small guy changed his demeanor and said the darndest thing. He said, "You got me. I'm a bitch." Adam followed that up with, "Damn right you're a bitch." I buddied up with the small guy's buddies, knowing that if Adam and Mini Me were going to go to blows, then I'd have to fend off three full grown drunk heathens. The situation slowly calmed and we dispersed. I learned then that he will back down from no one, whether he is right or terribly wrong.

Now, Adam was facing adversity, not from drunken hoodlems, but Cindy. He had the option to fight or let it go. Despite my attempts to play referee, the situation escalated until I was powerless and the two were going at it like cats and dogs. Cindy eventually called the peacekeepers, and my friend spent a night in the slammer. When they hauled him away in the paddywagon it was 5:30am.

Day 45 – November 27, 2011

If you've ever been through a situation like I just described, then you'll know that sleep was the last thing on my mind. My buddy was behind bars, and I was at his place with his significant other, who likely wanted to wring my neck for showing up and wanting to have some drinks with her man. Somehow I managed to get a few winks before waking up at dawn.

First things first, I had to see if there was anything I could do to get him out. Cindy suggested a few places to start. I had no idea how to go about getting someone out of jail on a Sunday morning in Texas. I wandered into the city on the Goose to see what I could do.

I visited the courthouse and the jail, looking for answers. A few guards hooked me up with suggestions. After a several-hour-long runaround, it became painfully clear that I was going to have to leave my friend locked up as I rode away from Houston. I did manage to talk to him through a small glass window of a heavy door for no more than ten minutes. I could tell that he was hurting and wanted to get the hell outta there. His eyes were bloodshot and holding back tears. He asked, "What did I do?" I told him in so many words. We said goodbye, and he walked away into a maze of solid walls, disappearing around a sharp corner. I, again, was completely powerless. As fate would have it, Cindy bailed him out the next day.

This time, as I left Houston, I didn't have the anxiety from the uncertain road ahead that I did when I left the stability of the multi-day stay in Key West. Instead, I looked forward to seeing the new countryside and inching my way west. The rest of day forty-five can be summed up as a short day of travel. About forty miles north of Houston, I stopped at an America's Best Value Inn. It was the extended stay version which featured a small kitchen in the room. For what I'd paid for rooms along the way, this was the best deal by far.

In the parking lot, with hours of daylight to spare, I managed to bleed my brakes. Weeks before, the fluid in my front brake reached its effective limit, and the feel at the lever was best described as crunchy. When I would lightly pull on the lever it wouldn't move. A slightly harder squeeze would have the lever go too far in, slowing the bike rapidly. I bled the front brake fluid, and the feel was great again. Then I serviced the back brakes. I tore into the rear brake caliper only to realize that one of the pads was worn to the metal and then some. That explained the complete lack of feel from the rear brakes. A few times, in heavy traffic, the inconsistent brakes made for some nail-biting situations. When I changed the rear brake pads before the trip, I kept what was left of the old ones, so now I just stuck those back on. They had about a month's worth of pad left. I finished up, pulled the Goose up on the sidewalk by the room, and locked it down like Ft. Knox.

Day 46 – November 28, 2011

A brisk morning warned of the day's ride. Cold, and his girlfriend Windy had made a lovely appearance. When those two controlled the weather it became demoralizing. The wind was coming from the north, the direction I was heading. I found from endless hours of riding that little things that are tolerable on short trips can drive you crazy on long ones. Headwinds take top honors. Fuel mileage dives like a submarine. My windscreen was too short to block the wind that jabbed me in the helmet. Some days it seemed that crosswinds were run by a perfect timer, hitting me every four seconds, and turning me into a real life bobblehead. Hours and hours and days and days of this were rather unpleasant. Oh, and let me not forget the ever-present scalp itch. This fun feature hit about once a minute every minute, also working by timer. You could've set an atomic clock to the regularity of my head itches under the helmet. Just when I got one scratched, the itch brigade supplied me with another one on a different part of my scalp. Fantastic! There was no way I'd make it back home sane if the itching kept up. Motivation was hard to find that morning.

Let me stop whining for a second and get on with day forty-six. I took I-45 N to Fairfield, Texas. Along the way, I made one stop at a Buc-ee's travel center. Adam had told me about the awesome restrooms. He said that they were the cleanest I'd find, and the most private that he had seen. I pulled in there, fueled up, and mustered up a deuce just so I could check out the stalls. I headed strolled past the array of everything convenience and the souvenir sanctuary that is the rest of Buc-ee's interior. The only convenience I wanted was porcelain.

I pushed the heavy restroom door open to find more doors, lots of doors, perhaps fifteen doors. All of them were solid. All of them were separated by manly concrete walls, eight inches thick, and full of clean tile, from floor to ceiling. *Which door will it be?* I slowly walked down the line. Door number one was occupied. Door number two and three were occupied. In fact, most of the doors were occupied. I found this a little surprising. *Do all these guys come in here with the same thing in mind?* I found an open door about halfway down.

I approached and entered. Inside, there was a single throne, sparkly white with crystal clear water, like the plumber had just installed it. If not for the seat still being warm, I would have believed it as a possibility. I imagine that the seats never cool in a place like that. I was in the first stall of my life where privacy came before economy. Men like privacy, and Adam was right—Buc-ee's didn't disappoint. If you're ever in Texas and need to unload, swing by a Buc-ee's. They have a dorky beaver character on the sign. You can't miss it, and I promise you the seats will be warm.

I continued on I-45 N to Fairfield. At Route 27, I veered west to Wortham, and was heading for Freestone County Raceway. I was after a visit to one of America's twelve professional outdoor motocross tracks. Passing thinly vegetated pastures full of cattle breeds unknown to me, I made it to Wortham's town limits without seeing any sign of the track. Wortham was tiny, dry, and modest. *A track that hosts an annual event with 20,000 spectators surely has to be a big deal here.* I stopped and asked a police officer running radar where it was. He told me to backtrack two miles and make a left. I did as he said and found the amateur track. By that time, it was getting late in the day, and I still didn't have a place to stay. I settled on seeing the track in the morning.

I retreated to Fairfield and found a place called Family Fun ATV Park that allowed camping. The price was twenty bones. I was directed to pick any spot on the property, being the only camper there. In a huge empty field far from anyone, I found a pretty little spot near a pond, beside a wood line and a few round bales. *Good enough for a hillbilly.* That night, I made a warm fire and spread out on the ground beside it for a few hours. Between light sips of whiskey, I admired a cold, but beautiful, Texas sky.

Day 47 – November 29, 2011

A frost-filled morning greeted me when I woke up. The night had been bitter cold. Not since North Carolina's Mt. Pisgah had my sleeping bag worked so hard. At certain points in the night, I had to get all the way in the thing and pull the drawstring tight. It worked brilliantly, and I didn't get cold unless I scurried out to take a leak. I packed up pretty early, squared up with the owner of the park, and took off for McDonald's, my coffee haven and unofficial office.

I searched for Freestone's phone number. After a few failed calls, the owner called me back. He and I made an arrangement that allowed me about a half hour to check out the track. He had one of his employees meet me at the gate to let me in. I rode back to Wortham and down the same road where I found the amateur track the evening before, only this time I went until I came to a T in the road. On my right, a large bearded man sat patiently in an old truck. He was parked at a metal gate and I knew I'd found the pro track.

If there ever was an old man that looked Texan, it was this guy, from his flannel to his beard, belly, and coveralls. He was the real deal. I followed his truck to the sign-up building where he presented me with a liability waiver. I signed it and he set me free to roam. I walked out and began a lap around the track, noticing that it was lined with a newer-looking, sturdy fence. The parking area had gravel roadways to keep the traffic organized. I was impressed by the facility and felt privileged to have the opportunity to explore.

I spent about forty minutes there in moto nirvana, running around snapping pictures and trying to imagine some pros ripping up the sandy soil. It only made me wish I had my motocross bike with me. Before I left, the old Texan told me of a short cut, involving a big tree, a Y in the road, and several sharp corners, which saved me nearly five miles on my journey to the interstate. My next destination was Billy Bob's honky tonk in Fort Worth.

Billy Bob's is the world's largest country bar. This converted cattle barn has a stage that's been graced by all of the great country music artists. Its tan stucco and maroon window accents hide its simpler past. The building looks slightly southwestern, but doesn't hint at being a drinking hole. It may even look more like a movie theatre. Two small awnings that say "Billy Bob's Texas" let you know that you have the right place. An even smaller awning with the words "Box Office" hint at its stature. I checked in at Hotel Texas and made a beeline for the big, bad, bar.

The walls were decorated with autographed photos, guitars, and cement hand prints from stars like Johnny Cash to Loretta Lynn. I stuck my hand in a few to size up the pickin' fingers. Most of them had rather small digits with Trace Atkins being the largest hand imprint I could find. Johnny Cash and I had the same size hand. There may have been forty patrons occupying the building; due to its size, it seemed empty and quiet, like a country music museum.

I sat down on one end of a wrap-around bar and ordered a beer. I took slow sips that matched the evening's pace. A couple was sitting a few dozen seats from me at the same bar. They seemed miles away. If I would've slid them a beer down that bar, it would have arrived tomorrow. *I might as well forget about talking to anyone here.* Billy Bob's may have been the largest structure that I've been in without an echo. It was large and cold and slow. I should've timed my visit for the weekend. Every Friday and Saturday they hosted live music, and Willie Nelson was known to just pop in and play a set here and there. My night ended with a stop at the White Elephant saloon. I drank enough to have fun, but had no luck meeting anyone. I was a stranger just passing through Fort Worth.

Day 48 – November 30, 2011

No continental breakfast? What! I gasped! While checking in at Hotel Texas the day before, the clerk told me that they'd have breakfast in the morning and that the place had Wi-Fi. She gladly took my money for the room without letting me know that I'd been duped. I walked downstairs from room nineteen to discover a coffeepot, and that was it. I thought about jumping behind the counter and putting a skillet in her hand; after all, the room wasn't exactly cheap.

The Wi-Fi was nonexistent, and several times during my stay I walked to the front desk to see what was up with it. Each time, she exhumed a large, red hardcover book. Inside the back cover were long combinations of handwritten numbers and letters. Most of them had been scratched out and replaced by others. These were supposed to be Wi-Fi codes. Each time I rounded the corner to the lobby and informed her that the last code was bogus, she confidently, but randomly, gave me another code and sent me on my merry way. I would've settled for a quick and easy "We don't have Wi-Fi."

I turned to the streets, or stockyards, as they were. I was after a breakfast that no microwave could prepare, or no spoon and bowl could handle. It was that time of year where all towns were decorating for the Christmas season. Fort Worth and its stockyards were no different. In fact, the Christmas decorations, the cowboy-ish theme, and the brick roads made the whole place feel like a trip to the past. As the brisk morning stirred to life, only a few were out and about. Three men were warmly dressed and cleaning up bits of yesterday's debris at a covered outdoor market. A lone woman walked in front of the Fort Worth Stock Exchange, through the brilliantly bright green grass, enhanced by the low morning sun. She was admiring the same tastefully decorated Christmas tree as me, and we both had our cameras pointed at its large red bows. She wandered off in perfect silence as I continued to look for anything opening up.

I walked by a plaque with a wonderful quote: *The Texans are perhaps the best at the actual cowboy work. They are absolutely fearless riders and understand well the habits of the half-wild cattle, being unequaled in those most trying times when, for instance, the cattle are stampeded by a thunderstorm at night, while in the use of the rope they are only excelled by the Mexicans.* (Theodore Roosevelt, 1885) What great, unbiased honesty President Roosevelt displayed. I bet even in the face of torture, one of today's presidents would try to bark out lies, over just a drop of honesty. I left the plaque with a slight sour taste in my mouth about our time's current state of leadership and continued on in search of breakfast.

I stumbled upon a wide plate of grub at the H3 Hotel Restaurant. It happened to be the only place open within reasonable walking distance. I had a heaping helping of eggs and toast with a never-ending stream of coffee, while sitting on a curved-back, leather chair underneath a chandelier of antlers. A hide, mounted high on the wall, was made into a rough map of the Chisholm Trail—a trail that stretched from central Kansas to southern Texas. I finished eating and returned to the Goose.

Right before leaving Fort Worth, I tried one last time to contact a friend of mine in Dallas, unsuccessfully. I had really hoped to see him while in the area, as it had been about two years. With Dallas out of the way, the flight path for the day was 35 S, one straight-ass shot down to Austin. For 187 miles, the highway cut through rural Texas past a here-and-there mixture of flat and dry towns. I passed through Waco and briefly entertained searching for the area where David Koresh started that cult and brainwashed all of those poor people, but that would've put me in Austin after dark, and it was no fun riding in a new city at night on a motorcycle. I made a few stops to fuel up, grab something to chew on, and scratch my head. The itch goblin was in full force.

At sunset, I arrived in Austin. A traffic jam had I-35 moving like cold molasses. It took an hour to travel three miles, and by that time it was as dark as it was going to get. To pass the time in traffic, I practiced balancing the bike. When the crawl slowed to a stop, I'd see how long I could keep my feet from touching the ground. It was tremendous fun, as you can imagine. Reality had me in a new city at night without a place to stay, again. The plan was to camp at

McKinney Falls State Park just south of Austin. I'd often reach the state parks or campgrounds by following signs directly from the highway. Interstate 35 didn't include a sign for the park, or if it did, maybe I was too busy balancing and missed it. Maybe I passed it by like a mindless body with a throttle hand.

Many miles south of Austin, I knew I'd gone too far, so I stopped at a Burger King to review the map. A local told me that I had to backtrack. The last thing I wanted to do was ride back into that traffic. I surrendered to exhaustion, found another America's Best Value Inn, and reserved a room. The Indian fella behind the counter was surprisingly so impressed that I was traveling cross-country, solo, on a motorcycle that he knocked $20 off the standard rate without me having to ask. Feeling grateful, I said to him, "Dhan'yavada" (Thank you, transliterated.) He smiled and I went on my way. The miles of wind and traffic whooped me into an early night.

Day 49 – December 1, 2011

It only took seven weeks to realize that buying more socks would extend days between laundry duties. Wearing pants and shirts a few times on the road wasn't a big deal if they didn't reek. After all, nobody knew me. Forget about wearing the boxer shorts an extra day, and wearing socks multiple days was entirely possible, but quickly became unpleasant. Trust me. One day was all that was needed to make those puppies smell, and two days, well that was just rude. My Alpinestar riding boots kept out the water and locked in the odor. Keeping fresh socks on also helped the sleeping bag make it more days between washes, and who wanted to be cocooned up in that thing with the smell of funky feet? To sum up the thought, clean socks are important to comfortable travel. Before I took off for the day's adventure, I disinfected my socks with the help of the hotel laundry room and was ready for another week.

I planned a short route that would land me at my day's destination before dusk. Yet, there was Austin sitting right there. Skipping it and moving on toward San Antonio crossed my mind many times. Backtracking into Austin had the price of daylight time to pay, but the reward of something new and exciting seemed worth it, so I settled on paying with my sunshine currency and aimed for a quick lap around Sixth Street. *Who knows if I'll ever be here again?*

Austin is the capital of Texas as well as the live music capital of the world. Downtown Austin was littered with proud signs and murals backing up its musical heritage. If great musicians are born in dive bars and trendy drinking holes then Sixth Street surely would be the place to be. Both sides of the street teemed with bars that looked thirsty for a guitar and good voice. I was eager to look around and expand my first impression.

It was still early as I set off on foot. Most of the doors were just swinging into action. Beer trucks were double parked and being unloaded by happy employees. Their restocking work would lead to many smiling faces later that evening. I could feel the college vibe in the air. Brick buildings with some years on them and brick intersections added character. Small oval signs with names like "Mooseknuckle Pub" and "Peckerhead's on Sixth" gave me an immature smirk as they hung over their respective doorways. I had completed a short walk up Sixth Street and back down and decided to leave.

Standing beside the Goose, I felt as though I was leaving without any sort of notable experience. The Jackalope Bar was right beside my parking spot and claimed to be the best dive bar in Austin. It was just before noon when I stepped in. Inside, the building was flooded with that eclectic/rustic style that you tend to see in old buildings after a few yuppies have made improvements. A giant jackalope figure greeted me at the door, and the walls were brick and dark. Paintings of large, perky-breasted women with wide-open blouses hung from the walls with other paintings of other things that I paid not a lick of attention to. I walked up to the bar, ordered a Yuengling, and was shot down when the bartender said, "They don't sell Yuengling in Texas." It wasn't that big of a surprise considering that Yuengling hasn't always been available in West Virginia when I wanted it. I then had him fetch a Shiner Bock, a native Texan beer, dark in color, smooth, and with an ever so sweet taste. I drank it quietly. The bartender wasn't too friendly. He moved and spoke like he was pissed to be at the beginning of a long shift, so after twelve ounces of silence I hit the road.

Lockhart, Texas, has become famous for its unrivaled brisket and BBQ joints. One, in particular, sparked my interest when I saw it win a head-to-head competition on the Travel Channel a few years back. It was Kreuz, pronounced "Krites" Market, founded in 1900 by Charles Kreuz Sr. The place was best known for its outstanding meat dishes served on nothing but butchers paper with a half loaf of bread as a standard side dish.

In Kreuz's parking lot, a vision I'd had about the look of the building disappeared immediately, only to be replaced by a massive barn-shaped building, one that looked like it should be packed with hay bales instead of hungry BBQ fans. The first step inside introduced my nose the smell of wood burning. It was coming from the rear of the barn where the huge brick ovens were stoked and cooking meat. The building was over-the-top Texan and had a real man's man feel to it. I questioned whether I had enough hair on my chest to push the front door open.

The meal that sat before me—huge slabs of beef brisket, a thick sausage link (best one I ever had), baked beans, and a half loaf of bread—threatened me in ways I never knew food could. Vegetarians beware! Leaf eaters may encounter spontaneous combustion upon entering. I could've used some help from John Wayne or Clint Eastwood to eat the last of it. "Finish it pilgrim," or "Go ahead punk, make the plate clean," came to mind. I just wasn't man enough. The half loaf of bread sat heavily in my digester like a clay brick. Stuffed to the gills, and a few more chest hairs sprouting, it was time to say adios to Kreuz Market and Lockhart.

A short ride through the Texas countryside past ever-thickening cacti and long, worn stretches of barbed wire fence, landed me in the slight town of Gruene, pronounced "Green." I secured a place to stay at Camp Huaco Springs, just a few miles from town for $15 a night. The campground was located against the easygoing Guadalupe River and was as pretty as a picture, flawless and secluded. I popped my tent up on the riverbank and headed back to town.

Gruene was a tiny town celebrated for being the home of Gruene Hall, the oldest continuously operated dance hall in Texas. Gruene's main intersection was T-shaped, and there I found Gruene Hall and the town's water tower. The modest, white, wooden dance hall would've been extremely easy to pass by if I hadn't read about it before.

Gruene Hall welcomed me with old, loose and creaky wood floors. While doing my best not to trip, I absorbed the essence of the place. Like Billy Bob's in Fort Worth, it had hosted most of country music's greatest singers, and the movie *Michael*, starring John Travolta, was partially filmed there. The walls were plastered with autographed pictures. Picnic tables with deep engravings made for the seating. Some of the engravings were so old that the original scars were worn round. They were the type of etchings that announced "Johnny loves Jenny" in the center of a carved out heart shape, whittled out years ago when the couples were in the midst of puppy love. The rear of the building was under roof, but had open-air seating. I fetched a Lone Star beer and parked my ass on one of those abused picnic tables. I wanted to just sit and listen to some live country and western while trying to sense what the walls had seen all of those years.

The band that had Gruene Hall's stage this evening set about playing their annoying songs. For eight originals in a row, a pattern exposed itself. Each masterpiece began with a super-slow ballad from the lead singer (who looked as though he popped right out of the grunge scene of the nineties), then halfway through the song, the whole lot of them would come to life, actually using their instruments for music production, only to finish with another super-slow and soft ballad from the lead singer. The band mates would just stand there and wait for him to finish, holding their instruments patiently, until finally they could play. I felt their pain. The eight somber songs drove me out of the place.

I spent about an hour roaming around town. There was nothing going on elsewhere. I briefly filmed a raccoon digging for grubs in a finely manicured front lawn. His antics would surely upset the homeowners in the morning. I laughed at his mischief and returned to Gruene Hall. The lead singer had ramped up the show. The band's first songs invited frowns, but in their last set they were redeemed; yet I had not found the good ol' Texan, old-fashioned country and western scene that I was after. My night ended by 10:00pm when I rode back to the Guadalupe's rocky, cypress-covered shore.

Day 50 – December 2, 2011

As I unzipped my tent to celebrate fifty days on the road, a pair of waddling waterfowl tamely greeted me. I really wasn't sure what species of duck they were, but they were brave enough to eat out of hand, and they didn't look like the mallards that I was used to. One was some sort of speckled species, and the one he was palling around with was some sort of all-white quacker with an oddly downward-curved orange beak. With no official duck food, I whipped out a bag of trail mix and tossed some peanuts and raisins their way. They rejected the peanuts at first, but then I guess they realized that they weren't getting any bread from me, so they started eating what I was sharing. I doubted that they came across many peanuts along the Guadalupe, or raisins for that matter. Hell, I didn't even know what ducks were supposed to eat in the first place. It was the first time I ever thought about what their diet consisted of, instead of thinking about them being part of mine. When I put the bag away, they lost interest and waddled back into the gentle Guadalupe.

It was an appropriate day to be a duck since it rained from sun up to sundown with no sign of letting up. My tent was completely exposed to the elements, and I frowned on packing it away wet, so I decided to stay another day at Huaco Springs. The price of $15 a day wasn't a budget breaker. The forecast called for rain for the next two days, solid. The storm was completely covering my route west. It was so large that two days of riding west still wouldn't have relieved me from its dripping clouds. *Maybe I'll wait out the storm here in the peaceful town of Gruene.* There wasn't much to do along the Guadalupe in the off-season.

Summertime's river enthusiasts had long since left the area. I planned to lay low and relax, hoping that the following day would be different.

I didn't do a darn thing until just before dusk when the motivation monster persuaded me to check out the River Road Icehouse, a mile up the road. In Texas, a lot of bars are known as icehouses. I had not recognized the River Road Icehouse as a drinking hole the three times I passed it by yesterday. I guessed that it was a river outfitter. The building was one of put-together architecture, like those you see where the owner built on here and there when he had the money. Once my grey matter made the icehouse-equals-bar connection, the thought of relaxing, grabbing dinner, and meeting some townsfolk sounded fun.

I ordered a pizza and shared the crust with the two in-house dogs that called the bar home. In between fetching a chew toy and racing down the long hardwood floor, they'd stop by my barstool for a doughy treat. Shortly after dinner, I met a young fella in a cowboy hat, who after seeing the Goose's make-shift luggage boxes, asked about my trip. When I told him that I was headed to Big Bend National Park soon, he called his dad, who was a long-time motorcycle rider, to get some advice for me about traveling that way. I told him that I was concerned about motorcycling in that part of Texas for its remoteness and proximity to Mexico. His dad recommended towns to visit and towns to pass by. He assured me that his dad had visited Big Bend a few times earlier in the year with no issues. There is a fine line between restricting yourself due to fear and traveling wisely. *If I take nothing else from this trip, I'd like to at least return to West Virginia a wiser traveler.*

Another hour or so passed and the first band of the evening cranked up. They called themselves The Phillip Thomas Band. They were there to open up for Curtis Grimes. I was told by a fellow icehouse patron that Curtis's band was picked as a number one talent from a contest that Kenny Chesney put on in Austin. I could see why they won. The band and singer were like peanut butter and jelly with none overpowering the other—the opposite of Gruene Hall's guest band the night before.

Before long, two gals—Rachel and her sister Jessica, from San Marcos, Texas—shared a table with me. All of the other seats were taken. I welcomed their company. Rachel, Jessica and I carried on for a while as Curtis kept the scene alive. Drinks flowed. Laughs shot out into the crowd, and I was happy to be in Texas.

Even though I was sitting and sharing drinks with these two gals, another gal had spotted me from afar. Her name was Julie. Like a dance hall ninja, she snuck up on me, latched onto my hands, and ordered me to dance with her. I fought against the whiskey telling me to "Go for it, man!" I politely tried to get out of it. It's not that I didn't want to dance with her; I was apprehensive because everyone in Texas, it seemed, was a great dancer, capable of fancy moves involving spins and perfect timing. To top that off, they were dressed in their best cowboy/cowgirl attire, leaving me to look like the odd one out.

Seeing that there was nowhere to run, I bowed to her request. Julie took it easy on me and actually taught me how to do the Texas two-step. She and I danced a few more times before Jessica cut in to dance with me. She noticed while I was dancing with Julie that I was a special needs dancer, in need of a whole world of help. The whiskey fought against the girls' best efforts to fine-tune me and my severe lack of rhythm. I tried like hell to keep time with them and was rewarded by having an absolute blast. In all honesty, it felt great to put my hands on the hips of a gyrating woman. It had been a while. The night concluded with Julie twirling under my hand to the last beat of the last song.

Day 51 – December 3, 2011

When I think of Texas, I think of dry, arid land full of desert landscapes or maybe large cattle ranches with cacti. Rainforest-quality saturation never crossed my mind. Here, the storm was so big that it covered most of Texas's 900-mile-wide surface. Sticking around Camp Huaco Springs another day seemed like the thing to do.

Day fifty-one started with black coffee and Wi-Fi at the campground store. When the friendly female office assistant opened the store, I was there like a droopy-eyed zombie, hunched on a picnic table and ready for a caffeine drip. Between hot sips, I told her about my fascination with River Road. It had to be one of the neatest narrow stretches of road that I'd ridden. Its thin ribbon of pavement curved through picturesque views of the Guadalupe River and surrounding hills. Caves and cliffs were everywhere. The only way not to see one was to close your eyes. The people who inhabited the roadside lived in village-like community clusters with river outfitters being the area's big business. I ended up riding a dozen-mile stretch of the road four times in two days just because I liked it so much.

With no solid plan for the daylight hours, I rode in the rain to New Braunfels, a nearby town, to escape the close quarters of my tent. There's only so much stimulation to be found in a 4' x 7' space. Other than eating at Whataburger for the first time in my life, nothing remotely exciting happened, unless you count mist from car tires sticking to your face shield while piloting a two-wheeler on unknown roads in the rain. On my way back to camp, I stopped at the River Road Icehouse to see who won the trip to Jamaica that I signed up for last night.

I walked in—fingers crossed, happy to be back—and was shocked to see Rachel and Jessica still there and still wearing last night's clothes, only much muddier. They were sporting smiles and holding cans of carbonated golden nectar. I joined them in laughs and cold ones. I inquired about their predicament, thinking slightly that they may have pulled an all-nighter. They told me that shortly after leaving at closing time, they tested their car's ability to handle ditches. What they found was that they had the wrong kind of car for the terrain and were struck with a flat tire. They called a friend who lived a few miles down the road to help. Now they were back and waiting on a tow truck. The timing was perfect for meeting up again. We made plans to hang out later that night.

The evening came, and tracked down this place called Billy's Icehouse that everyone was telling me about. A big-hair, mega-ballad, eighties cover band was scheduled to play. *Perfect.* Jessica and Rachel bailed on me, deciding to stay in and recover from their long night of debauchery, so I pulled up a chair and was going to take it easy until this feller named Bobby walked through Billy's front door (I had met him earlier that day at River Road Icehouse). He was old enough to be grey, but wild enough to be eighteen. He'd spent some of his life working on oil rigs; he was stocky and quick with the wise cracks. Bobby and some friends congregated around me as I sat alone at the last open table. With this rambunctious crowd of Texans ready to party, my switch flipped and I went after the night like an animal.

Another old friend/nemesis made an appearance to egg me on. His name is Jack Daniels; he likes to show up when everything is perfect and force me to get wild. Between Bobby and his clan, Jack Daniels, and free Redbull, I got as loose as pocket change. The band freakin' rocked! Their big hair, tight leathers, and wailing ballads lured all the ladies toward the stage. I followed like a fisherman with a sharp hook, hoping to snag a decent catch. The drinks, the music, and the women inspired me to shake a leg for hours.

The events that took place after Billy's Icehouse closed were not things to be proud of. It's no secret that alcohol, once heavily consumed, takes hold of the joysticks and controls every move. I was swimming in a pool of bad decisions. As the night wound down, I met a Latino fella named Luis and two of his lady friends, one of which took a nice fancy to me, and we planned to go to their place to "party" even more after Billy's closed. He said I could ride with him and that we would meet the gals over there. I left the Goose at Billy's and took off with someone I hadn't known for more than a couple hours.

Along the way, Luis wanted to show me where he worked. He was proud of his job. We turned onto some unknown dirt lane. Luis stopped the truck and pointed at buildings sitting in the distance like dark figures waiting our arrival. Once he finished explaining things about his job that I'll never remember, he attempted a U-turn via a freshly plowed field. The recent rains made sure that we weren't going to drive out in his old Ford truck. We were stuck in a foot of mud. Utterly stuck, and too drunk to figure out an escape plan. So, there I was on some back road in Texas, two hours past midnight, with a guy who I didn't really know; heading to a house where a gal was anticipating my arrival, who I also didn't know; and waiting on a tow truck to arrive, driven by Luis's older brother, who I also didn't know. Luis was terrified of his older brother. He talked of getting his ass kicked as we waited. He talked about it so much that I began to think that I may have to scrap with the guy. His brother was always on call and did not like to be called out for Luis's BS. A half hour later we were towed out, and Luis's brother took mercy on him. Luis dropped me off at Billy's and took off into the night for some unknown destination in rural Texas. I know I'll never see him again.

I sat there for a few minutes weighing the options. I felt that I'd sobered up enough to navigate a few miles back to the tent. I fired up my bike and took off. On a dark and slippery country road on the way to the campground, a deer decided to play chicken with the Goose. I missed the horned heathen by inches.

I remember the blank gleam in the deer's eyes and feeling like I could have counted individual hairs on its head. I was doing about sixty mph, and I can't help but shudder when the thought of what could have happened crosses my mind. I knew then that I'd have to get a handle on my drinking before the fat lady sang.

Day 52 – December 4, 2011

I stirred to the sound of rain still saturating everything around me. I had lost another battle with the Hangover Fairy. She had kicked my ass more times lately than I cared to admit. At the campground store, I skipped the coffee and asked the clerk to sell me a few shower tokens. I fought my way to the bath house and through a bite to eat afterwards. I needed hydration and rest. The rain held back the promise of a pretty day of exploration, so I retired to the tent for most of the day before coming back to life around three.

I had seen Gruene. I had visited the local bars, met a handful of great people, and even had a wacky adventure. The only things left in the area to see were a dry day and Canyon Lake. I picked the lake as the dry day just wasn't happening.

Canyon Lake is about a dozen miles away from Huaco Springs. To find it, I started on River Road and rambled through two or three other back roads. The Goose, very loyally, carried my nauseous ass to its shores. I parked on a hill and stood there weakly, wearing what felt like a set of heavy rubber trash bags. Not a soul was around. Clouds and drizzle mocked my hopes for a pretty view as the lake spread out into a murky horizon. I read a few fact sheets posted on a sign and roamed slowly along. Two deer were grazing on the wet grass and even they looked depressed. It had been wet enough lately to soften their hooves. I sat on a bench staring out boringly until a deer, or something large in the bushes behind me, let out an unidentifiable noise, something like a whistle and a snort combined. I whipped my head in that direction. It was close, but remained hidden. The little start that I got from the noise was all of the excitement I'd take from Canyon Lake. Everything else just seemed dull.

In Sattler, Texas, on the way back, I stopped at a Fox's Pizza Den. My head was thumping, and my belly was yearning for something greasy. I put an order in for a small pepperoni pizza. As they pushed it into the oven, I sat down at a table as a hungover mess, long faced, slumped, and barely breathing. The weather was killing my mood. To my left, one of Fox's walls was decorated with a few hundred one-dollar bills, most of which had generic artwork on them. I asked the kid at the counter for a sharpie. On one of my bills, I drew a pathetic-looking shape of West Virginia on one side of George Washington's head and wrote my blog's name on the other before stapling it to the wall. Even my drawing sucked. *Maybe one day I'll go back to see it still hanging there, if they don't take it down and burn it for lack of talent.* I'd seen dollars taped to walls, ceilings, bars and everywhere by now, but at Fox's I had the pleasure of seeing a baggie with four quarters inside taped to the wall. How's that for originality?

The day just couldn't have gotten any better. I left Fox's and Sattler for my sixth trip down River Road. When I rounded the turn into Huaco Springs, it was dusk. I climbed in the tent, reviewed all of my day's drab pictures, and settled in for a long, cold, wet night.

Day 53 – December 5, 2011

Man, I didn't want to come out of the sleeping bag. It was cold, but for the first time in a few days it wasn't raining. I had to make my escape from the campground and get on the road again. Get while the gettin' was good. Skedaddle before tent fever kicked in, ya know? When I unzipped the ol' Kelty to face the day, I was faced with another pair of waterfowl that I'd heard about, but had yet to see. Yesterday, one of Huaco Spring's permanent RVers told me about a pair of Egyptian geese that lingered around the campground. The feathery pair was vocal and suspicious, unlike the odd couple of a few days ago. They would beg for food but keep their distance, gently quacking as to say, "Don't get too close to the ginger. They're unpredictable." They had dark markings around their eyes, resembling a pharaoh, and hot pink legs and bills, like they were stolen from a flamingo. They seemed content in their adopted Guadalupe and probably have never known the Nile River. I snapped some pictures for the record books and wasted no time loading up my Goose.

At a Burger King in New Braunfels, I met an enthusiastic fellow named Jim. As I was shoveling in a pile of unhealthy rubbish, he came over to talk about FZ1s. He was in his mid-thirties, a die-hard Yamaha fan, and married (judging by the impatient looks he was getting from a lady in his car as he talked bikes with me). He was the first person I'd met on the trip who knew what my bike was on the first guess. I got a lot of, "Is that a BMW?" To which I'd proudly say, "Nope. That's a $2,500 Yamaha FZ1." So many motorcyclists were not familiar with the bike. Jim was very familiar, though, and his opinion was that the first generation FZ1s were better than the second generation ones. Jim was an owner of both. He lightened my spirits before giving in to his marital duties and making haste to the driver's seat of his car. I finished devouring three days of calories and headed south to San Antone.

Two of San Antonio's wonders are listed in the book *1000 Places To See Before You Die*. The Alamo is one. River Walk is the other, and both provide an excellent experience. I rode rather easily into downtown and to a parking area a few blocks from both attractions. The Alamo was priority number one, given that I had not a clue how long it would take to explore the grounds. When I arrived in San Antonio, I could spell Alamo and knew that there was a skirmish at the location, but that was the extent of it. Its historic significance had managed to elude me for my complete existence.

The Alamo began as a mission way back in 1724. Missionaries used the building as a place to convert natives to Christianity. It became a fort in the early 1800s, and became most famous on February 23, 1836, when a small group of brave men tried to fight off a massive attack by the Mexican army. Unfortunately, the men were outnumbered and lost their lives. Their cause was not in vain, and because of their actions against overwhelming odds, Texans can always feel proud knowing how hard a few fought for their liberty.

I was most intrigued to learn that Davy Crockett, the famed frontiersman, fought at the battle of the Alamo. It is now a museum, displaying many of his belongings, along with hundreds of other artifacts from the battle. My first impression was that the Alamo's unmistakably iconic front entrance was larger than I had thought. Inside, thick stone walls made the place dark and cold. Multiple stone structures accompanied that most recognizable building and made up the fort as a whole, again surprising me. I had always thought that the Alamo was just one small rectangular structure.

In the Alamo's central courtyard, a long and limber live oak, with branches lazily lying on the ground, lured me over for a look. It grew like an upside down wooden octopus. Beside it, a ten-foot-high structure full of neat stone arches and museum displays, stood strongly as one wall of the Alamo. The tree, the stonework, and the silent folks slowly moving about gave the old fort serenity.

From the Alamo, I trekked to the River Walk, carrying no pre-expectations. I knew there would be some shops and water there. *But what exactly is a River Walk?* To answer that, I'd have to take a stroll. What I found was a canal channeling the thin San Antonio River through an urban sidewalk paradise. On one side, cafés, beautiful hotels, shops, restaurants, and bars of the utmost style lined the esplanade. On the other side, the same exact thing. And in rare cases like this, that is a good thing. San Antonio's finest buildings line the River Walk. It's below street level, giving it a superbly charming and secretive feel. Arched bridges covered in leafy vines supply shortcuts over the river. Boats captained by men in Santa hats guided tourists gently along under the arched bridges and past small banks full of sleeping ducks. Huge cypress trees, jam packed with Christmas lights, watched over the canal as folks weaved their way down one side and back the other. If there ever was a place that looked like a fairy tale, or a place where you'd expect to pop around a corner and find a hobbit, this was it.

I popped into an English pub and sat down to an appetizer of nachos, chased down with a brew. Inside, business was slow and the attire was business. Like other stops along the way, I would have liked to have seen the River Walk and the English pub on a Saturday night. The River Walk is a place where one cannot, for a second, let his camera take a break.

From San Antonio, I stopped just outside of the city at a Bass Pro Shop/Outdoor World to get some bear spray. I'd be spending a week in bear and mountain lion country in Big Bend National Park, and I was looking forward to hiking without becoming food for one of the big predators. I knew that those encounters were extremely rare, but, like winning the lottery, it does happen. I also picked up a warming blanket for a few bucks that I could crawl into first, before my sleeping bag, if it got too cold. I was prepared materially for the cold, but not mentally. Texas was full of weather surprises. I missed Key West. After Bass Pro Shop, I rode a few dark miles along I-10 W, found a reasonable room, and settled in for the night.

Day 54 – December 6, 2011

I have to file a formal complaint about my digital camcorder before I get on with day fifty-four. Igor, my good buddy, my tech director, and the fella who recommended this camcorder, could not have possibly known how the camera would handle rigorous daily use in the cold of winter. So I don't blame him when I say that my camera wasn't cut out for winter road tripping. When the temperature dropped, my camcorder shivered as if it was mammalian. Literally, when the camera got cold, it would vibrate at such a high frequency that getting a good picture was impossible. I have no idea why it did this, and by golly I wanted it to stop.

The solution to one of its shivering episodes was to stick the darn thing in my jacket until it was warm. And only then was it ready to put in some work. I was in the hill country and it was freezing. The camera was having a much harder time with the low temperatures than my crazy, winter-riding ass was. And with that I say, "Ride on!"

Day fifty-four began under the sun. I walked out of my room at the America's Best Value Inn in Boerne, pronounced "Bernie" Texas, and thought that I'd stepped foot on the surface of another planet. That giant fireball in the sky hadn't shown its face in a week. My spirits were lifted and I was ready for a day of riding. The takeoff temperature in Boerne was forty-two degrees.

I was on a mission to find Luckenbach, Texas. From the hotel parking lot in Boerne, I misinterpreted the road atlas and wound up on Route 46 W. The mistake took a dozen miles to figure out. On a wide shoulder, I pulled over sensing something was wrong. Upon a closer look at the map, I reckoned the direction I was headed would still get me to my goal, while adding a handful of miles to the ride. I mounted the Goose and took off through the countryside, not knowing that I was headed for an unexpected point of interest. Route 46 W took me to 16 N and dropped me off in the town of Bandera, the cowboy capital of the world.

Bandera sounded familiar. *How have I heard of this place?* In the center of town, I parked the bike, dug through my side box, and whipped out *1000 Places To See Before You Die.* I thumbed through and found Bandera, Texas, and read that good ol' Arkey Blues Silver Dollar Saloon was in Bandera and remembered pegging its location on the map at home with a thumbtack. What caught my attention about Arkey's was its sawdust dance floor. I just had to see it. I turned my head to look up and down the street, searching for what I thought would be a big fancy backlit sign. Then its red door caught my eye. I had parked right in front of it. I took all of ten steps, swung the door open and looked down, surprised to see a set of stairs leading to the basement. I thought that the saloon would've been at street level with the neighboring shops, but it wasn't. Down the stairs I went, into a private feeling, sunken saloon.

I liked what I was seeing before I stepped off of the last step. Wood-framed pictures gobbled up wall space. Red and white checkered tablecloths covered each of a few long tables. An old Coors pool table lamp hung near a stuffed armadillo with a tip jar on its back. Beat-up wooden piers supported the rest of the building overhead, and real sawdust on the dance floor waited for nighttime to arrive and the tunes to crank up. The sawdust was actually spread on a hard-surfaced dance floor. I was mistaken in thinking that the whole dance floor was made of sawdust.

I ordered a Coca-Cola, and the pretty blonde bartender handed me one in a glass bottle. I smiled when I gripped it and tried to remember the last time I'd seen one. A few folks sitting at a table telling jokes and slowly drinking beer invited me to come have a seat. They all had me by more than twenty years, but accepted me as one of their own. Beside us, a fireplace warmed the air. In between a short history of Arkey's ninety-three years, the bartender said that the lone fireplace was the saloon's only heat. I liked the place even more. Once word made a lap around the table that I was planning to ride to Luckenbach and camp in a tent, a friendly lady spoke up and offered a place to stay for the evening since it was bitterly cold outside. It was beyond her reasoning for anyone to want to spend a night in a tent with temperatures where they were. I told her, "If it were later in the day, I'd take you up on your offer in a heartbeat," but it was only noon by that time. She gave me her phone number so I could reach her in case it got too cold to camp. With that, I thanked them kindly for the company, finished my Coke, and hit the road for some more of Texas's hill country.

Arkey's gave me a great first impression. It matched my country side, my drinking side, and a side that enjoys the company of real folks who find happiness where they are. Arkey's was a place with characteristics that reminded me of things I know. I would trade my complicated view of life to live simpler, stay put, and visit a place like Arkey's once a week if I was guaranteed to remain truly happy. When I left, I promised myself a return visit in the future, 'cause who doesn't want to slide around on a sawdust dance floor? Yee haw!

Taking 16 N from Bandera to Luckenbach is nearly a fifty-mile ride. The ride would've been absolutely perfect if not for the westward wind blowing colder 'n a witch's titty. I rode on, switching gloved hand from the warm right side of the engine to the left side of the engine through the hills. With those hills came corners, and believe me, the Goose was smiling as I blasted the first real corners that Texas had shown me. There was one section where I crossed over a mountain and hooked an ultra-tight off camber left. It damn near bamboozled me. I leaned hard to keep from ending up on the steep shoulder. A thin strip of gravel had collected in the center of each lane. Making it through unscathed was pure luck.

To survive the rest of the chilly miles between the two towns, I'd ride a dozen miles and stop for a minute to take pictures after the camera warmed up. As I passed through Kerrville, I noticed that the temperature had dropped to thirty-six degrees. In Fredericksburg, with only a few miles to go, I stopped at a motorcycle dealership in search of a balaclava—a piece of winter gear that covers your face and neck like a mask. That was the missing piece of my cold-weather gear. Now my neck had a wind block. For the remaining miles to point B, there was nothing to do but tuck behind the windscreen and tough it out.

I arrived in Luckenbach about an hour before dark. I rode through, snapped a handful of pictures, and continued a quarter of a mile down the street to Armadillo Farm Campground, where I planned to pitch my tent. The campground owner was a woman of strong personality and influence. She went roundabout with me over pitching my tent. I wanted to test out my sleeping bag; she wanted me to rent a cabin so that she didn't have to scrape my frozen body off of her property in the morning. Our strong wills clashed for a few moments until I just caved in to her wishes. She cut me a small break on the cabin. It was a tiny building that started life as your average storage shed. Bunks were installed, a nice dresser was added, and she supplied a small space heater. I unpacked, turned the micro heater on full blast, and walked to Luckenbach. The overnight temperature was expected to be twenty-one degrees.

How can you mention Luckenbach without mentioning Waylon Jennings's song, "Luckenbach, Texas"? In it he sings of getting back to the basics of love. Luckenbach is everything that's basic, not just love. It's "We only serve beer" basic. It's "You better eat somethin' before ya get here" basic. It's "How do you like hangin' out in a shack?" basic. It's "Ya don't mind chickens, do ya?" basic. It's "Insulation. Who needs insulation?" basic. It's "How do you feel about a dance hall with a breeze?" basic. It's over-the-top at being under-the-top, and a hard place to put into words. It's the place that defines the term unwind.

Folks come from miles around and across the planet to relax in its awesomely peaceful country and western atmosphere. A sticker stuck to the wall inside calls Luckenbach a mecca of music. It is exactly that, and has somehow managed to avoid an over-sponsored, resort-like feel. Instead, it feels like a farm, just a farm, a small and cozy one at that, where you'd expect to see grandpa pickin' on the back porch.

As you approach Luckenbach from Rural Route 1376, you'll see a sign that says "Luckenbach Town Loop." It may be the first real road sign that I've ever seen displaying sarcasm. A "loop" through town will take you past three or four modest houses, a few shacks (one is a bathroom covered in old license plates), a pole barn, a stone lean to, and a tiny pavilion/stage. The shacks are small, drafty, and highly weathered wood-sided structures, and are where the action happens. The most popular of these is the combination store/post office/saloon. My rough guess is that the whole combo might be 18' x 45'. As a visitor you'd park and probably look at this building first and notice the sign that says "U.S. Post-Office Luckenbach, TX." Two dates are on that sign. One is 1850 and the other is 1971. 1850 represents the birth of Luckenbach's general store, the first use of the property. 1971 represents Luckenbach's change to its current use.

A rancher named Hondo Crouch found Luckenbach (Population 3) for sale and purchased the borderline ghost town for $30,000 in 1970. A year later, Luckenbach's official zip code (78647) was retired. Hondo fancied using the town as he saw fit. His vision has brought us the Luckenbach of today. The population is still tiny, but it's far from a ghost town. Tourists like me won't let it be, so it lives as a country and western gem—an old worn slice of musical heaven, where chickens roam free, and a springy wood door just barely misses your ass when you step into the saloon. It's everything I wanted out of a blues experience in Clarksdale, Mississippi, but with a country and western vibe.

Speaking of the blues, I was in luck. Ben Beckendorf and a friend were slapped in a corner of the saloon and singing the blues as if they were invented right here in Luckenbach. His raspy tunes labored out like they had to cross through a filter first. Nearly twenty folks and I, mostly standing (seats aren't a strong point when you have 300 square feet of saloon), enjoyed the intimate live show. He rocked and raised his head. People smiled and held a look of appreciation that can only be found on a scale this small. I felt like a local and a friend already. Two thoughts hit me while sitting in that special little place: first, I can't believe this is free; and second, this is an absolutely perfect moment in life. I looked around to see guitars hanging from the pitched ceiling, walls literally littered with dusty pictures like they were part of a family album, folks in cowboy hats, wood stoves, and more weathered wood. It was a country boy's dream. I'd been to Texas's biggest saloon, its oldest saloon, and now its best. It had the least amount of space to offer on a cold night, but that was overshadowed by its deeply engrained, wholesome atmosphere, one that can't be rushed or synthetically reproduced.

Once the band wrapped up, I met some fellas in the back part of the saloon named Bob, John, and Ron. We had the most unexpected talk about motocross. This was the last place that I thought I'd meet people who knew about motocross. All three guys were sixty-five years young, and two were former Marines who served in Vietnam. Bob and John hailed from Crosby, Texas. John was a large man of few words and Bob's best friend. Through the evening he sat stoically and listened to Mr. Beckendorf play as if he was in the building listening alone. John seemed to be at total peace. His friend Bob was his opposite: clean-cut, talkative, sharp behind a photo lens, and a sponge for details. I listened as Bob told me stories about earlier years when his brother competed against multi-time national motocross champion and racing legend, Gary Jones. He talked of individual races, and of Jones's inventive dad. Bob knew my favorite sport well, and again, I was happy.

Ron matched Bob and John's age, but seemed to have taken a different life path. He was living as a drifter in a van with his dog. He had "hung around" Luckenbach for a couple of weeks by then and was becoming something of a fixture; he was often seen refilling the wood stoves with firewood that he snagged from the pile outside. He was tall, thin, wore a straw hat with a feather, had long, stringy grey hair, and had a very slight surfer twang to his speech. He grew up in south central Virginia and told me about spending time around the great David Bailey and his dad Gary Bailey as a young man. The Baileys are motocross royalty. He claimed to know them personally. Between Bob and Ron, my moto-pedia grew historically richer as they enthusiastically told tales of motocross from the days of low salaries, small transport vans, and dads who played the role of mechanic. It was one of those things that I recognized as road magic. It takes getting out of the cubicle to experience things like that.

Day 55 – December 7, 2011

Staying another day in Luckenbach was an easy personal choice, but there was another reason to stick around. Last night, I gave my new buddy Bob my word that I'd show up again. He told me that I had to hear one of his favorite Luckenbach regulars, Jimmy Lee Jones, play an afternoon set. He thought that I'd really enjoy it. I had some plans of my own until midafternoon that wouldn't let me return to Luckenbach until right before Jimmy put his guitar up for the day.

I stirred to life, nice and toasty in cabin number three at Armadillo Farm Campground. That tiny space heater had slowly created a warm microclimate in the midst of frigid outside temperatures. I felt fresh, youthful, and ready after sleeping like a baby the full night through. Perhaps it was the cozy cabin, or maybe it was the relaxing atmosphere of the tiny town that helped me catch some much-needed zzz's.

On the contrary, the Goose did not have the same sort of night. When I swung the cabin door open to greet the day, the twenty-one-degree air reminded me that I was in a T-shirt. I looked at my trusty steed all covered in a thick hair-like layer of frost, and almost felt sorry for the bike. It sat there cold and lifeless like it had an illness. Its headlights looked like big sad eyes that seemed to look back and say, "How could you do that to me, man?" Personally, I'd never seen such thick frost on anything. Ever the opportunist, I used my finger to push through the icy layer and spell Luckenbach across the sparkling trunk.

The polar temperature provided a perfect opportunity to test my cold-weather set up. Checkout time for the cabin was noon, and at 8:30, I took off for Fredericksburg with my appetite leading the way. Call it unwise. Call it bi-ased. Call it old-fashioned, or call it rebellion toward the wannabe, but I won't bow to the latest and greatest electronic warming jackets, $18,000 bikes with traction control, and GPS units that keep you from using your brain. These things take the excitement out of an adventure. They make you weak, and I say, "Man up! Face a bit of discomfort. And for crying out loud, get lost once in a while."

For cold weather, I've learned from years of wintertime construction work that nothing works better than layers, and there's no way in hell that I'm going to spend a grand on an electronic jacket. Those are for the men who want to zip their moobs up in artificial heat and ride when it's sunny on the weekends. I went at the cold by wearing all the gear I have at once, and if that wasn't enough, it probably wasn't sane to be riding a motorcycle. When I left for the twelve-mile ride to Fredericksburg, I was wearing a pair of thermal pants, a matching shirt, a T-shirt, two hoodies, a pair of jeans, one pair of socks, a pro-tective jacket and pants, riding boots, winter gloves, a balaclava, and a shit-eating grin. The only thing that I didn't have on was the rain gear. That was my last line of defense against the cold. It must be said that only the winter gloves were bought new for the trip; everything else was well broken in, and my secondhand protective gear had broken zippers.

Am I making the point that I can be as tough as an old leather belt, if need-ed? Well, I guess so. Twenty-one degrees did not bother me a bit, and I was happy to know that I still could have put the rain gear on over all of that.

Another breakfast bit the dust, followed by a bout of writing. I returned to Armadillo Farm with just enough time to take a shower and move all of my gear down the hill to the tent sites, where I'd be staying that night. I didn't want to go another round with the campground owner if I checked out late. The fore-cast called for another bitter night, and I was actually looking forward to testing my cold-weather sleeping arrangement before getting out to the very remote Big

Bend National Park and finding out that I'd need an extra blanket. I pegged the tent down in the lower right hand corner of the campground, tucked tight to a tattered split rail fence and just fifty feet off of the country road. Brilliant late afternoon sunshine pierced through each blade of grass, making them three shades lighter. A bright yellow armadillo crossing sign seemed backlit from the sun's outstanding glow. With my new spot all set up and the $10 tent fee paid in full, I walked to my new favorite place, Luckenbach.

It was well after three o'clock when I arrived. Bob and John were there. Bob wasted no time ribbing me for not being there earlier. He said that I had almost missed Jimmy Lee's set. It wasn't anything we couldn't laugh off, though. Bob snapped a few photos of me and told me that he planned to put them on a disc to be sent home to my mom. Unexpectedly, Bob and John briefly left for Fredericksburg to get a thermostat for Bob's truck.

As they took off, I walked into the saloon to catch the last half hour of Jimmy Lee's show. I opened the springy wooden door and stepped in. Ron, the drifter from last night, announced that the West Virginian had arrived. That triggered Jimmy Lee to start singing "Country roads," which makes a West Virginian's heart swell with pride. I've heard the song covered by rock, reggae, country, and pop artists. Back home, whatever local band is playing will perform their best rendition when the crowd needs a boost. That song has never failed to make me sing along, and from time to time while highly tuned in, make me raise a fist into the air. I'd been gone from home longer than any other point in my life, and as he was playing, an overwhelming sense of longing washed over me. I fought back a tear. West Virginia was a great place to grow up, being the outdoorsy type that I am. I love it and it will always be home. I couldn't thank Jimmy Lee enough for taking time to do the best rendition of that song that I'd heard. His voice was deep and scratchy and somehow still clear. Unlike John Denver's spiritual sounding original, Jimmy Lee somehow roughened the edges just like my mountainous state. He sang a couple more tunes and wrapped up just after four.

Another guy planted roots in the corner and kept the music flowing. At Luckenbach, the musicians simply popped out of the woodwork to play for free and fun in front of a small, appreciative crowd. They'd carry their instruments in, sit down, socialize, and respectfully wait their turn. Some of the musicians were just Joe Blows, and others were world-renowned, like Tanya Tucker, who rode in on the back of a motorcycle one afternoon to sing to the delight of a surprised crowd. It didn't matter who was playing; the place kept a low-key, raw country and western vibe the whole time. I'd never seen anything like it.

A bit later, Bob and John returned. We spent the evening listening to the random performers, snapping a pic here and there (none of which could do the moment justice), and getting to know the other dozen patrons. In just two days I felt like a local. They have a saying in their thinly populated town, "Everybody's somebody in Luckenbach." I knew I would be back there someday.

Day 56 – December 8, 2011

Luckenbach was better than expected, and I surely didn't want to put it in the rearview mirrors, but the trip wasn't over yet. I was headed for an expedition within an expedition, a multi-day ride into an alien landscape. The thought left me romanticizing about humankind's earliest travels.

Throughout history, man has made his way, step by step, across our planet, experiencing the moment of discovery—the moment where the land has never felt the impact of human toils, or has been recorded by human eyes, or has allowed an impression to be created in the soil by a five-toed biped. Along the way, he has crept upon shores where everything is the opposite of what he knows, where he is lost for words, and where his mind has no answers for his discovery, making him no more than a child in a strange place. He has found himself unable to identify edible plants or dangerous predators. He has encountered other cultures with ideas of their own that make him afraid. Reasons for these moments of no return, where the untouched land is trekked and forever changed, are many. Some have set out intentionally looking for trade routes or new resources, and some nomadically moved with the herd. But there has always been that first glimpse by someone, somewhere. Oftentimes, the journey had no known length or final destination, and returning home was only a wishful possibility.

It's the adventures where man has set out knowing he's going somewhere, but has no idea how long it will take or what he'll find when he arrives, that I long to be part of. Journeys like hiking Mt. Everest, or sailing across the Atlantic, or trekking through New Guinea are what I want. I utterly lose myself in these thoughts. Big Bend National Park was my expedition within an expedition. It was my far-off destination where I'd use multiple days to reach an unfamiliar end point. My reason for going rested on curiosity, and my alien landscape would be the Chihuahuan Desert, where I would be submersed in endless moments of discovery.

The brisk night had passed. I welcomed the morning sun with a smile and began packing. Last night's tent arrangement was an experiment in cold-weather camping. Instead of throwing the tarp on the ground as protection for the floor fabric, I put the tent on the grass, popped it up, threw the tarp over the tent, and put the rainfly over the tarp. This added a bit more protection from the wind and another layer to help keep whatever heat my body was making inside. Overnight, the temperature bottomed out at thirty. The setup worked great.

I planned for a three-day ride to Big Bend with two overnight stops along the way. One could easily do the ride in a day, with an early start on a more comfortable bike, but the Goose had a chafed-ass producing stock seat that turned a hind end raw after 150 miles. I had yet to come close to putting in 350 miles in one day. That was the distance from Luckenbach to Big Bend via 10 W.

Like any expedition, I needed to prepare with food and supplies. I'd ridden through the modest German settlement of Fredericksburg and noticed that it, too, had bowed to the usual corporate giants and was pimpled with a Wal-Mart. I scanned my road atlas to look for other options for supplies, but after Fredericksburg, the small black dots to the west that designate towns grew farther and farther apart until they seemed like rest stops for the monotonous Interstate 10. I didn't feel confident that I'd find the bits of supplies I wanted if I didn't just purchase them in Fredericksburg. For all I knew, Wal-Mart could've been the last real store I'd see before the park. I pulled up to its striped pavement plain, feeling that the store had somehow voiced, "Gotcha now."

Of course, everything I needed was under one giant roof. I bought a new tripod (old one broke), stocked up on food, more socks, and a mini backpack. An hour later, in the parking lot, I had the mini backpack zip tied to the backside of my wind screen (not that I needed more luggage room). It was just a really convenient spot to toss some snacks and the camera for easy access. To mount that sucker, I used my not-so-sharp knife to drill two holes through the windscreen for zip ties. The mini backpack fit perfectly.

I briefly spoke with a fellow motorcycle rider while spinning the knife until my wrist hurt. He stood watch for a few minutes, almost wanting to give me a hand. I never caught the guy's name and can't remember what he looked like. I kept my head down, focused on what I was doing while idly chatting. My normally friendly facial expressions were trapped behind my game face. I was a little intimidated about the next leg of the ride and more serious than necessary.

Taking 10 W out of Fredericksburg was a reality check. The terrain quickly settled into unmistakable desert, unlike eastern Texas where it feels like you're flirting with the desert, or just tickling it. This ol' country boy from the lush, green mountains of West Virginia felt a million miles from home. That's what I was after, seeing something different for a change.

The highway was lined with small plateau-like mountains thinly covered in red and green shrubs. Thirty miles from Fredericksburg, there was hardly a real tree in sight. It wasn't quite what I expected from Texas. I expected to see this sort of dramatically parched desert start in New Mexico. Along the way I made one stop at a small interstate pull-off town called Junction, where I would find one thing that certainly looked familiar: golden arches. I didn't fret. My camera needed to be recharged and I knew they had Wi-Fi. Hell, McDonald's on the moon would probably have Wi-Fi.

I sat there chewing on a McChicken sandwich with an extra dose of mayo. Folks came and went, all looking calm and bored. Western license plates dominated the parking lot. RVs hogged the largest portion. I could see from inside that two kids were finding pleasure in investigating the Goose. I already felt alone, and I had just arrived in this environment. A weird sense of uncertainty lingered. A half hour later, I hit the road again with a charged camera. Ozona, Texas, was ninety-four miles away.

Ozona is a strange place, stale and crusty, but somewhat of an oasis just when one is needed. A sign in the center of town proudly displays, "OZONA Biggest Little Town in the World." That designation comes from the fact that it is the *only* town in all of Crockett County, Texas. Crockett County, named after the one and only Davy Crockett, is 2,807 square miles of desert. Compare that with my home county's puny 212 square miles, and you can see why Ozona is kind of a big deal in Crockett County.

Ozona felt sleepy and dreamlike as if nothing had changed for decades. A bland vibe drowned out any form of excitement. Franchises that I was not familiar with, like a Fina gas station, speckled the town. I arrived there around 4:00pm and decided to ride around to check the rates for all of the motels. One franchise that I've become very familiar with, America's Best Value Inn, had the lowest price in town by $10, so I went with them. On a side note, I was turned down for a single night tent stay at Ozona's two RV parks. I really wanted to stay in a room anyway, because I'd be camping in Big Bend for a week and who knew if my stinky ass would get a shower.

Day 57 – December 9, 2011

I woke to find myself headed for the interstate in second place. As I slid the curtain aside in my room, a man in black denim jeans and a heavy leather jacket was standing beside his hog in the brisk Texas morning. He and I were the only motorcycle riders staying at the motel, and maybe the motel's only guests. I watched for a minute as his breath formed a perfect little cloud in between every careful sip of coffee. I thought about going out to have a chat but decided not to. If he was up this early and ready to brave cold wind at seventy mph on the back of his bike, wearing that little bit of gear, then he must be heading somewhere important, especially since there isn't a damn thing near Ozona. He was probably planning a few-hundred-mile day, and I didn't want to hold him up. As he fired up his V-twin and rounded the corner, I wished him luck.

Two hours later, after raiding the motel's Tupperware containers full of cinnamon buns, I geared up and hit the road west. The ride from Ozona to Fort Stockton is a desert wasteland, a no-man's land, or more specifically, Bum Fucked Egypt. I once heard the expression "Outer Mongolia" used to describe the middle of nowhere. It's safe to say that the emptiness between Ozona and Fort Stockton is the sister city to Outer Mongolia. Mile after mile, one big brown rolling hill after another, loosely speckled with the same red and green shrubs that encompassed my view the day before, dominated the roadside. If not for one small desert peak that looked like a breast with nipple and all, I may have succumbed to highway hypnosis and run into a ditch. It was on my right and shaped like a rounded pyramid. As I passed, I coined it "boob knob." Judging from the state of its erect peak outcropping, I'd say that I wasn't the only thing feeling the effects of the biting wind.

Here and there, the odd service station would appear on the horizon, accompanied by a few lonely wind farms. Interstate 10 cut through pristine West Texas like a cholesterol-hardened vein of human activity, linking one fragment of civilization to another. Everything to the left and right of the interstate's shoulders was raw, rocky, and untamed. I felt as though I'd finally made it to the Southwest, an area that had given me butterflies for weeks just thinking about it.

Still, it was new to me, and I appreciated the unforgiving terrain. When I'd stop for a quick picture, I imagined comfortable people whizzing by in their heated vehicles saying, "Hey honey. Look at that fool on the motorcycle. What the hell is he taking a picture of? There ain't nothin' out there. It's too cold to be riding in this weather. He must be one of those *special* people." It was barely above forty degrees.

Before I left Luckenbach, John gave me a pair of thin cotton gloves for the ride. I thanked him for his gesture, but I knew that I was carrying two pairs of gloves already and didn't expect to need any more hand protection. He must've known something I didn't. Just thirty miles from Ozona, I pulled to the shoulder. I reached into the rear trunk and fished out those bright white gloves. They went on first; then the winter gloves covered them. I thought that my winter gloves were impervious to the cold since they were the size of grizzly bear paws, but they weren't. The combination of the cotton gloves inside of the winter gloves did the trick, and the rest of the ride was a cool breeze.

I made it to Fort Stockton around 3:00pm. As expected, Fort Stockton was terribly plain. It was brown, dry, and dusty. Other than a familiar hotel chain, every building was short and squatty, rectangular and unwelcoming. Tall structures and architectural appeal seemed undiscovered here. Like Ozona, it felt like it cut off the switch of progress at least two decades ago. But why complain about it? There's something to be said about the hardy folks who call this remoteness home. I surely won't ever do the same.

I needed a place to stay and didn't feel like camping. I piloted the Goose to the town's golden arches where I wrangled some Wi-Fi and checked for the best rates in town. Budget Inn had everyone else beat according to the info on the net. I headed that way only to discover a place that didn't show up in the search. It was the Texas Inn & Suites. Its red, white, and blue sign said, "Welcome to the Oil Capital USA Fort Stockton, Texas." The building was your typical squared-off, U-shaped motel. A few unexpected palm trees grew on the edges of the parking lot, adding a friendlier look. I'd never thought of palms so far away from a beach before. Inside, the lady at the counter quoted a rate that was $10 cheaper than Budget Inn. That was great, but over time I learned to ask if that was the best they could do. Then she asked if I was a member of anything. I said I'm a member of the American Motorcyclist Association. She knocked another $5 off for good measure. I shot a "thanks" at her pretty little smiling face.

On the road, most small motel owners would quote their highest price and quickly drop it if I'd act like I was going to walk out the door. I paid my fair share of retail prices for a room before I executed this newfound skill. Being that the Texas Inn, like most small motels that I was staying in, was owned by polite and friendly Indian folks, I assumed (maybe out of a bit of ignorance) that they were accustomed to negotiable prices. From a very small amount of experience through three Caribbean cruises, I learned just how much haggling over price happens outside of America.

Once, on the island of Nassau, I gave a shot at bargaining with a large black woman selling carved wooden cups. I wanted one as a souvenir. I gave her a low price, hoping she'd take it without fuss, as I'm anything but confrontational. She didn't and quoted me a slightly discounted price from retail. I immediately caved and paid her the discounted price for the cup. Honestly, trying to low ball her made me feel bad, like it was immoral for someone who lives in a land of plenty to try and take away even more from a person who had it considerably less easy than me. But, here on the road, hotel fees (and sudsy alcoholic beverages) were destroying my budget. My mentality had to change, or I had to acknowledge that my money wasn't going to last forever.

I tossed the usual mess of gear onto the motel bed and headed for O'Reilly's Auto Parts, just across the street. Halfway across, and standing still on the yellow centerline like a white telephone pole, I nervously waited for a long lowrider, covered in a few coats of grey primer, to pass. When it reached me it slowed to a crawl, and I could see four young Latino men with shaved heads riding inside. The driver and a rear passenger leaned their heads and left arms out their windows and stared at me as if I had just tried to steal their rims or something. I stared back to fight off intimidation, but the red flags were going off like fireworks on the fourth in my head. *Are they gang members? Are they part of a drug cartel? Do they know where I'm staying? Shit!* I was freaking out without moving a facial muscle. They pulled their heads back into the car and kept driving. Why they did it? I have no idea, but it left me thinking about drug war issues near the Mexican border and questioning if I really wanted to go even closer. Against my character, I had just negatively profiled those guys, but their looks were not at all friendly, and the fact that they slowed to a slow drift unnerved me tremendously. I was happy when they moved on. I finished crossing the street, neck twisted in their direction, and opened the door to O'Reilly's.

O'Reilly's Auto Parts was a new franchise to me. Before arriving in Texas, I didn't know they existed. The store reminded me of Auto Zone or Advance Auto Parts, which we have a plethora of back home. They're the anti-mom-and-pop establishments that contribute to the ever-increasing, boring corporate monotony that is taking over our small towns. *But, guess what, they always have everything you need. Ain't it a shame?* I was there to grab oil and a filter for the Goose. Its black blood was thin and dirty and in dire need of refreshing. Not since Pat's house in Key Largo, Florida, had the oil been thought of.

Surprisingly, O'Reilly's had an oil filter for my motorcycle. Like I said before, they have everything. The guy behind the counter, named Guy, hooked me up with an old oil jug that I used as a drain pan. We got to joking around about his name. He said that when he was younger he would tell all the girls, "I am the Guy your mom warned you about." I laughed heartily. Then he said, "Now that I'm older, that line don't work so well." When I was finished changing the oil, I returned the jug to Guy at O'Reilly's, and he recycled the oil. The rest of my evening was spent on the phone, researching what to do in Big Bend, and wondering if I'd get a knock on the door from those young Latinos in the middle of the night.

Day 58 – December 10, 2011

At 5:57am I was awake. What was there to do in lively Fort Stockton before the crack of dawn? Who the hell knows? The answer that I found was to start packing. For what? For Big Bend National Park, a place that I'd been more nervous about visiting than any other place on the journey. Why, you ask? Well, the media's unending negative coverage of the Mexican/US border, and the fact that it is one of the most remote places in the contiguous United States, was enough to cause a mental raucous. It doesn't help that I've always been a champion worrier. Mom has always confidently said that I get that from her. Despite that, nothing short of abduction was going to stop me and the Goose from heading right for the park.

One hundred and forty-six lonely miles stood between me and Big Bend. Barring disaster, there was no way I couldn't make it before dark. That morning's frigid temperatures briefly spawned the weak thought of waiting another day before heading south. While scarfing down the best tasting and most complete continental breakfast of the trip, I canned that plan and turned to writing what I thought would be the last post in a week. There was no doubt in my mind that Big Bend wouldn't have a lick of Wi-Fi.

After breakfast, I headed for the room and crossed a rough-looking old man carrying a large television from one of the other rooms. He was hunched and straining and moving slow. I passed him by with a concerned glance, thinking "Is he stealing that TV?" and thinking "I can stop him if he is." In my room I turned and watched him load the TV onto the back of an old blue Ford truck. He then went for another room near mine. I stepped out to inquire about his activities. He said that he was working for the Texas Inn, and that they were changing out a few televisions. He was now smiling and overly friendly, unlike a thief. He asked if I could help him load the next one. I grabbed one end with an oomph and he grabbed the other with a raspy exhale. We waddled to his truck and slid it in the bed. I helped him with one more before taking off. He had a day's worth of work, and I needed to make some miles.

Thick fog and a heavy mist blanketed Fort Stockton. I fueled up at the local Fina gas station and made a call to Shane. I'm not sure what was going on at his end of the line, but on my end, I felt like I was headed for Oz. Cars appeared out of nowhere and disappeared into nowhere. People were bundled up and walking fast, and I could only see as far as the closest three buildings. The sunshine felt years away. It made my tone somber, like this was going to be our final conversation. He spoke positively and wished me luck. I locked the gas cap and rode out of town, into the ghostly air.

Visibility shifted from a couple of hundred feet to a quarter of a mile. As my speed increased the screen of fog seemed to thicken. Thousands of tiny droplets glued themselves to my visor, bringing visibility down to night levels. About twenty miles into the ride, I stopped to wipe my visor, both inside and out. There was no escaping this mist. It had seeped in between the little gap at the top of my face shield. The utter lack of visibility, thirty-four-degree temperature, and remote road made me seriously question why the heck I was doing this.

A pattern emerged for the first hour after Fort Stockton. I'd limp through ten miles or so until I positively couldn't see anymore, and then I'd stop and completely dry the face shield, snap a couple of blurry pictures (my camera was shivering again), and continue south.

Shortly after an hour of riding, the fog began to lift. I was rewarded with my first glimpse of southwestern Texas's mountains. They were sparsely dotted with plant life, yet impressive. The lush Appalachians were similar in height to these mountains but shaped differently. The Appalachians string together in one linear, uninterrupted patch of high terrain along the Eastern Seaboard. These mountains seemed to have randomly popped out of the region's flat land, often appearing as individual jagged peaks in the surrounding desert. Other than the next-to-freezing trip, the ride became quite relaxing. I pulled to the shoulder to have a chat with a herd of bison. They were fenced in and slowly grazing on a hillside. My multiple attempts to stir them up were ignored by the big-headed beasts. They were terribly uninterested in me. I imagined that finding something edible in that dry terrain was far more important than my entertainment. I was just north of the day's halfway point.

Marathon, Texas, is the midpoint between Fort Stockton and Big Bend. It's a tiny town with a fitting motto: "Marathon, where nothing ever happens." I stopped there to top up the fuel tank. Nothing was happening when a dark grey minivan with a canoe strapped to the top of it pulled into the parking lot. A short, bald man in his forties stepped out and headed my way. The fuel hose was hanging out of the Goose when he introduced himself. His name was Gary, and he hailed from Sacramento, California. Gary was slowly heading home after being on the road for more than seven weeks. He had visited family in Illinois and Florida. We swapped road stories and talked about Big Bend. Before I took off, he asked if I'd join him for a hot meal in Marathon, but with the goal of reaching camp before dark in mind, I politely declined. Gary seemed fine with it. He wasn't aware of how I loathed riding in the dark in unfamiliar surroundings. In hindsight, I wish I would've accepted his offer. We were both headed for the same park, so I thought that we might catch up with each other there.

South of Marathon, the mountains grew larger and the views even more magnificent. The journey that I was so afraid of was turning out to be incredible. Right before reaching the park, I veered left onto Rural Route 2627 and followed it for a handful of miles to the Stillwell Store. I read that I could find fuel there, and wanted to fill the tank before venturing into the remote void.

Pulling up to the Stillwell Store's ultra-primitive gas pump gave me the sensation of being in another country. Two large fuel tanks were perched above the pump. Each steel tank was about 4' x 12' and could have only been more primitive if a chimpanzee in a blue mechanic's outfit was spinning the gas pump's lever. I felt like a city slicker, clean-cut and sophisticated, standing next to the unfamiliar above-ground tanks. I walked inside to pay for my fuel first. The lady at the counter told me to fill first then pay, so I went back to the pump thinking about how long it's been since I pumped first then paid and how the world is changing. While pumping, I entertained a brief daydream that I was fueling up in Africa and about to set off into the wilds.

The Stillwell Store stood as a small, white building with plywood siding and a tin roof. A trailer, a few RVs, and a lone house complimented its solitary existence. It was the most remote business I had ever seen. In any direction from its gas pumps, you'd have to cover a minimum of forty miles to find the next slice of civilization. Marathon was like New York City to this place. If the Stillwell Store had a motto it would go "Bum Fucked Egypt feeling crowded? Come visit us at the Stillwell Store. Please. . . ."

Big Bend and its 810,000 acres of desert wilderness could make a man outta the most stylish, gelled-haired, pink-shirt-wearing, sissy boy. I had only just seen the park's entrance sign and got cold chills. The park's paved road and its single yellow dotted centerline led the way in. I followed it through a gap in the mountains. A tiny ranger's booth interrupted those yellow dotted lines a short distance later.

From inside her tight workspace, a female ranger popped her head out as I approached. I shut the Goose off and it was dead quiet. I fished out my national park pass, handed it to her, and looked around. The terrain on the other side of the gap seemed more dramatic. To my left, the evidence of a rock slide scarred the side of one range. To my right, distant peaks soared to the clouds. I made mention of the intense quiet to the ranger. She said that she had heard me approaching before I veered off for the Stillwell Store. She also said that the gap in the mountains amplifies vehicle noise as it's funneled through, making it all but impossible to sneak up on her.

Having no idea where I was going to camp, I changed the subject to campgrounds, asking her what campground would be best for a guy looking for the possibility of electric and a shower. She directed me to Rio Grande Village, another forty-eight miles south of the entry and right against the border of Mexico. *Ahhh!* I then began to question her up and down about the safety of the area. She confidently assured me that it was safe, and I'd have no trouble in that part of the park. With some directions and her solid advice, I took off south again to the part of the park that I had written off due to its proximity to Mexico.

The ride was phenomenal. The landscape was an intense contrast to anything I'd ever experienced. Huge, craggy mountains decorated the region. Miles of awe invited me to keep on riding. In the center of the park, the 7,800-foot peaks of the Chisos Mountains were smothered by clouds. Like a beautiful woman with a short skirt on and a lot of leg showing, I could only see the bottom three-quarters of the mountains, and the best part was left hidden away for a delayed tease.

Twenty miles later, the Sierra Del Carmen Mountains of Mexico came into my view, or I'd rather say, my life. They seemed close enough to touch, but were miles and miles away, on the other side of the Rio Grande. At first sight from afar, their peaks appeared to be high clouds, bluish and blending in with the sky. I said aloud, "Those can't be mountains!" Yet the closer I got the clearer they became. Distant blue gave way to desert brown and sunset pink. Just before entering one of the park's tunnels, sunlight highlighted the Sierra Del Carmen's massive vertical walls. I stopped the bike dead in its tracks. I was in landscape heaven. Right down the hill from me was the entrance to a sandy-colored stone tunnel and in the distance, the most breathtaking mountains I'd ever seen. On either side of me were alien ridges full of square stones and toughened desert plants. I stood for a minute, utterly alone, with my hands raised high and spirit even higher. It was a total moment of absorption.

Excited beyond reason, I pulled into camp around 4:00pm. The campground host intercepted me and helped me pick out a suitable spot. I picked campsite ninety-five in the no-generator section. It had a sturdy picnic table and was near a small restroom. Scrubby green trees separated the campground from the open desert. There were five or six RVs scattered about, but no tent campers. I was at peace and ready to settle in when the campground host came by to inform me that Rio Grande Village had a small store, hot showers, food, fuel, and Wi-Fi. *Wi-Fi all the way down here? No way.* And to think, I was nervous about coming here. I called it an early night shortly after dusk. The cold ride had taken its toll.

Day 59 – December 11, 2011

A clean cold morning arrived at Big Bend. I unzipped the Kelty and stiffly hobbled to the Goose. The sleep was still in my eyes as I pawed through the storage box in search of my stove, some water, and generic brand instant coffee. Like the moist mornings at Camp Huaco Springs, a fowl (this one land-loving) came over to inspect the ground for loose droppings. I was chewing on a bit of fruit and yesterday's bagel. This feathered friend was a road runner like the ones from the cartoons that honk "meep meep" and are perpetually running away from that poor coyote. He scoped me out, circling my campsite and waiting for the right time to pounce. His pointed crown, long sharp beak, and black and grey speckles reminded me little of the cartoon. He was fast, but not lightning speed. When he realized that I was onto his scavenging plan, he lost interest and disappeared into the bush. I finished eating, sparing not a crumb. Besides, who wanted to get a fine for feeding the animals?

A sign attached to the top of my picnic table warned of the park's javelina (hav-uh-leen-uh). It warned of unattended food loss, dangers of tent invasion, and issues between small pets and hungry javelina. My untrained eye had spotted one the day before on the ride down that had just been inducted into the road kill hall of fame. I pulled the bike over and inspected the wretched animal. I deemed it a wild pig. Although distantly related to pigs, javelina are small animals known as peccaries or new world pigs. This one was greyish in color, had a pig-like snout, hooves, and thick prickly hair that covered the body without hiding all of its skin, just like a pig. It was sleek, squinty-eyed, and short. The evening before, the camp host told me, "We've worked really hard to keep the new group of javelina away from human food." I wasn't sure of the fate of the old group and never bothered to dig for details.

I packed away the supplies and made my way to the camp store. It was a small brick structure, colored of the desert, with a relatively flat, noninvasive roof. Inside, a mini grocery store softened any thoughts of going hungry, and at the rear, a bright white laundry and shower room finished off the building. Outside the front of the building, a single Fina petrol pump stood ready for anyone in need. On the parking lot side, the roof jutted out over two picnic tables. I plopped my rear there and warmed my fingers with a bit of writing. Two road runners were making laps around the parking lot, looking for handouts like two seasoned panhandlers. All they needed was a sign saying "Will meep for food." Other than taking pictures of them, I tried to ignore their persistent begging. They even eyed up the Goose. The Goose eyed back with a cold glare. It was never one to be pushed around.

Before I left, a British fella came over. He was currently working in San Antonio and living in Vancouver, and came to Big Bend in his SUV a few days before. We talked travel, and he asked if I saw that motorbike movie with Ewan McGregor in it, *Long Way Round*. I said, "Man, I watched that thing twice! Movies like that make people like me do crazy things like this." He laughed and wished me luck. *If the trip didn't work out, it wasn't my fault; I could always blame my actions on Ewan McGregor and Charlie Boorman.*

I planned to let the Goose take a day off. It had been good to me and deserved it. Parking the bike allowed me to travel on foot while exploring what was closest to camp first. Right to the south of Rio Grande Village was a ridge with a three-quarter-mile loop and an absolutely stunning view of the Rio Grande River and the Sierra Del Carmen Mountains of Mexico, the same ones that I fell in love with yesterday. I was apprehensive about hiking even closer to the border, but I was practically on top of it. Rio Grande Village was tucked into a bend in the river. Pick up a stone, throw it twice and you'd hit the shore. A few people from camp assured me that there was nothing to worry about and that I'd be fine hiking alone. These were folks who have been there and done that, so I felt that their advice was solid. They did say that Mexican vendors would be set up along the path. That had me a bit nervous; I expected to round blind corners to find carts with mariachi music disturbing the silence, pushy Mexicans desperately trying to sell me a useless souvenir or tugging on my jacket, and shady characters in the background watching my every move, ready to overtake me. My imagination negatively snowballed out of control.

I took off on foot to the far end of the campground and onto a sandy trail that split those scrubby trees. The path gained elevation, leaving the campground and thick bush below. Thin logs held back just enough dry earth to make steps. I carried on, hyper vigilant. I rounded a corner, and wham! Relief washed over me as I realized that the vendors aren't actually sitting on the path. There were no carts or shady characters, just little piles of handmade crafts positioned strategically along the trail. Apparently, the talented Mexican folks would fashion painted walking sticks, decorated leather wallets, and beaded bracelets or necklaces of every color, and illegally cross the Rio Grande early in the morning to set up their bounty. They left horribly misspelled hand written notes asking for donations with suggestions like "walking stick $5," and expected to return in the evening to collect donations. Nothing was stopping hikers from just picking anything they wanted and heading back to the campground. Hell, I could've have stuffed my backpack full and thrown a dozen walking sticks over my shoulder, but I didn't. Signs posted by the park service along the path strictly warned not to buy any of the illegal merchandise. The penalties were confiscation and prosecution.

Tired from the steep climb, I summited the ridge and my breath was snatched from my lungs. Without a doubt, I'd never seen a view like that one. From the high perch, I peered straight at the majestic Sierra Del Carmen mountain range. Their grandeur dared me to look away, but I couldn't. Now that I was much closer, they had managed to become the most beautiful thing I'd ever seen, twice, counting yesterday's first glance.

The tiny Mexican village of Boquillas was the lone human fingerprint between me and the mountains. Boquillas's white, yellow, green, and pink mobile homes were clumped against the foothills. They didn't offend the view. Instead, they complemented it with simplicity. In contrast, a large hotel or golden arches would have infected the view like a boil on a forehead. *I can't believe this view.* No man could create a work of art as fine as Mother Nature had created here. Here was a scene that the whole of West Virginia could not match. Hours passed as I lost myself on that ridge.

I hiked back in the last bit of daylight. After dinner, I wanted to stay up and do some stargazing. The night skies of Big Bend are renowned for their lack of light pollution. I put the Goose on the center stand, my sleeping bag on its seat, my feet on the hand grips, and propped my head on the trunk. The stars were shy that night. Only a handful pierced the darkness before a silent herd of clouds snuffed out their view of Big Bend. I hit the sack after a short-lived moment of peace.

Day 60 – December 12, 2011

Just before dawn, a horrendous pair of yappy dogs mindlessly barked for an unfair amount of time. I was camping in the no-generator section of the campground and wished for it to be the no-yappy-dog section, as well.

Since the arrival of my mom's toy poodle eight years ago, I've developed an honest-to-goodness distaste for any dog that is defensive and obnoxiously loud for no good reason. Her poodle, appropriately named Spice, came into our household and tried to surpass me in the house's hierarchy just weeks after its arrival, like it had invited me to live there. I'd lived there almost exclusively since high school, when suddenly I had to fend off assaults from a skinny little cotton ball with teeth and beady, black, unforgiving eyes. Spice would yap and protest at my every move while sitting perched on the couch, coldly staring and visibly shaking as if suffering from hypothermia. No time of day was safe from her bark. If a floorboard creaked, that was enough for her to sound the alarm. If I bumped into a cabinet on accident or just walked in from outside, she would go bananas. She was a bona fide hormonal nutcase of a canine, and of course she only fully warmed to my mom. My stepdad, Tommy, has managed to stay above her in the pack order (no doubt working very hard at it), but Shane and I and everyone else who has stepped foot in my folks' house since the era of Spice has been greeted as a threat. She's lived an extremely spoiled existence without being harmed in the least, and I have wanted to kick Spice like a football since she was three months old.

So here I was, in close proximity to a few of Spice's distant relatives. I longed for the brutal hum of a five-horsepower generator to drown out the overly excited mutts. My ears picked up nothing in the desert's absolute silence, but yet they yapped with the stamina of triathletes. In the luckiest of moments, they would stop for twenty seconds. Then a spider would fart, or the wind would blow, or a star would twinkle, and that would make one of the wretched beasts squeak, sending the other one into a frenzy. After five minutes of warding off any nearby advances from say, a cactus, they would simmer down. I was a millisecond away from walking over to that campsite and unleashing a full can of bear spray on those bitches, giving them a legit reason to yap.

Speaking of peace and quiet, Big Bend's desert in the winter is one hundred percent quiet. When the wind was absent, so were sounds. There were no crickets chirping, no tree frogs calling, or spider monkeys howling. There were no background noises from modern life. There was nothing. Silence filled every open gap. I knew little of the desert's ways or how it functioned. Everything existed on a different plane from my part of the world, and its silence was a discovery that no book had prepared me for. I found it hard to sleep at night without some sort of ambient noise. My thoughts were never so loud.

The sun rose like a bright orange helium-filled balloon. I repeated the coffee and bagel routine without the company of any opportunistic birds. The morning had a dreary chill that fit my day's plan of visiting a ghost town. It sat fifty miles away, just outside the park's western boundary.

I was packing on clothes and packing away gear when a fellow camper and motorcyclist wandered over. His name was Don. He was wearing a modest jacket, a worn hat at a slight tilt, and glasses. He had noticed my bike and stopped by to say hello. As we spoke, Don's thoughtful demeanor shone through. He was a fella full of humbleness and wisdom, like the kind who listens politely and responds intelligently after a moment of consideration. I liked him from the get go. He and his wife, Ginnie, hailed from the world of permanent RVing, and hailed from Washington State before that. Like me, they recently sold their house to go mobile for a long while. When I asked him if he liked living like that better, he quickly responded, "Yes" as if it needed no consideration.

He and Ginnie were traveling in a large, flat-fronted RV with a small red Datsun truck in tow, and a small street bike in the bed of that. His real bike and favorite motorcycle was his Honda Goldwing. I told him that despite being a young man, I liked the Goldwing, and how if I had the kind of money for one I would have considered doing the trip on a Goldwing. We agreed that the 'Wing couldn't be beat for long distance travel and comfort. His was stored away in a semi-permanent location in the Northwest. We spoke some more of our shared mechanical interests, and he filled my travel plate with suggestions for Big Bend and its surrounding roads. I had just made a friend and had no idea of how good a one he would become. Our brief conversation ended, he headed back to his site, and I was off for my daily adventure.

The ride out of Rio Grande Village started off great. It was still chilly, but nice and clear. Twenty miles into it, at the foothills of the Chisos Mountains, fog had taken over, ushering me into a dream world. I slowed to match the visibility. The landscape became a hundred feet of pavement, a dotted yellow line, and scrubby bushes evaporating into the near distance on either side. It covered everything. My face shield moistened both inside and out. My mirrors were good for nothing. I kept on riding, making a giant gradual left turn, and once I reached a lower elevation, on the western side of the Chisos Basin, the desert reappeared. The ride turned amazing.

I left Big Bend's western entrance for a day at Terlingua Ghost Town. It's the skeleton of an old mining town and now exists as a hot spot to stop, grab some neat pictures, and find a place to stay while traveling the big open country in West Texas. I first heard of Terlingua from a man at Camp Huaco Springs. He gave me a mission of finding the famous porch and sitting down to a million-year-old view of the surrounding mountains. That's what I intended to do.

Out of the park, I joined Route 170 in Study Butte, Texas. At the base of a jagged mountain a sign read "Terlingua Ghost Town, 5." I continued on Route 170 until a slight right hand turn onto a beat-up paved road welcomed me to Terlingua. Stuccoed stone buildings with worn lengths of square timber made up the leftovers of Terlingua's remaining structures. Some of them were dilapidated beyond use, and some were like inhabited little forts. I rode straight through town to the far end.

A building called the Starlight Theatre sat within feet of the Terlingua Trading Post, where I instinctively knew I'd found the porch I was looking for. A short distance away, a sign with a phone number and "Upstairs at the Mansion" written on it, was an advertisement for the creepiest building I'd ever seen. The two-story building was windowless and veneered with worn stucco. So creepy-looking was it that I didn't bother to pay the place a visit. From my seat on the Goose, the windows looked like evil black rectangles. And whatever was upstairs, I cared not to find out. It looked like the perfect building for a large, greasy, long-haired, underdeveloped creature with fantastic chainsaw skills to be living. I have to be fair, though. If Upstairs at the Mansion is a motel, or B&B, or just a tourist trap, it probably is a neat place to stay and probably has nice folks running the show. I have no evidence otherwise, but man, that building looked wicked.

I pulled the Goose to the right and parked it against the trading post's porch. I clambered up the steps and turned around. The view was stunning. Huge mountains touched the sky as far as the eyes could see. The peaks of Big Bend's Chisos Mountains were clearly visible and accompanied by hundreds of pointy smaller peaks of the region. My camera couldn't quite record what my brain was storing away. I went inside the trading post for a looksee. There were goods and souvenirs, and quirky things not for sale like a stuffed bighorn sheep with its head aimed high and a bottle of Lone Star beer wedged in its mouth. Nothing, except for maybe that sheep, caught my eye enough to make a purchase, but where would it fit on the Goose?

I ventured to another part of Terlingua to satisfy an empty stomach. I found the Ghost Town Saloon, which only served breakfast. The building was made of stone and weathered wooden beams, under a collection of wavy tin roof panels that looked thirsty for a drop of water. The menu featured a large breakfast burrito (highly recommended) that touched both ends of my plate and then some. Before it arrived at the table, a fellow named Steve, who was temporarily living in a teepee down the street, pulled up on his Suzuki V-strom 650. Steve was a Vietnam vet, youthful, and clean-cut if not for his moustache. He was sporting a tan windbreaker and a backpack. He joined me at my table as we were the lone customers. I didn't mind a bit. The ten-inch breakfast burrito arrived, Steve grabbed a coffee, and he and I shared riding stories. His life had led him around the globe from the war to the present. I listened as he told me stories of long adventures, why he never made the choice to become a family man, and why he was completely fine with it. He shared priceless tips about getting the bike fixed on the road, while I made short work of the huge burrito.

We finished up and went to the saloon side of the building where Steve, a female bartender, and I sat at a table in the center. The room was dark and homemade-looking. Above us, the bottoms of the tin ceiling panels were visible. The stories went on. The bartender told us about the area's mountain lions and rare rainy days. Steve and I let her get ready for whatever afternoon rush that was ahead, and he and I ventured outside to our bikes. He volunteered to give me the unofficial tour of Terlingua with a small side of adventure.

Steve and I climbed down into a mini canyon formed by infrequent rainstorms over many thousands of years. It seemed like any average desert feature. I thought nothing of the canyon until we rounded a corner and came to the opening of a cave. The entrance hole might have been six feet high and four feet wide. I followed Steve in. We stepped over rocks and ruts into the increasing darkness until we could no longer see. He said, "Well, that's it." It felt incredibly surreal to be standing in a pitch black cave, in a ghost town, with an adventurous veteran, in the desert. It was awesome.

Lacking any light to guide us on, our only option was to back track, so we hiked out. I followed Steve back to the famous porch. He introduced me to some of his local buddies, all much older than myself. We sat side by side on long wooden benches, eyes locked on the mountains. Steve, his buddies, a stranger who rode in on a BMW adventure bike, and I casually shot the shit. The moment, the buildings, the men, and the mountains transported me to a simpler time when electronics did not exist and finding clean water might have been the most important daily task.

Steve and I left the porch and rode to Big Bend's entrance. We shook hands and left in opposite directions, he back to Terlingua and his teepee, and me forty-nine miles back to Rio Grande Village. As I rounded the Chisos Mountains, Emery Peak—the park's highest point—finally showed her face.

Day 61 – December 13, 2011

Before starting a morning's worth of catch-up projects, I had a steaming hot caffeinated beverage from the campground store. I can only make it so many days sipping generic instant coffee, and I'm as useless as tits on a warthog without a morning stimulant. Through the years I've cycled from sugary energy drinks to coffee, usually drinking more coffee in the winter months. I know the pros and cons of relying on stimulants, but haven't been able to shake 'em. Here and there, I've given it a go at giving up the drinks that give me a go, but my boycott never lasts much past lunchtime as my brain develops precise and convincing reasons why coffee and energy drinks are good for me. As the voice of reason grows louder on caffeine's side, I always cave like a sinkhole. Now, I can hardly imagine a morning without a liquid kick start.

I was awake and feeling great when I began a few minor Goose-related procedures. The road had been taking its toll on my homemade luggage racks. Rust began popping through the paint like an uninvited in-law. To take care of it I had to de-luggage the Goose, which meant that two bolts and a wing nut had to come off the trunk and three bolts and a metal plate had to be taken off of each of the side boxes. That took all of ten minutes, so before repainting the racks, I started the next project, the one that I thought would take days. I rolled up my sleeves and prepared for minor surgery involving the use of my electrician's hat, which has holes in it a mile wide. Electronics have always been my weak point, but never so intimidating that I won't give it a shot. I've been shocked by wiring household receptacles and switches more times than I can count. Each time, I've survived without learning a thing.

My mission was to mount a dc power outlet to the bike somewhere, something that I thought of doing while at Keith's in White Lake, North Carolina, but never did. I was carrying a dc to ac power converter, which was useless without a dc plug. Before I left home, Igor suggested that I mount it to the headlight circuit, and that's what I intended to do until I saw how exposed and easy the horn wires were to access. Without thinking, I went for the horn wires. Within fifteen minutes I had that puppy all tied in. I pushed the converter into the plug and hooked my camera up to see if it would charge. Failure. The horn wire didn't carry enough current.

At the moment of defeat, Don (my new campground buddy) came over and suggested that I hook the plug right into the battery. He said it confidently after listening to my trials and tribulations. He offered to help me out if I couldn't get that to work. He said that his RV was stocked with a substantial supply of tools, and from talking with him yesterday I knew that he knew his stuff.

His advice proved accurate. When I wired the dc plug directly to the battery, it had enough juice to run the converter. I became the proud owner of a Goose that could haul me around and charge my gadgets. Life was good. After that, a quick chain adjustment and lube prepared me for another day of Big Bend exploration.

Don also handed me a persimmon. It's a fruit that looks strikingly similar to a tomato. Being that I had never seen one before, I took the persimmon with a curious smile. It was reddish orange, shaped like a tomato, and had a few small green leaves attached where a stem used to be. I was highly unsure if I wanted to gnaw at it or not. He assured me that it tasted nothing like a tomato. Inside, I thought that he couldn't possibly be serious. I was totally judging a fruit by its cover. I have nothing against tomatoes at all, but I didn't want to bite into something even remotely similar to one that early in the morning. I told him I'd try it later.

When later came and I bit into it, my mouth recorded the taste of raw sugar. This thing was sweet. It lacked the bitterness of any apple or the citrus blast of any orange. It was sweeter than both, by miles. The texture was similar to a piece of cantaloupe. I was impressed. He had introduced me to something new. When I saw Don and Ginnie later on, I thanked them.

He returned to his campsite and I left for one final non-mechanical chore to check off of the list before sightseeing. Yesterday, when I left the park to go to Terlingua I forgot my annual national park pass, and the ranger charged me $10 to get back in. Steve, being the local, took a second to speak with her about waiving the fee before he parted for Terlingua. She didn't budge and claimed that the National Park Service had no way to look it up, so he and I negotiated a refund with her assuming that I brought my pass by before I left Big Bend for good. That meant that I would have to drive forty-four miles to the other end of the park to get my money back. In that park, that was a treat. Forty-four miles through absolutely pristine desert was better than any day at the office! My $10 were returned as promised, and I stuck around for a few extra minutes, talking with the pretty park ranger.

The ride across Big Bend to the ranger post was fantastic. Without the cargo boxes on the bike, the Goose was loose. It had been a couple of months since she was naked, and I'd forgotten just how peppy that puppy could be. And let me tell you, it felt so light and flickable, like a four-cylinder fighter jet. I was proud of and turned on by my motorcycle. The Goose begged to go faster while the signs posted a wimpy forty-five-mph limit.

On the way back, all the chores were done and the Chisos Mountains called my name. For the better part of the past three days they'd been covered in thick fog, so I decided to hold off for a clear day to visit. The highest peaks in Big Bend are the Chisos and can be seen from anywhere in the park on a clear day.

I rode to their access road full of anticipation and curiosity. I hung a right and began the six-mile climb to the basin. No less than a mile in, the landscape began to change dramatically. Yellow road signs warned of entering bear and mountain lion country. Gently rolling desert gave way to huge craggy cliffs and lush green forest. *Where the hell did this come from?* Big Bend was shocking me again. The ascent grew more spectacular by the foot.

I weaved and wandered and soon found the 5,400-foot Chisos Basin, or wonderland. My God, that place was amazing! Cliffs soared thousands of feet, surrounding the basin like a massive mountain fortress, and blocking nearly every view to the outside world. Inside this circle of mountain beauty, an alpine village and campground sat alone like a secret hideaway. It was perfect!

Millions of years ago, the area was covered by an ocean, and at the bottom of that deep, dark ocean, volcanic activity ran rampant. The peaks that surrounded me were born from that volcanic labor. Now, exposure to erosion had whittled them into a circular cluster of jagged points and spires. I felt as though I was standing in the middle of an ancient volcano, without the heat. I was fooled thinking that one lengthy volcanic episode created the ring shape of the basin's mountains. In fact, I learned that each peak in the circle was created from separate volcanic eruptions that formed nearly every notable mountain feature, except snow caps, in one flawless location. I mentioned before that the Sierra del Carmens were the prettiest thing I'd ever seen. That title was solidly ripped away while standing in the center of the Chisos Basin.

A lodge, campground, restaurant, park store, tasteful hotel, and visitor center made up the basin village. I grabbed a bite to eat at the restaurant and a coffee at the store and just chilled the heck out for a bit, taking in a view of what I thought Heaven would look like. I lost myself in the crazy thought that the Grand Canyon, Californian coast, Red Rock Country, and mountains higher than two miles were still ahead. For now, I was thankful to have experienced that place and was thinking about moving camp to the basin at least one day before I left Big Bend. The west had infiltrated my spirit and began to own a part of me.

After my moment of perfection in the Chisos, I motored down the twisty turns, out of the highlands, and back to Rio Grande Village. I was never more excited to write about an experience on the road. I wanted to get a post done fast and headed for the campground store like a missile. Inside, I ran into two fellas who I had briefly met there yesterday.

Roger and Jerry were young Latino guys, nineteen years old, and in Big Bend working on a project to create a new, unmanned border crossing in the park. Before they became co-workers, they were friends. They traveled from their home in Las Cruces, New Mexico, with the job's superintendent, who was Jerry's dad. The boys gave me my first glimpse of the laid back western attitude I had heard about. They spoke shy and softly, but never hurriedly. We got along great the evening before, and it was good to see them again.

A bit later, and without a word typed, Jerry's dad, Andreas, stopped by to get a shower. He was a much older version of Jerry, tired-looking but soft-spoken and friendly. He and the boys had been busy working extended hours that day. We joked about him not letting the young guys slack off.

Two hours had passed when Andreas finally rounded the corner to the shower room. He had taken the time out of his busy day to share with me an encyclopedia-like rundown on life in the Southwest. Jerry, Roger, and I sat quietly as he broke down everything from Las Vegas (his favorite spot) to Juarez, across the border. He spared no detail and assured me that travel in that part of the world was not as bad as the media made it out to be. He told me about his family in Juarez who lived lives free of fear. Occasionally, he visited them to find that nothing had changed. I wrote down some of his recommendations and sincerely promised him that I'd give 'em a visit.

It was 10:30pm when I made the trek back to the tent. Roger, Jerry, and Andreas were the last folks I saw that evening. They'd left for their camp an hour before, and now I was the lone person in the laundry room. Everything outside was cloaked in darkness as I sat illuminated against a painted cinder block wall. I typed the last words of the day's post, stuck the laptop under my forearm, and walked outside. It was quiet. The walk from the laundry room to my tent site was roughly a couple thousand feet. I'd made the walk in the day-time several times by then and at night once or twice before. The walk that I took that night turned out to be the scariest, nonhuman-related moment of my journey. *Why did I put myself in this position?*

Shortly after leaving the light of the laundry area, my flashlight began to flicker. It had done that before, but when it completely died and left me in the vast darkness of the remote desert, I began to panic. Big Bend's ravaging javelina, opportunistic coyotes, and each one of its twenty-four mountain lions dominated my thoughts. Again, I was familiar with the odds, but until one finds himself walking along a dark road, weaponless, it's hard to know the vulnerability I felt that night.

My eyesight was horrible in the darkness, and I was very aware that Big Bend's predators could see me walking along like a giant slab of slow-moving roast beef. I would like to compare the sensation to finding yourself in the middle of the Atlantic, in a few thousand feet of water with no life raft, knowing that hungry sharks will find you and capitalize on your misfortune. It was just plain uneasy. My strategy for making it back to the tent was to walk heavily, talk aloud, and move briskly. Folks along the way had said that coyotes don't attack adult humans. I believed it for the most part, but didn't even want to see the shimmer from their eyes in the dark night as they sized me up. It was common knowledge around Rio Grande Village that the coyotes would hang out, just out of sight, on the edges of the campground looking for a small child or a family pet to stray just a little too far from camp. I wished I'd never heard that. Eventually my tent came into sight. When I grabbed the zipper to open it, the anxiety evaporated. I was back in the presence of my knife, bear spray, and pistol.

Day 62 – December 14, 2011

Two months down! This short time has been the most incredible, life-enriching experience I'd ever had. I was tasting life at full throttle. To live exactly as you want longer than a long holiday weekend or two-week vacation, is special beyond words. I was just beginning to really meet my true self.

Daily exploration and writing posts to describe what I saw added a bit of structure to my trip. That was fine with me, though. Keeping up with the blog while traveling was the best pseudo job I could imagine. *Why can't I make a career out of this style of life? If there is a way, I will find it.* I was finally doing something worthwhile that didn't bother me a bit. I was focused more than ever on what I was doing, and motivated as never before. I was fantastically entertained, and found a pleasure in writing that I never knew existed. Folks followed along with me from home as if they were there by my side pounding out the miles. In fact, many of them called or emailed saying exactly that. My journey was no longer about me alone. I had a virtual crew of folks riding with me across America, and I was able to give a gift to those who may never take the time to do it themselves.

Daylight oozed through the tent, waking me, and spurring me on a stiff walk to Rio Grande Village's store coffee pot. I moved slowly—tired and oblivious to the irrational threat of a coyote attack that had chilled me to the bone on last night's walk. The sun's light had absorbed all feeling of vulnerability. I grabbed a hot cup of coffee and made small talk with some of my fellow campground mates. A half hour later, my involvement in the morning powwow at the picnic tables came to a close as I strolled happily back to camp.

Sixty-three miles away, on the far southwest end of the park, the energetic Rio Grande River patiently sliced through a wall of rock, forming the Santa

Elena Canyon. That's quite amazing, and I will go into further detail about the canyon later, but first I must point out something equally amazing and worth noting.

Big Bend is big, really big, even Texas big. It sits as an irregular blob-shaped slab of land in Brewster County, in Texas's southwestern elbow. Any dozen of my county's parks wouldn't come close to matching its designated area. What's more, my home county could fit inside Big Bend National Park four or five times. And on top of that, I could ride sixty-three miles from my home in Harpers Ferry and arrive an hour later in Washington, D.C. Or, I could leave the driveway and arrive in three other states in less than sixty-three miles. Up, down, and side to side, Big Bend is a beefy behemoth of undisturbed desert wonder. A fellow that I met at the campground store described Big Bend as the "last frontier" of the lower forty-eight. I'd agree.

Its interior is scratched only by a few hair-thin paved roads that take you from one end to the other while passing by years of potential wilderness exploration. Rugged dirt tracks do wander away from the pavement here and there on their way to some obscure location where a well once was, an old building still rests, or a hot spring was once used, but I never saw a soul on them. Primitive wilderness camping is allowed by permit for those crazies who have to get farther away than those rutted dirt trails will take you. After pondering its immensity, I learned that Big Bend is America's fifteenth largest park. *Kudos to the government for protecting so much land. They've done at least one thing right.*

I left Rio Grande Village and arrived at the Santa Elena Canyon parking lot 50,361 rear tire rotations later, or sixty-three miles. On the ride over, it seemed as though I was inching toward a ruler-straight plateau that hogged the horizon on both ends like an inescapable dead end. Then the Santa Elena Canyon boldly interrupted the perfectly vertical wall. I pulled over at my first good sighting. This was an elevated canyon, unlike the Grand Canyon where your primary view comes from the top down; I'd be looking from the water up. I became excited. From afar, I could hardly picture a more iconic western scene.

Sheer brittle cliffs, hundreds of feet high, highlighted Mexico's border. Gentle rolling desert graced the side of the Rio Grande that I was riding on, while what existed in Mexico beyond the cliffs remained a visual mystery.

I continued on; the cliffs grew larger and the Rio Grande came into view. In Mexico, horses were scaling thinly vegetated slopes of fallen rock at the base of the cliffs, as if they were billy goats. I had never seen a horse climb anything but a ramp into the back of a trailer before. I smiled, realizing that they were way more capable than I knew. Cattle and goats, with large dinging bells tied to their necks, grazed on either side of the river. Jokingly, I thought of how some were grazing legally and how some had rebelliously waded across the Rio Grande to graze illegally. I didn't blame the livestock. There were simply more tasty plants growing on the American side of the river. Their Mexican herders remained in Mexico as they kept a watchful eye on the wandering herbivores, all of which, I'm sure, made it home safely later in the day without any fines for their day of multi-country grazing.

Three cars were parked at the canyon's entrance. I walked along a raised, wood-slat path covering thick sand and winding through reeds and grass to the riverbank. Flowing into the canyon, the Rio Grande was little more than a shallow creek. The gravelly bank full of rounded stone was as wide as a football field, leading me to whisper, "Where is all the water?" I knew that I was located considerably upstream from the Rio Grande's final ending point in the Gulf, but just days before—when I hiked near the river at Rio Grande Village—it looked like an actual river. I stored the thought in my mind's file cabinet and proceeded on.

Santa Elena's cliffs now looked as though they could be a thousand feet high. They were mighty and required a head tilt where the skin on the rear of your neck folds into hotdog shapes as you look straight up to see the top. I headed for a makeshift concrete walkway that weaved back and forth, gaining elevation against a crumbly slope before leading into the canyon. At the top of it, and far enough in for the mouth of Santa Elena Canyon to frame a picture, I turned and could see the volcanic shape of the Chisos Mountains reflecting perfectly against the slow-moving Rio Grande. The mountains were upside down in the liquid mirror image. The view was magnificent.

I followed the trail deeper and deeper until I was again against the river's shore. House-sized boulders, obviously sent from above, littered the water's edge. Each turn in the path around the boulders was blind and silent. The farther I hiked in, the more I thought about rounding one of those boulders and finding a mountain lion drinking from the river. I gripped my bear spray as the hike lost a free and fun edge. *Doing this alone ain't all it's cracked up to be.*

I was surprised to find the trail end only a half mile in. I had walked as far as one could go without a raft. The canyon walls and the Rio Grande disappeared around a bend another half mile away. I sat on a high rock with good visibility and forced a moment of peace. I thought of the two countries sitting only a dozen steps across the water from one another. In that canyon the boundary seemed unimportant. Both sides looked identical but had different leaders, different laws, and a different language. It all seemed trivial. To me, Mother Nature ruled the slice in the mountain. She created it and will determine its path forever. She was mightier than the walls, the leaders, and the laws. I thanked her for not sending a flash flood.

I hiked out, sans mountain lion attack, and met a retired couple from Kentucky. They had not bothered to hike in. Instead, they sat back on two folding lawn chairs, feet in the sand, and found great pleasure in looking at Santa Elena's mouth. I told them how the trail stopped abruptly and about how quiet it was in there. They found my tiny adventure humorous. We smiled and talked about work and the East Coast and retirement. They were swimming in the kind of peace that I was looking for in the canyon.

I rode away from Santa Elena Canyon stoked for the granddaddy canyon of them all that was just a few weeks away, the Grand Canyon. On the way back to Rio Grande Village, I stopped by Cottonwood Campground to see what I was missing since I knew I wouldn't be staying there. It's the most remote official campground in the park with only primitive sites.

I followed that up with a quick visit to the Castolon Store, where I grabbed a couple of beers for later and wandered around the retired grounds of an old mill. Rusty antique wagons and tools were displayed near their adobe and wood beamed matching structures. I found it more fascinating to imagine that equipment in action and those buildings occupied, than to see them today as old relics from a time gone by. *Only the toughest sonsabitches could've handled life back then. Their lives had to be like life sentences of suffering and hard labor.* I rode on feeling male, but not manly.

Near Rio Grande Village sits Boquillas Canyon. I had hoped to hike it as well, but picture taking really sidetracked me on the ride back from Santa Elena. Enough so that I didn't make it to Boquillas Canyon with time to hike. (On the road, the short winter days sprinted by, often mocking my ambitious daily goals.) As I headed east toward Boquillas Canyon, the world was bathed in soft warm light, so perfect that I could barely ride a mile without stopping to take a picture. The colors were phenomenal, and I paid keen attention to every detail. Green cliff walls, bright red mineral deposits, bleached white ancient volcanic ash, purple cacti, purple rocks, peaks that looked like mule ears (and were creatively named mule ears), and a low-hanging orange sun were all absorbed by a crazy guy in a blue Crossroads Yamaha hoodie. The desert's array of colors was the unexpected highlight of the day. I snapped off a healthy 136 pictures.

Just before Rio Grande Village and in near darkness, I veered left for Boquillas Canyon. A quick and curvy road led me a few miles to a parking area near the canyon and in close proximity to the Mexican village of Boquillas. The light left me no choice but a quick glance around. I saw the mouth of the canyon but couldn't take my eyes off of Boquillas. I wondered what it would be like to live there in one of those colorful mobile homes. *How slow and simple their lives must be. I bet one of their lifetimes feels like two of ours.*

As I swung a leg over the Goose to leave, my jeans caught a sharp piece of steel on the exposed luggage rack that sliced clean through. A bloody hunk of meat was gouged out of my shin at the same time. I unleashed an "Ouch!" followed by two fun words that rhyme with brother trucker. I rode back to camp, gathered the laptop, and hiked to the campground store. My night ended with a huge burrito while hanging out like the village bum with a few new friends.

Day 63 – December 15, 2011

Campsite ninety-five had been home for my longest stop of the trip. I remember pulling into the campground last Thursday and seeing two javelina just a few spots up. Boy, I was so nervous to fall asleep that night with all of the warning signs around the park. Pictures, depicting javelina ripping up tents to get whatever or whoever was inside, were posted everywhere. Now, a week later, I had survived the dreaded thoughts of nighttime invasion.

Another nightly occurrence was the celebration that could be heard when the local campground coyotes scored a kill. I didn't know why they made so much noise for a minute or two, only to fall silent. I was informed by Don's wife, Ginnie, that coyotes do that after catching prey. The ruckus stopped when the coyotes began to feed. One night the pack sounded as if they were no more than 100 feet from my tent. Talk about uneasy. Several people reassured me that they do not prey on humans, unless they are very small humans, like sub-five-year-old children.

One of Rio Grande Village's store clerks told me about an incident where a woman who was shopping in the store looked out the window and noticed a coyote running across the parking lot with a small dog in its mouth. The woman cried, "That coyote has a dog in its mouth!" The store clerk spoke up quickly and said, "Ma'am, that's your dog!" The woman went berserk. Her toy poodle had escaped from its flimsy circular wire fence. A witness said the coyote had slowly approached the poodle in a submissive fashion, head down and squatting, so that the poodle would get close. Right at the last second the coyote snatched the poodle and darted for the bushes. I had no idea that coyotes were so cannibalistic. Despite being sinister to imagine, I couldn't help but picture how that situation went down for the poodle. My imagination would not give me a free pass on that one. The store clerk went on to say that javelina will also prey upon small dogs, cats, and other easily overtaken animals. Pet owners beware.

In my short stay at Rio Grande Village, I became a small fixture at the campground store. In the mornings, I was the quiet, disheveled, unshaven guy with a blue and gold West Virginia beanie on—prior to a cup of coffee—and the youthful, talkative, unshaven guy with said beanie on, after a cup of coffee. My nights were finished off with a hot shower, a day's worth of fantastic stories, and some finger tapping on the keyboard in the laundry room accompanied by at least one familiar face. This was the third day in a row starting the morning with the same gaggle of sleepy campers who flocked around the coffee pot.

We came from generator-friendly sections, from tents, and from RVs tagged with an assortment of state license plates. It had already turned into a routine. I suppose some things, like coffee in the morning, and reading the paper on the john once a day, are fine. Perhaps they're just a practical way to start every day. It's the week-in, week-out, year-in, year-out grind from unrewarding tasks that I'll never be able to handle.

An older gentlemen and I had a great morning chat over our steaming hot cups of brown stimulant. His name was Wiley and I'd seen him at least four times by now. He was a retired schoolteacher and now spent a large portion of his year playing a campground host by day and a retiree by night. Wiley brought a map with him that morning. It was an official Texas travel map that folded out so large that I'll never be able to return it to its original form. He had curiously listened in on a few of my conversations over the past few days and thought that I could use it. When he saw me that morning, he said, "I figured you would be up here." He was one of those familiar faces that I began to like. I was happy to talk with him and everyone there, the clerks, the campers, and the rangers. Being that I had not seen anyone I knew since Houston, it was pleasant to have a smidgen of familiarity.

Rio Grande Village and its fine folks would have to be put on the shelves of memory as I decided to move camp from there to Chisos Basin. *I just want to crawl out of my tent at least one time and wake up to that amazing view.* I planned for a hike to Emery Peak when I got there.

After breakfast, I began a few chores. Laundry was at the top of the list. I was down to my last pair of clean socks. Busting out the laundry in the morning took a good chunk of time, so to be efficient, I knocked out another post while waiting. An hour passed, the laundry was done, and I walked back to camp to begin packing. The Goose was waiting by the tent, still all sexy and nekked. I painted the cargo rack jet black, gave it a few minutes to dry, and remounted the trunk and storage boxes. By that time the Emery Peak trail was out of the question. It was a four-mile trip one way, and there was no way that I could move camp and hike nine steep miles before dark.

At the basin campground, I found a spot with a perfect view that was right across the way from a restroom, popped up the tent, and made a short hike to the basin store for a snack. I still wanted to hike some sort of trail while there since it was to be my last day in the park. The store clerk recommended the Lost Mine Trail. She said that it was two miles one way and was just short enough to complete before the mountain blocked the sun. Off I went, on my way to the trail head. I was pumped to do some hiking in that heavenly landscape.

Excitement quickly dissipated when I read the sign at the beginning of the trail. It stated, "You are entering mountain lion and bear country. Bears have been encountered at close range on this trail. If you encounter a bear or mountain lion, do not show fear and do not crouch or run. Make yourself look larger than normal (perhaps I could have stuck my thumb in my mouth and pumped up my biceps). Keep moving and do not linger. Shout and throw stones at the animal and report your sighting to a ranger as soon as possible."

With that information, the wind was taken right from my sails. I was unnerved and second guessing. My confidence for staying cool in a close encounter didn't exist. My pictures came out horrible because I didn't take any time to set up the shots. I didn't want to linger, ya know? The whole time I was thinking about a mountain lion jumping off a rock and landing on me so fast that I wouldn't have time to shoot it with my bear spray. I was much more worried about a big cat than a bear, even though neither is too fun to deal with in close quarters.

Think about your average housecat. Even those sneaky little clawed heathens will hide out, waiting to ambush their owners or the family dog now and then, and then take off like lightning into another room with their tail high and pride higher. I've seen it. Now picture a huge version of that attack. A man wouldn't stand a chance. Needless to say, I hiked about two miles total and was on high alert the whole time. In moments like that it would've been nice to have someone to hike with to take the edge off. At least I could attempt to outrun them—kidding.

The rest of the day was spent waiting for the sun to go down. I threw back a few and smiled as it turned dark out. A perfectly clear night was upon us, and the stars were guaranteed to give us Big Benders a show. Light pollution was virtually nonexistent in the basin. While getting properly tuned in for the galactic gazing, I unwittingly gave two Big Benders a show of my own.

I was standing beside the Goose and was five or six beers deep when I noticed a pair of eyes coming straight at me in the moonlight. The eyes were the perfect height from the ground for a big cat. I stepped back slowly to see what move the animal was going to make. It kept a slow, steady trot in my direction. The eyes were unwavering. My senses skyrocketed from drunken dull to just shy of outright panic. In a moment that sealed up the most embarrassing thing I did on the trip, I stepped forward one step, aggressively and simultaneously clapping my hands together, and yelled, "Get outta here!" toward the eyes. It was purely an instinctual move. Just then, the creature got close enough for me to see what it was, and the silhouettes of the folks who were walking their large dog came into view about twenty feet behind it. They had the dog on a retractable leash that was fully unreeled. They mumbled something sharply under their breath (probably about cutting off alcohol sales at the campground store) and yanked their dog away from my campsite. In that moment, my brother would have said, "You're cool."

A while passed before I let myself get over my stupidity. I stopped drinking to keep my senses alert. The stars patiently waited for me to rejoin the show. Never in my life had I seen a night sky twinkling so dense and clear. For hours, I gazed at our galaxy wondering just what is out there.

I'd learn later in the trip that my fears of a mountain lion attack weren't as far-fetched as some had predicted. Just weeks after camping at Chisos Basin, a six-year-old boy was ripped from his mother's grip by a mountain lion. The cat had the boy's face in its mouth. The boy's father chased down the cat as it could not escape quickly enough carrying the child. The father pounced on the mountain lion and stabbed it repeatedly with his pocketknife until it loosened its grip and fled. The family was hiking in a group of three with two strong adults on the easiest and nearest trail to the village, the Window Trail. I walked alone on the Window Trail on my first visit to the basin without thinking for a second that the lions would be so brazen around higher concentrations of people.

Day 64 – December 16, 2011

The stars' light dissipated upon arrival of the sun's first rays. I eagerly crawled out of my tent to meet Chisos Basin in the morning. The priceless view that I was expecting was there but had been one-upped by a familiar morning phenomenon. When I turned to my rear, fog was cascading down the peaks of the Chisos like an ancient river of cool white lava. It was moving swiftly and stayed tight to the mountains like it was partially adhered to them. It hugged the peaks the same way that water droplets stick to the side of a cup as they slide toward the bottom. I hadn't seen it so forceful since that evening on North Carolina's Mt. Pisgah. I stared quietly for a minute. Then the light bulb went off! I ran for the camera. I had to record its ghostly avalanche.

Camera in hand, I turned it on, and nothing. I knew for sure that the battery wasn't dead because I just charged it. This was just another one of the latest tricks learned by my little electronic frenemy. I'm not sure where he had learned to play possum, but he had it down. No matter what I tried, I received no response. I plugged the charger in, cleaned everything, took the battery out and reinstalled it, but still nada. The fog was fading fast, and I was cursing up a storm.

Plan B kicked in, and just before the fog faded away, I whipped out the cell phone and desperately snapped a few low-quality pictures. My day was doomed to be a cell-phone-picture-only day. *Shit! And double shit!* I had planned to ride west along River Road 170 to Presidio, Texas. I was told about that stretch of road and how it had recently been named one of America's best motorcycling roads by some popular motorcycle magazine.

My panic attack subsided while I was therapeutically packing up camp. I headed for breakfast at the basin restaurant. As I parked the Goose, a crowd formed on the sidewalk behind two rangers. Everyone was staring at a little black bear that just stole a bag of trash and darted for the bushes. I hurried over to get a glimpse myself, but the clever little scavenger had already disappeared. As he sifted through his bounty, we could hear plastic and cans crunching just out of sight. I seemed to be the only one who found the bear's antics amusing. *It's not every day that an animal pulls a fast one on the intelligent two-leggers that try to control the whole damn world.* After a couple of minutes lurking outside, waiting for him to come back for seconds, I gave up and went in to fill the gastro tank.

I was getting' the better of a plate of biscuits and gravy when the juvenile black bear walked around the restaurant and onto a hill in front of the lookout windows. Everyone sitting down for breakfast had a chance to see it before they left. He must have found enough grub in that trash bag to give him a pre-hibernation warm up nap. When I finished eating and took off for the Goose, the bear was still there and fast asleep.

The last great moments passed in Big Bend. It was a surprisingly awesome national park, but it was time to go. I left the basin and headed west past Terlingua. The roads became paved strangers again. Sixty-three miles separate Terlingua from Presidio. All but the first thirteen miles tightly hug the Rio Grande, giving a view of the border the whole way. As the Rio Grande came into sight again, so did a sign for Big Bend Ranch State Park. I had found Big Bend's little brother. Like the national park, Big Bend Ranch State Park encompassed an enormous helping of land in southwest Texas. From one end to the other, it's a solid forty-five miles of remote wilderness. The park has one peak over a mile high in its northwestern neck but comes up just shy of the real Big Bend in most other ways. As I rode through, I understood why that land had also earned protected status.

Whoever designated Route 170 as a great motorcycle road hit the nail on the head. I squeezed through tight mountain passes with cliffs hundreds of feet above the water. From up high, long stretches of lonely two-lane raced into the distance, teasing me with views of the curves ahead. That pattern of high climbs along the river, distant views of the road ahead, and lonely unmanned stretches repeated over and over. In sixty-three miles I only passed four cars, and two of them were white and green border patrol SUVs being relocated to an elevated point to keep an eye on the folks south of the border.

The Rio Grande performed a synchronized dance with Route 170 as it snaked through the desert moonscape. It's a lifesaving oasis for all nearby in-habitants. The green vegetation along its banks strongly contrasts the brown shades of the background. I longed for a good camera.

To be honest, the Mexican side of the river was twice as dramatic. Our side looked like a massive rock quarry most of the time, while the Mexican side flaunted endless mountain ridges. *What Mexico lacks in refined national conveniences is surely made up in its beauty.* I passed through Lajitas and Redford, Texas. Both were quite scrappy-looking and were matched by hungrier-looking settlements across the river. I imagined their Mexican counterparts as being the large, relent-less eyes of an owl, waiting for any lapse in vigilance to send groups splashing across the border. Personally, I don't have a problem with that. *Why is it such a big deal to share resources in a region so incredibly remote?*

Why the world isn't at peace and feels the need to build fences to lock out others—or lock in others—is beyond me. Here's my chance to say, "If I were in charge . . ." Well, if I were in charge, I'd set up a program where youths from all nations spend some of their childhood traveling the world to meet with youths of other nations. This introduction while the mind is young, open, and absor-bent would give the young people a first impression that would last a lifetime. That first impression would be "Hey, you're just like me." The time for children to develop nasty ol' traits like racism would be at least somewhat stifled, and they would stand the chance of comprehending their role in the larger picture. Closed minds are no better than infected wounds. Words like *them*, *they*, and *those* would no longer be used in finger pointing contexts.

When these children—the enlightened generation—reached adulthood, they'd carry with them the knowledge learned in youth that even though people may seem different, they still seek the same basic things: food, water, shelter, and healthy social relationships. They would become great leaders. And where would the money come from for this educational travel? In my perfect world, it would come from defense budgets, since childhood friends would not find it pleasing to bomb the pants off of one another. As I close this rant about being in charge, I'll say that I still appreciate and participate in activities like camping, fishing, hiking, and visiting the zoo because well-meaning adults introduced me to them as a boy when my mind was young, open, and absorbent. They are so deeply engrained in my psyche that I will always love these things as if I don't have a say in it. Breathe in . . . Breathe out . . . Back to the road. . . .

The ride along the Rio Grande ended in Presidio, Texas, where I fueled up at a pump that dispensed eighty-six octane, lowest I'd ever seen. I looked around, scratched my head, finished pumping, and took a hard right north, toward Marfa, Texas. Heavy grey clouds choked the sky and the mercury plummeted. About ten miles out of Presidio, I had to put my winter gloves on. Mountains gave way to an empty terrain full of yellow grass, cacti, and scraggly bushes. One ranch followed the next on either side of the road. In the fifty-nine-mile ride to Marfa only two things grabbed my attention. One was a large bighorn sheep that eluded a picture, and the other was Shafter Ghost Town.

I pulled over near the full skeleton of a deer. Stone ruins gobbled up most of the town. An eerie white church sat cleanly among shacks and mobile homes. A lone white cross overlooked the town from a nearby hill. I didn't bother riding through. Night was approaching, and I was reminded of that damn movie *The Hills Have Eyes*. I didn't want to show up at supper time and be the main course. Ya know what I mean?

Marfa, on the other hand, is quite the town. The 1956 movie *Giant*, starring Elizabeth Taylor and James Dean, was filmed there. The town also holds a claim to fame for being the home of a strange light phenomenon called the Marfa Lights. My mission for the arctic evening was to see the mysterious lights for myself. I found a room east of town at the Riata Inn. The Marfa Lights were eight miles east of that.

Nervously, I piled on clothes and gear and headed out to the middle of nowhere in complete darkness. The ride was endured rather than enjoyed. A fierce biting wind added to the already ridiculously low temperature. I pulled into a parking area alone against what looked like a round spaceship with red tracking lights. I was at the Marfa Lights observation building. I slowly walked into the open round structure. Everything except the orbs of light coming from the red bulbs was pitch black. My mind raced as I imagined some grotesque creature climbing over the rail in front of me. *I'd never see it coming.* The mysterious lights, the black angry night, and the odd building gave me the creeps. I was there to experience something interesting but couldn't keep focused on the task at hand.

I eventually calmed. I stood with a wall to my back and darkness in front of me, with one glove over my face to block the wind. In the distance I noticed one steady white light, a blinking red light, and four orang-ish lights that I thought belonged to a town. I remained still for half an hour waiting for something wild to happen, freezing my hind end off the whole time. A car pulled in beside my bike. A family hopped out and took a position beside me. They were native Marfans and filled me in on what was going on.

The Marfa Lights were the little orange lights way off in the distance that I'd been ignoring for the past half hour. Once I learned that, I gave them my full attention. They did disappear and reappear. They did seem to flicker. They did not move side to side, or up and down, or go shooting off into the distance, as claimed on the web. They looked like gas lanterns burning from miles away. I left feeling let down by the tiny, tiny lights in the black distance.

Back at the room, I read a few articles that leaned toward the lights being car headlights on Route 67 N—the road I took to Marfa. I could see that as plausible, but the kicker about the lights was that they were first documented by a cowboy in 1883, way before cars were in the area. The mystery continues. . . .

Day 65 – December 17, 2011

I awoke in a room with two beds, with one bed ripped about like it had been used as a trampoline and the other eternally untouched like a nun had lightly napped on it. I headed to the office for a small cup of motivation. The coffee pot was empty. In a joking, not really joking manner I made light of their clear glass pot holding nothing but air. The front desk clerk got the hint. For what I paid for the room, coffee in bed should have been mandatory.

The morning was cold and the clouds hung grey and flat. I began packing. Before I threw the camcorder in its spot, I pressed the power button to turn it on. Voila, it worked flawlessly. Marfa's mysterious lights must have had an effect on it. I raised my eyes and sighed, "Sometimes electronics just blow my mind." I may never know the reason why the camera took a day off, but inside I was happy to have it back. That meant that as I left Marfa and headed to the New Mexico border, my shots would be up to snuff. All of my cell phone pics turned out grainy and dull. On adventures of this sort, your equipment becomes less metal and plastic parts and more like a companion that you pray will be reliable. The Goose's ability to start every morning without a piston pumping hiccup is exactly what I'm talking about. I love that damn bike.

The plan for the day was a 195-mile dash north to the border that would get me out of Texas. There is nothing wrong with the giant state. I just wanted the feeling of someplace new. I arrived here on day forty-one and lived as a resident for twenty-four glorious days. The people I met in the Lone Star State were top-notch all the way. Lockhart's BBQ will make my mouth water for years to come, and the scene at the drinking holes tempted me to relocate permanently. I had nothing but the best time here. With pros there are cons. The only thing even remotely dissatisfying was the dreary weather. I was starting to forget what beautiful blue skies looked like.

Thirty-five miles north of Marfa sits the world's fifth largest telescope at the McDonald Observatory. Now, I'm no more qualified to investigate a place where superior intelligence sifts through the skies than a bullfrog, but back home, I have a wonderful friend named Justin who knows about these sorts of things. He is a grad student who will become a full-fledged astrophysicist later in life. He was the physics student of the year at West Virginia University and works on obscure projects involving gravitational waves. Recently, he wrote a paper involving said gravitational waves that, to me, looks like it's written in Mandarin. He's a fascinating individual whose life is beginning to take off like a rocket as he travels abroad frequently to discuss things that only people with perfectly designed thinkers discuss.

You may be developing a picture of Justin where pocket protectors, thick-ringed glasses, and socks up to his butt crack make up his appearance. That's quite the opposite of my buddy. He is fit, acne free, of average height, has a great head of hair, and best of all, has raced motocross and was good at it—I'm so damn proud of him. He may be just as well-rounded as Igor, but I'm not going to play favorites. I wanted to pay homage to Justin by visiting the observatory even if it meant holding a blank stare and nodding in agreement for extended periods of time.

To get there, I took 118 N through Davis Mountains State Park. Marfa's flatness took a hike as I climbed and climbed. Gently sloping mountains, clean earthy air, and fresh turns had me cheesing like a fourteen-year-old boy in a topless moon bounce. If not for a terrain of wandering pastures full of green shrubs that looked like tumbleweed before it tumbles and dry grass the consistency of long blonde hair, I could have sworn that I was in the Appalachians. The mountains were smooth and round and the grass grew right up the side of them, gracing the tops like a scalp full of hair. If it wasn't paved or owned by a hearty little bush, the land found a way to make the grass thrive. I wouldn't have been surprised to step off of the bike to take a leak and find a few pieces sprouting from my pant leg. It was a landscape fit for a comb and it was beautiful.

I hung a right at the last minute when I saw the observatory's entrance sign. I was now in blinding fog. Black Mountain at 7,544 feet and Casket Mountain at 6,183 feet loomed somewhere nearby. The telescope's high-altitude location strategically helped to ward off light pollution. I pulled up to a barely visible, domed building. Only the front doors and edges of the structure were dark enough to be seen from the parking lot. The door to the display area was open and no one was around. I walked in cautiously, wondering if I was supposed to be there. *Who leaves a building with technology this expensive unmanned?* Then I chalked it up to me being a nitwit. No person with half a brain cell would come here on a day of zero visibility. But that's just how it worked sometimes while riding around with no particular plan. Today, I just got the shit end of the stick.

Inside, the business end of the telescope was visible through a glass wall. I could see a moving platform, concave in shape, with mirrored plates attached. The plates worked in unison to collect light from far-off objects and just like a camera, the size of the lens (or mirrors in this case) dictated the amount of collectible light. The telescope was joined in the room by every sort of electronic widget, mechanical doohickey, expensive gadget, and scientific thingamajig that's required to translate the information from the collected light.

Justin probably would have been able to spin the thing in circles while measuring how much light was coming off the far side of Uranus, but me, I was left impressed by something in the bathroom. To my surprise, the bathroom was designed so that the exhaust fan was mounted level with the toilet seat, on the adjacent wall, just a foot away, instead of on the ceiling overhead—so efficient. *Who would've thunk it? Only smart people.*

The next leg of the day would take me to Interstates 10 E, 20 E to Pecos, and then to Route 285 N into New Mexico. As I rode north, Texas turned desolate, boring, uninhabited, and uninspiring. Big Bend's remoteness fools visitors with its three stores, post office, upscale restaurant, and abundant Wi-Fi. In the region of Texas surrounding Pecos, the land looked completely useless for great distances, like it had been cracked and sterilized by the sun.

Wretched and isolated towns teetered on the edge of becoming ghost towns. I rode by a small Texan town on I-20 called Toyah and couldn't take my eyes off it. Everything that makes a town, a town, was there. The problem was that it looked pitiful, dilapidated, and empty. I could see that the high school was boarded up and most of the houses had their windows broken out. Passing by, no signs of movement could be found. Toyah honestly looked perfect for the set of a horror movie. Riding on, thoughts of hardships that those folks must have endured to turn a town into a complete failure filled my mind.

In Pecos, home of the world's very first rodeo, I stopped at Subway for lunch. The town reeked of dullness. *I don't blame the folks who attempted to break their necks riding pissed off livestock.* In a land of so little to do, flinging yourself off of a horse or pissed off bull probably sounded like a good idea back then. Hiking or camping near a pretty lake for recreation just wasn't an option around there. So on I rode.

On 285 North from Pecos, I put the hammer down as the land lacked features of any kind. The terrain had absolutely nothing going on unless it involved oil fields. The big pumping rigs that look like masons' hammers pecking at the ground stole the show. Some were in use, and some were rusting away like iron tombstones in oily graveyards. *What a drab, brown, uninviting piece of earth.* Seventy-five mph was the posted speed limit, and I kept the Goose at a steady ninety-five. Despite the higher speed, the lack of relative objects nearby made my rate of travel feel sluggish. The slow feeling worsened as I cranked it up to 130 mph and back down to ninety-five. At one point, I counted a ninety-four-car train and could easily see every single car. Back home, the only way to see a train with ninety-four cars, all at once, was to get a view from some sort of aircraft.

Sure enough, Texas couldn't last forever. The border of New Mexico appeared on the horizon. I did the usual touristy thing and stopped for some pictures at the state line. I was greeted by a small green New Mexico sign with a sticker on it that read, "Don't mess with Texas." Man, I was brought to tears laughing. To me, Texas was like the big independent bully of the lower forty-eight; that sticker on the New Mexico sign was the equivalent of Texas marking its territory, much like a dog peeing on a fire hydrant.

It felt good to be somewhere new, and I looked forward to my New Mexican adventures. Thirty-three miles later, I found a really crummy room in Carlsbad, New Mexico. What a day! *(Whisper – still better than the office)*

Before bed I just had to find out why Toyah, Texas, was in such a state of despair. Tragedy struck in 2004 when a flood came through that area, destroying most of the homes. For years, the residents have fought seasonal tornadoes, and one of their biggest companies moved from town, taking with it a large number of jobs. In its heyday, Toyah was home to a few thousand. Now the number is unknown. The only info I could find on the population was from the 2000 census which stated one hundred residents. In 2011, I bet there weren't any more than forty survivors still there, barely hanging on.

Day 66 – December 18, 2011

I started my day out in a cave. Through sleepy eyes and on a bed with blankets no better than a pile of leaves, I looked around my room at the Caverns Inn of Carlsbad. The walls were textured with rough humps projecting nearly a half inch out like a bad concrete job. One of the walls was painted black from the smelly carpet to the low ceiling. The other walls were the color of stained drop ceiling panels. Lighting was up to nineteen-century standards. Throwing the curtains open to spunk up the room did nothing. The black wall yawned, as it seemed to say, "This room will look horrible no matter what you try."

Outside, the motel was veneered with every color of stone man has ever unearthed as if the masons installed it after eating a baggie full of magic mushrooms. Light green trim, so ugly that it looked like it had been on the bottom shelf of a clearance rack for fifteen years, adorned the windows and doors. Still, I've lived in places that would rival the Caverns Inn Motel. I didn't waste any time packing and getting the hell outta there.

Eighteen miles southwest of Carlsbad is Carlsbad Caverns National Park. I passed through a large area of the park that had recently suffered a wildfire. Trees were nothing more than coal black stumps, and mustard yellow cacti were sadly wilted over from the heat without looking burnt, like fire-retardant rubber pancakes. Fortunately, the fire didn't make it to the visitor center. It was a long and low building, desert tan in color with a flat, unobtrusive roofline.

I walked in, eager to find out how to enter the caverns. A small line was formed to my right. I hopped in and waited my turn. A young female ranger greeted me, smiling. As she was swiping my debit card, she asked if I had ever been in any other cavern. And she asked, "If so, how recently?" I spoke up proudly like a man with experience, standing straight and confident. I said, "I've been spelunking before, if that's what you're asking." I threw the politically correct word for cave exploring in there to leave no doubt that in front of her was a man who knew what he was talking about. A man who could hold his own if the park rangers needed a helping hand.

Then she hit me with, "Good. We need to know that because people who have been in other caverns stand the chance of spreading a serious fungal infection to Carlsbad Cavern's bats called white nose syndrome." I rounded my back as she questioned where and when I'd last been in a cave. I had to give in. I really wasn't all that experienced, and it had been a couple years since I set foot in a cave. She sternly listened as I told her that I'd been in Virginia's Luray Caverns and only a couple unknown cracks in the mountain along the C&O Canal, back home. She informed me that the spores could lay dormant for up to two years on clothing and that I needed to get my story straight. In all honesty, I told her that it had easily been longer than two years. She smiled, knowing that I had come clean, and handed me a ticket.

Carlsbad Caverns were formed millions of years ago as acidic water encountered weak stone and drained away, leaving huge, mostly dry, pockets of underground emptiness in the Guadalupe Mountains. These days, most of the cavern's activity comes from dripping water that seeps its way through the ground from springs in the mountains or rare rainstorms. Steady, painfully slow drips of mineral-rich water have created features in the caverns called stalactites and stalagmites. Stalactites are the formations that hang, or grow, from the roof of a cavern and, in most cases, are icicle-shaped. Some stalactites come out looking like drapes hanging from a window. Stalagmites are the opposite. They grow up from the floor and are the culmination of what's left after a drop of water hits the floor and evaporates, leaving the minerals to accumulate. Many times these rise up as thick formations, resembling ice cream scoops, stacked tall and round.

Anticipation was rising as I ventured to the mouth of the underworld. Caverns, per square foot, are the most fantastic places on the planet. Thick forests of pointed features poke and prod at the air space inside. I've found that sensory overload is easily reached within minutes of hiking through larger caverns.

Just before descending into the darkness, a park ranger gave me a quick safety orientation. She said the hike down may be hard on the knees. Hiking into Carlsbad Caverns is equivalent to taking the stairs down an eighty-story building, not an easy feat.

The cavern's massive entrance hole was breathtaking. I expected to climb through a crack or follow a creek-wide path in, but you could've flown a helicopter into this thing. A paved path weaved its way down into the blackness. That path would descend to the cavern floor where it meandered ever so gradually into more intriguing underground rooms. A section called the Big Room, which is the Western Hemisphere's largest natural underground opening, is comparable to fourteen football fields and has nearly 600,000 square feet of floor space. We're not talking flat floor space. We're talking fantasy floor space. Things that look like alligator teeth hang ominously just off the path. An area called fairy tale land is packed with waist-high stalagmites and resembles an enchanted city where you might see elves darting around in between the thick, rounded points.

Virginia's Luray Caverns, which are impressive and potentially more colorful, are splendid, but as it goes in the West, this place dwarfed its eastern counterpart. Although every color in the spectrum is represented in Carlsbad Caverns, most of the features share some shade of brown just like the desert above.

I wandered for nearly three miles in the land of no sun before taking an elevator 750 feet straight up to the surface. *What an amazing experience.* After reviewing the pictures, it became clear that I needed a better camera for parts of the trip that were going to be dark or dimly lit. Roughly ten out of my 146 pictures turned out with any sort of clarity.

Due to leaving the caverns late, Roswell was still obtainable, but my hope to mingle with aliens would have to wait until tomorrow. I finished my visit to Carlsbad at its local Radio Shack. I wanted to scope out their selection of cameras, before leaving for Roswell. My Samsung camcorder would film in high definition, but its photo capabilities were limited to five mega pixels, plus it had a tiny lens. I was carrying a Radio Shack credit card and knew if I bought a new camera it wouldn't kill the budget. They had a Canon Rebel T2i in stock that I really wanted, but I decided to do some research on the camera and sleep on it before spending the loot. After all, I thought I could pick one up at the Radio Shack in Roswell the next day.

I arrived in the odd town of Roswell around 4:30pm and found a place called the Trailer Village RV Park. For $10, only motorcycle riders were allowed the convenience of pitching a tent. All others entering the park had to have an RV. Across the street from the campground, a cream-colored sign announced, "Welcome to ROSWELL Dairy Capital of the Southwest." *Wait a minute. How can a place that's world famous for an alleged extraterrestrial crash not even hint at that on its welcoming sign?* My quick ride through had already shown a glimpse of an alien-crazed tourist town. Then again, denial goes hand in hand with the whole incident, doesn't it?

After setting up camp, night was in full swing. I rode to town to check out Radio Shack's cameras, and was disappointed when I discovered that Roswell's larger Radio Shack only stocked tiny digital cameras, like the ones that were popular before smart phones ruled the world. An employee said, "Wal-Mart carries it," referring to the T2i, but that was out of the question. Buying a new camera with cash would've severely injured the budget. Feeling let down, I coasted back to the tent and bundled up for a long cold night.

Day 67 – December 19, 2011

"Damn it's cold," I complained, while fortified in the coziness of the sleeping bag. My face was the only thing exposed as I smiled at the thought of the bath house a hundred feet away. It was heated and had hot showers. My brain gave my reluctant body a pep talk and the signal to loco mote. I made a mad dash for the showers.

All refreshed, hygienically ready for public encounters, and slightly warmer, it was time for an insane man's mission. I had thought about it all night and had to have that Canon Rebel T2i. The nearest one I could purchase with credit was in Carlsbad's Radio Shack. The weather wasn't on my side. The forecast called for dropping temperatures, rain, and snow all day. I knew that I'd only have a few-hour window in the morning to make it seventy-five miles south to Carlsbad and back. What sucked was that I had that puppy in my hands yesterday.

Sunshine lingered just long enough for us to have a sunrise before thick clouds with dark grey interiors showed up like an advancing army of strife. Temperatures were at thirty-four degrees and the weather was as nice as it was going to get. I etched a "ROSWELL NM" into the frost covered rear trunk with my finger and gave the Goose a pep talk. I threw a leg over my durable wheeled-horse and twisted the throttle heavy handedly. The Goose and I were on Route 285 again, heading seventy-five miles south, back to Carlsbad. We were hauling ass and burning gas!

I made sure that I got there just before the store opened up so no one could sneak in and purchase that bad boy before me. Murphy's Law states, "Anything that can go wrong will go wrong," so I wasn't going to take any chances. I have been screwed by Murphy so many times while taking something for granted that I'm now a devout believer in the law. With new camera in hand, I quickly raced back to Roswell. The storm in the distance was my competitor. I won, temporarily. . . .

   I was pulling out of the campground for a long overdue day of alien touring when I felt the dreaded loose feel in the rear of the bike. A quick look to the left rear, with my torso hanging over the side of the bike, confirmed that I'd earned a flat rear tire. This lovely little feature sported not one, but two punctures at once. Somewhere in my morning's scrambles, I must have run over an old utility knife. Two pieces of razor blade, from the kind of blade that's segmented so that you can break a short section off to reveal a new sharp point, was what I pulled out of the tire. I was glad to have made it back to Roswell before that sucker went flat. Erin, a man of seven or eight years my elder—the campground owner, and motorcycle guy—hooked me up with some compressed air after I plugged the holes.
   While we were manning the equipment, I lightly asked him to share his thoughts on Roswell's extraterrestrial connection. He wasn't certain exactly what happened, although he did speak enthusiastically about the event. He told me of a friend, an old ranch hand who lived nearby. His ranch hand buddy had told Erin that while riding and working on the piece of land where the supposed crash happened, his horses act up like there's something wrong with them. "The horses don't want to be there," he said. I found that interesting and so did Erin.
   Because no one seems to know for sure what happened, I choose to carry the opinion that in 1947 something special happened in Roswell. Call it naïve, or call it an uneducated opinion, I don't care. Who can prove it right or wrong? It's a back and forth issue that will linger for generations. I'll cross my fingers

hoping for indisputable evidence to surface one day. In the meantime, Erin will remain undecided as his buddy will continue to unquestionably believe. I thanked Erin for the help and rode to town to engage in all things alien.

I went straight to the source, the UFO Museum and Research Center. It is the thing to see if you come to Roswell. An elderly gentleman was collecting the $5 entry fee when I looked outside and noticed that the rain/snow mix had arrived. *No worries.* The tent was only a mile and a half away, and if I could ride 150 miles to get a camera in freezing weather, then I could handle a mile and a half in the slippery stuff. I moseyed along, into a light grey room full of out-of-this-world information. Entertaining exhibits featuring life-sized extraterrestrials stirred the imagination. Some of them looked like aliens that were killed and processed by a taxidermist rather than small inanimate mannequins. Countless pages of eyewitness testimonies were pasted to walls covered in pegboard. Most of them were accounts from retired military personnel.

I particularly enjoyed reading the statements that came from the locals when the word first got around, as the town stirred from the news. Their accounts gave simple and blunt impressions. Actions taken by the local police station and federal government were posted for anyone to sift through. To read it all would have taken a week. The Canon was pulling off incredibly clear pictures that my camcorder would've left grainy in the low lit interior. All was right in the world, or worlds, again. I walked out enlightened, with my passion for *wanting to believe* elevated.

From there, I used the wet sidewalk to bounce around from gift shop to gift shop. I was searching for a perfect sticker for the Goose. Businesses shamelessly played the alien card by decorating their storefronts with all things little green men. On one sidewalk, neon green humanoid footprints were painted right down the center. Murals showing space scenes occupied building walls. Extraterrestrials playing guitars, smiling and drinking Coke were everywhere—always watching with those hollow black eyes the size of sunglasses. I ducked into a store and purchased a bright green alien sticker and rode back to camp.

Chilly drops of rain limited my desire to be out and about on the bike. I decided to write up a post while the universal high was still lingering inside. From the campground's heated laundry room, I could latch onto a Wi-Fi connection. For the next hour and a half, I played my keyboard like a piano, writing like the wind. Then Murphy showed up. Unknowingly, I was kicked off of the campground's Internet connection from running over my allotted time limit. I had fifty-three pictures uploaded and a whole post written when I hit Wordpress.com's publish button. When my laptop's screen changed, I was slapped square in the eyeballs by that bright white, evil page that informs you that you are not connected to the Internet. Only eleven pictures and the first couple hundred words were saved. *Son da bitchin' bastards!* Defeated, I limped back to the tent and cocooned in the sleeping bag, bracing for a long, bitterly cold night.

Day 68 – December 20, 2011

Overnight, I had to pull what I'm calling the groundhog maneuver. It's accomplished by crawling all the way into the sleeping bag and pulling the drawstring tight, disappearing to the world like a groundhog in its den. Once I did that, I was nice and warm; however, claustrophobia would soon take over and I would have to let a bit of air enter to stave off a false suffocation. Repeat that cycle for a few hours, add a flat air mattress to the equation, and you end up with little more than a power nap.

I might have squeaked out four hours of sleep, tops. I was glad to see the sunshine when it hovered over the farmer's field next door. That meant that I could just go ahead and get the day started and forget about trying to get comfortable enough to fall asleep.

First, I was after coffee's promise of warmth and inspiration, and second, I needed to overcome the woes from the Internet issues faced last night. Not wanting to lose another bout with the campground's Internet, I decided to go to the place with the most reliable Internet known to man, McDonald's. I thought I'd get there, upload those pictures again, and write up a post in no time. I set about surfing around the home keys while stuffing fattening morsels from my deluxe breakfast into my largest head cavity.

I rewrote over 1,400 words of which I remembered from the previous day's attempt, and then, as they say, shit happened. Something went haywire with McDonald's Internet connection. I knew better than to close out of my work or change to another screen, so I closed my laptop knowing that the next time I opened it up, my work would be right there. I headed back to the campground, irritated but determined to finish what I started. *At least I have the typing part finished. Now all I have to do is upload the pictures again.*

At camp, I unfolded the laptop, linked to the Internet, logged in, and discovered that the post that I wrote was less than halfway saved. "Son of a bitch," I projected! To my dismay, Wordpress.com's autosave feature stopped saving my draft at 600 words. Again, son of a bitch! I was ready to slam the laptop on the ground like only a redhead can do when he's pissed off. Plus, I was reaching my tech edge for understanding what the hell I was doing, and why I kept losing the work. Not only would I have to remember and retype the 800 words it didn't save, but I still had to take an hour and a half to upload the pictures I wanted to use. Again, son of a bitch!

I was putting everything I had into recording the trip the best I could, and to have computer gremlins holding me up was nightmarish. Swimming in a shark tank with chum sacks tied around my waste would have been more pleasant. Eventually—sleep deprived and teetering on my last nerve—I took a couple deep breaths, put my nose to the grindstone, and finished what I started. In all, it took about five hours to do one short bit of writing. It pays to be hard headed.

Now I could move on with my life. I had some errands to run that would take me away from the older, alien-inspired section of Roswell to the side of town teeming with department stores, fast-food joints, and hotels. I needed to knock out Christmas shopping for the family and take a few minutes to go through all my gear and decide what to send home with the Christmas gifts. I'd been carrying a pair of toe shoes, riding boots, and a pair of regular shoes. I never wore the regular shoes, so they were the first things go. The air mattress was next. That thing had one patch in it already and after several attempts, I couldn't find this new leak. I had collected some brochures, notes, and maps that I wouldn't need for the rest of the trip, so they made the list of things going home. Finally, two cameras were sent home as well. One was an unused Sony Handycam, and the other was the shivering Samsung camcorder. Since I just bought the new Canon, those were rendered obsolete by both filming capabilities and picture quality. I found the local UPS store and shipped it all back to West, by God, Virginia. I couldn't wait for my family to get their gifts.

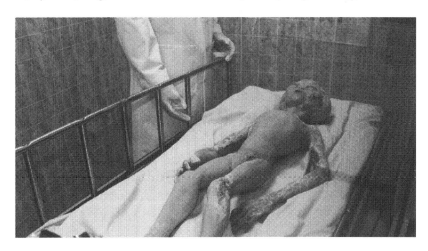

A whole day was pretty much in the books and night was falling. I rode to Roswell's Wal-Mart. There, the store's entrance windows and automatic doors were teaming with paintings of little green men. I thought of the Welcome to Roswell sign again and how it left out even the slightest hint of the theme that runs rampant in town. I went in expecting to find everything I needed. To replace my air mattress, I went with a thin blue camping pad. The trade-off saved about two pounds. I also bought a few more butane canisters for cooking and some bread for PB& J's.

Wal-Mart's painted windows sparked a quick ride around the more commercial side of town. I wanted to get a feel for which companies were advertising with aliens, while practicing night shots with the new Canon. Arby's, Comfort Suites, and McDonald's were just the tip of the iceberg of companies who adopted out-of-this-world advertising help. The town of Roswell even outfitted its streetlights with green glass globes featuring black painted eyes. I loved the spirit of the townspeople for going the extra mile to promote a bit of enjoyment. Now if we can only get them to change their damn welcome sign. I headed back to camp, cooked up some noodles, and ended my day with another groundhog maneuver.

Day 69 – December 21, 2011

I woke refreshed with a solid three hours of sleep. I really liked my new camping pad, but it could've used a little help from, say, another pad or a thick blanket. I weighed the pros and cons of each as if they were life-changing decisions.

A blanket would allow me to unzip the sleeping bag and spread out quite a bit more, but it would take up a good chunk of space on the bike. An extra pad would make lying on the ground more comfortable, but I'd have to continue to be crammed into the tightness of the sleeping bag. The sleeping bag hindered comfort by limiting adjustment for different positions. I like being able to spread my arms and legs out like I'm playing a game of flat Twister by myself when I sleep. On really cold nights, I'd find myself cursing with the tongue of a pirate as I stretched, strained, and shuffled for extra bits of room in the sleeping bag. I must have looked like a giant, wriggling, ticked off, red grub. So, what was it going to be, an extra pad or blanket? Decisions, decisions . . . Before I sold my house, I had to make decisions like buy food or keep the lights on. Now life was so simple and wonderful.

Two other convenient occurrences contributed to a not-so-good night's rest. I'm not sure if every Tuesday night in Roswell is locomotive night or not, but that's surely how it played out. For hours, in the early a.m. darkness, train after bleeping train would roll into town and honk the horn four times in this pattern: two regular honks followed by a third short honk, which was followed by the fantastic four-second honk. All of the engineers driving those trains must have had extensive on-the-job training to get the pattern perfect every time. I credited them for at least being consistent.

The second piece of the lack of sleep puzzle was the rooster that brought me out of my nighttime nap at 5:38am. It just wasn't my night. Oh yeah, did I mention it was cold? Well, it was the coldest night of camping on the trip thus far, colder than Luckenbach's twenty-one degrees.

On the bright side, the heated bathhouse was a hundred feet away. I made a beeline for the warm water and came out feeling nice and peppy. I walked into town to grab a coffee. Roswell was waking peacefully at sunrise. Cattle grazed in perfect light on ice-glazed blades of grass. Cars puttered by slowly with steaming clouds of condensation coming out of their tailpipes. Some windshields only had half the frost scraped off. It was anywhere America at 6:30am. Outside of downtown, Roswell felt really homey and normal. I walked back to camp past mud puddles with water trapped by brittle sheets of ice. I liked it there.

Soon, the twenty-four ounces of coffee had me wired. I was on the move, packing, organizing, cleaning up camp, and jamming out to some Motley Crew on my cell phone, all but hair thrashing. Before I got totally packed up, two of my fellow campground mates from British Columbia, Aaron and Linda, came over and we had a great morning chat about travel and blogging. They were down south for the winter on an annual sweep through the states and keeping a daily virtual journal similar to mine. I asked for advice on the BC region of Canada if I happened to make it there. They happily filled me in on anything from the best time of year to visit to handling grizzly bear encounters. They strongly suggested finding a walled place to stay each evening, as tent camping could lead to becoming an hors d'oeuvre. We exchanged info and bid farewell. I was ready to put the newfound familiarity of Roswell behind me. Days later, I found out that Linda and Aaron were stuck at the RV park in a snowstorm that I barely missed.

Not more than a couple of miles out of town, I saw it, a miracle in my small life. It was my first big mountain ever! Capitan Peak, at 10,083 feet, was on the right of the horizon, but the 12,003-foot summit of Sierra Blanca could be seen straight ahead, from seventy miles away. Hell Yeah! Finally! This had been a lifelong dream. I had never seen a mountain capped in snow with a base of uncovered vegetation. In my part of the world, if the top of the mountain is white, so is the bottom. The Appalachians are seldom tall enough to experience drastic differences in atmospheric conditions from their bases to their peaks. Big Bend's mountains and the Sierra del Carmens of Mexico broke many personal records, but these two peaks had them topped by nearly double. I rode straight for them.

One short pit stop in Billy the Kid's territory and I'd soon be at the foothills of those perfect giants. Linda and Aaron recommended that I detour through Lincoln, New Mexico. They had checked it out on their way to Roswell. Lincoln is a tiny western town in the thinly forested high desert of south central New Mexico, and it's where it all went down for some of history's more notorious Wild West legends like Billy the Kid and his band of Regulators, and Pat Garrett and his fellow lawmen. In Lincoln, five separate buildings make up the official museum. I saw everything in Lincoln as a sort of museum. One could start walking on one end of town, visit all the museums along the way, grab a drink and a bite to eat, and continue traveling with daylight hours to spare. It's that small.

The old courthouse was the most interesting exhibit for me. A bullet hole in the plaster from Billy the Kid's six-shooter is protected by a piece of Plexiglas. From a window on the second floor, I saw a square headstone that said,

"J.W. Bell DIED HERE Killed by Billy the Kid April 28, 1881." Unlike some of the other museums, it had been kept authentic. Unstable wood floors were partially covered by plywood subfloor. Plaster that has been chipped and stained has been left that way, and the ceilings were warped slats of wood in most rooms. All of the town's museums together told a great story of a time that won't soon be forgotten. I am a bit ashamed to say that I went there not knowing a darn thing about who Billy the Kid was (of course I'd heard the name), or what he did to become so infamous. I left with a decent understanding and was thankful that my BC buddies recommended it, and that Billy wasn't still roaming around looking for a fight.

Roads in and around Lincoln, New Mexico, are lined with gorgeous scenery that will make everything above your shoulders swivel back and forth until you get nauseous. The same blonde grass that I saw in Texas's Davis Mountains grew here. Small ridges with snowy hats lined either side of the road. The country felt big, open, and wild. I couldn't drive a mile without stopping and firing at something with the Canon. It was so untainted and heavenly that I had to force myself to keep riding. Scenery in the West kept getting better and better.

Ruidoso hit me as a surprise. Upon arrival, any trace of the desert was gone, and I felt like I was in Colorado mixed with a hint of Switzerland, not southern New Mexico. Sierra Blanca loomed overhead—shaking hands with the clouds—and every last building looked so damn rustic that I just had to stay a night. I wanted to push on to the White Sands National Monument, but there was no way I could simply breeze through a town like that. Ruidoso's style had my name written all over it. It gave me a mountain high.

I passed by an outfit called Rustic Expressions that had log furniture strewn about the parking lot and a sign along the street fully covered in antlers. I wanted to work there. Log buildings outnumbered Roswell's stash of aliens. Large Christmas decorations and sparkly garland hung from the street lights. It was as if a ski lodge blew up and a town grew from the bits of debris. I found a cheap room at the Indian-owned Budget Lodge, unpacked, grabbed my new favorite thing in the world, my camera, and trekked two miles into town.

The walk transferred me from dusk to night. In town, I found a bar called Quarters and scarfed down a fantastic plate of fish and chips. I wasn't looking for an English dish but was persuaded by the bartender. As I sat there growing a teeth-flaunting grin and fighting a losing battle with relaxing eye lids, he told me that their sister bar, the WPS Saloon, had live country music. I threw back a couple more, keeping a chameleon-like wandering eye on a pretty lady at the opposite end of the room, and soon headed that way.

The band at the WPS Saloon played all of the covers that I liked and just as in Texas, the New Mexican folks were excellent dancers. I was envious of them for shaking a leg for that many songs while looking professional the whole time. My unrefined dance floor gyrating would have had me two-steppin' on too many toes. I hung around for a few hours and had a wee bit of whiskey, okay a lot, before walking back in the snow flurries to the warmth of my cozy room.

Day 70 – December 22, 2011

White is the word of the day, and for good reason. The color lasted throughout the day, coming in various natural forms, all of which highlighted Mother Nature's beauty. It was snowing in Ruidoso when I left. I hoped to make it as far as *White* Sands National Monument to explore the rare patch of white dunes. A brigade of massive *white* cotton balls in the sky unexpectedly dominated my pictures all day. For the first time in my life I felt like I knew what big sky country meant.

Thumping pain had found its way from the beverages of last night to my head when I woke in Ruidoso. In life, I've sworn off of alcohol countless times. Here, I did it again. I promised I'd never have another drink. Instead of falling victim to a day pissed away in weak regret, I remained open to a choice: man up or wuss out. Normally I wuss out and end up sprawled out helplessly somewhere with low moans and small bitchy phrases seeping into the surrounding air. *But not this time.* I attacked the hangover full force.

Budget Lodge's lobby had a juice machine in need of draining. I marched in there determined to engulf as much fruit juice as possible. I found out a few years back that hangovers can be prevented by orange juice. The cause for the nausea and pain is not only dehydration, but more acutely, an abnormal drop in blood sugar that happens while taking in large quantities of alcohol. The natural sugars in fruit and real fruit juices are exactly what the body needs to stabilize its blood sugar level.

Last night, like most nights under the influence, when it came time to call it quits, the thought of drinking anything but more booze never crossed my mind. And therein lies the problem. When I remember to drink fruit juice before bed, I always feel great in the morning. Drinking water alone has never been enough to fight off my category five hangovers. At the juice machine, I forced down five cups of orange and cranberry juice. Back at the room, I tipped back some water for good measure and topped it all off with a couple of Tylenol Dayquil tablets.

It was thirty-two degrees when I left the mountain paradise of Ruidoso. Flurries happily danced in the air. Sierra Blanca's 12,003-foot summit still wore a blanket of clouds. The town was quiet and slow-moving, no doubt preparing for the winter weather fast approaching. I wanted to get the hell outta the high country before it really let loose. My flight path was a southwest dart on Highway 70 all day to Las Cruces, barring snowy disaster. Early on, it was apparent that my pace would be slow, but not because of the weather or the nausea— because of the scenery. Mountains, snowcaps, evergreens, twisty roads, it all was on the plate. And the morning's evergreens were especially phenomenal. They were dusted by a light layer of snow and frost. The sunshine made them sparkle and the snow-covered forest floor made each individual tree stand out. A big blue sky worked with the forest greens better than I'd ever noticed before.

I motored on, happy and feeling better, to the border of the Mescalero Apache Tribe's reservation, the second reservation of the trip. The first was in central Florida, and I remember thinking then that the government let them remain in control of the most useless piece of land. It looked great if you were an egret or alligator, but for human toils, it seemed like a subpar swamp. Here in New Mexico, the Apache Tribe's land was stunning. I pulled over about once a mile for ten miles. I did U-turns and cut through the median to get pictures. It felt fair and good knowing that the Mescalero Apaches' land was scenic and looked anything but useless. The mountains were thick with forests, the air brisk and clean. Between Ruidoso and here, these were parts of New Mexico more beautiful than I could've imagined. I came to the opposite border of their reservation. White Sands National Monument was forty miles away.

I passed through Alamogordo, a town sitting on a flat plain between the Sacramento and San Andres mountain ranges. I pulled over on the shoulder of Highway 70 near a stand selling hanging red peppers. To my right, I could see what looked like a long white paintbrush stroke at the base of the San Andres Mountains. *That must be the dunes.* I pulled out my zoom lens for a better look. Sure enough, there they were like a mirage, out of place in a land of brown earth and blue skies. They were about fifteen miles southwest.

I pulled up to White Sands National Monument visitor center. The building resembled a brownish-orange, rounded adobe structure and had the ends of log beams poking through the veneer. I went inside for a looksee. Interesting displays showing facts about the dunes' uniquely adapted white animals and quotes like "Those who dwell among the beauties or mysteries of the Earth are never alone or weary of life" (Rachel Carson) excited me further for my visit to the park. So what is so special about these dunes? Well, they're unique. That's it. Story's over. Nothing to see here. Move along. Exactly what were we talking about anyway? I'm kidding.

The white sand dunes are not actually like beach or desert sand. They are deposits of dissolved gypsum that washed into the Tularosa basin from the bordering mountains through rainstorms and snow melt. They are the world's largest gypsum dune field. Gypsum, unlike regular sand, absorbs moisture from the surrounding earth and creates dunes that are quite firm and easy to walk on. Water acts as glue in these dunes, holding all of the tiny grains in place. You won't find any standing water nearby, though, but a quick touch of the sand with your bare hand reveals the moisture locked inside. *It has to be great for making sand castles.*

I rode deep into the park. The vegetation covering some of the first dunes in sight disappeared, and a bleached landscape unfolded before me. The dunes became bald and ubiquitous. The park's road turned to pure sand. Banks of the gypsum sand were plowed to the side to keep the road open—just like snow. I stood up on the pegs as if riding in the dirt. I was ready for a washout.

The dunes unleashed a brilliant show when the giant white clouds parted and allowed sunbeams to reflect off of them, making the sand a piercing white. I didn't have sunglasses and paid for it. One eye rested in semi-darkness under my eyelid while the other held a near shut squint. I didn't let that stop my fun. I rode farther on, passing families sledding down the sides of untouched dunes, leaving them imprinted with shadowy zebra stripes. I was inspired by the fun they were having as I explored the strange landscape. It brought out the wild West Virginian in me, and the kid in me, the one who has never left. I ran around, jumped off of dunes, and rode the Goose standing up everywhere. It was truly a youthful experience.

When the weather began to change for the worse, I hightailed it for Las Cruces earlier than I wanted to. The next sixty miles were to increase in elevation again and become awfully remote.

White Sands Missile Range/Base was along the next stretch of road. Signs were posted everywhere warning about the potential danger. One is not supposed to pull over on the shoulder, but more than once I risked it for the sake of a good picture. I was lucky. Each time I stopped to snap the quintessential photo of a road and matching power lines fading into infinity, I was never bothered. Cars passed without even slowing.

I was impressed by the alarmingly straight thirty-mile stretch toward the San Augustin Pass. On the horizon, a snow-covered mountain was waiting. The Goose hummed right for it at 2,500 rpm in top gear for an eternity. I kept thinking, "I have to be getting close by now." Yet, mile after mile, it was still on the horizon. I inched forward until the distance was gone.

There was an overlook parking lot against that mountain on 70's eastbound side. I rode through San Augustin Pass and pulled a U-turn. A young Latino man was dressed warmly and parked facing the mountain in a stoic stare. He was still sitting on his motorcycle when I pulled up beside him for the same thing. He told me that he was from Las Cruces and that he'd ride up to the pass to clear his head once in a while. I said, "It's beautiful." The mountain looked like a perfect example of what you'd see in a Coors Commercial. Under heavy clouds, the snow contrasted with the mountain's jagged rock enough to make it look like it was in black and white. I sat for a bit breathing in the crisp wintery air. All full of humbleness, I rode down from the high ground and into Las Cruces, where I would find a reasonable room and call it a night. The Canon rolled through 237 photos throughout the day without breaking a sweat.

Day 71 – December 23, 2011

My eyes opened, feet traveled to the window, hand slowly opened the curtain, and my mind reluctantly recorded the weather conditions. My fate was sealed. Snow that had been forecast in Las Cruces had arrived. An inch was already on the roads, and it was only 7:00am. Checkout time was 11:00am. *Maybe it will be safe to travel later.* I patiently waited until then to scope out the road conditions. The storm that I'd been running from since Roswell had caught me.

I was stranded at the Century 21 Motel. The Goose's rear tire was getting pretty bald and to go out on those roads would have been certain doom, so I sucked it up, rented the room again, and vegetated all day. It was nice in its own dull, four-walls-and-a-window sort of way. I spent a few hours thumbing through my new camera's tech manual and got caught up on a bunch of digital errands that I'd been putting off for not wanting my fantastic lifestyle to be interrupted, even for a second.

Once in a while, I'd rise from my root-growing position to check on my trusty traveling companion outside. Its headlights stared back from beneath the tarp with a slight dusting of snow sitting on them like eyebrows. They looked sad and cold. I felt ashamed for standing in the heated room with a T-shirt on. I only left the room once for coffee, once for pizza, and once for ice cream. My hind end produced a warm spot on the bed that never really cooled. That was it, a day in a nutshell.

Day 72 – December 24, 2011

It was Christmas Eve, and I was in the mood to move. The snow in Las Cruces was still falling, but the temps were just high enough to turn slush into water. One thing dominated my thoughts: I just wanted to get to Arizona. There really wasn't a good reason to be in a hurry; in fact, the only reason I wanted to get there was to experience that slight rush of crossing a new state line. New Mexico had shown me some great times, and I'd made a couple more friends. It was a shame that I couldn't go north to experience the really rugged side of the state. Wicked snowfall from New Mexico's higher elevations dominated the state's northern roads. It was no place for a sport bike like mine. Perhaps those adventure bike guys, with their semi-knobbed tires, could've gotten around. New Mexico was so pretty, and I'd seen so little of it. My heart said, "I'll be back."

The Goose was packed and prepared for motion. I headed for the highway only to make it twenty feet. For the past two days, a BMW motorcycle had been covered up in the motel's parking lot near my bike. I didn't have a chance to meet the owner until he spotted me heading out and came out of his room to say hello. His name was Troy. He was tall, polite, and probably in his early fifties. He was taking the long way from Sacramento, California, to Los Alamos, New Mexico, and stopped to wait out the snow. We spoke mostly of long distance motorcycle travel. Troy was by no means a country-crossing rookie like me. He had racked up quite a few long trips in his years, some of which I mentally noted for future plans. One story he told disturbed me as much as if I had been there. It clearly bothered him, as he relived it to share the story with me.

At home in Sacramento, a few years back, Troy was rear ended by a car while riding his motorcycle. The driver of the car stopped to lend a hand. When the negligent driver realized that Troy was African American, he bolted, leaving Troy lying there with a shattered left knee. The driver did not know that he had smacked into one of our nation's military veterans and left him for dead. *Folks like that don't deserve the breath they're given.* When are we going to get over our different skin colors? It drives me nuts. We have a saying in motocross: "We all look the same with a helmet on."

Troy and I exchanged info, and I wished him safe travels. I fueled up in another part of town while watching an old lady roam against the curb on a busy street in one of those powered chairs. Cars whizzed dangerously by. She seemed alarmingly unaware of their proximity to her and even stopped once to lean forward and pick up a small green ball. I watched nervously. *This ain't gonna be good.* I couldn't have done a thing about it. There were no sidewalks nearby, and picking her and the chair up to carry her to safety wasn't even possible. I crossed my fingers that she wasn't going to nudge left on the joystick. She cruised along carelessly as if she had a death wish. She hung a right a few hundred yards later onto a side street. I sighed in relief, popped my helmet on, and headed for 10 W to crank in some miles.

I was amped to turn the throttle and head toward the western horizon. Nothing could stop me, except . . . except a fifteen-mile traffic jam. I'd only made it ten miles since Las Cruces. Road work was the culprit. I'm really not sure why it was so important to get that shoulder work done on Christmas Eve, a Saturday afternoon, with heavy holiday traffic relying on Interstate 10 as a major link to families across the South. *As intelligent beings, can't we just slow progress for a second and remember what's actually important in life, or will we always let the mighty dollar rule us?* Sometimes we humans can be the most brilliant, loving creatures imaginable; or we can be the lowest form of life—full of greed, destruction, and ignorance. I did realize that those guys were getting good overtime and holiday pay, but it came at the expense of creating stress for thousands of others. *The shoulder will still be there Monday, people!*

I coasted along at the mercy of progress, toying with the slippery mound of slush in the center of each westbound lane. My clutch finger (middle finger) cramped in the stop-and-go sea of cars. A coyote matched the pace of traffic for a bit. It was no more than forty feet away and trotting along looking for a broken spot in the fence to climb through. It stopped and looked at the traffic. I pretended that it was looking at me. This was my first up close glimpse of one. It looked exactly like an overgrown fox. I was taken aback. Its thick mesh of grey, white, and brown hair, bushy tail, narrow snout, and wide eyes all seemed to work as a creature, but I couldn't shake the thought of "Big fox. Really big fox."

Folks had told me that they were about the size of a German shepherd, as was this one, but I expected them to look more like a wolf. I smiled and made one of those "hmmm" noises that folks do upon a sudden realization. The traffic jam joyfully came to an end, and the Goose's clutch remained intact.

I stopped in Demming, New Mexico, to find warmth. The toes on my right foot were completely frozen. My left foot was exposed to the sunshine the whole time and was doing just fine. Who knew that a little sunshine could make such a difference while riding in near-freezing temperatures? I made another one of those "hmmm" noises. The mercury had risen all the way up into the mid-thirties by then.

Fifty-five miles separate Demming from Lordsburg, the next town along I-10 West. I tucked behind the windscreen as far as my tank bag would let me and kept the Goose around ninety mph. I arrived in Lordsburg feeling fine and a little surprised at how easily I handled the cold and wind. This is where I began to toughen up—or acclimate—and accept the fact that I'd left an inescapably cold winter in West Virginia for a wintery ride across the South. I thought that it was going to be all sunshine, desert heat, and bikinis. But I was wrong. Fate, and a constant push west, wasn't going to let me escape the chill of winter. I thought of Florida. In Lordsburg, I pumped yellow liquid into the Goose, sipped on a cup of hot brown liquid, and expelled yellow liquid into a porcelain pond. Arizona was only twenty miles away.

Arizona's big blue sign with the sun rays finally appeared. I was in Arizona—the Grand Canyon state. I was no longer in the Chihuahuan Desert but the Sonoran. I was just one state from the Pacific, in the Wild West, Red Rock Country, land of the saguaro cactus, and the Navajo Nation. I was glad to be there. At the sign, I snapped off pictures like I was firing an automatic weapon. Arizona felt warmer already and full of promise. I happily motored on.

Fifty miles in, in Wilcox, I decided to give Motel 6 a shot. All of this time I'd ignored them, thinking that they are a big, nationally known franchise and that their rates would be higher. I swung the stainless steel door open and approached the front desk, fully expecting to think, "That's too much. I'll look elsewhere." A young man of no more than eighteen with long brown hair told me that a room was $35. I damn near jumped over the counter and hugged him. I couldn't believe it. That was only $5 higher than popping my tent up at most state parks on the East Coast. It was almost half the price of tent camping in Key West and $15 less than primitive tent camping in Myrtle Beach, South Carolina. And I could take a hot shower, watch TV, and have a pizza delivered to my warm room. In hindsight, this began my quasi-love affair with the friendly motel chain.

The evening passed by watching *It's a Wonderful Life* all the way through for the first time, and if I may add, I love the way folks sounded in the days of pre-color movies. Their voices held an innocence that's been lost with time. It was a great movie, and like Motel 6, I waited too long to find that out.

Day 73 – December 25, 2011

I'd never been without family on Christmas. It did feel weird, but not because I wasn't back home. The strange feeling undoubtedly came from being in the rugged desert on Christmas and knowing that my plans for the day had absolutely nothing to do with the holiday itself. I was accustomed to cold winters like the one here in Arizona. And mountains, another feature of Arizona. And snow, which Las Cruces had provided. But here, the vast emptiness and dry earth reminded me little of past Christmases. There were no thick forests of bald deciduous trees, or rivers to speak of, no Christmas tree farms, no children running about. *Where exactly do desert dwellers get their Christmas trees anyway?* I looked around to see very little of any Christmas spirit in Wilcox. A heavy feeling lingered in the morning until the road soothed it away.

Riding west on Interstate 10, I came across a sign that reminded me of a recommendation that came from the Crossroads Yamaha shop back when I was in Albemarle, North Carolina. A customer at the shop that day, named Jim, had ridden across the U.S. a couple of times and told me about *The THING*. Exit 322 rolled around and dropped me off in *The THING's* parking lot. I had to see it for myself. A long, obnoxious, yellow store front was partnered by a Dairy Queen on the right and a blue, red, and yellow striped warehouse on the left that looked like it could be the factory where they made Fruit Stripe chewing gum, the one that tastes good for ten seconds then goes straight to the flavor of morning breath. Being Christmas, *The THING* had taken a day off. Jim had let me in on the secret of *The THING* while in North Carolina, and I'm glad he did. Jim said that *The THING* was a mummified Native American woman and child. If not for that, my brain would have exploded from the curiosity. I rode on.

Two nearby Cochise County towns rivaled San Francisco in the late 1800s. One was Bisbee and one was Tombstone. Both boomed in population and size from their mineral wealth, with Bisbee being richer in natural resources and Tombstone being richer in chaotic history. During Tombstone's most productive mining years, its growth briefly surpassed San Francisco while just a few decades later Bisbee became the largest city between San Francisco and New Orleans. Today they are simple relics of their former selves.

I planned to make them my Christmas present by unwrapping two brief experiences in these desert oases. From Wilcox, they're about forty and seventy miles southwest, with Bisbee being just minutes from the Mexican border. I thought the short ride would allow plenty of time to see both places.

In Benson, Arizona, I grabbed a snack, fueled up, and dove south on Route 80. Any traces of I-10 quickly disappeared, giving way to twenty miles of sparsely settled, rocky, rolling terrain. A green sign sat along the road by a mobile home park that said, "Entering Tombstone Elevation 4539 Founded 1879." I was unaware that I was cruising so high above sea level. I had never thought of deserts as having high elevation. The heavy chill in the air finally had an explanation. *If you're at 4,500 feet on the East Coast, then you're on top of an Appalachian mountain somewhere.*

When I drifted into town that was it for me. I looked around and was hooked. Tombstone was the epitome of the Old West that I had imagined, and it grabbed me with both of its ghostly gunslinging hands. Bisbee would have to wait until tomorrow.

Before Tombstone became legend, it was locked in a feverish gold and silver rush. Once the precious metals were found, the diminutive settlement flooded to the gills with all sorts of rough-and-tumble characters looking to get rich quick. Wyatt Earp, Big Nose Kate and her saloon, the O.K. Corral, Johnny Ringo, and Doc Holiday became immortalized in those frantic mining years. Their actions, along with thousands of nameless others, earned Tombstone's label as "the town too tough to die." Well, the Goose and I were there to soften the place up a bit. I rode past an old, beat-up hearse with a painted advertisement saying, "Why go around half dead when we can bury you for $49.50?" It seemed a fitting way to introduce such a turbulent place.

I exchanged Route 80 for a one hundred percent empty parking lot on the south side of town. Tombstone looked uninhabited. Being Christmas, the town was a borderline ghost town. A strip of small buildings, maybe four or five blocks long, was partitioned off to block modern modes of travel from entering the heavily visited part of town. The building nearest me was the Bird Cage

Theatre. It looked at odds with most of the other buildings. It had no covered walkway and appeared to be stucco. Tombstone's other buildings were wood sided and shared a covered walkway, with a brick structure thrown in at random. They were simple buildings, lacking all but the smallest amount of exterior trim. Even Bank of America had a red, white, and blue sign with letters so stressed that they looked like they were scraped up while a horse dragged the sign down a dirt road. The streets were deserted. Everything was closed, or "shut" as it's known by the locals, except the saloons. Hallelujah!

I made several passes along the strip before being lured into Big Nose Kate's saloon by live music. I had found everybody. Every tourist in town was in there. I pivoted my neck in various angles. The walls were busy with black and white pictures, paintings of nude women, western relics, old sayings on wooden plaques, and backlit Big Nose Kate insignia. The bartender was on my right and sportin' a brown, old timey moustache and period costume. I headed for him, smiling, and asked for a picture. He did me one better by getting the owner of the place to take a picture of us, both behind the bar, holding guns. Excellent! I had only been in there five minutes and already could've started a gunfight.

The Wyatt Earp imitating bartender was a hell of a guy. He made my experience at Big Nose Kate's top-notch. The lack of tourists (I can't imagine how packed that place would be on a good day) allowed him to give me a history lesson and show me a few old photographs around and behind the bar that were taken years ago, clearly revealing the ghosts of old cowboys.

He filled me in on why a shot is called a shot. The story goes, cowboys in the Old West seldom carried much money on them, but they always had a bunch of bullets. One bullet was worth about five cents. The cowboy would lay a bullet on the bar and tell the bartender to give him a bullet's, or one shot's, worth of whiskey. Days later, the cowboy would come back to the saloon after getting paid and buy his bullets back.

The bartender was proud to share his bounty of knowledge with an eager listener. He comped me a shot of Old Overholt Rye Whiskey. He said, "That's the stuff Wyatt Earp and the boys would order in Big Nose Kate's." For a lower end whiskey, it slid down the gullet warm yet surprisingly smooth. I chilled out there for a while until I felt the urge to search for lodging. The Trail Riders Motel came highly recommended. I reserved a room and went back to town. The sun offered a few more hours of daylight.

The Four Dueces Saloon was open at the north end of the street. The owners had fixed a feast for the townsfolk and the few tourists who were wandering around. It was a small joint that had a vibe that seemed to project a special welcome to those who were bored with the gunfighting. I scarfed down some lasagna, mincemeat pie, and chili. Grateful for the free food, I ordered a beer and tipped well. I sat alone at a small wooden table when a fellow motorcyclist, also named Mike, joined me. He had noticed the Goose lingering outside. He was twenty-nine, clean-cut as an active duty Marine, and currently living in Tucson. He grabbed a plate, and we yakked on and on about motorcycles. A while later, the door flung open without that lonely western whistle, and I could see that it was dark outside. The bartender from Big Nose Kate's had given it a mighty push. He recognized me and pulled up a chair. He merged right on in, in the Mike and Mike motorcycle mania, sharing stories about long rides on his hog.

The moon was in full control of the night when Mike decided to head home. Big Nose Kate's bartender and I hung about for a bit longer. When he left, so did I. I was off to see what Ringo's saloon was all about. I didn't stay at Ringo's long. It was housed in a much larger building that felt empty on the holiday night. A few stragglers, engulfed in karaoke, shared a microphone. Without them piercing the silence the place would have been dead. It was getting late and I was wiped out, so I walked back to my cowboy-themed room to lasso in some zzz's.

Day 74 – December 26, 2011

How someone can let their dog bark all . . . night . . . long . . . baffles me. My thin and permeable motel room walls were no match for the decibels that their wretched beast belted. I fell asleep quickly, but when bladder pressure woke me in the small hours of the morning, I was doomed to stay awake.

I lay there staring at the ceiling while listening to that mutt yap for an eternity. Once I looked out the window and got a location on it, the thoughts started rolling in about how I could shut that thing up. The most reasonable method would be to go next door and politely ask the owner to quiet their obnoxious dog. That wouldn't be any fun, though. Just like in Big Bend when those little shih-tzus wouldn't stop yelping into the darkness, I thought of getting the bear spray out and letting the dog have it. Other options frolicked in my mind. I could use a few zip ties and tie its mouth closed, or I could stuff some of my dirty socks down its gullet. I'm not a mean person; I'm just a light sleeper. Getting a full night's sleep is one of my greater joys in life. Perhaps I shouldn't have wanted to take my frustration out on the canine. After having plenty of time to think about it, it was clearly the owner of the dog who was guilty. I vowed, "I'll bear spray the next owner who lets their dog yap all night long within fifty feet of me." Don't say I didn't warn ya!

The sun rose, and yet again I drank as much coffee as humanly possible to feel normal. Checkout time at the Trail Rider's Inn was 10:00am. I hustled more than usual to get packed up. At 10:05 I was out of there. Getting jittery from a stomach full of coffee, I tracked down a place with Wi-Fi and hoped for a reasonably priced breakfast. At Morgan's Café and Pizza, for $5.50, I ordered a hearty combo of two pancakes, two eggs, and two sausage links. When the waitress brought the food out and I saw the bicycle-wheel-sized hotcakes, I felt like Adam Richman in an episode of *Man vs. Food*.

I attacked with dull knife and pronged silverware. The eggs and sausage links put up a pitiful resistance. Then I hit the proverbial wall halfway through the big doughy flapjacks. For the first time in my life, it felt as if even one more bite would send me to the nearest wastebasket. Although delicious, they were just too big for my capabilities. As I sat with my laptop opened on the table, I made a simple observation. The pancakes were no smaller than the area of the folded laptop and almost as thick. I found myself in a full-on fight against food coma. I downed another coffee and hit the streets in search of something to get into.

I decided to skip Bisbee, Arizona, altogether and stick around until 2:00pm to see the reenactment of the gunfight at the O.K. Corral. The ticket was $10, and since this was the thing to see in Tombstone, I felt the price was justified. Two o'clock came, and a hundred others piled onto the bleachers with me in front of a mock-up part of the old town. The show involved characters portraying Doc Holiday, Wyatt and Virgil Earp, Hattie Earp, the McLaury boys, Billie Claiborne, and a couple Clantons. The actors spoke loud and clear; they were funny and talented. They used real guns with blanks, and when the gunfight started I was looking through the viewfinder of my camera and about jumped out of my seat. It was loud! Every baby in the audience started crying. Actors who were "shot" remained motionless on the ground as we exited the set. Bravo! *Best ten dollars I'd spent in a while.*

If not for a teenage kid on a tall swing set outside of the show's walls, it would have been flawless. This kid had the crowd in a low chuckle. Looking to our right, his smiling head would crest the wall in two-second intervals. His long brown hair stood high in its brief moment of weightlessness. I laughed at his mischief.

On a side note, yesterday the bartender from Big Nose Kate's told me that only three men died in the gunfight at the O.K. Corral. He said what was really interesting was the gunfighting in the intersection just up the street from Big Nose Kate's: "Seventy men died there in a three-year period."

Now that I was an official super tourist of Tombstone, my time was up. Someplace new, someplace wild, someplace unknown was calling me. I knew the road would take me there. I planned nothing more than to ride until the sun set. I followed Route 80 back to Benson and back to Interstate 10. The vegetation seemed to thin ever so slightly as I eased northwest. Horizontal ground occasionally allowed a mountain to break the monotony.

Tucson came into view. I expected something more of it. Instead of a massive city with gangs of skyscrapers, only a few buildings rose high enough to see from the interstate. None of them rivaled Mt. Kimball and Rattlesnake Peak in the backdrop. I precariously parked the Goose at the end of a Jersey wall in between an on ramp and *The 10*. A desire to ride through the city just wasn't there, so I settled for a picture and tried not to get plowed over as I re-entered traffic.

Just past Tucson, I caught a glimpse of my first saguaro cactus. They are the ones that are shaped like a giant stick man with two arms sticking out and pointing up. They were way bigger than I imagined, taller than most trees in the area. I knew that one day I'd cross them, but when or where had escaped me. I left it to fate. Now, here they were, arguably the Wild West's most iconic symbol. I had no idea if I'd first see them in Texas, New Mexico, or Arizona. They were a most welcome surprise that brightened my day. Once again, I was feeling wonderful for having the chance to experience something new.

The sign for Picacho Peak State Park caught my attention while a magnificent sunset decorated the sky. I felt warm and free. As the elevation dropped from Tombstone to here, the temperature had climbed. I pulled up to Picacho Peak's gate in complete darkness. The stars were already out flaunting their stuff. I stuck $25 in a yellow envelope and watched it disappear into the park's metal payment box. The campground was just around the bend. Those brilliant saguaro cacti were growing thick here and looked a lot more ominous in the night. As I pitched my tent, their humanoid shape kept me company. I was not bothered.

Life was perfect. In the distance, a town's lights hung over it like an enormous purple bubble. Picacho's stars shimmered on, undeterred by any light pollution. The moon shyly played a game of hide and seek. It had not been dark long when I noticed that the moon was already descending on the horizon. Then, two hours later, it was gone. *That was odd. I'll have to look into that.*

Day 75 – December 27, 2011

A cold, cold morning brought me to life at Picacho Peak State Park. I've been a camper since childhood, but not a boyscout. My fire starting ability is about average, and I can pitch a tent with the best of 'em, but I'm no Bear Grylls. I still have a lot to learn. So, as I prepared for bed last night, I had a choice. Keep my pants and shirt on, to combat the dropping temperatures, or take them off and rely solely on my sleeping bag. It wasn't that cold when I climbed in, so I just slept in my under britches. That generally worked great for warm mornings. However, Picacho Peak had dealt me a harsh morning with temps in the low twenties. My bladder had dammed up a whole mess of urine overnight, and my clothes were lying next to my sleeping bag, exposed to the air. I really needed to make a run to the john, but the thought of stiffly easing into my pants, one leg at a time with heavily goose-bumped skin, and fighting gasps while gently cloaking the frozen shirt over my torso, made me hesitate.

Trust me on this one. In times like this, you don't want to crawl out of the warmth of the bag for nothing. No amount of wishing could change my reality; it had to be done. Soon the urge to take a whiz overpowered the fear of the cold clothes. While I was at it and freezing my hind end off, I gathered everything needed to take a hot shower in the bathhouse. Later, I would discover what intelligent people do in this situation. They sleep in their britches and keep their clothes in the sleeping bag with them overnight. In the morning, their clothes are near body temperature. I made one of those "hmmm" noises.

After showering, I exited the bathhouse bundled up like an Iditarod dog sled racer and ready for camp-packing battle. The sun had risen above the eastern peaks and the temperature must have already gained ten degrees. I shed a few layers and began loading the Goose just like any other morning. All was smooth as glass until every last desert fowl in the Southwest started hounding me. Like a pack of hungry wolves they watched my every move, waiting for me to slip up. They were looking for breakfast and apparently feared not of mankind.

I'd take something out of the tent and walk it to the picnic table or the bike, and as I'd head back to the tent they would pounce on my gear, searching for anything edible. At first it was amusing. I was having a close encounter with nature. Then one of those orange-eyed, curved-beaked, egg-laying bastards jumped up on my brand new camera and shit right on the ISO button. If he wasn't so fast I would've Ozzy Osbourned his ass. My vigilance heightened as I wiped off the camera. *I better not get salmonella from this bird shit.* Soon they realized that they weren't getting anything from me, so they disappeared into other parts of the park to continue their diabolical harassment.

All packed up, I hit the road north toward Phoenix. The Sonoran Desert took on a look of its own. Frail vegetation poked through parched sandy earth. Distances between each rugged plant grew longer. Out of nowhere, a cotton field appeared. I thought that I had left those behind in the Southeast. Irrigated trenches ran along the triangle-shaped field. It hardly seemed like a place fertile enough to grow the native plants, yet a thick cluster of cotton was thriving. I couldn't ignore how wasteful it seemed to attempt agricultural pursuits in a land of so little rainfall. Like the shoulder work on Christmas Eve, it just felt wrong.

Arizona's largest city materialized. I was in Phoenix and heading downtown. I wanted to hop off the saddle for a few minutes, maybe grab a sandwich at a one-off joint, and enjoy a midday walk. I headed for the center of the city, where the tall buildings blocked views to the outer world, but no matter where I went downtown, I would stop, look around, and without fail, find that a sketchy-looking character was scoping me out. I'd ride a few blocks and pull over again. The sketchy characters were there, too. Then I'd ride around a few blocks and try it again. I'd find more of them, glaring at me like a rolling dollar sign. The city was overrun by shady men, men who didn't move with the business folks, but loitered against buildings with sticky-fingered looks on their faces. They stared at me and my gear like they had X-ray vision. There was no way in hell that I was going to curb my bike and walk farther than eye shot from it. My hiking pack, sleeping pad, and tank bag would've been easy pickin's.

The bad apples, coupled with every last bus stop bum, gave me a terrible first impression. I watched as homeless folks slept on the bus stop benches, leaving everyone else to stand nearby. The folks standing looked like well-dressed, honest, working-class folks, like folks that paid the taxes to have public infrastructure and bus stops built. My stomach turned as I turned for Interstate 10. I had managed to roam all over Phoenix and not capture one picture for fear that my camera would get snatched. *When I get back on The 10 I'll pull over for a second and get a shot.*

That was deemed too dangerous, as the shoulders weren't all that wide, and a stucco wall lined the whole stretch of highway around the city. Defeated from Phoenix's unexpected variables, I headed off in search of Route 60.

In Surprise, Arizona, I stopped at Furr's Family Dining for lunch. The parking lot was bordered by profoundly fruitful orange trees. Oranges had fallen and carelessly lay all over the parking lot. The trees were still holding bushels worth on their branches. I snagged a few for a later snack and meandered in. I doubted that any would make it to the restaurant's cafeteria-like food counters. *What a waste.* The trees, like the cotton fields, looked incredibly out of place, like the exact thing not to grow if your goal is sustainability. Arizona doesn't begin to receive the rainfall that Florida does, but that doesn't deter man from trying to find ways to waste the vital resource as quickly as possible. I think that the sun has baked a few folks' minds out here. In fairness to Furr's, the food—especially the pie—was great.

Route 60 W would take me toward the towns of Wickenburg and Prescott. Both are mentioned in *1000 Places To See Before You Die.* Traces of Phoenix's burbs disappeared and were replaced by small hills and the occasional small town. In Wickenburg, I felt the day becoming long, so I reviewed the book again and decided to pick which town seemed more interesting and stay there. Prescott got the vote for being a mountain town with a college scene. That meant I'd have to cover another fifty miles before I could call it a day.

Before I left Wickenburg, I zigzagged through the old town for a peek at what I'd be missing. It looked fun and interesting, like so many other old towns that I'd seen by now. I imagined there was a rustic saloon where I could grab a cold beer and listen to some old tunes among folks in cowboy hats. I imagined being able to grab a bite to eat at a trendy restaurant inspired by a seam of culture that is lost in the present. I imagined meeting friendly folks and maybe a pretty gal to hang out with. But then I just bit my tongue and rode away. Our country is full of intriguing town centers where hip people of all fashions have neat little businesses. You'd have to live a million years to see them all. And, I wish I could. Life is so short.

On the way out of town, I ran across a car wash and gave the Goose its first shower since the wonderful folks at Crossroads Yamaha scrubbed off the road grime. In some strange way I think the bike was grateful.

I was now off to Prescott. The ride there was nothing short of phenomenal. I had no idea that I'd cross into alpine-like mountain country and ride thirty miles of the tightest twisty turns imaginable. From a two-dimensional map, you can't always predict these things. If you are ever in this part of the country on a motorcycle, do not miss the stretch of 89 from Congress to Prescott.

A long straight climb of maybe a one to one ratio (one inch per foot) teases you as you approach a mountain pass. To the right you can see a scar ascending across the mountain. You know that it's a curvy road taped to the mountainside, and you twist the throttle another 1,000 rpms trying to get there faster. The roadside grows green again with each foot gained in elevation. Bright yellow sharp corner signs are everywhere. The guardrails are short enough so as not to interfere with your high-altitude view, and are tall enough to protect the slow drivers who move along in utter terror in their four-wheeled safety boxes. You overtake them easily, thinking, *Move over rover! This is motorcycle country.* The only thing that stopped me and the Goose from destroying every last corner was the awesome beauty of the region. Cacti soon disappeared, giving evergreens center stage. That flat spot in the center of my rear tire took a breather. What a brilliant ride!

I arrived in mile-high-plus Prescott after dark and did a lap around town before opting to get a room. The temp was in the low thirties, and camping in the nearby national forest was possible, although I didn't really want to camp somewhere with no utilities in that sort of weather again (insert wussy here). Plus, I was feeling social. I found a reasonable room at the Pine View Motel and rode downtown.

Prescott is also known as Arizona's Christmas city. The town's lights were spectacular and fully contributed to the most colorfully decorated town square that I'd ever seen. The city center was completely surrounded by a wide brick sidewalk splitting two rows of trees. The trees wore multi-colored aprons of string lights, as if covered in thousands of fireflies dipped in food coloring. Among the holiday decorations, the Yavapai County Courthouse charmed passersby with ground-to-wall seasonal lighting. The Canon had a hard time doing the place justice. Every red strand of Christmas lights kept turning out pink upon review, and I couldn't back up far enough to capture the wide angle that my eyes so easily recorded. Yet, I kept snapping away.

Moctezumas was open for business along the town square. I stopped there for a bite to eat and a brew. It was your typical long, rectangular bar with pool tables in the back and a gathering of barstools along a lengthy wooden counter. Shiny stamped metal ceiling panels added a smidgen of character. A sticker behind the beer taps said, "Finish your beer. There's sober kids in India." I finished that last drop and last bite of food. The place was trendy, but empty—just like the streets outside. Either it was an off night, or the young folks were waiting until the crack of midnight to penetrate the town, or they had all gone home for the holidays. Whatever the reason, the scene was dead. I motioned to retire for the night. The Goose seconded and chauffeured me back to the room via a quick and intensely cold ride.

Day 76 – December 28, 2011

The day's ride started like it had finished the day before, curvier than a fat-bottomed gal with implants on the astonishingly twisty and beautiful Route 89A. I was motoring along, mentally ready for the fifty-six-mile ride to Sedona and short ride to Flagstaff afterward, when Jerome halted all forward momentum after just thirty miles.

When I arrived in Jerome, it seemed familiar. There was no way that I'd ever been there. *How do I know this place?* Then it hit me. I'd seen it on the tube twice before. The first time was an episode of the Travel Channel's *Ghost Adventures* when Zak and the guys did a paranormal investigation in one of the town's buildings, and the second time I'd seen Jerome was in a documentary about the rock star and lead singer of the band Tool, Maynard Keenan. The documentary focused on his newfound fondness for wine and the task of bringing a vineyard to Jerome.

Before I left home, I planned to visit Jerome, but out here on the road, I had forgotten about it. You can imagine my surprise when I accidentally drifted into town. Just minutes before, I was standing atop an overlook soaking in a long distance view of the desert. I could see Flagstaff's Humphreys Peak through a split in the mountain from fifty miles away. Below me, the road looked like the back of a garter snake. The pavement was dark and fresh and followed anything but a straight course. The sun reflected off the double yellows like two veins of gold. I had no idea that the road hooked left into Jerome directly after that split.

Jerome's terrain is fascinating. The town sits on a few steep terraces engraved into the side of a mountain. A large *J* labels the mountain above the town. That was the third time I noticed towns with large white letters on the side of a mountain above the town. Ruidoso, New Mexico, was one of the others, with an *R* labeling one of its peaks. When I arrived in Jerome it was about 1:30pm and my stomach was on E. In ultra-rare form, I had skipped breakfast. I tracked down a place to grab lunch by way of smell.

It was The English Kitchen and sat on one of Jerome's steep side streets that act as big steps leading up or down the mountain. Inside, bar-like seating accompanied a few tight booths. I pulled up a stool and slid my elbows out in front of me, hands holding a menu. I ordered their BBQ bacon burger.

My first bites confirmed that the town wasn't the only thing amazing here. Greasy slabs of bacon were glued to a man-sized patty of ground beef with BBQ sauce. It's not worth mentioning the bun or other trivial toppings. I had sunk my teeth into the best burger of my life and knew it. It could have been wrapped in shop rags and topped with pencil erasers; it still would have kicked the pants off of any other burger I've had. I knew that I'd reached the burger apex of my trip. I knew that no other combination of toppings, meat patty, and bun would be so unforgettable. It had a flavor that my taste buds would've died for. I tipped the pretty young waitress well and moseyed outside.

Finding Maynard Keenan's wine shop became my unexpected mission in Jerome. He named it Caduceus Cellars and I found it on the second or third terrace down from the top of town in a red brick building that shared a couple of store fronts and a sagging roof line. I'm not into wine at all, unless we're talking about me whining about the cold, but seeing his place was a treat. I've loved Tool's sound since I was a long-haired, grungy kid in the mid-nineties, and from the documentary, one could tell that Maynard was a laid back and respectable guy.

Here in Jerome he had set up a wine cellar of rustic sophistication. Red brick lined the interior walls, hardwood the floors, and rows of thin black track lights highlighted decorative pieces. The place was packed. Everyone in there, but me, was dressed nicely. I wondered if I was the only one visiting solely based on a loose connection to Tool. I'll never know. Jerome, as great as it was, would become my first stop of the day. I wanted to stay, but Red Rock Country was too alluring.

Red Rock Country and Sedona were twenty-seven miles northeast. Daylight wasn't on my side, but that didn't stop me from pursuing another mountain town experience. How can one describe Sedona? Let's just say I'm not the one. Immediately it took the honors of being the prettiest place I'd ever seen (Sorry, Big Bend). Heaven came to mind. The Yavapai Apaches consider the region sacred. If ever there were a spiritually inspirational plot of land, Sedona would be it. I had just arrived and felt lifted and light. Before I reached downtown, I pulled off into a housing development where I could see a mound of red soil poking through the evergreens. I headed for it. It was a cleared lot intended for a single family home. I rode to the top, working the Goose's suspension a little.

For a 360-degree view, white and red monoliths soared to the sky. I was wearing a smile like a surgeon had permanently fixed it there. I spun in a circle with camera in hand. The place was perfect!

And in such perfect places, you get droves of wealthy folks and flocks of tourists (like me). I rode into town expecting boutiques, coffee shops, and rustic restaurants—and they were there. But, so was a Burger King, sitting at a round-about like a diseased cat, spoiling a priceless view. My heart screamed, *Why? Why here? Why Sedona? Why can't they build that wretched thing five miles out of town? Is there no place that greed-ridden corporate America won't build, or will Wal-Mart flatten the top of one of these wonderful red monuments and put a plastic escalator in front of it so that our fat American asses can glide up it and buy forty flimsy plastic bags of junk?*

I hate to say it, but I may have just written an idea down that will inspire Wal-Mart's development crew to get to work on its next convenient location. The egos of these corporations make me sick. Mother Nature has worked way too hard in Sedona to have a fake ass adobe food box placed anywhere nearby. This was more tasteless than McDonald's building in the Biltmore District in Asheville, North Carolina.

I imagine that these companies gather at a yearly conference in Patondabak City, Missouri, to hand out awards for the year's most destructive, tasteless, and culture-killing locations. And, I bet there is some dilweed who goes home and hangs the award on the wall above his Ronald McDonald toilet and brags to his wife about how easy it was to get Egypt's consent, allowing him to place glowing golden arches on top of the Great Pyramid.

Because of Sedona, I snapped over 300 pictures. After reviewing them, none came close to portraying the majestic town. Sedona is a place that you just have to see for yourself. If a picture is worth a thousand words, then I'd need a bigger memory card to help describe the natural beauty. My visit was little more than a ride through. I wanted not to disturb the place or leave any trace of my encounter. Instead, I just wanted a minute with the megaliths. Mostly satisfied, I silently promised to return for a longer visit one day.

I pushed on via 89A to Flagstaff for the next leg and passed an elk crossing sign—a first for me. The snow along the shoulders was more than a foot deep. Flagstaff was going to be my original stopping point, but when I arrived, it was dusk and I still felt like riding my motorcycle, even though the temperatures were plummeting. There was something that I wanted to do in Winslow, Arizona. I fueled up with the plan of a next day visit to Flagstaff, and hauled ass through barren grasslands on I-40 E for fifty-seven miles to Winslow. A sign marking I-40 W had the words "Los Angeles" on it. I felt far from home.

I arrived in Winslow after a bout with Old Man Winter. I found another Motel 6. For dinner, I did my best gringo stroll into Alfonso's Mexican Restaurant. The food wasn't what made the experience memorable. I was the only patron, and Alfonso's lacked any neat angle to make my blood pump. Yet a weird teenage girl made my meal unforgettable.

She was a petite, pretty blonde and no more than fifteen years old. She wasn't eating. In fact, I have no idea what she was doing there. As soon as I walked in the door, she made it her mission to attack me with attention. She was carrying one of those plastic six-shooting snapping guns, which she used to shoot me about a million times during my dinner. At one point she came over, sat with me, smothered me with questions, made farting noises, asked for a ride on the bike (at which I responded very low under my breath with "If only you were eighteen"), all the while venting about how much she hated boring old Winslow.

I stuffed my face and nodded in polite agreement. She acted as though she had been dipped into a vat of Coca-Cola. Her hyperactivity was off the charts. I did my best to entertain her sporadic goofiness without being too much of a stuffy, uptight adult. After all, we were all kids once. She was still there when I left. I'm sure she was waiting to pounce on the next unassuming spud that walked through the door.

To end the day uninterestingly—like a stuffy, uptight adult—I finished eating and rode to Wal-Mart to buy a blanket for the increasingly cold nights of camping that I'd get in the high country of northern Arizona.

Day 77 – December 29, 2011

Standing on a corner in Winslow, Arizona—that's what I *had* to do in Winslow. I peeked out of my room's second-floor window and spotted the Goose down below with the ever-present frost on it. Glad that my trusty travel companion was still there, I began packing for the busy day ahead. Three stops were loosely in mind: downtown Winslow, to seek out *The Corner*; Flagstaff, for some pizza; and the Page/Lake Powell area of northern Arizona, for a unique visit with a new friend. All in all, it would add another 190 miles to the odometer and feel like a day of nonstop riding.

That was fine with me. I was getting somewhat used to the fact that if you want to get anywhere in the Southwest you have to dedicate a serious chunk of time. If I had started the trip with such large gaps between destinations, I may have ended it much sooner. The more compact East Coast broke me in nicely.

A couple strong blips of the throttle knocked out the quick two-mile ride from Winslow's Motel 6 to Standing on the Corner Park, at the intersection of Route 66 (Second Street) and Kinsley. The tiny holy grail of a park is big enough to invite you in for a picture but is still just a snag of a small town intersection. Winslow erected a mock-up building for the park. Distressed tan bricks and murals that looked like windows and doors gave it the feel of a real building. I happened to ride up from behind it where I saw that the structure was no more than four feet thick and made of cinder block. The faux building and giant Route 66 emblem, painted smack-dab in the center of Second and Kinsley, were nice touches that added to the attraction's charm. A sculpture that marked *the Corner* was of a young man with jeans and a leather jacket on, holding a guitar, and looking like the perfect hitchhiker. As he remained motionless in a distant stare, I ran across the street in search of a sticker for my bike and kept an eye out for that hot chick in a flatbed Ford. Perhaps she had errands to run or something and had taken off on foot, because there at the intersection, was an empty, pristine, cherry red, flatbed Ford.

I only noticed it after several minutes of wandering aimlessly and gawking at the sculpture, far longer than it should have taken to see it. Instead of being parked at sidewalk level within the park, it sat quietly along the curb like any other vehicle. If not for the wooden side rails along the bed, I think that I would've caught on quicker that the truck belonged to the park and not some old feller with a knack for restoration. Every time that I'd ever heard *"It's a girl, my Lord, in a flatbed Ford slowing down to take a look at me,"* I pictured a truck much like the one at the park, but without racks or bed rails of any kind. This is not to say that I was disappointed with it; the truck was perfect, even with its side rails. Winslow and the Kaufman family, who donated the land, had generously created a compact park that magically captured an idealistic moment in time.

I found it curious to see that most of the other tourists managed to take a picture with the sculpture while skipping the flatbed Ford sitting right there. I believe that they, too, missed the connection or thought that the truck was owned by one of Winslow's citizens.

I thought of a small piece of advice for the quiet town of Winslow. If they paid a good-looking gal to sit in the flatbed Ford, no one would miss the truck, tourism would be boosted, and I'm sure the business she would bring from being in the truck would supplement her wage. Personally, I would've loved to get a picture of a girl in the flatbed Ford looking at me standing on the corner, even more than a picture of me with the sculpture of the hitchhiker. Hell, in a year or two, the little blonde from Alfonso's last night could do the job. She was terribly bored and in desperate need of something to do.

Eventually, I came to the end of all that could be done at *the Corner* and had to leave. A feeling washed over me as I rode away from Winslow. It was a feeling that I'd never see the town again. Standing on the corner once is enough. It's not cool to stand on it twice. The lyrics aren't *"Standing on a corner in Winslow,*

Arizona, again," and there was nothing else going on there, so that was it and I was off to Flagstaff.

Humphreys Peak, Arizona's highest point at 12,633 feet, towers over Flagstaff and is clearly visible from Winslow. *It would be impossible to get lost traveling to Flagstaff from anywhere around here.* In the sea of grass and small hills, Humphreys Peak hovered in the sky like a big snow-capped buoy. I aimed and shot the Goose in Humphrey's direction. Sixty miles later, I hit my target of Flagstaff. Right away, I liked Flagstaff. It had that not too big, not too small, feel. The buildings were rustic and a lot of red brick and wood accents made them look that way. I parked among the old buildings on old Route 66 and found what I was looking for a few hundred feet away on a side street.

I was in Flagstaff to hunt down Alpine Pizza. The Travel Channel featured it on one of its pizza joint episodes a while back. I found the hip pizza parlor tucked back and wedged between two brick buildings. It had a tiny, café-style front porch where folks could dine on warmer days. The building was petite and cozy and felt more like a restaurant than a place to grab a quick slice. Inside, four booths—with wooden tables that looked like dwarfed picnic tables—were crammed into a dining room corner. Above them, a decorative, cedar-shingled roof added character. I threw my things in the first booth where a heart with "Cathy loves John" was carved into its wooden divider. In fact, every booth was engraved with a brief history of pizza-lovin', pocketknife-wielding couples.

I ordered a personal pizza topped with extra cheese, hamburger, and pepperoni, and can now vouch for the quality that put it on the map. The pie was anything but overly commercialized. It wasn't flawlessly round, and the toppings weren't laid out in checkerboard perfection. The right amount of greasiness shined up the cheese. I enjoyed it thoroughly, yet still gave the nod to Manhattan NY Pizza in Norcross, Georgia, as my favorite slice thus far. Alpine

Pizza and Flagstaff had the aura of places deserving a longer visit in the future, but I needed to push on if I were to make it to Lake Powell before dark.

I geared up, smacked the Goose in the ass, and made a beeline due north. Flagstaff's high terrain and foothills covered in golden grass faded away into a wonderland of color. I had reached the southern entrance of the massive Navajo Nation. A neat statistic that links my home state to the Navajo Nation is that both it and West Virginia encompass nearly 27,000 square miles, making the Navajo Nation the largest reservation in the United States. And worth noting, West Virginia may be the largest reservation of hillbillies in the United States.

About the time of passing the eastern entrance to the Grand Canyon, the landscape began to change drastically. This was the first time that the word exotic came to mind. The reds in the surrounding mountains matched that of Sedona, but they were accompanied by greys, violets, oranges, and a huge blue sky. Some sections of the ride through the reservation looked unnatural, like the soil and mountains were layered and colored by a team of designers. My pace slowed to a crawl.

It was so pretty and so unspoiled that it led me to complain. For forty miles I slammed the brakes on, took my big gloves off, untied my helmet strap, took the helmet off, dug the camera out, turned it on, set up a shot, turned the camera off, put it away, put my helmet back on, strapped it, put my gloves back on, and sped off only to stop a mile later because something awesome had caught my eye. All of that inconvenience couldn't erase my smile. A feeling of awe surged through my veins.

Page sits just inside the reservation's northwestern boundary, against Glen Canyon and the shores of Lake Powell. I crossed through a narrow, solid orange mountain pass. Snow clung heavily to the western walls on my ascent. The whites and oranges turned the land into a dreamsicle. I looked back through the pass to see a low sun perfectly in line with the road. The smooth pavement near me faded from pewter to a shiny, vanishing gold. I thought that I'd seen the day's best until the sun pulled one more trick out of its celestial sleeve.

I was a handful of miles out of Page and beginning a descent into town. Lights clustered together to form a civilization ahead, but overhead in the northeast, the sky was dark and purple. A thick, pink cloud underlined a set of orange, wispy clouds that stuck out like fingers into what was left of a baby blue western sky. It was so perfect that I parked the Goose for another picture. I walked a couple paces, set up the tripod, walked back to the Goose, faced the camera, went down humbly to one knee, raised my hands in the air as to become one with the sunset, and snapped a blurry feckin' picture. Perfection is hard to capture.

Earlier, I had searched for a campground online and found one simply called Page/Lake Powell Campground. It was well after dark when I pitched my tent. The temperature had already begun its evening dive, so I settled in for an early night.

Day 78 – December 30, 2011

I awoke well rested from one of the better nights of sleep I'd had. The strategy of adding another blanket to the gear paid off. This new blanket was folded over my blue camping pad, and by lying on it and using the unzipped sleeping bag as a blanket, I stayed nice and warm and was able to stretch out. It only took seventy-seven days to figure that out. Sometimes my light bulb doesn't shine so bright, ya know?

Page/Lake Powell Campground was once a KOA, and the residual facilities were still pretty nice from its former existence. Even with no real reason to improve their elevated tent sites, they were still making minor improvements. Before the frost had fully melted away, a bit of construction was going on in my sector of the campground. At first, thoughts of getting a discount because of the construction came to mind, but like many times before, a blessing was waiting in disguise.

One of the construction workers, Carl—a spiky-blonde-haired, twentysomething—took a brief break to come over and ask about the Goose and my journey while he puffed on a cigarette. I filled him in on my mad scheme. He dug it. In fact, he kindly invited me to the annual Frosty Balls Poker Run on New Year's morning with him and his fellow riders. I committed to it and planned to stick around Page until after the ride. Since I was sleeping in a tent every night in Page, my nards would be nice and conditioned for the cold ride.

Last night, in Winslow, I received an email from a feller named Mitch, who lived in Page and had been following my journey via ADVrider.com and my blog—since October. He first contacted me weeks before as he shared advice and recommendations for sights to see while visiting the Southwest. His messages were consistent enough that I began to look forward to hearing from him. When he sent that email to me in Winslow, the timing could not have been more perfect. I replied that I'd be heading due north to visit his neck of the desert the very next day—way sooner than he expected. He responded back with an offer of free lunch at a nearby restaurant. I didn't hesitate to accept the offer. Mitch did not know that visiting Lake Powell was already high on my to-do list. Because of him following along and our back and forth emailing, an interesting dynamic was born. He would become the first person who I met, in person, who found me via the Internet and my blog.

Mitch suggested that we eat at a floating restaurant at the Antelope Point Marina on Lake Powell. Although not the world's only floating restaurant, Ja'di To'oh at Antelope Point was the world's largest floating restaurant. Ja'di To'oh translates to Antelope Springs in Navajo, and the building was connected to the rest of the world via a long aluminum pier that scaled down the rocky shore and floated out into Lake Powell. Golf carts whizzed back and forth on the pier, transporting the out-of-shape, the elderly, and victims of food coma. Mitch told me that he'd meet me there.

I pulled up to an all-but-empty parking lot. The lake was mirror calm and reflected every feature that Arizona and Utah's desert could throw at it. I walked toward the shore for a better look at Ja'di To'oh. Then I noticed a motorcycle pull in and take a spot beside the Goose. It was Mitch on his Honda, PC800. Like me, he rode every day in all sorts of weather on his way to and from work. I turned and walked back to the Goose. Mitch was wearing a black protective suit, one that could take a hit and one that could fight off the cold. He stood tall and strong with salt-and-pepper-colored hair. He may have been in his late fifties or early sixties. His PC800 shone bright white under a huge blue sky. We shook hands with a smile and began walking toward the pier. When we got to it, we—being the big manly adventure riders that we were—took the golf cart to the restaurant.

Ja'di To'oh looked much larger and taller standing along its dry-stacked stone walls. It also seemed rather upscale. Inside, the ceilings were high, maybe fourteen feet, and the upscale feel abounded. I appreciated having lunch in such a place and surely would have missed Ja'di To'oh if not for Mitch. I ate a wonderfully prepared burger with cheddar and sautéed mushrooms. Mitch informed me that his son-in-law was the general manager of the restaurant and marina. He told me that they were planning a massive New Year's party with a wickedly upgraded fireworks show. A cover of $40 would get me in to see the live music, take part in the balloon drop, have dinner, and basically hang out at one of the coolest spots on the planet for the New Year's celebration. I was all in, except for the $40 part.

I love to party down, but that was just outside of the budget. I think that Mitch sensed that and somehow urged his son-in-law to come over with a comped ticket in the form of a blue, rubber wristband that said "Rock the Dock

II." I was so grateful for their generosity and couldn't wait to see the fireworks over Lake Powell. When Mitch and I finished lunch, I promised him that I'd see him at tomorrow's celebration. He headed off to tend to his duties, and I stuck around the restaurant for a bit to absorb some Wi-Fi.

I left Antelope Point a half hour later for a six-mile dart toward the Utah border. The 710-foot Glen Canyon Dam intercepted my attention before reaching the new state. The dam and the mighty Colorado River are responsible for Lake Powell's tremendous volume of fresh water. When the Glen Canyon Dam was built amid Page's arid land, the region gained an incalculable stockpile of fresh water. As a result of the dammed water, a lake formed with a shoreline longer than the entire West Coast of the United States—thanks to hundreds of nameless side canyons that took on water. On a map, Lake Powell looks unique when compared with the Colorado River's other dammed lakes. It has a shape that looks like the up and down ink marks that are etched on paper during a large earthquake, like dense spikes or fingers of water jutting away from the center. You don't see this sporadic shape represented as much in other popular lakes such as Lake Mead or Lake Havasu.

I parked the Goose and hiked along a smooth trail of orange rock to the dam's overlook. Glen Canyon fell away alarmingly. In front of me was a picture of the Hoover Dam's little brother. Beyond the dam, I could see the surface of Lake Powell, and immediately in front of me, and hundreds of feet below, the Colorado River looked dark and turbulent as it flowed uninterrupted through Glen Canyon. No one was around, so I quickly crossed a barrier to get an unobstructed picture. I crawled to the edge of Glen Canyon and held out my camera. I hoped that the wavy orange rocks would hold together for just a few more moments. I snapped a picture and pulled back. It looked as though the picture was taken from a helicopter. *Perfect.*

Looking away from the dam, Glen Canyon zigzagged out of sight. It was dangerously vertical and wonderfully beautiful all in one. A slight green carpet of vegetation hugged what little shoreline there was along the Colorado River.

With the Utah sign in sight, I detoured to a convenience store for some caffeine, and boy was I surprised to find the brand FMF (Flying Machine Factory), a motocross performance exhaust manufacturer, now making their own energy drink. Its motto was "Taste the Power." There was no way to pass it up. I wanted to taste the power! I excitedly bought a red-and-yellow-labeled bottle and twisted the top off. I snapped a corny picture of me taking my first sip.

Beside me in the parking lot two women from Utah were heading south for the winter. They recognized my West Virginia license plate and said, "Isn't your state motto for lovers or something?" I said, "No, that's Virginia. Our motto is Wild and Wonderful." I told her, "In West Virginia we get wild and then ride on over to Virginia for some wonderful lovin'." I told her that Virginians fear us. They enjoyed my motto modification. After my chat with the snowbirds, I headed off for the Utah border all amped up from my bottle of FMF power.

At the state line sign I let loose a bit and snapped off some really fun shots. Utah's motto is "Life Elevated." I did my best to get elevated in Utah by jumping over the Goose and capturing the action. As I built up a head of steam running toward the bike for the leap, I hoped that my foot wouldn't catch the seat and leave me tumbling in the soup of gravel on the other side. I had to jump over the bike three times to get the angle and timing right. My camera was on a ten-second delay and set for ten rapid shots. I was tired by the third jump, but managed to get it right. I left the sign for a short ride along a dirt road on Lake Powell's northern shore. It looked just like the southern shore, only more remote. I allowed a sunset and darkening sky to chase me back to civilization.

Being Friday and New Year's weekend, there was no way that I could settle for hibernating in a tent. Like it was my life's mission, I went to town to meet some Page-ens or Page-ites or Page-ers or whatever they call themselves. In a shopping plaza downtown, I found an aptly named joint called the Dam Bar and Grill. I strolled into that dam place like a dam high roller. The dam place was packed. The dam music was good. The dam bartender was hot. I found a dam bar stool, ordered a dam beer, and then sat there like a dam bump on a log.

A fella named Ryan sat down beside me, saving me from my boring self. He said that he was Navajo and that his home was on the reservation. He was in his late thirties, dressed casual, was dark-skinned, soft-spoken, and friendly. Ryan and I talked like old buddies for about twenty minutes until his wife called. He had to make a quick run to the airport to pick her up. At first, I thought he was bullshitting me. Page was so small that I could not conceive of it having an airport, but when he returned to the bar he had his supremely attractive wife by his side. She wasn't Navajo. Instead, she was of Latin American descent.

They joined me at our corner barstools. We yapped on about everything from riding, to taxes, and of all things, *Forrest Gump*. They lived in Kayenta, a town less than forty miles from the spot where Forrest stopped running in the desert to turn around and go home. The spot was in Monument Valley. I asked Ryan where it was, and he gave me his contact info and told me to call him tomorrow so that I could follow him there. Right then, it would be safe to say that I was stoked! I told them about my blog, my journey, and its unintended Gump-like theme. They couldn't believe it, and at one time Ryan actually said, "I'm just waiting for the hidden camera to pop out," like I was pranking them. We had a great time, shared a lot of laughs, and I found exactly what I had come to town for. I felt lucky. They left for their long ride home; I followed suit, making my way back to my lush palace at the RV campground.

Day 79 – December 31, 2011

On New Year's Eve, I awoke with one thing in mind, and it wasn't urinating, cold weather, coffee, or a steamy scene with Selma Hayek. I needed to get in touch with Ryan, ride thru the Navajo reservation to Monument Valley, and find the point where Forrest Gump stopped running in the movie—the point where he is in Monument Valley and turns to his legion of followers and announces, "I'm pretty tired. Think I'll go home now."

I didn't know the exact location, so I gave Ryan a call. He didn't answer. I called again, and again no answer. I waited a while and called again, hoping that I didn't come across as the loony type last night. Still, he didn't answer. I wasn't sure why. At the Dam Bar and Grill he was all about showing me where the spot was. I knew that the spot was within 140 miles from camp, so I decided to go for it anyway.

From my road atlas I couldn't tell if there were settlements along the way. The maps I carried left out most details about the reservations. I knew from talking to Ryan that the town of Kayenta was one of the bigger towns on the reservation, but that was ninety-five miles from camp. As if I need to mention it, the Navajo live in an extremely remote area of Arizona, and fuel stops are few and far between. With my bike gassed up, and the decision made to gamble on Kayenta having a fuel station open on New Year's Eve, I nervously rode into the complete unknown.

The Goose was getting about 160 miles to the tank, and to make it to Monument Valley and back on one fill would be impossible. Miles and miles passed with hardly any sign of life other than the random small herd of cattle. I was seriously worried that I'd have to abort the mission. I calculated my location and mileage over and over in my head in case I had to turn back. Then, as I rode farther along, things began to change. Tiny trading posts and the odd service station began to appear. They were rudimentary buildings. Some were without any external advertising, and some had just one or two ads—like for coffee or for fuel.

With about a half tank down, I pulled into a fuel station in the Black Mesa part of the reservation. Above the tanks, a blue and yellow sign read "Van Fuels." The store was deemed a shopping center but looked more like a business that had gone under. Inside, most of your everyday snacks and foods were available, along with crafts and clothing. It was far from being out of business despite the rough exterior. The anxiety that I had when leaving Page dissolved, as I kept an eastern path toward that unmistakable stretch of road.

At 120 miles from Page, I arrived at the Utah border again. I was in the heart of Monument Valley and unsure of where the movie scene took place. *Man, I could really use Ryan's help right now.* Twice, I was sure that I had found the spot where Forrest stopped running. Both times, I took the time to set up the camera for a couple pictures of me running through the valley like a crazy man running from the voices.

I pulled the bike over, ran up the road a bit, set the timer for ten seconds, hauled ass on foot down the road (counting 10…9…8…), then turned and trotted tiredly toward the camera. As I meddled in this silliness, I hoped that no one was watching. And wouldn't you know, hindsight is 20/20, and that, combined with Murphy's Law, worked against me in high concentration on this mission. Before I left for Monument Valley, I didn't take the time to look up the scene in the movie while I had Wi-Fi. I tried calling Ryan again. He snuffed me out for the final time. Only when I arrived back in Page and had Wi-Fi did I realize that I didn't ride far enough to get to the correct spot. *Son of a bitch.*

I had fun anyway. The formations in Monument Valley made up for every uncertain mile and every ignored phone call. They were spectacular beyond words. The monuments exist in an odd and lonely land of gently rolling flatness with long views of roads vanishing into needle points. Some of the peculiar pillars seem like legs to a missing table top. Others are long and narrow like a reverse canyon. You can't help but stare in wonder as they seem to reject any notion of becoming part of the normal terrain. Riding in their presence was a huge treat. I wondered if the Navajo still see them as miraculous as I did, or do they drive by desensitized with small worries like what am I going to eat tonight, or what's playing on the tube this evening?

On the ride back to Page, I stopped for a slice at Pizza Edge in Kayenta. I kept one eye wandering around the room in case Ryan walked in and the other on my greasy little slice of heaven. I was the only Caucasian around, but no one seemed to care. Being in such a place gave me a feeling of no longer being in the States. Pizza Edge's exterior was bare and beat-up, like a lot of the other businesses on the reservation. Down the street, I filled the tank again, left Kayenta, and focused on the terrain twice as much as I had on the ride there. As the day became long in the tooth and the sky grew darker, I hastened my pace to Page. I had a party to attend.

For the party, my wardrobe and everything from my shoulders up needed a tune up. I decided to cut my hair and buy a new pair of pants. Mine were stained and holey. I stood in front of a mirror at the campground's bathhouse holding an electric shaver in my right hand. I aimed at my mop of unkempt, reddish hair, and took a swipe with the electric shaver. It was a doozy. I had made a canyon on my head. At the bottom of that canyon, I now had hair the length of Velcro and an exposed scalp that hadn't seen light in thirty years. I stayed positive. The only way to correct it was to go ahead and cut all of my hair incredibly short. I had always been curious to see what it would look like anyway, and a new year was fast approaching. *Why not?* I went for it, leaving clumps of strawberry blonde fur all over the floor. The results were highly questionable. *It will grow on me—literally.* With a new bald head and a new set of jeans, I was off to the party.

I rolled up to Antelope Point at 8:30pm. Unfortunately, Mitch had already left. Not exactly knowing how to react, I decided to stick around for the celebration and fireworks. I was admittedly disappointed that I let him down after I promised to see him again the next day. In the days that followed, he told me that he had passed me on a golf cart on the way up the pier as I was walking down. We still kept in touch, and I was glad that my tardiness didn't change that.

Celebrating New Year's in Arizona, and in the Mountain Time Zone, brought with it an unexpected treat. At 10:00pm there was a balloon drop to mark the New Year on the East Coast, and at midnight the fireworks were lit to mark the New Year in Arizona. It never occurred to me that West Coasters would celebrate New Year's any different from us.

Just before the balloon drop, the restaurant manager pulled me aside and asked if I could pull one of the cords on a balloon bag. I said sure and was happy to lend a hand. For me, the party began after that. I met up with the bartender from the Dam Bar and Grill, whom I'd met the night before, and a few of her friends. She let me tag along to one of their houseboats floating on Lake Powell. Man, I'd a followed her anywhere. She was about five-eight, blonde, more fun than a barrel of monkeys, and had a hind end that would make you wanna howl at the moon. She introduced me to a slew of young, happy folks on the boat. The fun was flowing and the time sped up. I was partying like it was 1999.

Before I knew it, the fireworks had started. I sat glassy-eyed with my legs dangling from the restaurant's outside walkway over the calm waters of Lake Powell. Soft lights from Ja'di To'oh reflected off the water and the shiny boats docked nearby. Each huge, colorful blast invited hoots and hollers from folks standing outside. As the fireworks concluded, I spent the rest of the night shaking a leg with the best of them (I thought) on the dance floor until they shut the place down. Can't beat that!

Day 80 – January 1, 2012

2012 welcomed me with a sweet hangover. I swore I'd never drink again. Actually, I didn't regret it. I had a great time. Lake Powell and Page had shown me an unexpected side of life in extreme northern Arizona. The folks were great and the terrain one of a kind. I felt blessed to experience way more than I alone could have pulled off. One day I'd like to get back to the lake for some serious boating recreation, a swim, and another New Year's Eve party at Ja'di' To'oh.

But for now, I had my sights set on the big daddy of them all for New Year's Day—the Grand Canyon! Ninety miles separate Page and the Grand Canyon, which isn't too bad of a ride if the poison in your bloodstream isn't plotting against you. You have to pay to play, and I play hard and pay dearly.

Carl came over as I was packing my stuff and wanted to see if I was still in for the Frosty Balls Poker Run. I planned to do it, but once I found out that they weren't beginning the ride until noon, and having no idea what direction they would be traveling, I decided to skip it. The weather was warm and beautiful, making frosty balls out of the question. Besides, during my short stay in Page, I had managed to ride north, south, and east of town. Wherever the guys were going to ride, odds are that I'd already been there, as there are only a few ways in and out of Page. Getting to the Grand Canyon before dark was a definite priority. Carl understood, and we said good luck to one another. I stopped in town for lunch and supplies. At around 1:30, I was ten miles south of Page when I passed a group of a dozen motorcyclists heading toward Page. I lowered my left hand for the patented biker wave, as did they. I wasn't sure, but I'd be willing to bet that Carl and the guys were on those bikes.

I continued south, solo. I was backtracking on Route 89 through the reservation and through the same beautiful landscape that made me stop a million times three days before. A particular layered pile of sediment had caught my eye on the ride north, but I didn't stop to take a picture of it the first time. This time, I wasn't going to miss it. From the ground it started as a light cream color, like that of a book page; then a layer of grey with a twinge of purple sat on that. A thin stripe of deep purple rested on top of that, followed by a thin stripe of cream again. On top of that, a thick purple layer underlined the rusty-red top of the mound. Its shape mimicked a steep sand dune. It may have been thirty feet high and as long as a football field. I had never seen Mother Nature so precisely separate colors and combine them in a stack. The color lines were ruler straight, and even with thousands of thin erosion channels, centuries of water drainage was not enough to blend the colors together. It was a geologist's dream pile.

Route 89 intersects Route 64 at Cameron, the last bit of civilization before entering the Grand Canyon from the east. It was nearly 4:00pm when I wandered through Cameron's gift shop. My ass wanted a break from the saddle and my head needed hydration. Other than that, Cameron had nothing to offer a guy who was traveling through and already packed heavy like a covered wagon. An art gallery, motel, gift shop, and service station made up all of Cameron. I left the souvenir haven behind for the thirty-mile ascent to the Grand Canyon. Trees came back into my world; snow lay on either side of the road. *Where am I? This is not what I expected the Grand Canyon region to look like.* I had always thought of it as a mega gap carved in flat, brown desert, but at the Grand Canyon National Park sign, I couldn't see a hundred feet to my right or left for the thick forest that lined the road.

I ventured on in utter surprise. Desert View Overlook, the first overlook that visitors come to, invited me over. I parked in a well-established parking lot and headed for the good stuff. Then wham! *There it is, the mighty Grand Canyon.* I'm a bit ashamed to say that my first impression of the Grand Canyon was quite neutral. It looked almost exactly as I had pictured it (minus the surrounding forest) and as I'd seen it on hundreds of television programs.

I'd been a desert dweller for over a month and had seen tons of formations, some highly impressive and some not so. I was becoming used to the desert's tricks, and here was the desert's biggest trick of all. As I stood there, I hoped that there would be some other sections that would blow me away in the coming days. If I had flown from the East Coast straight to the Grand Canyon, the terrain shock would have been unimaginable. I expected my first time seeing the Grand Canyon to be like that. I wished that it would have felt as good as seeing the Sierra Del Carmen Mountains for the first time. Oddly, it looked as deep as I imagined but not as wide from rim to rim.

I hiked back to the Goose, nonetheless satisfied. In the parking lot, an Italian fellow was snapping pictures of my bike. I approached him curiously and introduced myself. He was a clean-cut, thin fella, and probably in his early forties. We shook hands and started ranting about motorcycles. He said that he liked my setup even though it was homemade. I listened as he told me of his recent motorcycle trip from Italy through Spain and France. His loop was 6,000 miles, and he did it in nine days. He was testing out a sport bike, and his only luggage was a credit card. *Man, I wish I could travel that light.* Before he mentioned that sort of motorcycle travel, I had never given it an ounce of thought about how convenient that would be. I rode away comparing travel the way I was doing it versus carrying nothing but a credit card. It sounded great.

Mather Campground is twenty-five miles from Desert View Overlook, and the setting sun raced me there the whole time. I stood up on the pegs while crossing over two long, thick patches of ice into the campground. It was heavily wooded with coniferous trees and moderately populated with campers. I found a camp spot, got set up just before dark, and headed back out to learn the area. I was in a semi-search for a Wi-Fi connection. After finding every convenience of urban life, except Wi-Fi, I rode back to the warmth of the sleeping bag for the first of several intensely cold nights.

Day 81 – January 2, 2012

The Grand Canyon is America's gem. As an East Coast native, I—like everyone I know—know something about the Grand Canyon. For my fellow road newbie, I thought it polite to add a few tidbits about its geology and Grand Canyon National Park. Take it with a grain of salt as I'm certainly no expert.

This epic hole is here for us to enjoy because of the Colorado River's tireless shoveling. As the river flows ever on, it whittles at the very ground that supports it. One by one, seemingly insignificant pieces of sediment get lifted, pushed, and carried farther and farther downstream by the water.

Millions of years ago, the Colorado began etching the soil high above the river's current surface, and as it cut deeper, erosion and gravity worked at the canyon walls. Rains, winds, and the freezing and thawing of soil made these walls weak. And what happens when weak, vertical walls meet a destabilizing force? They fall. When they fall, the gap grows wider. The canyon's rim, or top of the canyon, is where you'll find the walls that have been longest exposed to the forces of erosion, which explains why the Grand Canyon's rim is much wider than the Colorado River.

The part of the Grand Canyon that the National Park Service currently maintains is the eastern portion. The western portion belongs to the Hualapai Indian Tribe and is called Grand Canyon West. That's where the Sky Walk was built. In the national park, the only spots with dramatic visibility are the overlooks, due to the dense tree line. The North Rim of the Grand Canyon bests the South Rim by about 500 feet in elevation and was closed to campers during the winter. Mather Campground was the sole campground open during the cold months on the South Rim. And for the city slicker, Grand Canyon Village featured a full-blown grocery store, post office, and Chase Bank. There were several lodges with spacious lobbies, gift shops, bars, lots of rooms, and the worst Wi-Fi known to man. The Wi-Fi in the lodges allowed me to make it as far as my home page before rudely going on vacation. The library at the park headquarters was where I found the only Internet connection worth messing with.

A lot of folks along my journey told me that there wouldn't be anyone at the park during the winter months. Compared to the summer months, there probably wasn't, but there were still enough tourists running around in the cold of winter that parking at any one of the lodges, even on a motorcycle was damn near impossible. I couldn't imagine the sort of madhouse that the park becomes in the warmer months.

If you can handle the cold and don't mind foreign tourists, I would highly recommend visiting the Grand Canyon in the winter months. Doing so would allow you elbow room to move around in the park's buildings. English was a second language among the majority of folks that I encountered, minus park employees. Finally, to wrap up GC 101 for today, if we don't watch out, Wal-Mart will buy the whole damn thing, erect five super centers, construct Wal-Mart Dam somewhere west of the Grand Canyon, fill the canyon with water, and lease space to the titans of the burger industry for floating restaurants. . . .

The light of morning graced my Kelty tent, and the rush to get some hot coffee began. At nearly 7,000 feet, Mather Campground had air cold enough to freeze a stream of pee. I fired up the ol' Primus stove and popped some instant coffee in the pot. A few ravens, the size of roosters, lurked at the edges of my campsite. Until noticing a brochure about them, I thought that they were tremendously large crows. The story about a raven finding land after leaving Noah's Ark and Edgar Allan Poe's poem "The Raven" did little to prepare me for their size. I pictured them being smaller, and for that matter, I always imagined road runners being considerably larger. In the cartoon the road runner was as tall, or taller, than Wile E. Coyote.

Intrigued, I sipped my steamy cup of coffee until the caffeine took hold, then walked to the campground facilities for a $2 hot shower. That would get me a solid eight minutes of warm water. An engraving in my stall said, "$1.50 4 a shower, rip-off." I guess the park service didn't get that guy's memo before they hiked the price up fifty cents. I washed quickly so as to not have the water cut off and leave me full of bubbles.

The mission for the day should have been absorbing majestic views while snapping countless pictures, but it just wasn't. I had a serious hankering for a Wi Fi connection and was certain that one had to exist in the park. I just knew if Big Bend had solid Wi-Fi, then surely Grand Canyon National Park would match it. Going five days without an update for the family and friends back home—who knew that I was at the Grand Canyon—didn't seem right. I was their gopher, their test dummy, their expendable hillbilly adventurer sending stories back to the homeland. I only know of one person from back home who has seen the Grand Canyon and lived to tell the tale. Five days without a post wasn't an option.

My wild goose chase, via the Goose, took me all around the park, through all the lodges, and finally to the park headquarters and library, thanks to a tip from a guy at one of the visitor centers. By that time, it was after two o'clock and most of the light of the day had passed. *No worries. I'll be here for a few more days and have plenty of time to mess around in the canyon.*

I left the library for a short hike along the rim near the visitor center, past Mather Point. The paved trail was only 1.3 miles long, and meandered along the canyon's edge. I'd cross a few overlooks and peacefully stroll through the woods. I wouldn't be too far from civilization but just far enough to get myself into trouble. It was the perfect solo break-in hike.

I set about walking. The trail was flat and easy. It hugged the rim closely, but was far enough away that you could trip and fall two or three times and still not plummet to your death. Railings protected folks at the overlooks. Everywhere else, the invisible railing of sound judgment kept my legs from having one of those involuntary jumping reactions that you fear when you're up way too high and way too close to an edge.

The Grand Canyon's rim zigzags its way along the Colorado's course. At some overlooks, I was able to look right and left and see other humans at other overlooks. Only when that happened did I realize just how big it is. As they stood at the end of some eroded peninsula, a half mile or mile away, they looked like little pieces of moving peach fuzz on top of a gigantic cliff. The whole seeing-people-as-ants-from-an-airplane effect was going on in a horizontal plane. Without them standing out there at the edge, I found it hard to grasp the scale of the colossal canyon.

The rim trail weaved and wandered. On one side of it, base jumping country loomed, and on the other, vast forest lay. I hiked casually without ever being able to see around the next corner, and one of those next corners got me. I was strolling around like the pale picture-taker that I am when I rounded a corner and bam! Right beside the trail were three huge elk. In this situation, I have hunting friends that would've bonered out immediately, but the elk made me nervous. The shrubby trees weren't big enough to climb, and if one of those beasts wanted to charge I'd have nowhere to go. Backtracking would put me in the forest way after dark. I had to get the hoofed herd to move.

I reverted to some trail knowledge that I learned along the way. Signs had recommended that if you encounter wildlife, you should make noise, throw rocks or sticks, and keep your distance. So there I was, raising my voice, demanding them to move, and throwing anything I could find at them, while trying not to actually hit them. They didn't give a flying rat's ass about my protest and just kept grazing. For a brief second, one looked up as I was waving my arms around. When they were good and ready, they simply walked far enough away from the rim for me to safely pass. Relief! The Goose wasn't far away. Still walking back, I came across a mule deer with a massive rack. He was old and far off the trail. I figured that I could make a mad dash away if needed, but like the elk, he wasn't worried about me either.

After the wildlife fun, I headed to the Bright Angel Lodge to charge some batteries. I asked a fella behind the desk if the elk had ever attacked anyone in the park. He said, "On about five occasions. The people they charged were tourists who thought the elk were tame and managed by the park." He also said a few of the unaware tourists even tried to pet them. The only thing owned and managed in the Grand Canyon are the mules, folks. Everything else is as wild as a West Virginian and can hurt you. Yee haw!

Day 82 – January 3, 2012

I'm going to skip the morning routine mumbo jumbo and focus on the day. Of course I didn't sleep well, and of course I had some coffee first thing. Instead of wasting time on that, what's important is that I'm at the Grand Canyon, baby! Give me a fanny pack, a tropical shirt, and socks and sandals combo. It's time to sightsee and point my camera right down into the massive hole in the ground just like millions of other tourists have done before me. Maybe, just maybe, if I'm lucky, I'll pull off a bit of originality in one of my shots.

A few days ago, when I first arrived at the park, I whizzed by most of the pull-offs on my way to Mather Campground, so there were twenty-five miles of overlooks with my name on them. The stop and go and brief hikes would leave plenty to do in one day. I headed back to Desert View Overlook for a better view.

Desert View Overlook has a small gift shop, fuel station with twenty-four-hour pumps, lookout tower, and café. I hit the café up for another coffee and hobbled over to the lookout tower. It was cylindrical, faced with dry stacked stone, and three or four stories tall. A few coin-operated telescopes were placed at the upper level windows. I checked out the high perch for a bit, realizing that everywhere around the rim of the Grand Canyon is a high perch, then stepped outside for a better look. Nothing had changed in two days, so I headed back to the Goose, satisfied with stop number one.

In the parking lot, I ran into a French fellow, whom I had seen at the Bright Angel Lodge bar. He was a young guy, had dark hair and eyes, was newly twenty-one, fresh off the boat from France, and was getting solidly rejected by the bartender while trying to get a beer last night. At first he pleaded with the bartender to take his word that yesterday was his birthday. The bartender sent him to fetch ID. He walked away flustered. He came back confidently with a white and red French ID of some sort. The bartender denied it like a blocked shot. The guy became visibly upset. The bartender sent him on his way again, and this time there was a spirited verbal exchange. I thought he wasn't coming back, but lo and behold he showed up with his passport. The bartender popped the top off, handed him the brew, and he took a seat and let the best beer of his life cool him down. I smiled at his persistence.

Now, in Desert View's parking lot, he recognized me and was surprised to see that I was riding a street bike in such cold weather. I smiled again and welcomed him to the USA. He was taking a few weeks to see some of the country's more famous sites. I didn't get his name, but it didn't matter. He was a nice fella and thrilled to see the Grand Canyon. We wished each other luck and he left.

Right after we finished talking, another French guy, this time a French Canadian from Quebec, came over to talk bikes with me. Neither one of the guys spoke English very well, and my French is about as good as a coat hanger's, nonetheless I found it quite intriguing to experience their accents back to back. The first French guy's accent was twice as thick, but his English was much better. The French Canadian guy was a motorcycle guy and wanted so badly to tell me all about his bikes, but his English vocabulary was just too thin. We patiently came to the understanding that we both love motorcycles. These guys broke the stereotypical stuck-up-French-guy mold. They were cheerful and interested. I was glad to meet a few more friendly foreigners. Speaking of foreigners, they have completely taken over the park. I think they are in the know about the least crowded time to visit the GC, or perhaps they are just hardier.

While hopping from one pull-in to the next, I studied my camera. To me, it was a piece of equipment with more features than the Grand Canyon itself. *Is there a better place to take a gazillion pictures for practice than the Grand Canyon? Of course there is. It's the Playboy Mansion.* Anyway, by the end of twenty-five miles of overlooks, I had clicked off several hundred half-sketchy pictures and had gained a decent understanding of the Canon. I also learned how to get better shots than the automatic features allow. It's all about light control. That's what I figured out. Many of the automatic settings allowed in more light than necessary, dominating the pictures with solid white skies and tan and beige earth tones where deep reds and oranges should be. My eyes were telling me to keep trying until I got it right. When I reduced the light intake, the colors came back. It's all very interesting, I know. The rest of the day was spent bouncing around the park buildings like a bum looking for a barrel of fire, trying to keep warm, before inevitably ending up mummy-shaped in the Kelty.

Day 83 – January 4, 2012

Those pesky elk were at it again. It was early morning, and I was following two cars across the park to a trail head when an indecisive herd of horse-sized beasts snarled traffic. Some had already bolted across the road, but most were lurking just out of sight in the woods and on the shoulder. There might have been ten left, waiting to follow the leaders. Their long heads were up in the air and their eyes were opened wide and alert. They stood broadly from the first car to nearly the Goose's side. Clearly, they were waiting for the next bravest elk to make a move, which would send them all scurrying across the road. I'd seen this play out all too many times in West Virginia with white-tailed deer. Once one goes, those damn things will commit to following, regardless of the danger, like they have a thing for suicide.

For the folks driving the cars, this was a chance to point their cameras out the window and get a shot of Bambi. To them this was a magical encounter with nature, something to look back on and tell the grandkids about. For me, the elk were too close, too strong, and too heavy. If the elk panicked, I could have been flattened. Instinctively, I revved my engine. The howl of the Goose sent them running the other way, just like it had done deer and many, many cattle along the way.

One of the ladies from the car in front of me aimed her large, ignorant head at me and said, "Why did you scare them off?" in a pissy British tone. I responded, "One of those things could charge my bike and flatten me. You're not the one sitting on the motorcycle." She was in the safety of her enclosed vehicle, and that was as far as her forethought had made it. She leaned back in and wound her window up before I could yell, "Why don't you get out and pet one. Park ranger says they're friendly."

I didn't let it get to me. I had bigger fish to fry. A day of testing my luck solo in mountain lion country arrived again. A trail at the far west end of the park had gained my interest. It's the South Rim's most remote trail and fittingly named Hermit Trail. For nine miles, it plunges to the Colorado's Hermit Rapid and loses 4,240 feet of elevation. It rarely receives maintenance, is steep, rocky, and had packed snow along the shadowy parts, making a slip and tumble all the more likely. The trail log posted an angle about hiking the Grand Canyon that I had not considered. It said, "Here the easy part—downhill—comes first; the tough part—up and out—comes when you are already tired."

A story of a gal capable of running a sub-three-hour marathon was posted next to the trail log. She and a companion set out hiking in the Grand Canyon with inadequate food or drink and no map. When the companion could no longer continue, she went off alone in search of help, but her fitness was no match for the Grand Canyon. Her friend remained still and was rescued. She, on the other hand, was found two days later; she had died from dehydration. *Why do I want to do this?*

Some of the park staff at the visitor center talked me out of doing the entire hike by myself in one day. They warned of ice and fatigue like I'd never experienced before. I listened thoroughly and considered the trail log's warning as well. I gave myself an hour descent and planned a two-hour climb back out. I ventured on cautiously. Near the rim, Hermit Trail was mild with a smidgen of rocks. Once out of sight of the rim, it became steep and icy, and remained rocky. My view of the canyon changed. No longer was I just looking down. I looked up and to the side. The trail steepened some more. Earthy steps made from logs holding back dirt became more numerous. I was dropping elevation quickly. Tough plant life clung to the canyon side as cliffs looked larger than they had from above.

I continued on with a growing feeling that around the next blind corner could be a mountain lion. Those things must rent space in my head. I believe my fear of the mountain lion began from watching a show where an elderly lady told the story of her husband being viciously mauled by one on a mountain trail in California as they were hiking. She said that the lion was ripping the scalp off the rear of her husband's skull. He was old, weary, and losing badly in his attempt to get away. She grabbed a stick and smacked the hell out of the mountain lion over and over with no success. Then she began poking it with the sharpest end. The mountain lion responded to the stabbing motion by letting her husband go. His scalp was hanging off the back of his head like a shop rag. The image that my brain created of the incident will never leave me, and only grows crisper when I hike alone. Still, I continued on.

I may have dropped 2,000 feet in elevation as one hour passed. A rounded peninsula poked into the canyon. I could see Hermit Trail continue to the left and out of sight. Two women stopped to have a look off the peninsula, joining me. They were hiking back up from a four-mile descent. This did not make me feel brave and manly. For a split second, I thought to match them, but I remembered the trail log and my goal. From here, the Colorado River looked thin and twisty. It was still so far away. The sky was blue, and across the canyon, the horizon beyond the North Rim was no longer visible. The women left, and I stayed behind to soak it all in.

I climbed back out in almost the exact amount of time that it took me to hike into the canyon. If I would have known that my legs—full of metal from old motocross injuries—could do so well, I would've gone further.

On the way down, a father and son combo whizzed by at breakneck speed. They didn't have anything to drink and were going like their lives depended on it. The dad was overweight, hyperactive, and talked confidently about the canyon. I felt for the boy. His dad could have led him straight into an emergency rescue. On the way up, I slowly passed them. Ol' dad was huffing and puffing, often taking time to rest his hands on his knees. The kid looked fine. I kept an eye on them for a while before their pace and mine left a substantial gap between us. I take it that pops didn't read the signs. Near the top, I stopped for a moment to enjoy the scenery.

The hike back to the rim was over sooner than expected. I needed something to do, so on the ride back to Grand Canyon Village, I stopped at every overlook on the west side of the park, finishing them off. There were about a dozen that I had not seen. I came away most impressed with an overlook where one vertical mile of wall could be seen without interruption. Trees lined the rim, and at the bottom a dry creek bed could be seen strewn across the ground like a spaghetti noodle. It was an awesome yet intimidating view. Most views of the Colorado River and canyon floor are hidden by an outcropping somewhere far below, but here, the only thing that could break the view would be fog. I had never seen anything like it and I loved it!

I motored on to the Maswik Lodge, which is home to a food court that covers all the cultural culinary basics. It's the Grand Canyon's buffet without being a buffet. Separate stations offer anything from burgers to egg rolls. I scarfed down a pound-and-a-half burrito with rice and black beans on the side. Any more and a brass button would have shot off of my jeans, ricocheted off a timber beam, and landed in somebody's soup. My gut was busted.

Remarkably, the sun was still hanging around in the sky, so I just horsed around. A few hundred feet away, the real workhorses of the park, the mules, were stationed in their three muddy pens. Something compelled me to stop for a chat. I walked to the fence and became the life of the party. Everyone came over for a quick scratch and a how do you do. Then a mule sporting a wicked mohawk selfishly hogged my attention. He chased the others off and kept them at bay for the rest of my visit. When another one of his penned up compadres would try to come in for a pat, he would lower his head and throw his ears back. That must have been donkey language for, "Don't mess with me, jackass!" Full of all the farm-filled fun I could handle, I rode back to the tent for one last cold night at the Grand Canyon.

Day 84 – January 5, 2012

Overnight, the mercury plummeted to a hypothermic fourteen degrees. The tent was set up like I had it at Armadillo Farm Campground, where it was first covered by my tarp and then covered by the rainfly. The blanket was strewn across the tent floor as insulation and I slept on top of it in my bag. Before last night, it had hovered around eighteen degrees every night at the canyon. They were all groundhog maneuver nights, but fourteen degrees was just low enough to make me lose sleep over the thought of having black toes by morning.

When I drifted off, my toes were ten cool nuggets attached to my foot. When the sun welcomed me to another day, my Field & Stream mummy bag had kept me alive and frostbite free. It boasted a minus-fifteen-degree rating, which I didn't plan to test out.

Time to leave Grand Canyon National Park had arrived. The Goose and I traveled every road in the park, stopped at every overlook, saw bald eagles, elk, mules, mule deer, French fries, French folks, walked on ice, rode on ice, hiked, sat for moments in awe, shivered, and smiled. The experience was fulfilling. One day, I will surely return to that giant hole. Perhaps next time, I will be able to see the canyon by way of a whitewater raft on the mighty Colorado River, or share the experience with someone. For now, though, the road was calling and I was answering.

Morning consisted of the usual routine with a side of laundry. I was outside of the bathhouse folding clothes and cooking Ramen Noodles for breakfast on a picnic table when a traveling trio took a seat at the table next to me. They had been bouncing around the states in a worn out mid-nineties minivan with scenes of mountains and brown bears painted on it as if painted in a hurry or by a class of fifth graders. It had Canadian license plates, which hinted at the origin of two of the three in the group. Those two were college age Canadian bomb- shells, and they had been packed in that van for weeks with the luckiest young Australian lad on the planet. These girls had morning hair and were wearing baggy sweatpants. They were showing off yesterday's leftover makeup and were still better-looking than anyone I'd ever met. One was a blonde-haired, blue- eyed Canadian queen, and the other was an exotic brunette with dark eyes that I could've fallen into like a black hole. The Australian chap was just an average- looking bloke. I envied his ass.

As I slurped my noodles and folded my clothes extra slowly, we shared stories about our time on the road. I could hardly look at the girls without thinking about how I'd crash that beat-up van into a deep snow bank the first chance I got, forcing the girls to snuggle up close to keep warm as we waited for help to arrive. I'd fake my way through a series of phone calls to 911 and promise them that help was on the way. Then I'd get back to snuggling. When help that I didn't call, didn't arrive, I'd wait until sunset to mention a survival tactic that I learned way back. You know the one. It's the one where you shed all of your clothes and jump in the sleeping bag together, fighting the cold as a clump of nude bodies. The girls would reject that notion almost immediately, questioning my motives.

Then, recognizing that they're on to me, I'd hop out of the van and pretend to look for firewood in the shrinking evening light. I'd keep at this just long enough for them to wonder where I went. Then, like a rocket, I'd burst into the van with the news that "There are wolves out there!" This would scare the girls into survival mode—the exact mode I needed them to be in so they would jump into the sleeping bag with me. I'd smile in the darkness as all three of us tried to squeeze into one bag.

And this, my friends, is why the Australian fella is on the trip with the gals and I'm riding solo. *Unless he's missing a few chromosomes, I know that this option has already crossed his mind.* I could see that he knew what I was thinking while folding my clothes. Their laundry finished drying and they began packing. I wished them safe travels and left the park, all horned up and ready to ride.

At the southern entrance to the park, I had another run-in with a small herd of elk—could have been the same ones as before. This time, they were far enough away not to involve me in a when-animals-attack moment. I hopped off the Goose and set up a shot. A man in a gold-colored SUV with California plates jumped out and joined me. We watched as they lazily plucked off whatever vegetation they could find poking through the snow. When they vanished into the evergreens, I hit the road again.

I was heading due south toward Williams, Arizona, when Fred Flintstone pulled me over. He was twenty feet tall, four-fingered, smiling, barefoot, and pointing at the Flintstones Campground sign. *Oh man, what is this?* This campground had it all, especially if you owned a barking dinosaur named Dino, were married to a woman who wears an animal hide, and had feet made of concrete calluses.

The campground office was straight out of the cartoon. It had three rooms that looked like hollowed-out boulders. Its windows were deep and round, but not perfectly round; they were more like hand-chiseled round. Three huge, flat, stone slabs sat on top to make a roof. Dinosaur bones poked through the grass around the parking lot. I was in Bedrock and it was great! It's too bad that the campground wasn't farther away from the Grand Canyon because I would've loved to stay there a night. Once my camera was nice and warm from the bucketload of shutter snaps, I gave a hearty "yabba dabba doo!" and headed off toward Williams.

Thirty-four miles later, I arrived. I did a quick ride down Main Street, hit up the visitor center and museum, and planned to continue riding west. On the way out of town, I spotted a Motel 6. Just out of curiosity, I stopped in to check the rate. It was only $36. I hadn't made it far, but Williams had a look about it that was neat enough to earn an overnight visit. It was a small main-street sort of town, like Arizona's version of Mt. Airy, North Carolina.

Sadly, in 1984, Williams became the last town along Route 66 to be passed over by the interstate. A sign at the museum read "The last stoplight between Chicago and Los Angeles was at the corner outside this building." I felt sorry for Williams, and what do you do when you feel sorry for a town? You boost its economy and tip its people well. I checked into Motel 6 and footed it downtown and back to the nineteen fifties.

I walked up and down Main Street twice before stopping for dinner at a funky little place named Twisters 50's Soda Fountain. Its checkered floor and white and red Route 66 décor smacked me with contrast as I walked inside. It was alarming and ultra-perky. My blue hoodie, jeans, and toe shoes clashed with Twister's theme like fire and water. I felt like a bipedal blueberry as I scrolled through the menu. On it I found a Big Bopper Burger, and couldn't resist. The service was fast and polite. I destroyed the greasy burger and a Coke and strolled over to the other side of the diner where I'd fit in—Twister's had a bar.

The room was darker; beer taps shimmered in the low light. Padded stools welcomed me to have a seat. An attractive brunette was running things on the opposite side of the counter. That was enough for me to send some stimulus money Williams's way. I ordered 'em tall and cold and she kept 'em coming. She and I jawed on about Arizona and higher education. We spoke of our shared interests in becoming multilingual, and all the while she kept the other patrons topped off. She gave me a burrito shop recommendation for San Diego. I told her I'd give it a whirl if I made it that far. And thus my night in Williams began.

The sun had set and I was feeling social. I had a hankering for something with whiskey in it. I demanded my legs to find my ass another barstool. Up the street, the Canyon Club looked promising enough. It was low lit, long, and narrow. People who were hunched over at the bar paid me no mind when I wandered in. Another attractive bartender (albeit fifteen years my elder) poured me a stiff glass of Jack and Coke. I sipped through three or four glasses and patiently waited. I know from experience that in these situations someone always gets curious and asks something like "Hey what the hell is that on your feet?" which leads to hours of best buddy bar banter, or if you're lucky, a long evening of flirting with the former local high school homecoming queen. On this random night in Williams, I met a female helicopter pilot who flew Grand Canyon tours, an old, long-haired man who seriously pushed his welcome by promising to pay his tab next time, and a couple from California.

The Californians were both in their twenties. The gal was about twenty-seven and from what I can remember, looked pretty good after six or seven shots. She had long, dirty blonde hair and a severe interest in me, or at least that's what the whiskey said. Her boyfriend was maybe five years younger and a laid back type. They were good folks, and we all got along well. I'm not the home wrecker type, after all.

They and I palled around for most of the evening, starting in the Canyon Club. At some point, we shared the bright idea to leave the Canyon Club for another joint. My memory strains to remember, but while at the other bar, we tried to go up a set of blocked-off stairs and were kindly asked to leave. I can recollect no other details. We were three sheets to the wind when we stumbled back to the Canyon Club and reconnected our bottom sides to barstools. This was an evening that wrapped up like many before it. The Californians and I philosophized about life, music, travel, and the paranormal. I was glad to share an evening with them but will never remember their names. The music died out as "last call" was announced. I walked Main Street one last time to the unfamiliar warmth of my room.

Day 85 – January 6, 2012

Last night's shenanigans left me in search of morning hydration. I lumbered downstairs and into the lobby, all sleepy-eyed and irritable, ready for an assault on the coffee maker and juice machine. Back at the room, I packed—slow and steady—while waiting for the familiar jolt of caffeine to sharpen up the day like a focusing lens. Checkout time was 11:00am, and I was out of my fine Motel 6 suite at 10:59 and a half. The day was looking bright.

Williams is on a portion of old Route 66 that parallels Interstate 40 so tightly that the two roads were indistinguishable on the road atlas. I pulled away from Motel 6 thinking that I'd have an easy ride to Oatman, Arizona, on old Route 66 all day. Williams's Main Street was behind me as I ventured away from town. A couple of miles passed, and I found myself at a turnaround point. I was lost. Not terribly lost by any means, but just a bit out of sorts.

Two women in a truck with a bed camper were pulled to the shoulder. I parked and walked over, hoping that they were locals. I said, "Hello" and followed that up with "Where the heck did Route 66 go?" They didn't know. They were at that turnaround thinking the same thing as me. I looked at my map again. Interstate 40's thick blue line seemed like the only option for heading west. I reluctantly took it.

I tried to hop back on Route 66 at Ash Fork (the flagstone capital of the US) but was rejected and redirected again to I-40. Ash Fork looked small and lonely. My experience there was little more than a ride through. Like Williams, Interstate 40 had taken the wind out of its sails, and—unlike Williams—the Santa Fe Railroad left it for dead in 1960 when it moved ten miles north.

I was parked at an Ash Fork community memorial and reading a little ditty about the town's history on a black and gold metal plaque when an overweight gal in her late teens wandered by. She was alone. I pretended to continue reading as she passed, but I was really keeping an eye on her, for she carried an awfully suspicious demeanor—made all the more evident by her cantankerous facial positioning. She was scowling at me like I was there to burn the place down. No cars were whizzing by, and no one else was out for a stroll. The only thing going on was me. To her, I may have been the first person to seem at all interested in reading that plaque. She wandered out of sight, looking as lonely as her town. On my way back to the interstate, I explored a side street, hoping to see Route 66 lead away from the boring highway, but instead I saw a line of signs—like the Burma Shave signs—that together make a bit of poetry on the side of the road, and one of them read "KEEP ON GOING." *I think I will*, so I left Ash Fork like so many have done before.

I rejoined Route 66 five miles later. I came off the ramp, crossed a cattle guard, and headed into a grassy no-man's land. Mitch, from Page, recommended that I ride that section for the scenery and over-the-top Route 66 vibe. The retro colors and style of the fifties that he told me about came out of nowhere when I rode into Seligman. I wasn't prepared for it. For a town hardly longer than a few football fields, it packed a serious 66 punch. A plain Jane hamburger painted on a big retro sign above a burger joint welcomed me to Seligman. Matching Coke, malt, and shake advertisements adorned the rest of the eatery.

Seligman exists today by riding the wave of tourism. If location is everything, Seligman doesn't have that. Instead, it has locked down on its unique past and plays the hell out of the Route 66 card. For the passerby, it's a visual pleasantry in a land of bland features. It looks more fantasy than real town, kind of like Helen, Georgia, but with a different theme.

In a matter of seconds, I drifted through at an idle. Two small children ducked behind metal posts at a service station. They looked shy and curious. Most businesses flaunted some version of a big, round-bodied American vehicle from the slicked-back-hair/pack-of-cigarettes-rolled-up-in-a-shirt-sleeve era.

I stopped at the Rusty Bolt. I had been lured in by the mannequins. The damn place was carpeted with them. The Rusty Bolt was a gift shop displaying an eye-catching assortment of no less than twenty period-dressed mannequins positioned from the rooftop down to the front entrance of the building. Inside, souvenirs were plentiful. I was on the hunt for a few more stickers to add to the Goose's metal skin. The Rusty Bolt had more on display than you could shake a stick at. I bought a handful and walked outside.

While slapping the stickers on, I had a nice chat with an attractive rubber woman in a long, orange dress sitting on the bumper of a 57 Chevy. She was a lanky brunette with perfectly plasticized features. I had been on the road so long without so much as a hug that her unblinking, lifeless figure was looking pretty damn skippy. She was a great listener, but ya know . . . I never got her name.

From Seligman, Route 66 returned to an arrow-straight, desert road lined with huge grassy fields. The lack of corners and abundance of open space got me in trouble. Somewhere before the town of Peach Springs, I was riding heavy-handed on the right grip. I was moving swiftly, not light speed, but fast enough for the officer who popped over the hill, coming in the opposite direction, to jump on the binders and whip around. I knew that I was caught as soon as I saw his brake lights in my mirrors. I made life easy on him and pulled over. I stood beside the Goose as he approached. I could tell that he was younger than me and worried that he might have something to prove.

He asked for the paperwork and my ID. I went about unloading my pas-senger-sized gear bundle so that I could fish it out from under the seat. While setting stuff aside, I practiced my polite good-ol'-boy routine that has got me through more than twenty-five of these encounters in the past. I was spitting out the book of manners while fearing that he would search the bike and find my pistol. In the end he let me go due to my hasty pull over. He said, "Most bike guys just hammer down when they are in your situation." I told him, "With all this gear, Sir, and not knowing the roads, I had no choice but to pull over" in a light and clear voice. I asked if he would let me take a picture of the scene, and he agreed as long as I kept him out of the frame. Soon after he left, I reloaded the gear and took off gently. Luckily, he didn't see the sweet wheelie I pulled while leaving Seligman.

I set a grandpa pace for the rest of the day. Route 66 arches north for a quick swipe through the Hualapai Reservation. Short, smooth mountains with table top outcroppings lined the road. I passed a herd of black and brown cattle. They were clustered inside of a fence made of branches. Not one of those knot-ty fence posts was straight, yet it worked. Each post had its own unique bend, like letters of the alphabet. Thin metal wire tied it all together. The cattle seemed indifferent to the homemade fence. I imagined that they would let cau-tion tape hold 'em back from the greener grass on the other side.

I kept riding until another embodiment of Route 66 popped out of no-where. Rolling grassy fields had disappeared, and I was again in a rocky moun-tainous desert. I had found the Hackberry General Store. It was an oasis of old. Geriatric cars sat around falling to pieces ever so slowly under the cloudless sea of blue above. Weathered wood, ancient gas pumps, galvanized tin, and a treas-ure hunter's Shangri-La of signs came together to form a makeshift store. Cattle heads in various states of decay hung from posts, like gruesome contestants— along with the rusty cars—in the world's slowest race to total disintegration.

Inside, an old feller manned the counter. License plates hung from the ceil-ing. Like Luckenbach, Texas, it had so much character that the only possible way to make it cooler would be to whip out your pocketknife and scratch some-thing. Everything was over-the-top neat all the way down to the store owner's donkey. The old feller cracked a knowing grin as I complimented him on his seasoned collection of antiques. I left there feeling like I just visited one of America's truly special spots.

On the road again, and still not at my destination, I passed my indirect destination. The sign said, "Mike's Outpost Saloon." Two of my favorite words, and another cool word in between, were combined to name a drinking hole. Merely passing by was not an option. The building was modest in size and had two rickety, wooden wagons on the roof, and paintings of cacti and six-shooters on the exterior walls. *On the East Coast, those wagons would rot to pieces in no time.*

Two Harleys were parked outside. I wondered what sort of motorcycle folks they belonged to. I walked in and spotted them, decked out in leather. The guys were massive and rattlesnake-mean-looking with grey beards and bandanas. I kept a couple of barstools in between us just in case I had to make a break for the door. All of that precaution faded within minutes. The bikers were suitably named Buck and Buzz and turned out to be two really good dudes. We shared brews and laughs. Buck and Buzz left at sunset. Their Harleys disappeared into the orange glow like a movie scene. I watched with a sly grin.

Mike's Outpost Saloon's bartender warmed up to me nicely after a bit. When I first arrived, her petite frame, blonde hair, and dark eyes warned me to behave without saying a word. Since I was new on the scene, she was a little quiet and short with me as she handled the sober side of the counter like a professional. Through time and a constant trickle of curious questions, I had her talking to me like an old friend. She politely listened to my story and whipped out a book about Route 66 from behind the bar. She showed me the best place to stand to see the sunset, cooked me up a pizza, and told me about her daughter, who was a Playboy Playmate. I listened with the utmost interest. She secured a spot near the parking lot for me to pitch my tent, and I lingered longer.

Soon the place began to fill with locals. I had been there for a couple hours and was tuned into the social station. The evening blessed me with interesting encounters from an assortment of characters. I met two local lime miners from Hackberry, who loved their jobs; a young fella from Georgia and his Japanese girlfriend, who were stopping in for a break on their way to San Francisco; two pretty gals from Kingman, Arizona; and most interestingly, a Sioux Indian couple, who moved from North Dakota to the desert.

The names of my Sioux friends escape me now and it may be better that way. We began talking about their move to Arizona. I told them my story, and we kept it light for a while. Bottles clinked as the bartender tossed away the empties, and all seemed good in the world. Then alcohol allowed religious and political stances to come flying out of our yappers. The Sioux lady soon joined friends at another part of the saloon, and I became a giant ear for Mr. Sioux.

This man, a Native American, a man of maybe his early forties, broke down right in front of me. His back was facing everyone, but the pain in his face was there for me alone to witness. He told me of his life in the military. As he spoke, he was slow and deliberate. Some of his words were interrupted by long reflective pauses. He recounted a stretch of service in Mogadishu, Somalia. Tears slid down his cheeks as he told me about a young, armed male whom he shot and killed there. He found out afterward, after it was too late, that the boy was only thirteen. He said that the decision to fire was out of fear for his own life. He reflected on the age of his children and thought of the Somalian boy and cracked even more. I watched and listened. For a few minutes, he looked tortured. I felt for him, knowing that the memory and moment will follow him to the grave.

He calmed on his own accord after several more minutes, but wasn't the same for the rest of the evening. I really wasn't either. He has that vision of the gunshot in his mind forever, and now I have the vision of him crying over the terrible tragedy in my mind forever. *Why do we let violence get that far out of hand?*

At eleven o'clock, Mike's Outpost Saloon closed. I pushed the Goose into a brushy area near the edge of the parking lot. I dug out my tent. The sky was clear. The moon and stars shone bright enough to put away the flashlight. I thought of everyone I met as I set up camp and was thankful for the experience.

Day 86 – January 7, 2012

A morning warm enough for a T-shirt! My desert hideout behind Mike's Outpost Saloon proved to be a good start to an amazing day. But first I had a race with a train to win.

The perfect morning was no match for the movement in my abdomen. Mike's saloon was closed, making the bathroom off-limits. Below me, a housing development full of unsuspecting innocents was waking up, and across the way, a massive field full of promise. My only option for finding relief was to enter that field, cross over the raised railroad tracks, and quickly drop a deuce before the approaching train arrived. The train was probably a quarter of a mile away—incredibly long, and moving slowly—eliminating the option of waiting for it to pass, but just fast enough that I'd have to hurry through my business once I made it across the tracks. I didn't want to wave at the engineer while I stood beside a pile of soiled white paper. This was it. A move had to be made, literally.

I clinched, snagged a roll of TP from my side box, and bolted across Route 66 into the field, over the tracks, and positioned myself just out of sight of any

132 DAYS

prying eyes. The beauty of the West is that you can see things from great distances. I knew that the hourglass would grant me a solid minute to fertilize before the train arrived. Sure enough, I carefully crossed in front of the train, with just feet to spare. Either way, waiting for the train or not, that one was going to be a close call.

It didn't take long to pack up and hit the road. I had my sights set on Lake Havasu by nightfall, with a stop in Oatman, Arizona, on the way. Kingman is about halfway between the saloon and Oatman and would be my first stop. Of all places, Kingman's McDonald's would become unforgettable. I was there for breakfast, a spot of writing, and juice for the batteries.

As soon as I plugged in and began writing, a fellow walked in with a huge pack on his back looking to do the same. He was wearing worn jeans, a sweaty tank top, and a loose grey hoodie. A head full of jet black hair and a dark complexion hinted that he was of Asian or Latino decent, but that's trivial. His big bright smile proved that he was a man happily living life to the fullest.

He was looking for a power receptacle and was talking to a group of young folks. I overheard him, and having already scoped out the dining room receptacles, I directed him to the only other one available. I went back to typing until I again overheard him eagerly sharing his story with the same group of youths. It sounded like me talking to the people I'd met along the way. He was giving the why's, the where's, and the how's of his journey. I stopped what I was doing and walked over to chat with this fellow, camera in hand.

His name was Sam and he had been on the road for twelve days longer than me and had walked from Tacoma, Washington, to Kingman, Arizona. He was wandering America with a greater cause than mine. He called his purpose a "Unity Walk" and was raising awareness about basic problems that we can overcome if we start asking the right questions of ourselves and making more positive decisions. It goes far deeper than that, but that is my best quick description. He and I shared nearly identical views on countless topics. Sharing his concerns with me was like preaching to the choir. I thought it uncanny meeting Sam in such circumstances. Our paths crossed after so many days and nights on the road as if guided by a higher power.

He wasn't the only traveler I'd meet at Micky D's that morning. Sam and I were conversing when a lady spoke up who overheard our stories. Her name was Betty; she and her husband William had traveled extensively across America. They chose not to walk, or ride a motorcycle, but to loco mote in a domesticated bus. They were a few years shy of retirement age and had a hardiness about them that you'd expect from Alaskans. They shared the same love for travel and adventure that Sam and I had gone on and on about.

So there we were, all engaged in a great bit of storytelling, a sort of travel triangle, if you will. I forgot about why I came there as we spoke. It's not every day that you come across such like-minded, awesome folks, who take real steps to get more out of life. We hung around for two hours before Betty and William split, followed by me. Sam, Betty, and William wrote down their contact info and shared great advice about the Pacific Northwest. I rode on smiling.

[254]

From Kingman to Oatman, the terrain morphed into a fantastically prehistoric vista. For miles the pavement was light and faded by the relentless Arizona sun. I leaned in and out of corners, hugging dangerous cliffs, only protected by square wood beams linked with corroded steel cable. A washout in one of those corners surely would have led to me and the Goose sliding under the bottom cable to a prickly desert death. But it was awesome. I kept it on two wheels past each and every toothed mountain and absorbed the scenery. The landscape made the word "rugged" seem girly. I'm going to go out on a limb and guess that every engineer who designed the section of Route 66 from Kingman to the Colorado River was a motorcyclist or had been in a past life. It was biking perfection. I'm certain the Goose was grinning.

The fascinating western town of Oatman entered my world through a few friends that I'd made along the way. Mitch from Page, and Don and Ginnie, who I met in Big Bend, said that it was a can't-miss while in western Arizona. Oh man, that place was cool! The spirit of the Wild West was runnin' wild in Oatman. Its mountainous background made it even more dramatic than Tombstone. Dusty wood buildings with creaky floors lined the thin road in and out of town, and clapped-out overhangs shaded open front doors. It had a put-together feel as if modern building codes meant nothing in Oatman. It was perfectly unrefined and waiting for a gunfight. And that's exactly what happened.

I was walking along a wooden sidewalk and noticed a group gathered around a couple of men in cowboy attire. The daily gunfight had begun. Loud words roared from the actors; pistols were drawn and shots fired. When the smoke cleared, the men who played dead in the dusty street were bank robbers who got robbed by a bank robber, robber. I thoroughly enjoyed the act, yet gave the nod to Tombstone's longer gunfight. However, I did like how it felt more spontaneous here at Oatman. The gunfight began without warning among wandering tourists. Tombstone's Gunfight at the O.K. Corral is a bit commercialized.

One of the things that I had to do while in Oatman was grab a burger at the old Oatman Hotel. Mitch, from Page, confidently recommended it. I ordered a buffalo burger with Swiss and mushrooms. Just as he had predicted, it did not disappoint, yet remained in second place to The English Kitchen's BBQ Bacon Burger. Inside the Hotel, the walls were lined with thousands of dollar bills from all sorts of patrons of the past. I'd seen this several times by now. *How about that for a great insurance policy when business slows?*

On the cramped street outside, Oatman's famed wild burros roamed among the trucks, tourists, and dune buggies. These *wild* burros were not penned up; they ran loose. They seemed tame and used their cuteness to beg for food. And let me tell you, I didn't see a skinny one in the whole bunch. They've carved out quite a niche for themselves. The grandparents of today's beggin' burros were released into the hills years ago as gold mining evaporated in the area. Oatman, unfortunately, didn't have any place to camp, so I moved on toward my end goal of Lake Havasu City.

Route 66 came to the bank of the Colorado River. California was on the other side. I wanted to wait until after Vegas to cross into the massive state, but the lure of the sign being right there was just too much to bear. I crossed the bridge over the Colorado River on I-40. Being in California gave a whole new meaning to being far from home. Long, lonely rides on deserted roads in Texas now felt like eastern memories. I looked at the sign in disbelief. *Have I really made it this far?* Instead of continuing farther west here, I crossed back over the Colorado and stuck to the plan. I'd be spending a bunch of time in California in the near future, and hopefully a mega earthquake wouldn't send it all crashing into the Pacific before I got there. In Arizona, on my way to Lake Havasu City, the feeling of rushing the next leg of the journey through Nevada and Utah dominated my thoughts.

Upon entering Lake Havasu City, I found another set of golden arches and finished writing my morning's work. As I was wrapping it up, the folks at the next table struck up a conversation with me. Their names were Paula and Rich. They were a classy, well-dressed couple from Santa Monica, California, and incredibly interesting. Paula was once married to a master Russian painter, and Rich was a sailor, with boats docked in both Los Angeles and Washington State. Again, I had a highly unexpected, great time in a McDonald's with some fascinating fellow Americans. We talked about travel with big smiles and peaceful hearts. Before leaving, Rich offered an overnight stay on his sailboat if I passed through Los Angeles. He said that he'd tell me where it was and where he hid the key. I couldn't believe it.

I finishing writing and checked into another Motel 6. I freshened up for a night on the town and then flipped the tube on. The first round of Supercross was on Speed Channel, and there was no way I was going to miss it. The rest of the night I sat in front of the TV watching my favorite thing in the world. Man, I missed my motocross bikes. *What a day!*

Day 87 – January 8, 2012

Motel 6's mattress took care of me last night. Without question, it contributed to the best night of sleep of the journey. I felt so rested in the morning that coffee wasn't my first thought. It would've been a great day to travel with all that energy, but I was staying put, kind of. I had a notion to hunt down Lake Havasu State Park and move my operation there. After that, I had no idea what to get into.

I packed and took off. My eyes were wide and ready to spot a sign pointing me in the right direction, but it never appeared. *Either I missed the park or it doesn't exist.* I found myself fifteen miles south of town at Cattail Cove State Park. I looked at my map again to confirm that I wasn't imagining a park named Lake Havasu State Park. Sure enough, it was there on the map, just outside of city limits. I did a U-turn and headed back. Still, no sign for Lake Havasu SP was found. Instead, the city had posted a sign for Windsor Beach in its place, which is all fine and dandy for the folks looking for Windsor Beach, but it was as helpful as a hole in the head to this unacquainted hillbilly. My map indicated the park's location with a little green tent but said squat about Windsor Beach. I strained my thinker to figure out the problem. When two and two came, I realized that Windsor Beach was in the state park.

For twenty bucks, I wrestled my tent up on spot twenty-six in ferocious wind. Lake Havasu was choppier than a haircut from a blind barber. The wind was so bad that I had to move my tent closer to a terraced hill for fear of it blowing away. One of the rangers told me that the lake's effect on the climate made the wind strong. He said that air above the cold, deep water collides with the desert's dry warm air and funnels through the shallow canyon along the lake, increasing its velocity. I made one of those "hmmm" noises.

Lake Havasu State Park was like a KOA with less to do. I browsed the campground map for any sort of hiking trail. One short line squiggled across the map along the lake. Given its urban proximity, I wasn't really surprised. I strapped on the toe shoes, grabbed the Canon, and headed off, hoping for something unexpected. A sandy path worked its way through the brushy shore from one end of the park to the other.

This was the kind of trail your grandparents would be disappointed with. It was flat, easy, and invited boredom. Lake Havasu stayed in sight the whole time. I should have just left my camera at the tent. I wanted mountain trails with great views, gnarly terrain, and ferocious wildlife—minus the ferocious part. The mountain trails were probably on the other side of Lake Havasu in California's Whipple Mountains. They poked wrinkly and royally into the sky. *If I only had a boat.* The Goose is a poor swimmer, so I decided to see what the retirement community of Lake Havasu had up its sleeves.

I found a big surprise. In the late sixties, Lake Havasu City purchased a bridge from London, England. It was disassembled piece by piece, and transported to the young Arizona city for a whopping $2.46 million. Each piece was numbered and shipped to California via the Panama Canal then trucked from California to Arizona. What an effort! Total cost, including purchasing the bridge, was $6.96 million. A small replica of an English Village now complements the bridge. Shops and restaurants entice tourists to lighten their wallets.

I walked across for a closer look, whispering "London Bridge is falling down, falling down . . ." Bringing the bridge to Lake Havasu was an enormous project, but the bridge itself isn't mind-blowing. It's not all that tall and it isn't even long. Its sturdiness matches its plainness. Four stone arches support its span. From the top you get a view of a clean, commercialized Lake Havasu City and the channel that separates Havasu Island from the mainland. Golf course living and imported palms create an idealistic backdrop. Fancy cars and expensive hotels dot the shore. I was overwhelmed with white-collared delight. In fact, so much excitement surged through my limbs that a reaction almost happened. I wandered back to the parking lot. Being Sunday, almost everything was closed. The day was still young, so I had to find something to do.

I mounted my iron goose and aimlessly throttled around town, desperate for something, anything, when an old familiar friend caught my eye. It was the Happy Kitty Biker Bar (big surprise). Chromed out and exhaustively polished Harleys sat outside in formation like jets on an aircraft carrier. *Why not try my luck with the biker crowd?* I walked in hoping for a pleasant evening among new friends; however, the music could have stopped when I crossed the door jamb.

I had strayed into a hive of your typical Japanese-bike-hating group of Harley riders. They welcomed me with dirty looks and sneers. Apparently my bright blue Crossroads Yamaha hoodie didn't have the same street cred as their leathers (that only see perfect sunny days). I sat there for nearly three hours, not wanting to go back to the tent and not wanting to let them chase me off easily, and only managed to talk to two people. One was a local fellow, who wasn't a biker, and the other was the owner of the place.

She was an eye-catching blonde—a cougar in tight clothes—and patient enough to answer my question about the bar's name. I asked, "Why Happy Kitty?" She said that she also owned another bar in Lake Havasu City called the Mad Dog and simply chose the opposite. I know, I know, interesting story. Well, that's the best that day eighty-seven would bring. It was one of the least eventful days of the trip, and I couldn't wait to hit the road again. *Still beat an effing cubicle.*

Somewhere around 3:30am I woke thirstier than a camel with a mouth full of flour. Across the way from my tent was a drinking water pipe. I snagged the flashlight and moseyed over. It was a night where darkness seemed to stop at sixty percent. I turned the flashlight off. Lake Havasu's white caps were visible from a couple hundred yards. I filled my bottle confidently without spilling a drop. The moon was acting like a baby sun without the heat. It hung clear and bright, inviting me to stay out. I gazed for a spell in utter peace.

Day 88 – January 9, 2012

I stirred at sunrise. The moon had clocked out and handed the keys to the heat ball. I packed up camp and headed to Denny's for breakfast and a morning finger jog across the keyboard. Denny's lacked a connection to the worldwide web, so I aborted and swung by Burger King. They too were without Wi-Fi. That forced me to suck it up and head to the one place that I knew would have it, McDonald's.

I pulled up and looked around. Beside me, an old man was packing his breakfast into the rear trunk of his mini scooter. Inside, except for one child of preschool age, I was the youngest customer. Lake Havasu City was crawling with snowbirds and silvers. Everywhere I went, folks of the age of wisdom drastically outnumbered the youth. They owned the place. Just a quick look around and you'd find a person of advanced years zipping around on a golf cart, scooter, or some other non-full-sized vehicle. Lake Havasu City felt like my safest stop of the journey so far.

With a deluxe breakfast down the hatch, and another post up and running, I was off, north again, toward Valley of Fire State Park in Nevada. My early course backtracked to a portion of Route 66 that I rode days ago and then veered off for new ground along the Colorado River and through Bullhead City. I stopped to fuel up and munched a half pack of M&M's while the pump did its thing. When the nozzle clicked, I threw the rest of the bag of candy in my tank bag and continued on. Five miles later, something thumped, rubbed across my leg, and disappeared. I was ascending a long gradual corner into dark brown peaked mountains and whispered, "Oh crap! What just came loose on the bike?" I whipped the Goose to the shoulder beside a sign that read "Hoover Dam 67 Las Vegas 97." I hopped off the bike and looked at the road behind me. Something brown and flat was lying in the center a short distance back. It was my log book. It had bumped the tank and hit me on the leg on its flight off of the Goose. If not for that, I wouldn't have noticed my unzipped tank bag. Priceless notes and contact info could've been gone forever.

Let me tell you, it's a weird feeling when you are riding a motorcycle and something unseen hits you. If it's bigger than a cricket, it could be dangerous. Take for instance, a rock flung up by a car and ricocheting off of the ol' Adam's apple, or a plastic shopping bag that finds itself covering your face shield. In this case, it felt like something the size of a small cat had jumped off my leg. I was relieved to find that everything was alright and continued on with a toughened up log book in my fully zipped tank bag. I got lucky.

Ever the one to fulfill a recommendation, I noted my proximity to a point of interest just ahead. Folks had told me about a ghost town named Chloride. It sits on the seventy-mile, dead-straight section of Highway 93 well south of the Hoover Dam. I had no idea what to expect from Chloride, but secretly I hoped that it would be like Oatman, or Tombstone, or Luckenbach. I wanted my imagination rocked again. I wanted to slowly look around and find someone staring at me with concern for my irrational ear to ear grin. I wanted to fall in love with another one of the West's treasures.

Well, Chloride is no Oatman, or Tombstone, or Luckenbach; it is about seven times the size of Luckenbach. Don't let that fool ya. It still was a tiny ghost town but less interactive than the others. A menagerie of rusted pots, barrels, and coffee cans hung loosely from the town's entrance, like half art—half ran-out-of-space-for-this-at-the-salvage-yard. Chloride's place in the world is marked by a giant white *C* on a nearby hillside. It was once a bustling gold mining village and now clings to life by drawing in curious onlookers with its leftover ruggedness.

I walked from one end of the town to the next. A squeaky, decorative windmill spun in someone's yard. It was the only audible noise. I felt as though I was being watched through small cracks in venetian blinds. A few mock-up shanties saying things like "Arizona Central Bank/Museum," "Old Red House," and "Rickedy Ass Saloon" stood empty and dilapidated like failed attempts to draw in tourists. When I was far from the Goose, two men at separate times walked by my bike and stooped down to check out my license plate, but they didn't take the effort to wave or say hello; they just stared at me. I stared back. With my riding gear on, I probably looked like a wandering and confused astronaut. Being the only tourist in town, my experience was rather strange.

I stopped at a gift shop to buy a Chloride sticker. The gift shop was also the owner's home, I believe. I crossed through a short gate belonging to a chain link fence, into a yard, and walked up and actually knocked on the door, even though a sign said "Open." A lady with long, dark hair invited me in. I told her what I was after, and she earnestly searched for a sticker, but came up empty-handed. She was the only person I met from Chloride. She fixed my flawed impression of Chloriders being derelict desert dwellers distrustfully doing dastardly things to do-gooders. She was a nice woman who had moved to the desert for peace and quiet. I left satisfied enough and still had Valley of Fire State Park in mind.

Miles later, the sight of dark chocolate mountains, irregular-shaped, and piled-up-looking, was grand enough for a photo. A setting sun made for warm, detailed browns. I pulled over to the steep shoulder. The Hoover Dam access road was three miles away. Cars flew by as I snapped pictures in all sorts of contorted angles like some phony professional. When I finished, I was standing on the left side of the bike. I threw my right leg over the Goose and started a landslide of bike and rider off the shoulder and into a rocky gulley. My right leg had not yet hit the asphalt when the bike started falling fast to the right. When I realized that there was no stopping its five hundred pounds, I pulled the clutch in and yanked the handlebars to the right. The Goose lurched forward in a tight lean, down the hill and into the ditch, without crashing over. I thought nothing of it. I like off-roading. But, when the rocks started smashing against the low-hanging exhaust pipes, and the sandy bank kept giving way to failed attempts to ride out, I got a little worried. A few hundred yards later, I popped back on the highway at a more shallow point. Folks driving along had to be thinking, "What the fuck is that idiot doing down there?"

Valley of Fire State Park became a future plan as I rolled up to Hoover Dam. I had not the willpower needed to ride by it now and then visit it in a week when my family arrived in Las Vegas. Curiosity had taken over.

Hoover Dam is as iconic as anything else in this country. If I demanded, "Quick, name ten things entirely American!" the Hoover Dam would probably come flying out of your windpipe right after the Grand Canyon or Elvis. By itself, it is so impressive as to make it unforgettable. However, the 890-foot-tall Pat Tillman and Mike O'Callaghan Bridge—newly erected beside the dam—also highlights the natural canyon, making for an awfully dramatic spot on the planet. Not to mention, Lake Mead and its whitewashed shore. Breathtaking, it is.

Until now, my impression of Hoover Dam came from the television. Like the Grand Canyon, I thought that in person it would look wider, but by no means was I disappointed. I was riding in a post card. A cotton candy pink and blue sky put a cherry on top of the terrain. I parked the bike and walked across. It felt mighty. Looking down at the Colorado River from the road surface made my knees vibrate. Lake Mead's deep blue water looked as deep as the ocean. No one walking around looked bored. We were simultaneously in a moment of awe. We were all kids again.

I hung around until dark. Soft, yellow lights dotted the dam and the road out. The beautiful chocolate mountains were now black with power line tower silhouettes protruding above. I filed out as one of the day's last visitors.

Nevada and Arizona are on opposite ends of Hoover Dam. As I left Arizona behind for a dark ride toward Las Vegas, the huge state of Nevada welcomed me to stay for a while in the West Coast time zone.

A few miles from the Hoover Dam, I crested a hill on Highway 93 to see Sin City and all of its lights in action. I pulled to the shoulder. Cars flew by dangerously. The lights of the city were colorful, compact and clustered like stars toward the center of galaxies. Beyond that, the desert was as black as coal. I wondered what it was like to be among all of that glowing energy. Seeing Las Vegas at night for the first time fired me up for the days to come.

Vegas's lights remained in the distance as I pulled off the highway in pursuit of a Motel 6. I stopped by a local pizza joint for directions. They told me to forget about a Motel 6 and look for a place called Fiesta Casino. They also told me that I could get a room there for $32 a night. That was enough for me to bolt off toward the casino. Once there, a pretty Latina quoted "$169 a night" with a smile. *Ain't no way!* What I didn't know was that the casinos were booked solid for the week's mega electronics convention. I left Fiesta, dejected, and rode around town looking for a room.

In the sky a supremely orange, low-hanging moon puzzled me for a few minutes. I pulled into a parking lot to stop for a better look. *Is that the sun or the moon?* It had been dark long enough to make headlights necessary, but still, the ball floating in the sky resembled the sun. The silhouette of a mountain scraped across the bottom of it. The moon's diameter had never looked so wide. It looked fat and heavy. A dark sky bordered it, making this look like some sort of evil sunset. I remained locked on it for several minutes to see if it was indeed rising or sinking. As its color brightened into a shade of cream, I knew that I had been fooled by the moon. Never had I seen it look as big as here.

Intrigued, I roamed around town until I found an America's Best Value Inn. The room was more than three times cheaper than Fiesta. Exhausted and starving, I checked in, found a Jimmy John's sub shop nearby and hit the sack early.

Day 89 – January 10, 2012

Although seeing downtown Las Vegas from my room at the America's Best Value Inn was no problem, I didn't realize until morning that I was actually within Henderson's city limits. I wasn't bothered by that, though. One look at Las Vegas in the morning from afar and you can thank your lucky stars that you are not breathing in that awful, brown smog. Yep, smog, thick and brown like the surrounding mountains. I had never witnessed the human created side effect. To say it looked like fog, but light brown, would be correct. From where I was standing on the balcony of the motel, it loomed over downtown Vegas like a soiled snow globe.

I wondered what Vegas smelled like, after seeing it covered in dirty air. There was only one way to find out since no one is bottling the stuff and selling it on the Internet. I packed up and rode right into it in search of Interstate 15. Cruising amid Vegas's heavy traffic didn't smell like Irish Spring soap, a mountain meadow, flowers, fresh laundry, a pretty girl's perfume, or an apple pie in a window sill. It smelled like truck exhaust and hot asphalt. It smelled of industry the way cities often do, but more *city-ish* than I've ever smelled before. Even Baltimore's industrious smell—a smell that I've known since being half the height I am now—will throw you a salty Chesapeake Bay breeze once in a while. Here in Las Vegas, things smelled stale. But gosh, I was still excited to see familiar faces there and party it up in the wild-ass city.

Las Vegas Motor Speedway sits on the outskirts of town where the desert takes over again. I flew past it not knowing what it was until I was right beside it on the interstate. An emergency vehicle crossover was a quarter mile up. I used it to pull off an illegal U-turn, irritating a semitruck driver in the process.

I love motorsports, and this was a prime place to get a bit of a racing fix. My stepfather is a huge Nascar fan, and I wanted to snag some pictures for him. I stopped at the ticket center and gift shop to find out what sort of cars were on the track. I could hear something going on in the distance. The friendly female clerk told me that a Richard Petty driving experience was on the big track, and the exotic cars were on the infield track. She said I could ride over and watch, no charge. *Sweet!*

The Goose and I found the infield and caught the last three laps of the guys driving on the Nascar track. They pulled off before I got my camera out. Then, like a distant echo, I heard the sound of super-revved pistons being slammed up and down at 10,000 rpms. The exotic cars had taken the infield track. I rushed for the Canon and hurried to the fence to keep from missing another opportunity. You name it and it was there, piloted by some fortunate, deep-pocketed motorhead. Lamborghinis diced with Ferraris. Corvettes gave rear-wheel-powered pursuits to all-wheel-drive Audis. Suped-up Mercedes supercars whipped in and out of Porsches. I was in a motorhead's dream world, and from the looks of it, I could have been the only spectator there. Everyone else was right next to the cars and looked involved in the workings of the operation. I chilled out trackside for another half hour before checking out the rest of the facility. Some motorcycle police were taking a training course, folks were learning how to drift their cars around corners, and I noticed Rob Maccachren's Rockstar-sponsored trophy truck leaving the dirt track.

Before I left, I called my friend Paul back. I had missed his call earlier. He mentioned that while in Vegas a while back he stayed at the Circus Circus Hotel for somewhere around $19 a night. For that price I could hold off on traveling north and get a day in Vegas that wouldn't break the bank. He recommended calling first to confirm. I relied on my unwavering superior wisdom and simply rode back into Las Vegas. *Even if it's twice that much I'll still get it.* Little did I know that the convention in town that got me the night before was to shaft me again. Circus Circus, as big as it is, only had a few rooms left for the hefty price of $130 a night. *Next time I'll listen to Paul.*

Directly behind Circus Circus was a KOA. *KOA in the city? Weird, but okay.* I rode into the concrete campground. Everything that you'd expect from a KOA was there, minus dirt. Neat RV pads consumed the space. At the office, a happy young gal with fire-red hair and the enthusiasm of an overgrown girl scout smiled wide as she said, "We only cater to RVs." I was shot down again.

My mind wandered to the last option on the table: I could pop my tent up with the homeless folks and their tents in the rough part of town that I passed through on my way to Circus Circus, north of the strip. It looked like Phoenix had been concentrated and poured out as a human paste on a few of Vegas's city blocks. Riding through that section, there were a few long red lights that I thought about running. Sitting there idling, I felt like a sitting duck—sitting on a Goose. I concluded, "I wouldn't last a second there."

Valley of Fire State Park is forty miles north of Las Vegas. The day was getting long. I stopped at a fuel station for gas and whiskey on the Moapa River Reservation before entering the park. Late dusk was fading to night as I pitched my tent in a tucked back cove of Martian rock walls. For the last fifteen miles I had traversed a terrain that I could not explain. Mountains with the region's common look shared the park with mountains seemingly from another world. Reds and oranges comparable to Sedona existed in globby formations on either side of the road. One looked like a beehive; others were smooth, Swiss cheese monoliths.

I couldn't decide whether they were slowly working their way out of the ground or laying on the surface and eroding away. All of them sat heavy and unsettled, similar to boulders being spilled out of the back of a dump truck. A sign at a pull-off said that the wild orange formations are the leftovers of ancient sand deposits. I can believe that; however, "What's up with this brilliant desert moon?" I whispered at 2:00am while outside of the tent taking a leak in the near daylight.

Day 90 – January 11, 2012

I awoke in a dazzling land of complementary colors. A huge baby blue sky, cloudless and clean, hung over Valley of Fire's outrageously odd orange outcroppings. When I arrived yesterday, I had little time to get a feel for the park. Sure, I crossed enough formations to gain an appreciation, but they were near the campground not far from the western entrance. Today, on my way north-east to Utah, I hoped to fill my eyes with the rest of the park's wonders.

I broke down camp, hopped on the Goose, and rode all of forty-five sec-onds to an empty circular parking lot at the base of Atlatl Rock. The engine was still as cold as the other side of the pillow.

Atlatl Rock is home to petroglyphs scratched into a flat portion halfway up its height. It's bulky and rounded and mostly orange, with a smattering of rust coloration throughout. I climbed nearly ninety metal steps, clinging to Atlatl Rock's exterior, to reach a steel viewing platform in front of the petroglyphs, knowing that the ancient artists had to scale the rock risking a life threatening fall. In front of me were scratched-in depictions of herbivores with long, swept-back antlers, and tongues like dragons; droopy-looking trees that put me in mind of wilted saguaro cacti; dancing stickmen, hands raised to the sky; and symbols shaped like targets, crosses, eyes, hands and feet with all fingers and toes accounted for. They were primitive in detail, like drawn by children.

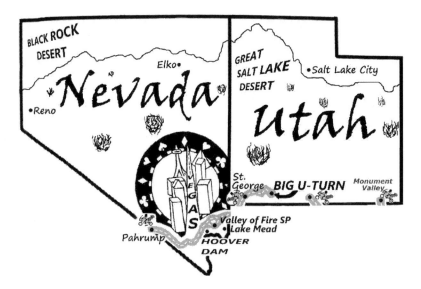

Unfortunately, some dimwit named Ike decided to add an idiot-o-glyph. His autograph was carelessly etched into the rock big enough that it could not be ignored. A sign in the parking lot said, "These petroglyphs were made by an-cient tribes. Respect their antiquity. Help preserve them." My guess is that Ike the genius failed to spot the suggestion. If he felt the need to destroy something so priceless to have his name seen, then maybe Ike could've carved his name in his forehead. I continued on, slightly perturbed.

Valley of Fire State Park had a dynamic visitor center. Inside, interactive displays invited chances to learn the park's "whys" while timelines broke down the geographic events that led to what we see today. Artifacts unearthed from the land's natives rested in permanent preservation. A taxidermist's sculpture sat in a glass case. It was a fully mounted bighorn sheep. *This has got to be the animal in the petroglyphs.* But most of all, I liked the mini-zoo of live desert wildlife that the visitor center displayed. Lizards, small mammals, and arachnids lived in adjacent terrariums, each looking peaceful and well fed. I had not seen live animals on display in any other state park.

Outside, droves of desert fowl and ground squirrels took advantage of small feeders placed there by the park staff. I sat and watched as they darted about from bush to bush just feet from my feet. To my left, the park rangers' white trucks glowed so brightly that I could hardly look at them. Then again, anything brighter than a burning cigarette tends to make my eyes squint.

I motored on to the park's eastern entrance where I took some time to play in a hollowed-out formation. This rock was more Flintstone than the slab houses in the cartoons. It had a round door that I could walk in at a slight duck, had round windows that let bright light in, and was shaped like one hemisphere of a basketball. I climbed in, smiling. I peeked out the windows and looked up and around. It was nature's perfect shelter and was a perfect way to end my visit to the park. Valley of Fire is a region of extreme contrast where taking a bad picture may be impossible. Just point and shoot. Pictures come out good. Close one eye with a hand behind the back, or better yet close both eyes and spin in circles; odds are you would still manage to capture some of the park's fiery beauty. Everything against the blues and oranges seemed brighter and alive.

Overton is the first town one enters upon leaving the park's eastern entrance. I stopped at a building with a big yellow *M* for breakfast and Wi-Fi. Nothing special happened, no lengthy encounters or wacky incidents. Instead, I typed vigorously without interruption. I barreled through coffee and a deluxe breakfast of sausage, eggs, hotcakes, and a biscuit. (So many mornings like this were beginning to add more "me" to my abdominal area.) Overton looked just like any southwestern town not famed for a mining past or gunfight or exotic natural feature. It was just overly ordinary Overton.

On my run to 15 N, I was a few miles from town when I noticed a spec of an American Flag perched high atop a rocky sand-colored peak in the desert. It stood there solo and strongly against the wind. *Why not spread some pride? I'll take a picture and share it for the efforts of the folks who had to lug it up all the way up there.* I swapped the short lens for the long one and shot five or six photos of Old Glory flapping from afar.

I was about to take off for the interstate when the morning's coffee pressed against my bladder. I ventured down an embankment to take a whiz. It was steep and full of marble-sized rocks. Before I knew it, the gravel broke loose and my hands hit the desert floor, gloveless. Bad mistake! I stood up quickly like I had bounced off the ground. I looked like Edward Prickly Hands. There were easily 100 tiny thorns lodged into my hands and backside. At first it didn't seem that bad, so I went for the camera, but after a minute a slight pain, bad irritation, and severe itching set in. After a half hour the symptoms wore off and my grippers were back to normal. Moral of the story: If you have to take a leak in the desert, look for a flat spot. Everything in the desert is spiny, unforgiving, and wants to hurt you.

Interstate 15 N would leave Nevada, take me through the extreme north-western corner of Arizona, and into the state of Utah. By the time I crossed into Mormon country, it was 3:30. I was tired and feeling pretty burnt out on the bike. All day I fought a tremendous side wind that had the Goose swerving like a drunken texter. I arrived in the town of St. George, Utah, and made up my mind to head to Zion National Park the next day. I just didn't feel like camping, plain and simple.

St. George was spread out among a rolling terrain of brown, bald, and rugged mountains. It felt urban and regular. Tall restaurant signs poked into the big blue sky, and a fair amount of cars filled the streets. I followed my deal-seeking radar to St. George's Motel 6. Their tall sign poking into the sky advertised "$33.99." I checked into a warm room, absorbed a hot shower, and then walked down the hill to the town's one and only bar, named One and Only Bar. In St. George everything is up to par with the rest of the nation except for the bar scene. I was only out to have a brew.

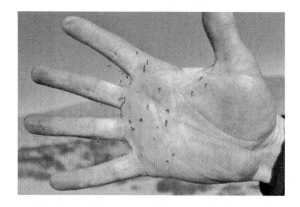

Upon entering I thought the place was decent, although women were no-where to be found. A large round bar with plenty of room for the bartender to move around in sat under dimmed lights. Two pool tables were tucked to the side like any other place I'd seen. No one was talking. Men sat around quietly, hunched over, as if in deep thought. They looked uncomfortable, like they were only pretending to know what they're doing with a beer sitting in front of them. Other than noticing it, I made nothing of it. I knew that I was in Utah and have heard about the reserved nature of its citizens.

I plopped down on a barstool opposite the front door so that I could see who was coming in. A nice fellow named Kevin sat a couple stools down. He was in his early fifties and had a scruffy beard and rust-colored hair. He and I broke the silence as we talked about travel to the East Coast. His dad had told him, "Nothing is worth seeing east of Colorado," and he had lived his life by that motto. I told him that it is worth at least one visit in life, just to experience the vast difference in terrain. Kevin and I drank another beer, and all was well in St. George until a fellow who looked somewhat like a long-haired cult member, wearing a homemade white shirt, walked over and introduced himself to me for reasons unknown. Perhaps he picked me because I was new to the bar or similar in age.

This idiot had found the bottoms of more twelve ouncers than he could handle. I'm usually a polite and patient listener around strangers, but all he wanted to do was vomit mouthfuls of close minded garbage about his religious beliefs, the Old Testament, taking pills, and using religion as a reason for violence or "protecting his religion" as he would've wanted it to be known. He topped that off with being a close-talker, where his face was more often than not too close to mine. I told him, "There is never a reason to be violent over religion," and then I tried to change the subject several times. Every time I mentioned something different, he would completely ignore my motion and jump back on his high horse, yapping on about the Old Testament.

When I just would not agree with him on his views, he gave me a sinister glance, walked to the next guy over, and started preaching to him. I admit to being freaked out enough to grab my belongings and head for the door. I really had no idea what the weirdo was capable of. I was in an unfamiliar town around unfamiliar folks. As I crossed the parking lot on the way back to the room, I looked back a few times to make sure that a knife-wielding lunatic wasn't following.

If you are religious, that is fine with me, and I will like you the same, but I see no need to use the actions of pushing, forcing, manipulating, convincing, or using violence for any reason when practicing your religion around others. Why not try accepting, caring, helping, understanding, and for crying out loud, loving others? This cat was truly a religious extremist, and I wish that I'd never met him. I don't remember his name, but I'd be willing to bet that it was Ike.

Day 91 – January 12, 2012

I rose with the sun and headed for Utah's Zion National Park. That seemed as good of a place as any to knock off a day or two of the countdown to seeing family in Vegas, but deep down, I just wanted to skip to the following Monday. Right away I was fighting a fairly substantial headwind, and the temp was in the upper thirties. Zion National Park is about forty miles northeast of St. George, in some of southern Utah's more rugged terrain. The higher elevation would promise even colder temperatures.

As I rode farther on into the cold and away from civilization, I became overwhelmed with a thick bout of loneliness and indifference toward exploring a new national park, so much so, that I stopped along the side of the road to take a deep breath and ask myself, "Do you really want to camp in the wilderness for the next few days?" I heard the answer I was looking for loud and clear. I plainly did not want to camp at high altitude, freeze my ass off, and isolate myself from people for the next few days. Two other things supplemented the decision, as if I needed more justification. I was simply ready for some warmer weather. It had been a bitter, cold ride since Texas, and the incident last night with the crazy cult guy—who looked like a blonde Charles Manson—put a bad taste in my mouth for that general area.

Las Vegas is at a lower elevation than Zion and would be quite warmer. The decision was set. From the side of the road, I did a U-turn and backtracked a few miles to a Maverick convenience store. I was parked along the front of the store and leaning against the outside of the building eating a Slim Jim. I watched as a man curiously wandered over to my bike. He was reading my stickers when I approached for a chat. He told me that Zion was a can't-miss park. He tried to persuade me to keep going, but I wasn't having it. I made a mental note of his strong suggestion and told him, "I plan to see the park later on. Maybe on the ride back East." Even though I didn't follow through with his advice, our brief conversation, coupled with the decision to head toward warmer weather, lifted my spirits almost instantly. I felt so much better about the day. It was like I could breathe again.

More times than not in life, I've gone against my grain to tough out situations that I really didn't want to be in for the sake of fitting in. I've indulged in unfulfilling, monotonous employment while ignoring my interests to avoid being called lazy. There, on the side of that road, I listened to my inner self completely and made a decision based on being happy.

Still, one other player factored into the whole mental mess. When traveling this extensively, I found that being impressed becomes more difficult. Just as a drug user moves from weaker substances on up the ladder to heavier stuff for bigger highs, I was beginning to suffer a sort of *lack of novelty*. I was getting antsy and longing for a change. I had really enjoyed the West thus far and whole-heartedly looked forward to experiencing more exotic landscapes. Countless highs had come in the form of desert gifts, and I was thankful for them, but . . . *some ocean waves and green vegetation would be great*. I knew it was coming, and all I'd have to do was be patient, which has always been one of my really weak points. Shamefully, I can't remember a time where I didn't want everything yesterday. That leads me to wonder if that's just how I am, or has our fast paced society made me that way?

Much happier, I hit the road back through St. George, northwestern Arizona, and back into Nevada via 15 S. I stopped at a McDonald's in Mesquite, Nevada, and ran across a woman working there whom I had met yesterday, fifty miles away at the McDonald's in Overton. She was a pretty, mid-thirties brunette, well-spoken, and friendly. She was out of uniform and said that she oversaw every McDonald's in the area. We spoke briefly about travel, as she was heading to New York in a few weeks. She returned to her duties, and I returned to people watching and lunch. It was bizarre to come across someone twice while being so far from home at two completely different locations and times. Yet, her familiarity proved slightly comforting.

From Mesquite, my ride was a seventy-two-mile blitz to Las Vegas. I arrived before dark and found a Motel 6. I did some research on Couchsurfing.com before heading out on the town. There were plenty of people on Couchsurfing.com willing to host in Las Vegas. I chalked it up as a possibility for the next few days. So there I was in Las Vegas, Sin City, a gambler's paradise, a party animal's heaven, and a wonderland of great drinking establishments. I really wasn't in the mood to drink and live it up, but a thought hit me that got my blood pumping. The thought was, "You only get one *first night* in Vegas," and with that, I tracked down a taxi next door at the Boulder Station Casino and ventured to the strip with wild in my eyes.

The Canon stayed put at the room, so my memory will be the only tool that I have to remember my first night in Las Vegas, and trust me, I did my best to make sure that I wouldn't remember a thing. Most of the night, I palled around with these two young cats from Minnesota, who I met at the PBR Rock Bar, named Lukas and Jesse. They were newly twenty-one, which helped to keep our energy high and the fun level through the roof. Lukas and Jesse were buddies on vacation together and in Vegas for their first time. From what I remember, coupled with the evidence that was on my hands and wrists (entry bracelets and stamps), I bar hopped like a drunken wild hare, smack talked for hours, and belted out some powerful, eighties-hairband karaoke at Coyote Ugly when the hot gal, who was dancing on the bar, lowered the mic to within inches of my teeth-showing, gut-wrenching, off-key-singing mouth. Somewhere in the night, a taxi driver even gave me my tip back because I made him laugh so much he almost pissed himself. *VEGAS BABY!*

Day 92 – January 13, 2012

It's safe to say that day ninety-two wasn't exactly productive. When I get real loose—beyond the point of worry or decency—I call the creature that I morph into the Zombie. The Zombie is the opposite of my sober being. He's loud, a ladies' man, a world-renowned dancer, a whiskey aficionado, never has a deep thought, and is as shy as a nudist. Despite his name, the Zombie shouldn't be feared. He's an all-around peaceful being in search of music with a fun beat and people capable of translating the best slurred slang known to man. Preparing Mike for battle with the Hangover Fairy is not one of the Zombie's strong points. If it's taking shots and climbing street lights you're talking about, then the Zombie has me covered. If it's time to crash and you need to drink plenty of water, take your shoes off, and brush your teeth, the Zombie will leave you hanging every time. I know this creature well.

When I awoke, I paid my dues for having too much fun. I spent the first half of the day in deep recovery. The second half began around the crack of 5:00pm. My aim was simply to head to the strip with the camera and make up for last night's lack of photography. All was going as planned, and I was being a good guy by staying away from any liquid influence until I received my first tweet ever. It came from Jesse. He and Lukas were at the PBR Rock Bar again. They made it known that they were ready to party. I shit-canned willpower and tracked them down like a bloodhound. It had been a while since I saw anyone familiar, and those guys were the closest I was going to get to a good set of buddies in Las Vegas.

It was their last night and they wanted to live it up. To make things a bit more interesting, I spiritedly mentioned that I wanted to get married in Vegas. They took my joke and ran with it. The next few hours were some of the funniest I've ever had. I don't think that those two crazies let a single female walk by without proposing for me. They would approach like two stealthy dung beetles ready to give the gals a big line of shit. Jesse would talk straight-faced, and Lukas would be standing with an irremovable grin, ready to chime in. Often they'd turn and point to me, and I'd do something dorky like wave and say "Hi." Lady after pretty lady took it well, as they politely declined our irresistible offer.

Then one beautiful young cocktail waitress did give me a *yes,* and from her expression she may have been interested—at least I thought. She was about five foot ten and looked like a Brazilian swimsuit model, perfect from head to toe. We talked over the ins and outs of the wedding ceremony as she held a tray of cocktails. She was obviously on the clock and entertaining our hijinks. But as she walked away, she gave me one last wink, and my dreaming, drunken, squinty eyes married her right there. If only we were both serious. . . .

Somewhere between the brews, the babes, and Lukas's intimate encounter with a sexy, headless mannequin on a sidewalk outside one of the strip's gift shops, Jesse mentioned staying up until sunrise. *What the hell, I'll give it a shot.* It had been a few years since I pulled that off.

Well, I did make it to sunrise, but the guys didn't. They called it a night around 4:30am due to their nine o'clock flight to Minnesota. My strategy for making it long enough to greet the sun was a huge breakfast at the strip's Denny's paired with coffee and orange juice. I arrived at Motel 6 just before 7:00am, removed my shoes, brushed my teeth and settled in.

Day 93 – January 14, 2012

Three hours after falling asleep, I was awake and seriously thinking about reserving the room again. I needed more shuteye. Checkout time was 11:00am, and I was as tired as if I'd been out all night partying or something. Getting the room again would require a short, groggy walk to the front desk, about three minutes to process the card, and a walk back. Not getting the room again would require some serious determination and an all-out assault with regard to packing my things and trying to squeeze out a shower before eleven.

Very, very reluctantly, I cursed like a baseball had just impacted the family jewels, and started packing. A short walk to the front desk with intentions to reserve the room again went awry when the clerk told me that the price had increased by $20 since yesterday. Damn weekend rates. The Goose was loaded, and I was drying off from a shower with five minutes to spare.

Boulder City is twenty miles southeast of Vegas and is the closest town to Lake Mead National Recreation Area. It's a place out of sight from Vegas's stream of lights, seemingly unaffected by the big city just across the hill. It exists at the base of those dark chocolate mountains that surround Hoover Dam. I passed through here at night a few days before without giving it a thought.

At Burger King in Boulder City, my brain manifested enough words to pull off a day's writing; then I searched online for a campground. I found one along the shore of Lake Mead. It was part of the National Park Service, and I could use my annual park pass to get in free. For $10 I'd be permitted an overnight stay with every convenience, except showers; they were twenty-five miles away along another portion of Lake Mead's shore. That surely beat the $55 a night at Vegas's Motel 6.

With camp set up and the sun setting, I took a stroll to the lakeshore. My body was arguing with my mind. My body was saying, "Get your ass in that tent and get some rest," but my mind was saying, "That'll be a really long, boring night." I reached the shore of Lake Mead talking on the phone with my mom. I did this often enough to know that nothing new was going on back home. The darkening sky and foreign surroundings looked nothing like home. Sublime thoughts crept in while we spoke: *I've been on the road a while now. It's a different world out here. I miss my folks.* I bent down with one knee straight out and one knee pointed up, neither touching the ground. My left hand was touching the water's cold surface. Mom and I finished talking, and I remained there—taking it in—until it was thoroughly dark.

Light may have been gone, but it was early when I arrived at the tent, so I did what I thought I would do much more on the trip: I read a book. The

Zombie purchased one a few nights ago at the MGM Grand. It was *The Man's Manual* and covered damn near everything a wussy type of man would need to know to be, well, not a wussy. The chapters followed an order that saved the best of the book for last. I read three chapters and skipped around the book a bit. I, being the ex-construction worker that I am, didn't think that I could possibly learn anything else new about hammering a nail through wood, but I sure did. If you're nailing through extremely hard wood, and you don't want to bend the nail, you can put soap on the tip of it to kind of lube it. Or, if you think you may split the wood with the nail, you can flip the nail over, point up, and smack the sharp side with your hammer to dull it a bit. A dull nail splits less wood than a sharp one.

I am open to my strengths and weaknesses, and for the most part I still need some help here and there. Before that book, I never knew how to skin a catfish or gut a deer. No one has ever taught me. And the same can be said for my encounters with women. No one has ever taught me how to skin or gut one. In all seriousness, though, I've never learned how to deal with them. By default, I'm on edge around them. I don't have the slightest clue what they're thinking, yet I feel that they can read my mind. I don't know why they need so many damn shoes, or why they always go to the restroom together, or why they get all fancy-looking to go to work and come home, remove the makeup, and turn into a sweatpants gremlin. I'm not lying when I say that I could have a better conversation with a walnut than anyone of the female persuasion. *I'll have to read the chapter on women a dozen times.*

Throughout the pages, I learned some, laughed some, and the author, Greg Stebben, is the cleverest of writers. If you know about anything manly, you'll get the jokes. With my newfound awareness of my half-manliness and extreme lack of sleep, I called it a night when the short arm pointed at nine.

Day 94 – January 15, 2012

On October 14, 2011, I clicked the Goose into first gear in my brother's driveway with no clue as to how life would change in the immediate future. On November 14, I felt like I was on an extended vacation. Good times were had every day with an overwhelming feeling of peace, and I had money to burn. A lifetime of being stifled by the greenbacks had magnified my desire to have fun and blow some money. On December 14, I was still in vacation mode without really thinking about the big picture. New landscapes were taking my breath away almost daily.

Now it was the day after the three-month mark, and there had been a change. Vacation mode had all but vanished. Preservation mode was now nearly in full control. This change came, primarily, from my declining bank account and an awareness that I had no idea what I was going to do when all of this was over? An answer eluded me; however, thoughts were creeping in.

I thought of motocross, but wasn't thinking about making another push to become pro someday, but rather, using the best thing that I'd ever been involved in to save my butt again. Before I found motocross as a teen, I was in experiment mode, like many of today's youths. I was drinking too early and fooling around with the wrong things. Then, at seventeen, I started racing mx, and until twenty-one, I stopped every negative influence, just shy of cold turkey, in order to do my best on the track each weekend. I learned about setting and achieving goals, exercising, and socializing with good, decent people.

Then it all changed when I let my motocross life take a back seat to my nightlife. Weekend parties and drunken craziness came to plague the majority of my free time. Alcohol-fueled nights became addictive, desirable, and most of all, stimulating. I contemplated, "Have I replaced my adrenaline rush from moto-cross with something a lot worse?" I began to think, "If I get myself involved in the motocross industry, it can get me back on the right track. . . ."

As for good ol' day ninety-four, excitement was hard to find. Laundry du-ties returned. Unlike the first weeks of the trip, I was getting awfully used to wearing my pants and shirts three or four days in a row. A habit learned from a lifetime of practice was breaking. Before leaving home, it was inconceivable to wake up in the morning and spend a whole day wearing yesterday's outfit. Per-haps that sort of strict tidiness came from the early school years where you nev-er ever wear the same clothes two days in a row for fear of ridicule from your fellow classmates. I was seeing how silly and impractical it is to live like that. Nonetheless, the last straw still remained dirty socks. When they were all used up, it was time.

I went to Sudz, Boulder City's laundromat. While waiting for the spin cycle, I half-heartedly searched the web for a place to take a shower. I had nothing better to do with my time. I found Canyon Trail RV Park. It was right up the hill from the laundromat, and the fellow who owned it generously opened his office for a second on a Sunday to let me get clean. He charged $5 for the favor. I justified the price of the shower as the cost of fuel spent riding the fifty-mile round trip to Lake Mead's bath houses.

I folded and rammed my clothes into the Goose's trunk and set about find-ing a place serving food that didn't belong to a chain of franchises that exist in every small town from here to the Atlantic. Downtown Boulder City hosted a tiny business district full of shops and restaurants. There I found Tony's Pizza Pasta & Subs. It was a stucco building, light sand in color, with five arches de-signed into its front entrance.

I ordered two slices and slowly ate them while fighting off the urge to wan-der into the bar in the next room. The damn place was packed with rowdy football fans hooting and hollering at the flat screens mounted high around the bar. A playoff game had 'em all stirred up. It looked fun, but I had to keep in mind my dwindling checking account.

The sun was gone for the day when I rode back to camp for another early night. I was lying in the tent bored out of my mind and thirsty. Earlier in the day, I noticed a water spigot at one of the other campsites down the hill. I un-zipped the tent and crept into the darkness. A big fat owl startled me as it flew past. I ran back to my site to get the Canon while hoping that it would still be perched at the same spot when I returned. It was, and I tried to sneak up on it for a close up. The owl allowed a thirty-five-foot comfort zone before flying off. That was my first close encounter of the owl kind. The hooter's silhouette reminded me of a bird with a cat's head, thanks to its pointy head feathers. Each one of my pictures came out blurry. I was shaking and carrying on like Barney Fife from the excitement of it being right there. The bird won this time, but next time owl be ready.

I fetched the water that I'd come for and walked back to the tent. Through sixty more pages of *The Man's Manual*, I learned how to tell a good suit from a cheap one and how to wear it. I also learned how to make a small plane out of matchsticks that's powered by flies. You put the flies in a freezer (in a jar) until they are cold, then put drops of glue on your plane. Take the flies out of the freezer; put them on the glue drops, facing in the same direction. Breathe warm air on them and watch them take off on that sucker. I vowed to try it the next time I owned a refrigerator. Speaking of flies, I didn't know that trout will not bite on anything but flies. That's why fly fishing is such an art. The fake flies made by fisherman have to look and act exactly like the flies that the trout want to eat. A bit wiser than when I woke up, I turned out the tent light and wormed into my mummy bag.

Day 95 – January 16, 2012

Day ninety-five, a big day, and it all started at 4:00am. I awoke in complete darkness in my lavish tent erected along the shore of Lake Mead with the wheels turning in my head. Night is the greatest time for solid thinking. Being a really light sleeper, I get more than my share of this quiet time, and frankly, more than I want of it. Excitement for the midday meeting with family, and a few thoughts that had been weighing on my mind, kept me up. I tried to fall asleep, but it just wasn't happening. Two and a half hours later, the sun had brightened the sky enough to go ahead and crawl out of the sleeping bag and get on with the day.

I zipped up the hill to the grocery store to buy a healthy breakfast, then jetted over to McDonald's for coffee and Wi-Fi. An hour and a half later, a new post shot out into the world, and I left to gather my things for a skedaddle back to Las Vegas.

The twenty-one-mile ride from Boulder City was over in a flash. A sign at Walgreens on the strip said 11:22am. Planet Hollywood would be home for the next few days, and at 11:30, the spot where I'd meet my family. I darted through heavy traffic full of finely detailed cars. I hoped to make it to Planet Hollywood's lobby before they did. I wanted to surprise them with the Canon and capture some first reactions.

I beat them to the punch by less than two minutes. I was standing in the registration line when I noticed the East-Coasters walk in. I took cover behind a pillar to get my camera ready for the sneak attack. With the Canon turned on, my eye socket against the view finder, and my ball cap on to throw them off, I made an approach. It was as stealthy as possible for being in a crowded hotel lobby. Kayla spotted me walking their way. She cracked a big smile. Tomato Joe and Tomato Pam turned and smiled as well. Shane was beside them and talking on the phone. He noticed their reactions and turned toward me. His reaction was disappointingly neutral. I've seen more excited reactions from the well placed smiling mouth of a Mr. Potato Head.

Shane has been my favorite person to spend time with for as long as I can remember, and my reaction to seeing him after three months apart was of joy. My legs were vibrating in my baggy blue jeans kind of like a shiver without the cold. I was enlivened and anxious. In all fairness, I may have just confused him a bit as I poked a camera in his face while he was on the phone. In no time, it felt like the three months on the road never happened. It felt like we had all just flown in for vacation. I was happy to be reunited.

We headed to registration where Joe handed me a ticket stating that my room was comped. He had earned enough gambling credits to receive a free room for two nights. I knew of this possibility before they arrived in Vegas. I thanked him sincerely, and we packed into an elevator destined for the thirty-fifth floor.

The four of them stayed in Planet Hollywood's Panorama Suite. From the rectangular windows situated on the room's curved exterior wall, we could see the fountains of the Bellagio shooting into the air. Vegas's Eiffel Tower Restaurant almost looked within reach. The outrageous energy of the city could be seen clear to the distant mountains.

Planet Hollywood's rooms were fantastic. The Panorama Suite's movie theme was based on Marilyn Monroe and featured two of her dresses. One of them was a sexy red dress from her movie *How to Marry a Millionaire*. A set of her white gloves were placed in a glass-topped coffee table. Pictures of her hung everywhere. Just stepping foot in the classy darkened suite made even the most hillbilly feller from West Virginia feel like a big baller. Vegas was written all over its perfectly decorated interior. It was the coolest room that I'd ever been in.

My room paled in comparison to the Panorama Suite, yet it blew me away by being ten times better than any standard hotel room. A giant soft bed sat in the middle of the themed room. It was long enough from front to back and side to side for me to lie either way without any limbs hanging off, like a super king size. My room's theme centered on that wacky 1987 movie *Space Balls*. Bill Pullman's futuristic white jacket hung in a glass case to the left of the bed. Like the Panorama Suite, memorabilia and framed photographs decorated the walls. A huge flat television, far too complicated for me to operate, held a big black stare toward the bed. I knew that I'd not turn that thing on the whole stay.

We finished unpacking and descended onto Planet Hollywood's buffet. They were hungry from hours of flight, and I was ready to eat better than I had in three months. The buffet extended for what seemed like miles. Food was piled high. It seemed so plentiful that you'd swear you could walk outside and find yourself standing in a rich agricultural region and not in the middle of the desert. *How long can Las Vegas keep this up?* We pigged out. The food wasn't free, and I cleaned up two heavy plates, followed by a heaping helping of ice cream.

The folks gambled for a while after eating. I stood by quietly, watching greenbacks get lost forever to the Vegas nightlife. Gambling, thankfully, has never marked a spot on my list of guilty pleasures. The opportunity to lose money rapidly has always been a turn off. Back home, our county has had a horse racing track and casino for decades. In thirty years, I may have entered its doors fifteen times. That's not to say that I think of it unkindly. There's no doubt that the casino has strengthened our county financially. In fact, I can't imagine how derelict Jefferson County would be without it. And for that, I appreciate it; however, the brainwashing sounds of the machines endlessly going "boop bee boop," paired with the lifeless expressions of the human ATMs sitting before them, has always weirded me out. I've only had one great time where the racetrack and casino were concerned and that was when they hosted the mega rock concert Lalapalooza, back in the nineties.

So here I was, standing quietly and watching my brother gently donate dollars to the mouth of the machine, like he was feeding a baby, when I sucked it up and put $5 in the next slot machine over. Two turns of the wheel later, I won $4.50. I cashed that ticket out faster than you can yell, "Jackpot." *Making money gambling, I could get used to this.*

The rest of the evening was spent with Shane, out on the town. The others called it an early night. I moseyed on over to the PBR Rock Bar for a bit of nostalgia from my previous nights out with the Minnesotans. Shane followed suit five minutes later. It was on from there. I mean, you only get one first night in Vegas with your brother. Shane and I attacked the night like animals. Each escalator and each flight of stairs became a king-of-the-hill footrace to the top with yours truly always coming out the victor. Hey, my book, my story! Actually, he may have got me on a few of them. We bebopped, bar hopped, and cat called. We threw 'em back, downed 'em, and chugged 'em. We went full force. Somewhere along the line, two wild-asses from Colorado joined in on our shenanigans like reincarnations of Lukas and Jesse, and before we knew it, Vegas delivered what it was built to do: provide fun-filled, high-energy experiences for all.

Day 96 – January 17, 2012

Quality time in Vegas is an oxymoron. Time in Las Vegas is usually described with terms like wild, crazy, blasted, blurry, or broke. My day began around noon due to the long, wild, crazy, blasted, and blurry night before. The folks had breakfast delivered to the Panorama Suite. Unfortunately, I missed it. I woke up sideways on the bed, shoes still on, with an awful taste in my mouth. I headed for the bathroom to brush my teeth and noticed the toilet filled with remnants of yesterday's buffet. I did not remember eating vegetable soup, but that's surely what it looked like, only more grotesque. I flushed the half-digested scraps and went for the toothpaste. On the bright side, if I had not heaved all that mess into the toilet last night, the Hangover Fairy would've had her nasty hands around my neck. I really didn't feel that bad.

I walked to the Panorama Suite to meet them. Shane asked me, "Where did you go last night?" Apparently, I had left him with the guys from Colorado at

Coyote Ugly when I felt the urge to vomit coming on. I must have made a mad dash back to the room. I told him, "I guess I had to get the heck out of there before I yakked everywhere." I didn't remember the incident at all, being at Coyote Ugly, running back to the room, or projecting stomach soup into the commode. He filled me in on the night, saying how much fun he had hanging out with the Coloradans. He smiled as he shared hilarious details that I was sorry to have missed out on.

For the day, I third wheeled it with the family. They did a bit of gambling and I did a bit more watching. Vegas provides plenty to see and do, but that was a secondary concern for me. I wanted to spend some quality time with them, time that I'd remember.

Just before dusk, we sardined into a cab and headed for the Rio Hotel and Casino for a huge seafood buffet. My taste buds barely let me veer from plates piled high with Alaskan crab legs. Those brave fishermen, who have become so popular as to earn a television series, can rest assured that their hard work has not been in vain. Everyone pigged out on everything from duck, to corn on the cob, to swordfish. My assault on the buffet was solely aimed at crustaceans, not only because I love crab meat, but I was going to get Tomato Joe's money's worth. I thanked them for sponsoring a homeless wanderer with another meal.

The buffet proved too big to conquer. We left the table with stomachs at maximum capacity and hailed a taxi. Little did anyone know, we were about to receive the most educational cab ride of our lives. The cab driver was a Native American descendant, writer, traveler, trivia buff, and all-around intelligent fellow. For the ten-minute cab ride across town, we said nothing as our driver blurted out a minor geography and history lesson. He spoke of ancient giant sequoias, the Russian language, and whatever else you may ever need to know if you find yourself in the Discovery Channel's *Cash Cab*. Unfortunately, he wasn't quizzing us and no prize money changed hands. No lights popped on in the cab's ceiling, and we couldn't go double or nothing on a video bonus question. Instead, we listened quietly. He was a fascinating man. Just about everything he mentioned was a huge interest of mine. When we stepped out of the cab, Shane looked at me and said "Between you and him there were more useless facts in that cab than one should have to put up with." I just smiled, knowing that he was right.

We were back at Planet Hollywood and preparing for the evening. Everyone, minus me, was going to see a comedic ventriloquist show. I could have gone, but chose the frugal route. While they were out, I holed up in their suite. Vegas's show of electronic color surpassed my laptop's glow. I was writing and observing. Dark maroon curtains were opened wide on either side of the windows, framing the energetic picture. The lights inside were low. Flawless furniture surrounded the flawless chair where I sat. Behind me, the Panorama Suite's bar held a gallon of Jack Daniel's. The shiny brown liquid went down smooth as I sipped it on the rocks in silent opulence. I couldn't help but feel lucky in the moment. I looked around and thought, *This room, this hotel, this city is unbelievable. Where the hell am I, and how did I get here? Somebody pinch me.*

They returned in a fit of chatter and laughter. They were all ramped up for another shot at the slots. Everyone spilt up to try their luck once again. I tagged along with Shane and watched him give the blackjack table a go. He sat on a stool, and I stood behind him and to the side like an awkward type, unsure of what to do. I didn't realize that this was frowned upon by the dealer. Three times, I announced that I was just watching my brother and that I didn't know how to and didn't want to play.

Card games, like gambling, have never interested me. For that matter, board games and video games have always been a bit dull as well. As a kid, I remember being frustrated when my friends would sit in front of the TV screen and fight over the video game controller. I thought, "Why sit here and play pretend when we can go outside and play football or basketball or build a fort?" Shane is like me in that sense, but with a more developed tolerance toward games. He fared well for a while before succumbing to blackjack's odds.

A bit later, we all met to decide where the rest of the night would go. It seemed like everyone wanted to gamble some more before calling it a night. I was tired and mentioned that I really wasn't into partying down. Secretly, I wanted to spend some time with my brother where alcohol didn't control the pace of the night's activities. I wanted the moment to last as long as possible. I wanted to feel like I had spent some quality time with my brother. I wanted to remember our visit to Las Vegas. Last night, although incredibly fun, was over way too quickly. Our heavy drinking made it that way. I was really close to Shane and missed him. I hoped that a few months apart wouldn't damage our relationship, and it hadn't. At 1:00am the night got the best of me. As I fell asleep, I knew that I had gotten some quality time with my brother.

Day 97 – January 18, 2012

I opened my eyes to unfamiliar walls. I was in a king-sized, cloud-like bed without the slightest clue of my earthly coordinates. I sat up quickly and looked around in blank confusion. It was obvious that I was in a hotel room, *but where?* For thirty seconds, I was more lost than a set of keys when you're late for work. When the flood of mental activity rushed through my brain, bringing with it awareness and taking away grogginess, I whispered, "Oh yeah, I'm in Las Vegas."

This has happened throughout my life many times, as in the case of mornings waking up on vacation, or at a friend's house. Never had it taken as long as it had here to pull through this strange morning misperception. I chalked it up to staying somewhere different every day for nearly three months. Give it a shot and see if you don't wake up thinking you're somewhere that you're not once in a while. This wasn't the first episode of the trip, but by far the most intense. There had been mornings on the road where I expected to see my house's greyish-blue bedroom walls when I opened my eyes. These instances were always amusing after the twilight zone feeling wore off.

It was too early to see if the folks were up and moving, so I got to work getting my things ready to carry to the bike. A few minutes after 8:00am, Shane texted to see if I was up. I responded and headed for the Panorama Suite. Joe and Pam were still visiting the Sandman, so Shane and I spoke quietly. Then, as if shot out of a cannon, Joe came rip-roaring out of his room. Shane and I were startled. Pam's James Brown cell phone ringer sounded and must have awakened them. Joe was bouncing sideways singing, "I feel good! I knew that I would." To see a stout man of six foot eight bouncing sideways on one foot first thing in the morning singing James Brown fit Vegas perfectly. Joe had a sense of humor to match his size and plenty of energy to boot. Joe slowed to a walk, and we followed to the breakfast table. A few hours hanging out in the morning and a big breakfast with everyone gathered at the table seemed a fitting way to spend my last bit of time with them.

My short stay with my brother and extended family had to end. Vegas was entirely too big and expensive for my vanishing budget. They planned to stay there until Saturday, but I had to continue on. Money willing, I would have stayed until Saturday as well. We took a few pictures, and I said my thanks and farewells to Kayla, Pam, and Joe. Shane helped carry some gear to the bike. I loaded up, thinking *this is it—the last time I'll see my little bro for who knows how long.* We said goodbye to one another with a handshake and steady eye contact.

I was about to ride away when I realized that I had left my phone in their suite. Shane volunteered to run up and grab it for me while I kept watch over my things. Ten minutes later, he was back. "It wouldn't be normal if I didn't forget something," I said as he neared the Goose. Now it was time to say goodbye for real. We shook hands again; I took off and that was it. I was on the road again to places unknown. My chest felt tight and my soul lonely as I rode away.

The feeling faded slightly when I arrived at Gold and Silver Pawn Shop. That was the pawn shop where the *Pawn Stars* TV series was located. A few folks, including my parents and Bob from Luckenbach recommended seeing the place. I wanted to follow through to help satisfy their curiosity. I had seen a few episodes on the tube sporadically over the past two years. From what I gathered from the show, I liked the no-BS, cut-and-dry deals made with patrons and respected the consistent use of experts when negotiating a price.

I pulled into the small, crowded parking lot. *That's it? Where's the big over-the-top Vegas façade? Where's the bling bling? I've seen more elaborate pawnshops in Myrtle Beach.* Instead, what I saw was a heavily used, single-story building with hardly any bells or whistles and a sign hanging from it that was anything but impressive. I guess you don't have to look the best to be the best, and these guys were doing something right if they had their own television show. If not for the hour-and-a-half wait to get inside, I would've ventured in. Filming was happening while I was there. A man on a loudspeaker kept telling the tourists to get away from the front door while the cameras were on. I lurked around for ten minutes then hit the road west.

My path would take me to Highway 160 and over the hump, to Pahrump, Nevada. Pahrump is a small town that caters to everything you need, and I mean everything, except vegetation. There are the ubiquitous franchises recognized across our great country, and then there's legal sex with strange women for money: legal prostitution, legal and managed brothels. You say, "I thought Vegas had that." And I say, "Vegas does not, but I thought it did too." And so, we learn something new every day. These legal brothels do exist in Nevada, but not in all counties. Some counties have just a few, and some counties have none. All are regulated by individual county law, and in places of high population, like Las Vegas, they've been shown the door. Perhaps somewhere between twenty and thirty exist statewide.

I was gliding through Pahrump's parched town when I noticed a billboard pasted with a scantily-clad female attracting "business." Without an inkling of hesitation, I thought about going for it. Unlike Houston's underground sex rings, here in Pahrump it was okay, and presumably less skeevy. Plus, there was no chance of being arrested in an undercover sting operation.

I had been on the road for three months, traveling the U.S. not unlike a monk. Every night, in every drinking establishment, and every chance encounter with a nice young lady thus far had left me high and dry. (Although I'll never forget her for all of the wrong reasons, I have to acknowledge the opportunity to get lucky with Cynthia from Club 19 in Florida. No amount of whiskey was gonna trick me into believing that she was something other than a corn-fed buffarilla. I still shudder when I think about her eyes wandering up and down my poor body and her aggressive pick-up lines). Here in Pahrump, I knew that I was a man poisoned by his own lack of game and flying mere millimeters higher than desperate. The thought of a warm touch and zesty session for all of a minute and a half—counting disrobing—was enough to make the ol' springboard gain weight.

Thus, through every tire rotation in Pahrump, I thought about sex. While at McDonald's searching the web for routes through my next two days, I thought about it. I chewed on a McDouble and fries and thought about it. In the parking lot, I met a fellow from Switzerland who moved to Nevada two decades before. He might have been in his early fifties, had brown hair, and had lost most of his accent. As he talked, I nodded and smiled to be polite, but I couldn't stop thinking about the brothelly possibilities. He spoke kindly of his home country, and I kept thinking about sex. He mentioned how Switzerland felt so crowded, and I thought about paid sex. He said that he liked Nevada for its open space and sparsely populated areas, and I thought more about legal prostitution, huge boobies, and long smooth legs. For a brief second I entertained my unproven impression of Switzerland being one of Europe's more rural countries, and again my thoughts were yanked back to my proximity to the brothels. Conversing with anyone was useless. I had a decision to make—go for it, or not.

I left Pahrump a victim of a self-administered cock block. In all frustrating honesty, I did not have the money to go for it. Literally, the money was in my checking account—if I wanted to turn tail for the East Coast in two weeks. The thought of ending daily travel at all was enough to make my stomach turn, let alone ending the ride prematurely. I knew stubbornly that there were things that I wanted to do in California and that I'd not deprive myself of them. The mortality of my journey became increasingly clear. I rode on to Death Valley.

Before this trip, the thought of even going to Death Valley would make me nervous. The name, the remoteness, and the distance from home was enough to give me the willies, but now that I'd grown used to this region—and with Big Bend, Texas, under my belt—there was no reason to think that our nation's national parks would be anything less than amazing and well facilitated. I headed toward Death Valley with one minor concern—night was fast approaching—and no matter where I was going, I just didn't like riding after sunset.

Dusk rewarded me with amazingly colorful skies as I left Nevada for Inyo County, California. A spray painted line on the road with "NEVADA" capitalized separates the states. From there, long stretches of empty, rolling road welcomed the light feel of the Goose's tires. The temperature comfortably dropped to the upper sixties. Pressure from a perfect mix of cool and warm air brushed across my hands and neck, awakening my soul. I was happy to be motorcycling.

I arrived at the visitor center after dark, got directions to the campground, and set my tent up. Ramen noodles were on the dinner menu. Shortly after eating, I crawled in the tent to lie down. I was gaining comfort and nearly faded off to sleep when some sort of animal bumped against my tent three rather hard times. The right front corner of the tent shook rapidly as if the animal ran into it totally without seeing it. For the slightest of moments, I tensed up.

This used to freak me out a lot more at the beginning of the trip, but I got over it through experiencing it enough and developing a guessing game. *What sort of furry four-legger is it?* My guess this time, a raccoon. Almost without fail, a UFO (unidentified foraging omnivore) would visit camp at some point during the night, and most times I heard them as they scampered about, climbing on the picnic table or messing with the tarp covering the Goose. It's just part of camping. Usually they left the tent alone. A couple swift claps of the hands was generally enough to motivate them to move on.

That didn't always work, as with the case at Thunder Gulch Campground in Florida when something was messing with my tent. When I clapped my hands, instead of running, it growled at me. This happened three times. It made the hair on my neck stand up, and that sucker got the best of me. To this day I still don't know what sort of animal it was. . . .

Day 98 – January 19, 2012

Morning came with a decision. Take the high road or take the low road. Either one promised a special encounter with one of America's great landscapes. My map presented two escape routes from Death Valley for the day's ride. The high road involved leaving camp and taking the northwestern exit out of Death Valley via Route 190. I'd ride along the eastern side of Sequoia National Park, and maybe catch a glimpse of Mt. Whitney, California's highest peak, at 14,494 feet. The low road consisted of leaving camp, heading south out of the park, and visiting the United States' lowest elevation at Badwater Basin.

As much as I love seeing huge mountains, I picked heading due south to Badwater over a chance at seeing Mt. Whitney, based on Badwater Basin's number one rank on a national scale. If Mt. Whitney was our nation's highest peak, there's no doubt that I would've headed north to see it. In turn, that would've made for a cold day of wintry high-elevation riding. Sliding south through Death Valley promised a day of warmer riding in terrain unfamiliar to snow. I didn't like being in the position where I'd have to choose one over the other. I wished that I could split myself in two, go see both attractions, and rejoin at the end of the day somewhere south in the Mojave Desert.

Now decided, my morning was one of standard preparation with a side of a $5 shower. Death Valley's Park Village is like Big Bend's Rio Grande Village. It's a hub of civilization sitting in a supremely harsh environment so far in the middle of nowhere that its existence seems frail and hardly makes sense. It's also known as Furnace Creek Ranch. Below a sign stating "Highest recorded temperature 134°F July 10, 1913," it calls itself Furnace Creek Resort. It's a small place of many names that supplies everything you need from bottled water, to gas, to a shower, which leads me back to the morning.

I tracked down the shower house among a smattering of small wooden buildings. They were painted yellow and used as hotel rooms, a post office, and a village store. A giant swimming pool was next to the shower house and surrounded by small patches of green grass being watered by sprinklers. An odd palm tree or two were imported and planted for a somewhat tasteless, unfitting feel. Beyond that, a varying landscape of rocky browns, severely in need of a drink, finished off the view. I took my pricey shower in a spacious tiled stall and thought about how I didn't like seeing those sprinklers outside, and how that pool fit the land like a square block in a circle hole. It felt odd and wasteful.

Furnace Creek Ranch grew from the discovery of minerals in Death Valley. Subsequent mining activities required shelter for living on-site. The oldest house in Death Valley (1883) is now a museum at the ranch. It's a small, unpainted, weathered wood building. Inside, I gained an immediate appreciation for how incredibly hard life was for the first non-natives to inhabit the region. Hanging on the wall, a few journal entries, from a German fellow trying to make it across Death Valley to join his company, gave a stark impression of his time here. He wrote of an ox that reached its physical limit and died, supplies sacrificed, friends lost along the way, and his wife that he longed for back on the East Coast of the United States. Despair poured out in his words. Hopelessness lingered in his notes. And matters weren't helped at all as settlers labeled the region with forlorn descriptions like Death Valley, Furnace Creek, Badwater Basin, Funeral Peak, Last Chance Mountain, Hell's Gate, and Devil's Golf Course. Psychologically, the names were uninspiring, yet inspired by scorching realities.

Behind the museum, an outdoor display of mining equipment sat in perpetual sun. A sixty-ton Baldwin 280 oil burning locomotive topped the low-tech equipment. It began hauling ore in 1916 in Death Valley. There were mine shaft carts made of wood and steel, once pulled by mules. A wagon with wheels made from tree trunks—sliced and wedged into steel rings—rested heavily on the sandy soil. Rusting and rudimentary mining equipment told the story of Death Valley's late nineteenth and early twentieth centuries. I could still feel the heat, sweat, and labor of the men and mules emanating from those primitive machines.

Badwater Basin is about twenty miles south. I fueled up at Furnace Creek Ranch and had my first experience with California's ridiculous fuel pumps. I pulled up to the pump, hopped off the Goose, and was going through the motions. The nozzle was in the bike, electronic payment had been made, I pulled the trigger, but no fuel came out. A thick rubber cone was attached to the nozzle. It was designed to compress like an accordion when the nozzle is inserted into the tank. I thought that it was there to prevent spilling and really paid it no mind. Four or five times, I put the damn nozzle in the tank and pulled the trigger, only to be denied a drop of fuel. The service station attendant came to my aid and said, "If that cone isn't pressed hard against your tank it won't work." He then asked if I was new to California. He gave me the lowdown on California's pumps: "They're all a pain in the ass for motorcycles."

The problem lies in design. The cone is meant to cup a car or truck's fuel tank fill spout (the cylindrical piece that your gas cap screws into), while the nozzle is inserted and transferring fuel. Its purpose is to keep fuel vapors from entering the atmosphere. Most motorcycles don't have the raised fuel spout like a car; they have a flat opening recessed in the top of the fuel tank that is accessed by a metal flip cap. Because the opening to a motorcycle's fuel tank is recessed, a gap is formed when attempting to fill the fuel tank, which causes an inappropriate seal, or vacuum, or pressure to be read by the pump, making it not work. It's as if the pump thinks that someone is trying to dispense fuel with the nozzle still inches away from the car's fuel spout.

I concluded that the design, the application, and the law that made the cones mandatory, was just another spoonful of bullshit passed without enough research showing effectiveness, and without consideration to the population as a whole and what they drive. Thousands, if not millions, of motorcyclists fuel up in California daily, and all the while, fuel vapors are escaping the most poorly designed piece of rubber crap that I've ever seen. Hey, whoever is in charge in California, your work is subpar and thanks for the headache.

I had a tank full of fuel and was throttling south when I passed a sign that read "72 miles to next services." Looking back, that was the greatest distance between resources that I'd see on my journey. Badwater Basin appeared on the right not long after. I hopped off the Goose and looked around. A small black and white sign was mounted to the mountainside behind the parking area. It said "Sea Level." From where I was standing it was about 250 feet overhead. Badwater Basin is 282 feet below sea level and was spread out before me as a giant white plain. That sign and a couple of informational boards were the only things to show the non-geologist that even the ocean's surface was higher than this. If not for them being posted, I wouldn't have known. Minus the salt flat, everything looked like standard desert.

Note: The lowest elevation on Planet Earth is the Dead Sea in Jordan/ Israel at 1,388 feet below sea level—'case you was wonderin'.

I left the bike for a short walk to the lowest of the low spots in the basin. Badwater gets its name from highly concentrated saltwater that pools there. The story goes that a surveyor working in the area long ago couldn't get his mule to drink from the standing water; thus he coined the spot "bad water." I trekked about a half mile out to the official salt flat area to get a feel for standing in the center of the valley. Where visitors had trampled the salt, it was hard as concrete and full of engravings. In the undisturbed area, it held a brittle, crystal like shape and uneven roughness. There is only so much one can do out there on the salty plain, so I fought the urge to bend down for a lick and got moving again, heading south.

Just out of the park lies the small town of Shoshone. I was fueling up much more successfully this time when an old woman came over with a strong recommendation for the nearby Tecopa hot springs. Not wanting to be rude, I told her I may visit them. She spoke of their healing power and refreshing nature. She said that she moved out here from the city because of them and that they've made her pain go away. What I didn't tell her was that I had to be moving on to reach my goal of "a foot in the Pacific" on day 100. It was an unforeseen goal a week ago, but now reachable.

The journey to my next stop in Baker, California, was pretty unexciting until I passed Dumont Dunes. The dunes were a holy grail in my eyes for their quick appearances in several of the off-road motorcycling movies that I obsessed over in the nineties. They were in the distance, maybe a few miles out and accessed by way of a dirt road. I'd always pictured them as being closer to the ocean and looking grander. In reality they looked like specks of pale land in a desert valley wilderness. The parking area for dune visitors was all but empty.

From a distance, I could see a few ATVs roaming around on the sand hills. I wanted to ride over and watch them, but I kept on moving. It would have done me no good to watch other people enjoy such fun riding. I promised myself once again that I'd get my motocross bikes out here one day to ride Southern California's dunes. I snapped off a bunch of pictures to drool over later on, when I'm back on the East Coast, and rode away. Twenty miles south of there, in Baker, I stopped to stretch the legs before hopping on I-15 West.

The goal was Barstow, for no good reason. Except for seeing two fast and highly horsepowered Baja trucks racing through the Mojave, kicking up long plumes of dust, nothing remotely exciting happened on the way to Barstow. I found a KOA, again, that catered only to RVs. Barstow was small, dry, and average—with everything that every other small and average American town has these days.

I found a Starbucks for Wi-Fi. It was to be my first ever Starbucks experience. I have always shied away from the place for feeling out of tune with its image. I admit to being ignorant of what's currently trending in pop culture or how to be stylish and fashionable. To me, Starbucks is the place where city folk of the aforementioned qualities hang out—with the latest electronics, wearing scarves, sporting clean fingernails and perfectly parted hair, and talking about college days. Admittedly, I'm somewhat intimidated by that crowd's tidiness and intellect. I have the fashion sense of a blind homeless man; and most days, I'm not even wearing matching socks. Only recently have I been filled in that a brown shirt and black pants don't work.

With that, I went in. Instead of grabbing a coffee that late in the day, a Panini and yogurt parfait had to suffice for a first impression. *So far, so good.* On my laptop, I tracked down a Motel 6 while trying to look like I was doing something important. Clean-cut individuals lurked all around, ordering coffees with descriptions harder to pronounce than most species' scientific names. Motel 6 was right up the street, so I got out of there as fast as possible without having to engage anyone wearing a vest and scarf with a question like "So where did you go to university?" In which case, I would grunt, yell "Yeehaw," do a square dance maneuver, try to bite them, and run out the door.

At the room, I sacrificed a few hours of daylight to catch up on the little things that I'd been neglecting, like updating my map online, categorizing posts, and transferring a bunch of stories to another motorcycling website. I called my friends at Crossroads Yamaha and left a message to check about getting a tire. My rear Michelin Pilot Road 2 was finally giving up after 11,189 miles. I hoped to make it to a dealer before anything serious happened.

Day 99 – January 20, 2012

I awoke with a mission. Like Igor's dilemma on day one, the Goose was hurting for a fresh rear tire. The last bit of rubber covering the cords was beginning to flake off. It's completely possible to ride on a tire where the cords are seeing the light of day, but risky. In the best of circumstances, I'd squeeze two more days out of it before it let go and left me stranded on some unfamiliar California road.

Fortunately, I had teammates on my side. My good friends at Crossroads Yamaha-Suzuki in Albemarle, North Carolina, had my back, and Carmen was at the lead. On day eleven they told me that if I needed anything along the way to let them know. They had predicted that I was going to go through tires quickly due to hauling so much extra weight. At 10:00am, Carmen responded to last night's voicemail. After finding out where I was and where I was headed, she set up a plan to find a fellow Yamaha dealer in the greater Los Angeles area that could give me a deal. Barstow is no more than a half day's drive to anywhere in Los Angeles, so I remained flexible to whichever dealership she found.

I told her that I was heading west to Malibu Creek State Park and that Thousand Oaks Yamaha was somewhat nearby. I first learned of Thousand Oaks on a visit to Loretta Lynn's Amateur Motocross Championship in 2001. Thousand Oaks was sponsoring one of America's fastest up-and-coming teenage racers, Mike Alessi. For that, I hoped to work with them. Carmen contacted a gal at Thousand Oaks, and they agreed to help me out.

I was stoked and satisfied, but Carmen kept looking, feeling like she could do better. She called me back about another friendly dealership willing to work with Crossroads. She said that she had contacted Dave from Chaparral Motorsport's tire department in San Bernardino. We decided on Chaparral as the place to get a tire because of its proximity to Barstow. At her request, I too called Dave to work with him on the plans. I knew that he would hook me up with a free tire change if I bought the tire, and I knew that Carmen had negotiated a good deal for me. That was enough to put a smile on my face for weeks. I packed my things and prayed that the tire would hold to San Bernardino.

Eighty miles later, through terrain growing slightly greener, suburbs growing denser, and a high pass through the San Gabriel Mountains, I pulled into the warehouse-sized Chaparral Motorsports. I have known of Chaparral for years despite its opposite-coast location. In the late nineties and early two thousands, I ordered their free catalog for the great deals and surplus parts availability. I stopped ordering from them when I started working at bike shops myself. I remember them sponsoring Jeremy McGrath and Jimmy Button through the Chaparral Yamaha race team. In the world of motocross, that was as big as it gets. In the nineties, Jeremy McGrath was the Michael Jordan of our sport. In 2001, I attended a Supercross in Atlanta, Georgia, and took photos of McGrath and Chapparal's race truck while there. Back home, I had those pictures hoarded away like little treasures. They're priceless to me.

Now here I was in Chaparral's parking lot. I was looking at the font used on the store sign. It was the same one that had graced those mail order catalogs. It was the same one that was on the race truck. It was the same one on Jeremy McGrath's jersey. I was star struck by the damn building. I gathered myself, yanked the Goose's rear tire off in the parking lot, and wandered inside to track down Dave.

I stepped into a huge world of everything motorcycle. Not sure where the tire shop was, I wandered around for a few minutes lost. When I discovered it and walked inside, Dave greeted me with a smile. With his big and energetic voice, he looked squarely at me and said, "You know that they (Crossroads Yamaha) are going to take care of this tire for you." I didn't know. I thought I was going to pay for a nicely discounted back tire. Boy, was I surprised. It was one of the best feelings of my life, just knowing that good people were looking out for me. Then he spontaneously said, "You know what? I'm going to go half with Crossroads on your tire." *Holy moly!* Here I was, a simple ol' country boy from West Virginia, riding a scratched-up, decade-old bike, in a building that I can only dream about, and talking to a fellow who wanted to help me out. *What have I done to deserve this?* Insert speechless right here. Decent rear tires start at nearly $200 and only go up from there. I mustered up a "Thank you," but I wanted to shout from Chaparral's rooftop. The fellas took the Goose's back tire to the service area to put on the new rubber and went back to business as if they did this for every customer.

I took off with the Canon in a giddy daze to explore the huge showroom. I'm not sure of the square footage of the sales floor, but without question it was the largest motorcycle sales floor that I'd ever had the pleasure to wander. Its three massive sections housed hundreds of off-road and street bikes, quads, and side by sides, plus a parts and accessories department. That didn't include the huge helmet room and the attached tire shop. Then, folks, there were three other on-site detached buildings. One was a 110,000-square-foot tire storage and shipping warehouse, sitting beside another 110,000-square-foot parts and accessories distribution center, and finally, a massive service shop that would be any man's dream shop. Believe it or not, there was another 50,000-square-foot building in Ohio that served as Chaparral's East Coast distribution center. Had I died and turned up in motorcycle heaven? I thought so.

Walking through Chaparral brought back memories from my former days as a parts-counter guy and new-bike-setup guy. I was a kid with nothing more than motorcycles on my mind back then. Here, the smell of new tires, the look of squeaky-clean bikes, this year's awesome new riding gear hanging on slick displays, and the excited looks on the customer faces were as familiar as if I'd never left that line of work. After a massive circle around the showroom, I headed back to the tire shop to get the newly mounted tire.

I thought it would be time to go, but Dave one-upped it again. He took me on a behind-the-scenes tour of Chaparral through the huge buildings mentioned above. I met the service shop manager and the distribution shop manager and saw what it took to make their operations run; it was impressive. Chaparral's inner workings resembled a factory more than hobby based retail. A truck with a load of tires was being unloaded by three guys, conveyor belts ran without ceasing in the accessories warehouse, and a guy on a forklift was carrying something to the dumpster. These were but a fraction of the people involved. Dave gave me the shop's full history as we walked along, starting with how the shop was named. He said that Chaparral's name came from a race car that the owner took a liking to, and not from vegetation or scrubby bushes. I walked along listening like two big ears with legs.

When the tour was over, Dave and I headed back to his tire shop, and I briefly grabbed the guys for a quick picture. Again, they went the extra mile by hooking me up with a free Chaparral beanie and a sticker. I said another thank you and farewell to the guys. In the parking lot I mounted the new meat. Twenty minutes later, the Goose had its second leg back on and I was off, trying to beat the sunset to Malibu.

The ride from San Bernardino would welcome me to State Route 210, State Route 134, and Route 101—in other words, those famous Los Angeles parking lots known as freeways. Malibu Creek State Park was eighty-two miles away, and I would have made it before dark if not for the thickening SoCal traffic.

Out here a legal phenomenon occurs where traffic is creeping along on the freeway and motorcyclists ride on the white dotted line that separates each lane.

I was passed by several sport bikes and even a BMW adventure bike with panniers. They were flying through the slow-moving herd of cars, seemingly unconcerned that someone might make a lane change or open a car door.

When the traffic got real slow I thought about trying their method but decided not to when I saw a big white work van swerve sideways across two lanes of traffic to keep from rear-ending someone. Plus, the Goose's side boxes were a bit wider than your average motorcycle luggage. I couldn't help but watch, half cringed, as the motorcyclists played Russian roulette with their safety. If they had been injured as bad as I had in past motorcycle crashes, perhaps they'd think twice too. Soon I lost the race with the sunset and found myself riding past Hollywood looking for the park amid heavy traffic, in a new big city, in the dark.

I stopped at a Shell convenience store on Las Virgenes Road. I parked the Goose on a section of blue stripes that marked a handicapped parking spot. I was tired and looking for a quick in and out snack attack, gambling the spot wouldn't be needed in the two minutes I planned to stay there. A woman in a sleek white Porsche pulled up beside me at the next nearest spot. I didn't catch the exact model of her car but knew that it was only a year or two old. She stepped out, looking upper class and elegant, dressed nicely to match her car. She may have been in her fifties, but I'd never find out. I know better than to ask a lady. She looked at me and politely warned, "The cops will get you for that," speaking of my parking job. I replied with something like, "Right now I'm so tired that I don't care," in a mild joking manner, but just stiff enough to assert that I wasn't planning to move the bike. I had no idea where our next few words would take us. I was truly tired and semi-lost, a bit impatient, and ready to be defensive if she pushed me to move the bike. We exchanged a few more sentences, each one lightening the mood, and walked inside separately.

Inside we crossed an aisle and ran into one another again. This time she had a question and a short conversation evolved. She was a Malibu native, writer, and all-around welcoming soul. I told her about documenting my journey and my newfound love of writing. She told me about a children's book that she had recently published. She was a great listener with an engaging and intelligent way about her that made her a pleasure to chat with. We spoke about life in Malibu, a little about work, and a lot about travel. She had worked on cruise ships before. Neither one of us had moved an inch since bumping into each other in that aisle. Minutes passed quickly and I forgot that I had my bike parked in the handicapped spot. We exchanged info before parting.

She was the most interesting lady, and as I rode into the night I reflected on the chance encounter, thinking that I shouldn't have been defensive or in any sort of hurry. I found the park a few miles later and pitched my tent in the dark, *grassy*, Malibu hills. Perfect Day. Perfect Day.

Day 100 – January 21, 2012
In my unofficial rule book I was officially hard-core. On day five I said, "Five days in. That would sound so hard-core if it were a hundred days in."

Well here I was, one hundred days on the road and having survived it without so much as a splinter.

What had I got out of it besides a ton of fun? It was the most interesting period of my life. Interesting didn't exactly mean easy. Most days whizzed by magically, like yesterday, but a few were painted with trouble like day thirty-nine. Most days, I fought a chilled wind from the seat of the bike when I would have preferred a tropical ocean breeze. I was unendingly unfamiliar with my surroundings but also inspired by them. Through every mile, I felt incredibly lucky to have made it this far. I gained a new respect for the vastness, beauty, and diversity of our great country and its people, and I gained a greater appreciation for my family. I love the thought that I had the chance to be a quasi-tour guide for people back home who kept up with my journey on the web. Some of them were seasoned travelers and some had hardly left their birth towns. I was happy to exist outside of my comfort zone. Life was anything but structured and boring. *How long could I go on like this?* I wanted to answer that with forever, but even the best loner soul traveling or escaping reality reaches the limits of his capabilities.

I'm reminded of a program on public television called *Alone in the Wilderness*. It was about a man named Dick Proenneke. He left society behind at fifty-two years old for a life of retired solitude in the Alaskan wilderness. For thirty years he existed as little more than a hermit in his handmade log cabin, using his handmade tools to survive. He received small shipments of supplies from the outside world once or twice a year through an acquaintance who had a bush plane. He seldom returned to civilization to see his family.

Like my journey, Mr. Proenneke showed the world what his life was like by diligently recording tasks such as fetching water, shoveling snow, and building a bear-proof wooden lock for his cabin. He kept the lifestyle going strong until he reached eighty-two when he decided that Alaskan winters were more than he thought he could handle. He wisely abandoned Alaska's back country for California and a world that he had left decades before. His alternative would surely have been to wind up as a human popsicle for a pack of wolves. It was far too early to know if I had Mr. Proenneke's stamina, but at 100 days I was nowhere near ready to quit. I am made from some of the same ingredients that he was. The money, or lack thereof, will decide when I have to quit. Mentally and physically I could keep riding and writing long into the future, no problem.

I started the landmark day with an appreciative hand stroke through Malibu's dark, green, dewy grass. Grass—the resilient plant that we attack weekly with hyper-spinning blades from our chore-inducing lawn mowers—I missed it. It looked great, smelled great, and felt great. It held a piece of home in it. It had given me peace of mind as I pitched my tent the night before. I knew that it wouldn't puncture the tent's floor like the desert so desperately wanted to do. It had been far too long without feeling the natural green carpet between my toes. Each blade suddenly had more value as they covered Malibu Creek's enchanting, steep hills. The grass looked happy to be growing in such rich soil. I was happy too. This was the California that I'd been waiting for.

My moment of Zen and exuberance was short-lived as I slid a few tokens into the campground's shower stall. I waited a second and eased into the water droplets. They were cold as shit, as expected. A minute later, they were still cold. I fumbled with the handle but nothing happened. My allotted minutes were dwindling away as the water remained icy. I cursed and gasped for air when I stuck my head under the showerhead. I cursed winter, I cursed the cold water, and I cursed the park. I paid $35 last night to pitch my tent, and $2 for the Californian water torture that I was experiencing. Goosebumps had me looking like a plucked chicken, only whiter.

I toweled off and walked outside. It was chilly and clear. At my feet, strange black worms—as thin as four hairs braided together and a foot long—were squirming across the concrete trying to escape the bit of water from my shower that had seeped outside. They too looked uncomfortable in its frigid wake.

Time had come to fulfill my lone purpose for waking up on day 100. I had to get my pale hillbilly feet in the biggest pond on Earth, the Pacific Ocean. Malibu was the nearest place to make that happen. I rode through the beautiful, but crumbly, Malibu Canyon on the way to the beach. The rain from last night had triggered several mini landslides along the canyon road, leaving bowling-ball-sized rocks everywhere. The steep mountainsides here were loosely covered in vegetation. I assumed that plants played hell trying to take root in the fast-eroding soil. More debris was scattered from one rainstorm than I'd seen in any three.

The canyon road weaved right and left precariously. A man in a foreign sports car hooked a turn—with wheels squealing—coming from the opposite direction. I was in a sharp lean and, like him, rather enjoying myself. Then I rounded a corner and spotted the unmistakably level, blue horizon that only an ocean can make. *There it is.*

I parked at an overlook and looked at the ocean hesitantly, in wonder. I wanted to go to its shores, yet prolong this moment at the same time. It meant that there would be no more heading west for me and the Goose. Heading west has a ring to it. I liked the feeling of heading toward a seemingly endless frontier. Adventure is always just around the corner.

I motored into Malibu. As expected, Malibu was a beach paradise. Its homes were sturdy, modern, beachside marvels. The mountains that I'd just ridden through provided a scenic backdrop. I had always thought of Malibu being a little flatter. Once again, the moment of discovery left me amazed. I found a place to park at Malibu Lagoon State Beach and took a narrow, sandy nature trail down to the ocean. The coast was rocky and alive, keeping me from wandering in barefoot there. Ocean plants and animal life filled the gaps between these rocks more fully than I'd ever noticed on the shores of the Atlantic. The carcass of a sea lion stretched out on the sand as a treat for scavenging birds. *Never seen that before.* I followed the shore for another mile in search of a place suitable for putting my stompers in the surf without cutting up the bottoms of my feet.

A dark sandy stretch near a pier supporting a large white building would be the spot to host my fair-skinned walking sticks. I rolled up my blue jeans and moseyed in. The water was nearly as cold as Malibu Creek's shower. Little waves chased me back to shore as I tried to keep my pants dry. When settled in for a second, I said aloud, "I've crossed the United States." I felt like I had accomplished something, even if it was at a snail's pace. I called my mom while standing in the freezing cold waves like someone who calls their mom after winning the lottery, or to let her know that there's "one on the way." People walked by slowly without even a look. I absorbed the cold water for several minutes.

I turned away from land, taking a moment to think about the Pacific's other shores—like I've always done while standing in the Atlantic imagining a voyage across the sea to Europe or Africa. From this shore, places like Hawaii, Japan, China, Australia, and Russia were out there. These were places that sounded much more exotic to me. They were places I wanted to visit some day. Inside, I hoped that the mighty oceans wouldn't be like giant watery fences, too big for me to cross before I die. I walked back on shore to snap pictures and trekked barefooted back to the bike. I was as happy as a clam. There was plenty of time to take a long lunch before battling Los Angeles's heavy traffic. I had made my mind up earlier to go to the third round of Supercross at Dodger Stadium.

I missed riding my motocross bikes so much that I counted on Supercross to get a quick fix. Monetarily, it wasn't practical at all to go. I checked the map for a less jammed way into the city. Sure enough, it looked as though I could jump on Mulholland Highway near Malibu Creek State Park, follow it to Mulholland Drive, and connect to the 101 after Beverly Hills, just a few miles from the stadium—all the while riding through twisties in the Santa Monica Mountains.

I took off like I had just discovered a secret road. I passed through patches of residential areas, all perfect-looking and clean. The roads were twisty and all was well. Then I became out of sorts. I wasn't sure if I was still on Mulholland, but I'd seen nothing to contradict it. I kept riding. The pavement deteriorated and altogether vanished. I continued riding, now on a dirt road full of rain ruts. I stood up on the pegs, arms and knees bent in racing form. I gave the Goose a little workout while thinking that the dirt road had to lead to pavement soon. I wheelied over small humps and spun the rear tire like I was on a motocross bike. It was fun until a dead end appeared. A brown sign read "Santa Monica Mountain Zone Parkland." I could see that the road continued to the left through a locked gate. I realized the time I had lost and made a hasty retreat to the nearest freeway. Going back down the mountain, I passed a man navigating his family van ever so slowly through the rain ruts. I passed him standing up on the pegs and hauling ass.

I made it to Dodger Stadium with little time to spare. A special section was quarantined off for motorcycle parking. Convenient it was; however, cheap it wasn't. The ticket to watch the race was $27, even as a last-minute purchase. The parking pass was $20. *Twenty dollars for what? There's nothing to see in the parking lot.* The only thing going on there is a headache-causing traffic jam in which they wanted twenty bones to participate in. Rip-off city! And inside, the food was so expensive that I'd rather go hungry than pay $5 for a small tray of fries or $9 for a tiny personal pizza the size of my hand.

I paid for parking with a halfhearted smile, happy to be there, yet feeling like I'd been bent over and probed at the same time. I found my seat and forgot about the parking lot. The track sat before us fans like a finely sculpted wedding cake. Each jump and each berm was shaped with a surgeon's precision. It was beautiful. Looking at the track brought back thoughts of my mindset when I was racing every weekend, hoping to someday make the big show. Back then, all I wanted was to be pro. My life felt singular and balanced. Since then, I've lost that feeling of purpose. I sat in my seat and wondered how life would be if—after recovering from my broken femur—I had put the effort in and not let other influences get me sidetracked. Would I have made it? Who knows? But one thing was for sure: I was still spectating, and still in love with the sport.

A laser show was getting the fans amped up. Music thumped through the stadium in tune with highlights playing on mega-sized flat screens. Sponsors like Monster Energy, Honda, Suzuki, Dunlop tires, and Parts Unlimited provided banners to line the pristine track. Fans filed in and took seats. Everyone looked happy. I felt like I was meant to be there.

The show started. One after the other, qualifying races wrapped up. Guys jockeyed for position, scraping plastic, (as we say in mx, referring to our plastic fenders and body panels) each one trying to make it to the night's main event. In the qualifying heat races, factory riders raced away from the pack—teasing us with short glimpses of their unbelievable speed. They are the riders directly assigned to race for companies like Honda, Yamaha, Suzuki, Kawasaki, and KTM. They are backed by those manufacturers' endlessly deep pockets. No performance part or high-paid athletic trainer is off-limits to these guys. They are usually scouted and supported in early childhood from said factories. They walk around light and thin, with the physical stamina of Olympians.

Indeed, the way they ride a motocross bike on the track defies physics. They fly their motorcycles over sixty-five-foot triple jumps and land with more precision than a licensed pilot. In loose corners, they can hold a lean far enough to scrape the handlebar ends. I'm a decent rider who caught on quickly. To become professional, though, I would still have had a huge mountain to climb. The guys that I was here to watch have the ability to make me look as slow as if I were galloping around the track on a horse. These guys are my heroes.

The main events were fantastic. I watched a rider in the smaller 250cc division conquer a triple jump that no other 250cc rider would try. Hell, most of the 450cc riders weren't doing it. He not only cleaned house in his class, but set the fourth fastest lap time of the night out of all racers. When the big dogs hit the track (the guys who make millions racing dirt bikes), the stadium went bananas. Twenty athletes, the crème de la crème of motocross, all dressed in battle garb, lined up behind the gate. When it dropped, they thundered to the first turn like red, green, yellow, blue, and orange bullets. I had seen this battle play out before. Only one could win, and second means better luck next week.

For twenty laps they rode at insane speeds over obstacles meant to slow their pace and provide a challenge, but they never slowed. Whether in a corner or laying it flat over a jump, every rider looked forward with his right wrist locked at wide-open. I was hoping that one of my two favorites would take the win, but each suffered a minor crash while trying to make two knobby wheels grip soil like super glue between your fingers. The ever consistent Australian native, Chad Reed, came out victorious. I had watched him face our sport's best for nearly a decade and applauded his effort. Every racer who competes at that level works extremely hard and should be appreciated for his talent and dedication. Motocross is the ultimate man and machine combination sport and a great man versus man competition as well. I'll always love it for that.

To change the mood, leaving Dodger Stadium was a nightmare. Due to detours, I got lost a dozen times, found myself taking completely unfamiliar roads in Los Angeles at midnight while utterly confused. The police gave horrible directions and then sent me on my way over and over again. After an hour of wandering around Los Angeles, I found 101 N and made a beeline for the safety of my tent in Malibu.

Day 101 – January 22, 2012

Nightlife activity started my day. The first hour of Sunday wasn't yet complete. It was nearing 1:30am, and I had just settled in after Supercross. A band of ornery teens had overtaken a campsite a few spots down on the opposite side of the road. To them, it was Saturday night extended. Loud music thumped from one of the cars. A weak campfire illuminated bottles and red solo cups strewn about in the beautiful grass. They were partying, and I thought nothing of it. I'd survived many, many weekend nights like the one they were having. Through the years, I've beer ponged myself blurry, pulled off one-handed keg stands, leaped from balconies, walked through screen doors, experimented with a lil' bit of this and a lil' bit of that, all of it in the name of fun. It doesn't matter what sort of wild-ass antics they were up to, I've done it.

From my tent, I could hear them talking and laughing faintly over the tunes. I remained still, waiting for my eyes to get heavy enough to start sleeping. Two voices soon grew louder than the rest. They were growing closer and emitting from a highly pissed young female and a young man, plastered beyond awareness. He was lagging behind in an obvious stumble. She had caught him cheating, and they were headed my way in a full-blown war of words.

I listened to the footsteps. The girl marched up the road until she reached the entrance to my tent site. She turned and gave him another tongue lashing. The guy responded back defensively. I was fully awake and lying down on my back with eyes focused on the roof of the tent. I studied its soft lines as I hoped they would simmer down or keep walking. But they didn't. Instead, their argument escalated into a heated explosion of tears and pitiful apologies. I could hear their clothes ruffle and their feet skid across the pavement as they stumbled and changed position. They were no more than twenty feet from my tent and going nowhere. The girl kept up the hysterical crying while the guilty party, with a voice sounding like a surfer mixed with an Abercrombie enthusiast, grew frustrated that she wasn't getting over it. I listened more, because I didn't know what else to do. They kept at it for another dozen minutes.

I weighed the consequences before interfering. If I broke it up and the guy became an offended drunk, I could end up holding the shit end of the stick while he and his zombified buddies gave me a beat down. If I didn't do anything, I'd have to listen to these two turds hash it out. I sat in silence waiting for them to calm. Their arguing was going nowhere fast. Romeo had spewed all he could think of, and Juliet wanted to go home.

When the same story began to repeat, I grew frustrated. I could feel my face's surface gaining heat and my cares slipping away. Soon, each word that they vomited out of their drunken teeth holes angered me. Seeing that they had no regard for anyone else, my blood boiled over. I went for the zipper of my tent like an animal. The flap whipped and slashed as I tried to get my whole body out all at once. Before I managed to straighten all the way up, I shouted, "Take that shit back down the hill! I'm trying to sleep!" Their heads swiveled rapidly in my direction. The drunken ladies' man said without hesitation, "Yes sir." The noise stopped, and the girl quietly followed him down the hill.

I went from seeing red to sheer perplexity in seconds. I couldn't believe it worked. If I was as drunk as him and someone came at me like that then we'd be havin' words. *That was almost too easy.* I climbed back in my tent reflecting on him referring to me as "sir." For a moment, I felt old. No one had ever referred to me as sir outside of the business world. It was after 3:00am when I finally dozed off. Stiff, cold air hung in the Santa Monica Mountains, forcing me to pull a groundhog maneuver in the sleeping bag. I just couldn't get comfortable.

Nature's alarm woke me at seven. Unless I'm sick with the 'itis, if the sun is shining, I can't sleep. You could say that I'm disproportionately diurnal. I was stiff and tired, slipping around in the dewy grass when another campground neighbor came wandering over. He had long grey hair pulled back in a ponytail. His face was serious, and I guessed that he wanted to talk about last night's campground ruckus. His name was Henry. He was a fellow motorcyclist from the outskirts of Chicago. We set about talking bikes without ever mentioning the party brigade that infiltrated the park. Henry and his wife were on a four-month tour around the states in their truck with bed camper and enclosed trailer setup. He kept his Harley in the trailer until they'd become stationary for a day or two; then he and his wife would sightsee using it. They left Chicago on November 28, 2011, and were planning to return at the end of March, 2012.

I liked Henry. He and I got along well. He was a man who just liked to ride, never looking down on me for having a Japanese bike. I was curious as to how he made the time for himself and his wife to travel for four months out of the year. He told me that he owned a small-scale landscaping operation back in Chicago. He and one employee held down the fort, working long weeks for eight months out of the year. His elbow grease, sweat from his brow, and low overhead allowed him to get ahead just enough to take a few months off annually.

He confirmed a suspicion that I'd had over the years. Whether it is landscaping or any other sort of work, I think the key to having more than average free time is to be in charge—a leader not a follower. He said that he didn't mind doing the labor, knowing that the long vacation was on the horizon, and I wouldn't either.

We spoke of some of the other places that we both had been on our trips, and he left me with recommendations for great roads to ride in the northern states, most notably the Beartooth Highway. A ton of folks had told me about that stretch of road. Henry and I shook hands and began our days. He wandered back to his camper, and I took off for Malibu again.

I found a McDonald's right on the ocean, where I could squeeze out another writing segment over breakfast while staring at the mighty, blue Pacific. The chore of writing a daily post was something that I'd rather do without mentioning. I wanted folks to be able to read about the journey without thinking about the time that I had to hole myself up somewhere, forcing words to navigate from my brain, through my fingertips, to a blog's maintenance page, to the web, and finally to their eyes. I wanted them to be able to read about the journey like they read the paper—consistently, without ever thinking about the person working the giant roll of paper, or the person making sure the ink doesn't run out. I wanted the adventure to feel seamless—like uninterrupted, constant exploration—but like it or not, writing took up a sizeable chunk of the day, nearly every day. I was about to find out that this was an intriguing time to be writing in a McDonald's in Malibu.

All cylinders were firing smooth as I crunched on an oatmeal, fruit, and walnut bowl and typed away. Then a woman in her late fifties—with wild, grey, curly hair, glasses, frumpy clothes, and a face as flushed as a heavy drinker's—wandered in. Her arrival was comfortable the way that shaking hands with a person who has just peed on his fingers is comfortable. She was clearly schizophrenic and off her meds. She walked in, sat down, and began having a loud conversation with the voices. At one point she bent over to tie her shoe and while in the squatting position, looking at the floor, she yelled, "Eat!" Her voice was gravelly and rumbled like a man's.

Later, some unsuspecting folks sat next to her. They were ten minutes into their breakfast and had yet to see her wild side. She looked over at them and said, "I'm sorry. I'll go get that hamburger for you right now," speaking fast and apologetically. They were perplexed. Once she announced, "Tickets will be on sale right here, tomorrow morning" in a voice loud enough to make everyone in the dining area look her way. I did my best to be respectful and not get involved, and I wasn't even going to write about the encounter.

As I was typing, I was sitting, facing her, in the opposite corner of the dining area. I kept my head down, my ears open, and allowed an eye to wander in her direction every minute or so, but even with those precautions, she picked me out of the crowd. Damn! She began mimicking me. She blurted out some "do do do do click click click" noises followed by other typewriter sounds. She sat up in perfect posture with her head swaying back and forth as to enhance the importance of what she was typing on her imaginary typewriter. Then her head stopped moving and she turned toward me, laughing hysterically while her hands continued air typing. I ignored it and it eventually stopped. I was embarrassed for being put on the spot, but much more embarrassed for her. She let up on me and went back to rambling about something else. When I left, she was still there and still going strong.

I set an easy goal for the day. I wanted to see the Pro Circuit race shop in Corona, California, sixty miles inland. Pro Circuit is a legendary motocross institution. It's a Southern Californian race shop that competes with the big four Japanese manufacturers and KTM for Supercross and outdoor motocross national championships. It's owned by a hardworking fella named Mitch Payton, who has a reputation for selecting the best up-and-coming professional racers, putting them on Pro Circuit modified bikes in the 250cc class, and winning championships, sometimes with such efficiency that it looks easy. Racers like Jeremy McGrath and Ricky Carmichael have blessed the shop with championships along the way, but its reach goes further than the race track. Pro Circuit manufactures performance engine and suspension parts, and sells anything from handlebars to T-shirts. Like Chaparral, I've known of Pro Circuit forever. The mere thought of visiting the shop made me foolishly excited.

The Goose and I wandered twenty miles south along the gorgeous Pacific Coast Highway and then turned east on Freeway 91. Along the way, I rode past Angel Stadium in Anaheim. Supercross would be coming back to Anaheim in two weeks for the fifth round of the series. I took a mental snapshot of the stadium's location for future reference. Then it was on to Corona and the Pro Circuit race shop.

I found the white architectural wonder and was disappointed when I walked up and tugged on the door only to find that it was locked. Right then I realized it was Sunday. Once again, I had lost track of the days. With no scheduled workweek, this happened quite often. Days blended together like kool-aid and water. So much was going on in the present, and so much was waiting around the corner, that time often disallowed nostalgic reflection. I just kept moving, every day, all day. I preferred life feeling like an endless weekend, but who wouldn't? It pains me to say that I can think of a couple people who like grinding out five days on the clock and resting for two.

So Pro Circuit was closed. That was evident. I needed to find another option. Earlier, I made a tentative plan to visit the shop, snag some pictures, and head west to Bolsa Chica State Beach, in Huntington Beach, to camp. Now it was clear that I needed to stay in Corona overnight if I were to see the inside of the shop and meet the folks that worked there.

After unsuccessfully finding a campground nearby that would let me set up a tent, I tracked down Corona's Motel 6 just before 4:00pm. It was not an architectural wonder like the Pro Circuit building, but it was priced identically to Malibu Creek State Park's camping fee. I looked forward to its familiar wacky and colorful blankets that I'd seen in every Motel 6 since my first stay in Wilcox, Arizona. They were a wild collage of blue, orange, white, red, and yellow with images of cars, cities, people, dogs, bears, waterfalls, and of course Motel 6 signs. I knew the room would be clean and the shower hot.

I was exhausted from lack of sleep and had not showered since the icy droplets smacked my skin on Saturday morning. My armpits had a sexy musk reminiscent of workout clothes that have been worn twice and not washed. The rest of the evening was spent in the room, desperately researching how to get sponsored and watching the last two quarters of the 49ers and Giants game.

Day 102 – January 23, 2012

Corona and the moto fix. It's a phrase that portrays day 102 best. However obvious it may sound, it does not mean that I'd been drinking Mexican beer and working on the Goose. The Corona I'm talking about is the city of Corona, California, and the moto fix is how I'm describing a day of exploring Corona's unexpected saturation of motocross-related businesses. I had not planned to stay in Corona for another day; I wanted to visit the Pro Circuit race shop and then head north, back to San Bernardino, to a state park I had noticed days earlier.

A storm moved in overnight, bringing with it relentless rain that pounded Motel 6's roof and the tarp-covered Goose. It was that type of thick, watery assault that overwhelms gutters and cleans streets of leafy debris. From my stint along Interstate 10 in Louisiana, I was aware that my wet weather set up was only mediocre. It was warm enough outside that I wouldn't suffer if I headed north; I could pull off a short day's ride in the wet stuff. But why? I'd surely end up fighting low visibility in heavy traffic.

Dave from Chaparral had warned me about the drivers in this part of the world. He said, "Be careful as you ride around L.A. Everyone drives at eighty or faster and acts like they are racing in Nascar." He also said that they have no regard for motorcyclists. Most of this I had already witnessed firsthand. Dave was right. Hell, even the motorcyclists had no regard for motorcyclists. His warning and the heavy rain was enough for me to stay put.

I started the morning by finishing some unfinished business. I slid into my rubbery rain gear and rode through Corona's side streets to the Pro Circuit race shop. You may be wondering why a guy who has ridden almost every day for the past 101 days needs a moto fix and is willing to find it in the rain. The answer lies in the difference between street riding and off-road riding, and is simple. I haven't found anything quite like racing motorcycles off-road, slamming corners, twisting the throttle until it stops, and getting airtime. Although the Goose and I had been airborne on a few sets of railroad crossings, I still yearned for the real thing. The high gained from riding a machine with a little too much power, through an ever-changing landscape of dangerous obstacles, is heavenly. Flying through the air without wings gives you the feeling of weightlessness. Astronauts have found this feeling in space, and pilots have forced large expensive aircraft into free falls to get it. But folks like me and thousands of other motocrossers, skateboarders, bmx'ers, snowboarders, skydivers, and base jumpers have found ways to achieve it consistently with fewer resources.

The high is found on the motocross track by approaching a jump with anticipation. Your brain and right wrist work together to find the correct speed. Your elbows and knees bend in attack mode, ready to handle the G-force. You launch off the jump. Your legs squeeze the side of the bike keeping the soles of your boots on the footpegs. For a brief second you can relax your grip on the handlebars and find yourself flying. You rest assured knowing that your bike and its long suspension is flying right under you, waiting to happily absorb the landing. You take hold of the grips, your tires touch down, your feet are supported by the footpegs, and you turn the throttle wide-open, only to fly your motocross bike a dozen more times on the very same lap. It's a sensation that leaves you feeling as if you are more than you are. It's an extension of the same rush perhaps experienced by the first man who ever climbed on a horse. It starts out unnaturally and ends up the most welcome of experiences. It's downright addicting. Every day that passed on the road, I missed my mx bikes more.

Getting back to Pro Circuit, I pulled up to the front of the building again. The door was open this time when I tugged on it. The large, tinted windows that had blocked my view inside yesterday were now behind me. The building was clean and bright inside. To my left, a glass case was filled with championship plaques. Motocross memorabilia hung from the walls, making it more than just your average dealership. I rounded a corner to find a room holding all of Pro Circuit's championship winning motocross bikes.

There were twenty-five of them sitting on bike stands facing me. Most of them I'd seen in action, and I could place a face to every championship bike. To me, they were shiny treasures sitting in a perfect moto museum. They couldn't escape my hand as I grabbed the same throttle that was twisted at the championship winning checkered flag. I analyzed them one by one, squatting down to see if I could find a trick "one-off" part still bolted on. I was starry-eyed and kid-like. After asking permission, I snapped many, many pictures like the bikes were about to be sent to the crusher and I needed to record every detail.

Here was a room full of motocross greatness. I marinated in it for a bit and was just about to ask about a behind-the-scenes tour of the shop when a dozen British lads walked in and swarmed the employee at the counter. With that, I geared up and headed for the next rainy destination, the Monster Energy warehouse.

My reason for going there was to investigate what path I'd need to take to get sponsored by them. I needed money to keep the trip going and could think of no better way to raise it quickly than sponsorship. The overly friendly guard at the warehouse gate sent me down the street to the Monster Energy corporate headquarters. There I told the receptionist what I was doing and asked who I needed to talk to, to inquire about sponsorship. She gave me a card for consumer relations, a free energy drink, and sent me on my way. I planned to take care of that later on in the day.

From Monster Energy's headquarters, I was headed for lunch when I found Race Tech's headquarters. Race Tech makes performance parts for motorcycle suspension. I squished and squeaked into the Race Tech lobby. Three employees immediately stopped what they were doing and focused their attention on the dripping wet hillbilly who just walked in. I looked back at them with a smile and said, "I really don't have any reason for being here other than to ask if you guys have any stickers." They all laughed and very kindly handed me seven or eight Race Tech stickers. Nice folks they were.

I continued on and was again drawn to a bike shop, this one called Pit King. I walked in and met the owner of the one man operation. His shop was tucked into a long complex filled with other businesses. It was small, crammed with bikes that would be sitting outside on a clear day, and loaded with motorcycle accessories. Since no one else was there, he and I talked for a while about business, the economy, desert riding, motocross industry jobs, and my journey. He was such a genuine guy. I wished him luck after he described the recent downturn in business. He seemed to be chasing the dream of self-employment while fighting hard against the rigors that come with it in a recessed economy. From what I told him about my blog, he directed me to a motocross magazine office down the street and said that he wasn't sure if they were still in business or not. He thought that maybe someone there would be interested in my story.

It was close and worth a shot to see if they could use a contributing hand, so I rode over. The foreign fella who answered the door informed me that MX Illustrated moved out of that building four years earlier. Oddly enough, the sign was still hanging on the outside of the building. I wondered what sort of business he was running where he had the loot to rent that size building but didn't need his own sign to get customers. Seemed pretty sketchy to me.

That completed my moto fix around Corona in the rain. Back home, there's no place like Corona. We have a bike shop here and there, all scattered a healthy drive from one another, but we don't have famed riders at our tracks. We don't have famed shops with championship bikes. Corona is part of Southern California's motocross mecca. It hosts a small, densely arranged motocross empire among its many ordinary businesses. It showed me how much folks value recreation on the West Coast. I liked Corona a lot.

I arrived at Motel 6 at dusk and gave the Monster Energy consumer relations department a ring to not only seek sponsorship, but to learn the process. A nice lady on the other end of the line was patient enough to listen to my babble, but politely declined my request. She informed me that Monster sponsored professional athletes and events, not trips, although she said, "We get requests for trip sponsorships all the time." I asked for some advice for a guy in my shoes, and she said to try the other energy drink brands. I chalked it up as a learning experience and not a failure. I set about further research online, inside knowing that I'd waited too long to start looking.

Day 103 – January 24, 2012

The rain subsided in Corona. I started packing in the sunshine for a ride west, back to the ocean, this time to Santa Monica to meet some fellow travelers and friends.

Before I get on with that craziness, I have to explain the long way around detour used to get back to the beach. I could have hopped on Freeway 91 and jetted perfectly west all the way to the ocean, but an unseen force was urging me to make a pit stop in San Bernardino again to visit the Glen Helen raceway. Glen Helen was home to one of the twelve stops on the AMA outdoor national motocross tour, and the second national track that I visited on the trip. The first one was Freestone MX in Wortham, Texas. Since it was Wednesday, I didn't expect much action at the track, and I was right as far as the motocross track was concerned.

Glen Helen was a muddy quagmire. I was the lone fool standing at the gate looking at its rain washed turns and steep inclines. Then I heard the sounds of motocross bikes nearby. Up the hill and thinly hidden out of sight, to my surprise, was the Pro Circuit Kawasaki test track, and coincidentally a few of our nation's top pros were there pounding out laps. Broc Tickle, Darynn Durham, and Tyler Bowers were absolutely killing the practice session. *Oh man, here's my chance to see my dream life in action!* I cranked up the Goose and rode to the gate of the test track. It was set against a loosely vegetated, crumbly mountainside. The track was a dream. Each of its jumps had pointed peaks built to perfection. It had whoops and berms that were symmetrical, and was only slightly moist like it had not rained there at all.

Not wanting to be too pushy or invasive, I sat there at the opened gate for a bit before creeping inside on foot toward one of the rider's mechanics. I politely asked if it was okay to watch the guys ride and snap a few photos. He didn't mind but told me that the pictures can only be used for personal use and can't wind up on the Internet. I promised him they wouldn't. A few minutes after being inside, next to the track, the riders pulled off. The mechanic took over track maintenance duties on the skid steer, and the riders sat down for a breather. I felt like the odd man out. They were talking about how to go faster in this section or through that corner and joking around as a group of young men do. I stood there silently, trying not to stare too hard. It was obvious that they'd be on break for a while, so I revisited the Glen Helen track for a track walk.

I stomped through foot-deep mud, imagined racing there, and chased the track dog around. She was some sort of playful mixed breed about the size of a Rottweiler with brown fur and a black snout. I watched as she flew down a hill full speed right into a mud pit. Her chest bottomed out on the mud's surface. It slowed her progress like quicksand. I could see every muscle in her body working to escape it. I laughed heartily.

The sound of high-revving four strokes filled the air. The pros were practicing again at the test track. I went back to watch them ride and daydream about how fantastic their lives must be. These were guys who've known no other way of life. I'd seen them on TV and read about them in magazines for years. I don't like to admit it, but I envied their fortunate circumstances. When months ago I was sitting in a cubicle at the Assessor's Office, trying to stay awake overtop a pile of paperwork, they were out here on any given weekday riding the best bikes money can buy.

I left the test track and Glen Helen with a void of curiosity filled. For years I had wondered just how steep the huge hills around Glen Helen were and what the professional racers did mid-week, between races. These guys were unquestionably living the life I would've chosen for myself if only we had the choice to decide how we come into this world and had control over circumstances there after. Maybe in my next life. . . .

I was off to the Pacific again, this time to meet Igor, Caleb, Hilton, Kevin, Amelia, and Rosy. Igor and Caleb were already friends of mine, and the other folks were Igor and Caleb's friends. These guys had been traveling the western United States for a couple of weeks in a Ford Flex, packed tight and often crossing the same places just days behind me. They were quite the mixed bag of journeymen with many miles around this planet under their young belts. All of us came from wildly different backgrounds but shared a deep desire to travel.

Igor was the Ukrainian of the bunch; Caleb and Kevin hailed from North Carolina; Hilton was born in South Africa; Amelia was our fun-lovin' British gal; Rosy was all the way from Norway; and I was the lone hillbilly. Put us all together and you'd get a thick traveler stew. Caleb, Hilton, Amelia, and Rosy had just completed an eighteen-country, seven-and-a-half-month tour of Europe, Asia, and Australia via the OzBus—an overland, heavy-duty cargo bus.

They had escapades in China (where the Chinese military had to free the bus from a precarious position), camped roadside in Romania, and bungee jumped in Nepal. Caleb went on to work in Australia for a bit to gain enough money to complete a full circumnavigation of the globe. He left Australia for a hitchhiking and bus tour through South America (where he outran a couple heathens in Columbia), before eventually arriving back home in North Carolina. Hilton had jumped off of a few of the world's highest bungee locations and was a traveling been-there-done-that machine.

As this was Hilton and Amelia's first time in the states, we met up in Santa Monica for a glitzy tour of Hollywood, Beverly Hills, and the Griffith Observatory where we could see the Hollywood sign and every light in Los Angeles.

At the observatory the Hollywood sign barely poked through the darkness. Igor and I did our best to get a few night shots of it. A pack of coyotes could be heard somewhere down below. It sounded like they had just made a kill.

We went on to partake in the typical oohing and aahhing on the walk of fame, and generally goofed around. When it was time to grab some grub, our clan chose Johnny Rocket's Diner. Our energy was high and the chatting frantic. We laughed and played around like we were wired to do nothing else.

The movie *Rock of Ages* was being filmed at the Chinese Theatre. The actors and extras were decked out in flawless eighties attire, and the street was lined with vehicles from that decade to provide an accurate setting. For me, this was almost like being home. Vehicles from the eighties still grace the roads all over West Virginia. Hell, some of the cars looked familiar. But the tight, bleached jeans, tall, puffy hair, and men wearing makeup sure was enough to give a sense that we had traveled through a wormhole back to the days of mega ballads. I can't describe how nice some of those cutoff faded jean shorts looked all hiked up on the derrieres of a few of those actresses. It's a style they can bring back if you ask me.

Our action packed tour of Tinseltown ended as we scooted back to the room in Santa Monica. The day where worlds came together wrapped up with a few dozen cocktails, a drinking game, some wholesome camaraderie, a fireman's hat, and strong bouts of laughing.

Day 104 – January 25, 2012

Seven of us had spread out on any surface we could find last night when the lights went out. Caleb and Rosy took a bed since they were the only couple. Igor and Hilton took a bed and kept some distance between one another, unlike their first night together when they had an experience of the unintentionally intimate kind (let's just say that Hilton's nickname, Snuggy, was born then). For their sake, we'll agree that they were both asleep. Amelia and Kevin couched it up, and I used my camping pad on the floor. Four walls and a roof in Santa Monica beats a tent any day.

We woke at different times. A few of us strolled to the local deli for some bagels and coffee. When we got back, everyone had their eyes open, took turns in the shower, and began packing. Their agenda was to make it to Caleb's friend's house in San Francisco before dark. My agenda was to split with them and hang around Santa Monica and Venice Beach all day until it was time to meet up with another familiar face.

We gathered our things and footed it to the parking garage. I didn't have room for the plastic fireman's hat on the Goose, so I attempted to give it to someone. Hilton took the hat and made a donation to my trip. *What a top-notch guy.* We stood a few moments for pictures, and they scoped out the decal-laden Goose. Then we said our goodbyes and parted ways. In that moment, I wanted to go along with them so bad. I wasn't terribly excited about being on my own again after having one of the better nights on the road. It was over too quickly. Like when I left my brother in the parking garage waving goodbye in Las Vegas, I had that same tightness in my chest and feeling of loneliness.

The crew had visited Santa Monica Pier and Venice Beach yesterday. They highly recommended it to me. Igor told me that the Santa Monica Pier is the western end of Route 66. On my own I may not have realized that. It was nothing like the portion of the mother road that I traveled in Winslow, or Williams, or Oatman. It didn't have that spirit of a time long ago in a forgotten town, and it isn't in the high desert.

The pier is situated in fantastically beautiful Santa Monica. Around it, massive yellow and blue circus tents poked into the sky. A Ferris wheel and small roller coaster sat atop it, lending to an atmosphere based on fun and excitement. It jutted into the Pacific like a wooden colossus. Snack stands, gift shops, and a restaurant all called the pier home. Street performers, similar to the ones I saw in Key West, lured in tourists. Fisherman cast into the day's calm waters hoping for a bite. Santa Monica's palms grew on the bluff overlooking the beach. It was anything but forgotten.

The walk from Santa Monica to Venice Beach was a sandy adult's playground. Bicyclists, in-line skaters, workout buffs, runners, volleyball regulars, and surfers all made up the group of active outdoor folks. *When I grow up, I want to hang out on the beach and play all day too.* Along the way, I indulged in a set of swinging rings. The object was to latch on to one with one hand, swing to build up momentum, snag the next ring, and make it all the way across, via the other six or seven rings. I made it but could've used more hand strength. Wearing a backpack loaded with a laptop and camera didn't help at all.

I arrived in Venice Beach, aka the freak show capital of the United States. Unless you're a tourist going to people watch or a man with hulk-like muscles minus the green skin, then you're an eclectic artist looking to sell your work or gain attention in Venice Beach. I saw an old Indian man gliding on wacky oversized in-line skates, playing eighties-hairband music on his electric guitar, wearing tattered clothes, and sporting a turban. Interesting feller, he was. *Don't see that in West Virginia.* Gift shops abound, painters and photographers display their best work, and no shortage of guys pushing their music cd's walk up to you. Venice Beach is a colorful 3-D collage of life and art, moving at its own pace, following none along the way. It was neat for a one-time experience, but I preferred the walk along the beach on the way back to Santa Monica better than the wild and somewhat sketchy people of the vendor area.

I strolled slowly on the hardened, wet sand. I messed with the pesky seagulls that were messing with me. They stayed close by, swooping and following me the way a spy would until I crunched my last Cheeto and stuffed the small orange plastic bag in my pocket. When I'd stop walking for a look at the sea, they'd stop waddling behind and pretend not to be looking. Clever, they were. I continued on, chancing upon a large group of really good surfers.

On the Atlantic, I've seen one surfer at a time, here and there, but this was different. The waves were bigger, and the guys and gals were exceptional. I had never witnessed surfing of this caliber before. It looked like a lot of fun. Pilgrimaging out west to live that sort of life finally made sense even though it isn't exactly my cup of tea. I don't have long hair, talk like I am cooler than I am, or have a tan. Plus, I've always fit the bill as a land lover. In time, I made it back to Santa Monica and rode south to Manhattan Beach to meet up with Harvey just before five.

Harvey is Kayla's dad or Shane's father in-law; he was in Los Angeles for work. He's a military type without the tough guy ego. He does well, travels the globe enough to write a book, and is quick to smile. He and I spoke a few days before about hanging out while he was in town. He offered to let me stay at his room for the duration of his trip. Harvey, from the first time I met him, has been one of the nicest and most generous people in my life.

Harvey agreed to let me grab a quick shower upon arrival. It had been two days and ye ol' armpits were pleasantly ripened. He and I hunted down a Mexican restaurant, caught up on things as we do when we run across one another back home, and generally had a good time. I welcomed the sight of another familiar face.

Day 105 – January 26, 2012

Staying in Manhattan Beach with Harvey was a nice change of pace. My body rested from the endless miles of riding, and I appreciated a bed that I didn't have to blitz away from in the morning. The temperature hovered in the low eighties; for January, you can't beat that. If I had the loot, I would've planted roots right there until late March. Harvey headed to work at 7:00am. A whole day of trying to keep myself entertained was ahead. In an area as pretty as Manhattan Beach, with so much laid back energy, I didn't have to look far to find something to do.

I awoke from a solid night's sleep, brewed a few cups of coffee, and hunted and pecked my way through an hour's writing. I walked in perfect warmth to Target for breakfast and a new toothbrush. Twice on the trip, I'd left my toothbrush behind when I left a room. My hurried packing always overwhelmed my thought process, often resulting in undesirable souvenirs left in the room for the cleaning ladies. *No worries, I'm in the land of conveniences and a toothbrush is never far away.* Back at the room and approaching lunchtime, I decided to explore the shoreline in and around Manhattan Beach.

Only a few miles of aimless exploration landed me in Hermosa Beach, south of Manhattan Beach. I parked the Goose and went on foot from there. One beach town blended into the next. One superbly clean, angular beach house blended into the next. The tan surfers with pecks and the skinny little blondes blended in well also. Call it California camouflage, if you will. One redheaded biker with pasty white skin, a receding hairline and developing moobs, wearing black boots, and holey jeans didn't blend in at all. I'd never felt like I needed new clothes and a tan more in my life. Another important accessory I noticed in the beachfront communities was the skateboard. Man, I couldn't believe how many folks were skateboarding. It didn't matter if they were five or fifty, man or woman, tall or short, fat or skinny, from Mars or Venus—they were skateboarding everywhere. Looking back, I find it funny that no redheaded pale folks were seen skateboarding. They were probably inside hiding from the sun. That's where I should have been. *Who the hell let me outside anyway?*

However old-fashioned on the East Coast, here in-line skates weren't dead. Personally, I hadn't seen them for years. Every form of locomotion not involving an engine was going strong at the beach. The vibe was so surreal. It was like being surrounded by a bunch of adults who never grew up. I think with a little more time in the sun and the coolest pair of shorts that money can buy, I could've fit right in. Who wants to grow up anyway? That's no fun.

While in Hermosa Beach, I tracked down a gnarly little pizza joint for some lunch (notice my use of gnarly). Two slices of pepperoni, a salad, and a drink for $6. That was a deal anywhere in California.

After lunch, I was heading back to the room when I spotted a Pep Boys. *Perfect time for an oil change.* I hadn't changed the oil since Fort Stockton, Texas, and it was long overdue. With three quarts of the cheapest oil they sold, I rode back to the Residence Inn to replace the Goose's black gold. It was still hours before Harvey got off, and the only plan I had was to head back to the beach to catch the sunset, so I had to find something to get into. *Why not workout?*

In the presence of so many fit humans, I could use an assault on the growing abdomen. I had gained a good ten pounds of shade for the tool during the ride. Spending time in so many fast-food establishments was the culprit. I had eaten what I wanted when I wanted for months. When I left in October, I was a month into the Insanity workout program and in pretty good shape. I didn't have two pennies to rub together for food in those days and was eating considerably less. After a few months on the road, I was getting winded just staring at the hotties running around SoCal. My button-pushing fingers were the only things that had gotten any exercise.

For twenty minutes, I bounced around the room, running in place and pulling off moves similar to those made by a one-legged man who had tripped on something. I was trying to remember some moves from workout videos of the past. When the jumping jigglefest was all said and done, I had built up a sweat. Mission complete. Still, there was a ton of time to burn, so I looked up the person in charge of sponsorship from the Stanley Tools Corporation and gave him a ring. I left a message regarding my use of their toolboxes as panniers and thought that it was an idea that was now time-tested and worth sharing. As time would prove, they would never respond to my voicemail. Hey, I was desperate. What can I say?

Harvey arrived, and I suggested that we catch the sun before it disappeared into the ocean. The warm colors created by a vanishing sun against the deep blue Pacific are worth the effort. Some days, writing seemed a task in need of force to complete, but never did it cross my mind to skip a day of using the camera. Harvey agreed to ride to the beach and off we went. The darn traffic kept us from seeing the sun go down, but the cotton candy remnants of the sunset were nonetheless brilliant.

Harvey and I walked to a pier. The ocean breeze and perfect light had us in a great mood. Down below, a swarm of volleyball nets stood empty and ready for the next day. We grabbed dinner at the Rock Fish Restaurant. I had the best pulled pork sandwich of my life. Harvey ordered prawns for an appetizer, making a food first for me. They were great; dinner was great; the day couldn't have been more relaxing; and it was perfectly warm out. *Why can't they all be like this?*

Day 106 – January 27, 2012

I slept until the crack of nine. What! How did that happen? Well, I don't know, but it felt great. Harvey was long gone. His day at work started two hours before while mine was just beginning. I immediately jumped out of bed and ran out the door to see if it was snowing. Sleeping until nine without staying out all night long is one of my life's rarities. Harvey told me that the lobby at Residence Inn had continental breakfast until 9:00am. *If I hurry, they might still have part of it open.* I missed it yesterday and paid for breakfast from the produce department at Target. Could have saved some loot, had I known.

The hotel staff was slow to clean up the breakfast counter, and everything was still out for me to enjoy. I loaded up as if this was the last chance to eat in a week. With my belly full and the coffee desperately trying to counter the effects from an expanded stomach, I walked back to the room to knock out a post.

That morning I was having trouble finding something to get into that didn't cost anything. Being Southern California, I decided to fall back on the heart of motocross again. I knew that somewhere out there in the great expanse of city was the FMF factory. I mentioned FMF when I found their new energy drink in a convenience store near the border of Utah weeks ago. I've been a fan of the brand for a long time and I've used their exhausts more than once on my race bikes. They are just like Pro Circuit, only different, if you catch my drift. Both companies sponsor elite riders. Both are performance-based shops. Both have changed the sport in immeasurable ways. Both demand and deserve respect.

Before I took off for FMF, I suffered through another short workout, recovered in a cool shower, and searched for an address. To my dismay, FMF was located in the well-known and gang-ridden city of Compton, a suburb of Los Angeles. I mulled it over in my head for a while whether or not to ride out there. I just couldn't understand why such a wholesome company would be located in a place with such a hard-core reputation; albeit my information regarding Compton's reputation comes from lyrics written in nineties gangster rap.

For all I knew, Compton could have become a retirement community where the most violent dispute arises after someone takes a geriatric stumble through someone else's azaleas, or it could have deteriorated into a Goose-thieving, hillbilly-whoopin', drug-running, grandma-smacking city of rebellion.

Eventually, I settled on the thought that Compton probably has a section that is really bad, and the rest of the city is where the safer folks live. After all, from my bit of traveling, I realized that most people are up to good, not up to no-good. The directions would take me on the freeway all the way there except for the last half mile. That didn't seem so bad. In fact, the only thing that gave me trouble was the heavy traffic.

I pulled up to the right address, but the building was unrecognizable. If it weren't for one yellow FMF box van on the side of the building, I wouldn't have had a clue that I was there and would've turned tail. FMF's heavy, automated gate reminded me of what city I was in. I had to pull the Goose up to the gate and honk before it slid open. FMF, like Race Tech in Corona, was located in a huge building in an industrial park. My visit landed me there smack-dab in the middle of a warehouse remodel.

The fellow at the front desk filled me in on the building's unfinished exterior and the good and bad sides of Compton, saying that if I had gone left off the exit ramp, it would have only taken me a few blocks to find myself in the troubled areas. He said that FMF is in the midst of putting a shiny new, metallic veneer on the front of the building. He also told me that the empty waiting room will possibly be transformed into a café.

He attempted to get me a behind-the-scenes tour but was denied by upper management. Remodeling was the priority at the moment for the company. I didn't mind since I had no expectations when I arrived. I was there solely to fulfill curiosity. Before I left, I asked him if I was in the building where the exhausts were handmade. He confirmed that I was. With that, he padded my palms with a hefty handful of stickers. I left for Manhattan Beach, happy to have gained a small experience.

A couple of days before, Igor and I met these gals just outside of our room in Santa Monica. They were dead sober. Igor and I had our beer goggles strapped on tight. These were the gals that gave me the plastic fireman's hat. There were three of them, all brunette, all attractive, aged mid-twenties, and all in town for business training. The fireman's hat came about through the trade up system, which is based on the story of a person who started with a paperclip and traded up the ladder, finally trading something for a house, and using no money along the way.

One of the girls had gained the fireman's hat by trading something for it. She was after whatever she could get from us that would potentially hold more value than the hat, thus helping her trade up to her eventual goal of world domination. Igor gave her a mini tripod for the hat. Like I said, we may have been a bit tipsy. At any rate, they mentioned that they would be at Busby's Sports Bar on Friday night and that I should come out with them. Their plan was to get the rest of their group together, about twenty folks in total, and hit the town. I told them I'd give it a shot.

I left Manhattan Beach for Santa Monica. I found Busby's and wandered inside around 7:30. It had low ceilings, and the rooms were dark, small, and sectioned off from one another. It was the opposite of an open floor plan. I walked around awkwardly looking for them, popping into rooms full of people quietly drinking or having a bite to eat, and often causing them to stop mid-sentence. People looked at me like I was lost, and I don't blame them. I think that my face easily displays the features of a man out of sorts. My squinty eyes, crooked teeth, gaping nostrils, and protruding ears share the characteristics of a backwoods feller who may have had a banjo-playing uncle pappy, brother daddy, or an aunt mommy. I'm all too aware of this, and it does nothing but breed anxiety in the presence of strangers. Even at my most confident, I can rest assured that I still look like fucking Opie. Yet, I carry on hoping that life will bless me with a lottery win or something to balance me out.

And so it goes, the girls weren't in the joint. I'd been in this position before and knew quite acutely that there was a slim chance that they would show, so I just did my own thing and enjoyed a plate of surprisingly tasty chicken tenders, while sitting alone at one end of the darkened bar. I dabbed deep fried slabs of chicken into a puddle of BBQ sauce and chewed to my heart's content.

But then, a different group of gals grabbed my attention. They wanted me to take a picture of their girls' night out. *No problem here—wink, wink.* For a moment, I felt like I was back in the game. Then another thought occurred to me: *They probably find me harmless like a "special" sort of guy.* One of them handed me her cell phone. I pointed and shot, but it couldn't handle the low light. Ever the self-critic, I recognized what needed to be done here. I knew that if I whipped out the Canon, the picture would turn out great. However, I knew that once they saw the size of my glorious, electronic photo weapon it would wipe out any chance of snaggin' one of 'em out of the herd. What girl is gonna want to get to know a guy who carries around a huge digital eye?

Nonetheless, I used my camera to take a picture for them. They were tickled pink with the results in that "thanks buddy" sort of way. I did manage to get an email address from the hottest one. She strictly clarified that it was for sending the picture at a later date. The group that I was waiting for turned out to be a no-show. At 9:30, I left Busby's for Manhattan Beach. I had to get back to the room by a decent time in order to be respectful to Harvey's working hours. Did the fireman's hat group show up after I left? I'll never know.

On a side note, Busby's Sports Bar was rated the third best sports bar in the nation, so that in itself was worth a visit. A couple of months ago, you couldn't have pulled me out of the door until last call. I felt a change a brewin'.

Day 107 – January 28, 2012

Morning began with immediate packing. At 7:00am I forced the gears of my body into motion. Harvey needed to be out of the room by 8:30 in order to grab a quick breakfast before his flight from LAX to San Francisco. He was traveling there for another week of work. Part of me wished that I could head to San Francisco with him. The fourth round of Supercross was scheduled in Oakland that night, the city adjacent to San Fran, and I would have loved to go, but reality would have it no other way. I thanked Harvey, wished him safe travels, and he headed off to add another piece to his interesting job-related travel puzzle. I packed up and headed south for yet another familiar face.

This time the familiar eyes, hair, nose, mouth, ears, and body belonged to Brittany, my ex-girlfriend. She was flying into San Diego on Sunday to see me and do a bit of vacationing. She planned to stay for about a week. We'd explore the southwestern city's attractions together, both of us being newbies to San Diego.

Leaving Manhattan Beach and riding south to San Diego is pretty straightforward. You can take the fast road, the scenic road, or the Pacific Coast Highway, aka Route 1, which I'm dubbing the middle road. Knowing that the freeway would be full of traffic, and Route 1 would be full of traffic lights, I set my sights on the scenic road—the unofficial stretch of pavement that hugs closest to the Pacific's beaches. I wanted to ride tight against the coast all the way to San Diego, if possible, through every residential area, through every curve in the coastline—always keeping the Pacific to the right and within sight. From the road atlas, it looked doable.

I left Manhattan Beach slowly and surely. Beauty abounded along the elevated Californian coast—Hermosa Beach, Redondo Beach, Torrance, and along the peninsula that is Rancho Palos Verdes. All were a picture perfect treat.

Side roads paralleled the shore, often making the orange, terracotta roof tiles of gorgeous seaside homes visible down below. Rolling green hills and sweeping turns stopped just short of falling a hundred feet into the ocean.

Rocky cliffs sometimes had homes built precariously atop them and sometimes looked even better when they were doing nothing more than making a cove with gentle waves for long boarders, or just doing what they've always done, stopping the Pacific's forward progress. Hiking trails made steep descents to the sandy beaches below. Jagged rocks forced their way up out of the surf.

This stretch of coast was like the first world of the first world. The homes matched the cars and matched the people. Shiny Mercedes Benz's were a dime a dozen. Folks with running or biking gear looked ready for a triathlon, regardless of their age or shape. Most actually looked very fit and active, and I admired them for being outdoors. In such great weather, why the hell would you ever want to be inside? My worn gear, holey jeans, stickered-up bike, and its ripped seat did not fit in well.

Just as I was reaching sensory overload, I came across the Port of Los Angeles. It's a stretch of the coast that forces a driver inland near Long Beach. I suppose that I could have taken more side roads here, but I didn't. For a moment, I gave it a shot and became disoriented on a back street looking for a bridge to continue south along the ocean. I regrouped and hopped on Route 1, the middle road. From the map, it clearly dodged the port. Traffic lights increased, and before I knew it, I was back in Sketchy Peopleville. I couldn't see the ocean anymore, and I wouldn't call it the ghetto, but it might've been one liquor store away from it. Children as young as four were running around on the sidewalks with no adult within arms' reach. The roadsides were dirty, and it kind of smelled. I hoped that I wouldn't see a kid trip off the sidewalk and succumb to the cars racing from stoplight to stoplight.

Arriving in Seal Beach changed that. I started hugging the coast again, following it tightly to Huntington Beach. I stopped to stretch the ol' meat stilts at a dog friendly beach. The dogs looked tremendously happy to be running around in the sand and waves. Occasionally one would drop a landmine, with tongue out and panting in the perfect sunshine, seemingly smiling. A mile offshore, oil rigs mucked up the view more than those canine landmines ever will. I rode on through Newport Beach and Laguna Beach where I stopped for lunch.

Jack in the Box looked like the cheapest place around to grab a quick bite, so I grabbed a number three and recharged the body. Those beach towns along the coast were just hard to imagine. They were so clean and full of the coolest shops. The weather was unreal, the people were fit, and it was so close to heavenly that I really couldn't relate. I'm from a completely different world. Though I did like it a lot, I could not imagine how such extravagant lifestyles could be maintained for long periods. It seemed too perfect.

I did find one real blemish that didn't have a thing to do with offshore oil rigs, or an unrefined area near the port. It was a stretch of road that had a warning sign: "Constantly moving ground next 0.8 miles." If that doesn't throw up a red flag that something may happen in paradise sooner or later, nothing will.

From Laguna Beach, I rode south and jumped on Freeway 5, the fast road. I quickly became bored with that and went back to riding the coast. Then I quickly bored of that part of the coast's abundance of traffic lights, so I did what was inevitable and transferred back to the freeway for a sprint to downtown San Diego. I found that there was a large portion of relatively undisturbed land in between Los Angeles and San Diego from south of San Clemente to Oceanside, where taking the freeway was the only option. Marine Corps Base Camp Pendleton comprised a fair portion of that land. I enjoyed seeing a smidgen of SoCal coast not yet overrun by development.

In San Diego, sunset was beginning to spread soft light on the boats docked in the harbor. A cluster of medium-sized, shiny, glass-covered skyscrapers rested beside the water, changing colors in the light. San Diego looked clean and orderly. Its sprawl disappeared over the surrounding hills, giving it a smaller feel. It had a safe, friendly vibe before I even took my foot off the peg and laid my first step on its pavement. San Diego didn't feel like a few of the industrialized, oversized, and homeless-ized cities that I'd seen. It felt welcoming.

I rode around San Diego International Airport to familiarize myself with it before meeting Brittany there the next day. I tracked down the cheapest motel closest to the airport. Can you guess what I found? Good guess. Motel 6 is correct. It was cheaper by more than $10 over the next closest room. Brittany planned to sponsor our lodging expenses for her visit, so I reserved the room for two nights. She didn't mind, knowing that I was nearing a Ramen and PB&J bank account. After unloading the Goose, I scrambled back to the harbor for some shots of the sun before it went to sleep beyond the horizon. Back at the room, a long evening teased me as I fought off the desire to blow money on drinks out on the town.

Day 108 – January 29, 2012

January wound up a being a month of surprises, starting on a floating restaurant on Lake Powell and ending immersed among familiar faces, most of which were like me, 3,000 miles or more from home. Now I'd be sharing some of it with a person who knows me a little better than a handshake and a couple of nice words. Brittany would be here in a few hours, and I couldn't help but think about why.

I'd left her behind, physically, cold turkey on day two. I claimed single man status to anyone who asked along the way. I'd made it clear where I wanted my life to go, yet she held on. A little known secret was that Brittany and I talked regularly as I traveled, not every day, but a couple times a week. Some mornings she woke me up with a call, and some days she knew where I'd been and what I'd done before I wrote about it. While we talked, everything inside of me wanted to keep it as just friends, but she wanted more. I left her and home for time to heal, time to find myself, and to live life. When we'd talk, she never failed to express her interest in traveling with me. I'd explain how I sacrificed everything I had for this trip, and she always seemed ready to abandon everything she knew just to be with me. I didn't understand her, and probably never will.

The thought crossed my mind a million times on long days of riding: *Why doesn't she just give up? I couldn't have made myself clearer.* Our relationship started in turmoil, whether she could see it or not. I wasn't in love with the girl. I believe that love is a two-way street if a relationship is to work, and it has to happen in the purest of ways—you just can't force someone to love you. With that, I'm enough of a softy that when she phoned, I answered. I saw no reason to hurt her by denying her a voice to hear on the other end of the line. I have felt the pain when the one you love stops picking up with a sweet "Hey Babe."

Brittany and I had been separated for 106 days. In that time, somewhere in the remote Southwest, I caved a little and agreed to let her meet me in California. It may have been during a dark night alone in my tent, or it may have been after sipping my third glass of whiskey, or it may have happened while staring at the Grand Canyon thinking, "It would be nice to share this with someone." I don't recall. Now, here we were, about to meet again for another ride on the rollercoaster of life. . . .

A beautiful Motel 6 morning greeted me in San Diego. Brittany was scheduled to land at the airport at 11:26am. I snagged some coffee and a quick shower before trekking two miles west to terminal number two. I knew that she would have a few bags with her and that both of us and the bags couldn't fit on the bike. At the airport, I found the baggage claim that she would be passing through and waited patiently, camera ready, for the first sighting. I had my hat pulled down low, with a kiosk helping to block her view. Somehow when she rounded the corner, she turned her head to the right and immediately spotted me. My incognito mode was busted. The chance for a surprise picture was ruined. We hugged, and I welcomed her to California. She was all smiles, and I thought about how good the hug felt. I let her know that we had a long hike back to the room. She didn't mind.

At the room we had some *catching up* to do. If you've followed along, you know that I'd been on the road a long time as a two-wheeled lone wolf with as much game as the Pope. Seeing women had become a highlight of my day, especially along the beach. Ten days ago, as I was riding through Pahrump, I damn near went nuts over the possibilities to be had within the walls of a brothel. I'd love nothing more than to describe what it's like to make moves similar to the game of Twister played on a trampoline in the dark by two wild and wonderful West Virginians—with my newfound fondness for writing—but I'll spare you the details. It's better that way.

We based the rest of our day around a plan to visit the San Diego Zoo. It's a place that's been on my radar since first hearing of it on Jack Hannah's Animal Adventures as a kid (my favorite show then). We secured the directions and were pleasantly surprised to find that it was only a mile away. This would be the first time having the luggage boxes on the bike while riding double. The Goose handled it without a complaint.

San Diego Zoo is located at Balboa Park, San Diego's big green point of relief from the concrete jungle. It's an amazingly attractive getaway from the hustle and bustle of city life. We had only been there an hour when I began to forget about the hard grey corners of sidewalks and dense population outside. Striking sand-colored, stucco buildings with intricate Spanish Colonial trim and accents make up the park's central area. Plants flourish here. They weave and wrap their way around every last corner, often so thick that they make you feel like you've entered a jungle full of ruins.

Balboa Park is a wonderful home to not only the zoo, but a host of other recreational and educational buildings. I noticed a science center, natural history museum, and indoor botanical garden. We went there for the zoo but submitted to those types of exhibits. By the time we found the zoo's ticket booth, it was after 2:00pm. Entry was $42 a head. That would give us less than three hours to get our money's worth. We decided to wait until the next day to see the zoo.

While the animals were forced to patiently stand by for our visit tomorrow, I decided to take Brittany to the coast so that she could see the Pacific Ocean for her first time. We bypassed the harbor and airport, and rode through a pristine residential area to Sunset Cliffs Boulevard. We found some shoreline. I stood beside her and proudly gazed at the mightiest of oceans the way a father does when he hands his son the keys to his old hot rod. She looked at its infinite blue glory and said, "That's pretty." She and I look at the world a bit differently. What can I say? We soaked up some sun just like the folks a half mile out in a small white sailboat, snapped pictures, and headed back to the room to get ready for an early dinner.

Fifth Avenue lies in the center of San Diego's happening Gaslamp District. This area is like New Orleans's infamous French Quarter drinking streets with an English and Irish flare and minus the hooters and debauchery. The streets are of average width and wedged between a mix of short and squatty and modern, vertically-superior buildings. Our evening began with a couple of burgers at a sports bar on the street level of one of those buildings and ended at a funny little place called the Tipsy Crow. We shared enough drinks to have fun without losing our legs navigating back to the room, where we spent some more time catching up. We fell asleep to none other than another airing of *Forrest Gump*. I positively love that movie.

Day 109 – January 30, 2012

Hello. My name is Mike. I'm a thirty-year-old native of West Virginia. Like many of you gathered here today, I have an issue. They say that the only way to get over your problem is to admit that you have a problem. Well, folks . . . I really, really like animals!

It should be no surprise by now to hear that Brittany and I spent a full day at the San Diego Zoo, the nation's best! If not for my passion for motocross, I'd surely be in some sort of animal-related career. Being at the zoo brings out the kid in me like no other place. While standing on the edge of an exhibit, I found myself competing with people half my height for the best view of some hairy four-legger. Most folks my age seem to have grown out of this fondness for nature and its wonders. Not me, though. Not even close.

I have always fully appreciated the other species that we share this small planet with, both plants and animals. Many of their jobs in nature make our existence possible. It pains me to no end knowing that a large portion of the human population exists unaware of the chain of life that makes the environment tick. Sure, a few lesser known species have made the extinction list over time, but now, due to man's toils across the planet, larger, more well-known species have their existence teetering on a non-renewable edge.

The African lion, or king of the jungle as we've named it, is one of those species. I once heard a statistic stating that within the last seventy years, their population fell from 450,000 to a meager 20,000 surviving in the wild. That's a population decline of ninety-six percent. And we all know whose population has grown exponentially since then—ours. In the last seventy years our population has more than tripled.

As for the lions, they don't know that they are teetering on the edge of extinction while we sit back and hog a disproportionate amount of resources and have the large asses and an obesity epidemic to show for it. Their decline is solely based on man's mismanagement of land, poaching, and our blatant ignorance.

At times, man has it in him to be Earth's lowest form of life: lower than the cockroach that never pollutes, lower than the vulture that never wastes, lower than the hardworking ant, and even lower than the snake that swallows its prey whole but never takes more than it needs and never kills for pleasure. I cannot imagine a world without lions in the same way that children born in the twenty-first century can't imagine a world without the Internet. Thanks to places like the San Diego Zoo for tirelessly working to raise awareness about our non-human neighbors, they still have a fighting chance. Without zoos, parks, and designated wildlife reserves, we might have already lost a few significant animals like the lion. . . .

Our hike at the zoo started with a loop that led us to a giant male African elephant. This fella was the biggest pachyderm I'd ever seen. He was using his trunk to pull straw out of a raised metal feeder no more than five feet from us. It was the closest I'd been to an elephant. He was impressive from his trunk's dexterity to his prehistoric-looking toenails. He was a great ambassador for the rest of the zoo.

Next, we were off to check out the big white polar bears. These guys, like the lions, are in a ton of trouble due to habitat loss, and it's important that we know this. We can change that! This was my first time seeing a polar bear. Their cuteness was almost enough to fool you into thinking that they are nothing but gentle giants. To survive in the conditions that they call home, polar bears have to be undeniably accurate hunters. One slip during an opportunity to snag a seal, and they may not see another one for a week or more.

From the polar bear exhibit, we meandered through the zoo's many twisty, heavily vegetated trails to the gorilla pen. I could have spent all day zooming in on their facial expressions. Their hands' similarity to ours is beyond peculiar. Zookeepers threw heads of lettuce and bunches of broccoli into the gorillas' enclosure. I wish I could say that humans were the only ones capable of thieving, but it's not so. I saw more dirty food snatching in the gorilla pen than was called for. However, none of it went to waste.

We continued on through aviaries full of exotic birds, past reptile exhibits galore, cats of all shapes and sizes, and crazy little monkeys. All of them kept us stimulated for hours. I could write a book on each creature if time allowed.

We wrapped up the hike at a section called the urban jungle. This was a loop near the entrance and exit gates where the massive rhinos and giraffes are found. I couldn't help looking at the giraffes and thinking that they looked like hairy dinosaurs, and the rhinos seemed like the modern-day mammalian versions of the triceratops, powerful to the tenth degree, with horns capable of making your knees tremble.

The last exhibit we passed was perhaps the most unexpected. It was a long, narrow pen with a cheetah and a golden retriever in it. At first I thought that the golden retriever was in there for food—kidding. It turned out that the exhibit was full of domesticated animals, even the cheetah. Zookeepers displayed those animals to local schools or walked them around the park to help kids gain a fondness for wildlife. That's where it all starts. If you don't gain a healthy respect for our planet and its non-human inhabitants as children, then, odds are, you won't gain one as an adult. Brittany and I were wiped out from the miles of walking. On the way out, we grabbed a bite to eat at a Mexican restaurant and called it a very early night at the good ol' Motel 6.

Day 110 – January 31, 2012

Motel 6 near the San Diego airport sufficed for the last couple of days. Our time there had been pretty smooth with just one unsavory incident happening mere minutes after Brittany arrived at the room for the first time.

We were staying in Room 237, and our not-so-lovely neighbors were in Room 236. These folks sounded as if they were going to win a million dollars for taking the human decibel level to new heights. It was a fight to the finish for this couple. Motel 6's interior walls allowed Brittany and me the pleasure of listening to the whole thing go down. Sharp shouting went on for several minutes. We didn't think much of this. Brittany and I had been there and done that.

During the initial escalation, the fighting couple even threatened to get their "mamas" after one another. We managed a slight laugh from this, and judging from the way they described their mamas' name-taking, butt-kicking capabilities, I could tell that these two came from respectful backgrounds. The fighting continued through the levels of relationship drama. Belittling comments were speared at one another. Racial cruelties were used against the man in the ultimate low blow, and then their argument turned frightening. The woman began screaming, "Rape!"

My mind began to race. *Should I bust down the door to help this gal? Should I bang loudly on their door and threaten to call the cops?* All of the consequences had to be weighed first, and believe me, my brain was in overdrive. I was carrying a pistol but didn't want to be put in a position to use it. Being caught in California with a pistol was instant jail time. *Is this girl bluffing?* I had no idea.

Brittany and I held out action, listening just a little longer. The simple act of waiting in a situation like this could mean life or death. I hated not knowing what to do. Obviously the two were dating or married and knew one another well. The longer we listened, the better our understanding became that they were having a severe argument without rape. We could hear them stomping around and throwing things. I did not hear choking sounds or slapping; however, it was obvious from the heavy thuds coming from the dividing wall that they were shoving each other.

I called the front desk to have them send someone up to check out the disturbance. The front desk told me to call the police. I told them that one of their guests could be in potential danger. The gal at the front desk didn't seem to care and repeated her demand for me to call the police. With phone still in hand, I watched a gnarly Hispanic woman, not unlike a hairless Sasquatch, leave Room 236. She looked frustrated yet unscathed. Her debate partner, saying it politely, stayed in the room. I had seen him the day before. He was a black male, possibly older than me, thin and short, not the sort who could hold a woman like that down.

Situations like that perplex me. Getting involved could lead to getting shot. Who's to say when it's the right time to step in? This woman's bluff could've led to a real dangerous situation if I would have tried to intervene. Thankfully, it all worked out this time. Brittany and I agreed that we wanted to get out of there and around more decent folks.

We decided to move on. We were in the mood for camping. With Google Maps, I found one lone KOA near San Diego. It was located twelve miles south in Chula Vista. Since the Goose only had so much load capacity, I had to take Brittany and her things to KOA first, return to Motel 6 for my things, and ride back to KOA. These logistics were developed on the fly.

Chula Vista's KOA was beautiful. Its grass and mulchy tent sites surrounded leafy trees and palms. Its camping infrastructure was manicured to perfection. Small log cabins were rustic and shiny as if the first coats of stain were still drying. There was a laundry, indoor game room, Internet connection, hot showers, and anything else that anyone who wants to sleep outside but not really get away from it all could ask for, and all of it for the low introductory fee of $39.95. KOA was $5 higher than Motel 6. I just don't get it. We volunteered to move from a room to a night full of back pain from sleeping on the ground, and it cost us more.

Well, we were committed anyway. I dropped her off and gave her the task of setting up the tent while I was gone. After a few pointers, she gave it a whirl. I expected to come back to a completely set up tent with a nice and tight rainfly covering it. Instead I came back to a tent in shambles. Brittany was lying down in defeat on the picnic table's bench seat. She managed to put the tent and poles up to ninety percent complete, but the rainfly was on backwards and not secured. It looked like a fort made from kitchen table chairs and a sheet. I just laughed and chalked it up as a learning experience for her. Unlike my family, hers didn't do one single night of camping during her youth. I finished off the tent setup, straightened out the rainfly, and secured it properly.

We showered and turned our attention to lunch. A mile away, a restaurant advertised authentic Hawaiian food. My Mikey-likes-it food discretion told me to talk Brittany into having a bite to eat there. I wanted to try something new, but she was unsurprisingly hesitant. Toward food or drink, Brittany has an annoying compulsion to blurt out "That's gross." I've seen her do this with things as benign as orange juice, whereas I'm always glad to have a bit, pulp or no pulp. I went in prepared to lecture her about cultural food differences and about being more open-minded. As I've discovered, she doesn't like to veer far from the deep fried chicken strip.

My brother may be the only person I know who's pickier. I can't remember the last time I saw him eat anything remotely green. It's a wonder he hasn't fallen to scurvy by now. Once, as young teens, I became so offended that he wouldn't try Mom's broccoli that it escalated into a verbal assault. From that, we now have lingering mental scar tissue and an unforgettably funny story. He and I both came from a clean-your-plate background, and I think that all of my mother's cooking is top-notch, so for him to refuse it struck a nerve. To his credit, plain hamburgers don't stand a chance when he's itching to eat.

Inside the Hawaiian joint, the place looked like the remnants of a KFC with Hawaiian accents, kind of one-off, but kind of not. We ordered the barbecue mix plates and they were okay, but I should've gone for a bolder menu item. Most things on the menu reminded me of some version of Chinese food seen at any old buffet. Our late lunch was over, and our plan evolved into a trip around Chula Vista to get familiar with the area since we'd be there a few more days.

We returned to camp at dusk for a relaxing evening in the indoor-outdoor essence that is KOA. I was mentally ready for a few hours of vegetating by a fire with Willy Nelson playing on Pandora and some roasted marshmallows—really roughin' it. *This will be great!* That was until . . . until I split the first piece of wood with my hatchet and lodged the world's gnarliest splinter under my right thumbnail. The dimensions on that bad boy were no less than an inch long and every bit of three-sixteenths of an inch thick. It was a real teeth-clinching, I-just-fucked-up moment. I was making out alright with the hatchet while using it to shave off some kindling for the start of the fire. Then I planned to take our larger chunks and split them for the next phase before putting the biggest chunks of wood in later.

Here's a slow-mo version of what happened. I grab a full piece, stand it up on the ground before me, hold it with my left hand, steady it, rear back with the hatchet (with my right hand choked up on the handle a little too far), move my left hand out of the way, and then whack the piece of firewood with a swift blow. The hatchet makes great contact in the center of the standing log. The wood splits and begins to fall to the side. During follow through, my thumbnail on my right hand slides down the hunk of wood falling to the left until it finds a sharp splintered piece. The splinter spears into the soft nerve-laden tissue from the tip of my thumbnail to within a centimeter of touching my thumb knuckle. I let go of the hatchet. My body moves to a bolt-upright position. I yelp. My muscles tighten, my face squints, and my ass cheeks clinch. My left hand grabs my right like it was trying to steal something. I dance a little pain jig in the mulch. Brittany yells, "What's wrong?" I start pulling out shards.

It felt like I had just hammered a finishing nail right under my thumbnail. To say it sucked is an understatement. I got a pair of mini scissors and went to work. When I could get no further, I just left what was left under there and did my best to ignore the throbbing. A few cold ones helped dull the pain. Brittany and I chilled by the fire for a few hours before retiring to the cramped little tent.

Day 111 – February 1, 2012

Trying to sleep was a pain in the rear with the pain in my thumb. I couldn't get the throbbing to stop, even if my thumb wasn't touching anything. It was hard to find a position to lie in where my hand remained elevated and my thumb wasn't resting on something. Eventually, pure fatigue set in and I fell asleep for a few solid hours.

We awoke and started the day with showers. While Brittany was still doing her thing in the warm water, I hunted down a sewing needle that I packed in my hiking pack. The aim was to get the rest of the wood out from under my thumbnail. Let me tell you, buddy, nothing will wake you up quicker than sticking a needle underneath a sore thumbnail and digging away. One by one, I dislodged piece after dripping bloody piece until my thumbnail almost looked normal again. When all of it was out, my thumb felt ten times better. That was an episode sent straight from the seventh level of Hell. I can only imagine one place on the body worse to have a large splinter introduced.

Brittany wanted to visit a beach. For miles around, the choices were endless. I suggested that we follow through with another recommendation from my friend Don, whom I met in Big Bend, Texas. He told me that he grew up in La Jolla, pronounced "Luh hoya" Beach. He said that I should check it out while in the area. La Jolla Beach was twenty-two miles north of Chula Vista's KOA. We packed our things and took off north on Freeway 5, past downtown San Diego to exit 26, then headed west until the ocean was in sight. I didn't exactly know where La Jolla Beach was according to my generic map, so our first stop landed us at La Jolla Shores Beach.

This area was nice and included free parking. Brittany and I walked across the sand to the water. It was pretty; however, I knew better. If this was the beach Don was talking about, then his credentials would have taken a shot. His recommendations up until then had been nothing less than fantastic. Brittany took a moment when I wasn't looking to further her agenda. She drew a large heart in the sand with "Mike + Brittany 12" etched into the center. She frowned as I made jokes about the high tide coming in. We found a maintenance man who directed us to the La Jolla Beach that we were after. It was a mile from where we were, so we rode south until we found downtown La Jolla.

The place looked like a slice of Heaven on Earth, like "almost Heaven West Virginia," but with Pacific Ocean, sea birds, gorgeous coastline, fit people, crafty shops, surfers, and snorkelers. We found free motorcycle parking, and wandered down a steep, paved hill. We had not traveled farther than a hundred feet when we spotted our first wild sea lion. This guy, like many coastal Californians, was just chilling in the sun without a care in the world. We rounded a corner to find life at its best. A sign said that we were at La Jolla Cove. This was the place Don had described.

Sea lions, pelicans, and seagulls wrestled for rocky real estate along the shore while we gawked at Mother Nature's creation. A small stretch of sandy beach, shaped like a horseshoe, was surrounded by a rocky bluff. A man who was painting a portrait of La Jolla's hillside looked as though he was standing in a painting himself. Snorkelers explored the blue water just past the breaking waves; farther out, boats with snow white sails cruised along silently. This was paradise. Don had come through again.

We walked down a flight of steps to that hidden stretch of sand where man and nature seemed to symbiotically share the beach. We were foolishly excited. Brittany and I let the waves chase us up the sand. We climbed through a small cave hollowed out by the ocean, took pictures full of big smiles, and jabber jawed about how we would like to be out there snorkeling too. We were playing. We felt laid back. The scene was growing on me.

On the high ground, we found lunch at a restaurant named The Spot. I ordered a Chicago deep-dish pizza, with chunky tomatoes instead of sauce, while Brittany ordered a tasty chicken sandwich with sweet potato fries. That place knows their pies!

From there, we bounced through a few gift shops. Brittany was on the hunt for a cute La Jolla T-shirt. On the way back to the Goose, our path led us straight into one of Peter Lik's photo galleries. I saw a photo from the sidewalk and instantly recognized it as his work. I learned of Peter Lik through the Weather Channel. He had a half-hour show on there where he perfectly captured incredibly remote landscapes, in all sorts of weather. I looked up to the guy. I saw one of his other thirteen galleries while in Key West on Duval Street.

Before the trip, I cared little about photography, but that changed, and I morphed into a photo fiend on the road. One of Mr. Lik's more famous shots came from underneath the pier at La Jolla Shores Beach. The pier's supports created an endless, shrinking-doorway effect over the ocean water. It was a shot equally beautiful and mysterious. The gallery assistant taught me a few things that he'd learned about various papers that photos can be printed on. He gave us his card, as if we had that kind of money, and I thanked him for his time. We looked at the rest of Mr. Lik's gallery and were off to KOA at rush hour.

Back at the tent, we agreed to check out the night life in Chula Vista. Brittany wanted to sing karaoke. This, my friends, is third to the fear of hangovers and spiders for me. She, on the other hand, had the voice of Patsy Cline reincarnated. She loved to show it off, and I loved to encourage her artistic side. Chula Vista enticed us to try Manhattan's Bar, a lively enough drinking hole, small and full of folks who looked of the working class. Brittany sang a few and did great as usual. I chickened out. If the place were empty, I would've mumbled through Guns-N-Roses' "I Used to Love Her." I introduced Brittany to that song earlier in the day as a joke. She didn't think it was funny.

When she had the mic, I had the duty of meeting drunken horn-dogs who stumbled over to our table to find out if I was with her or not. I was used to this. Back home, it happened all the time. When they'd come to me to express their interest in her, I'd always think, "Keep it in your pants dumbass. She's going home with me," while wanting to karate chop them in the Adam's apple. I have never in my life been so disrespectful as to go up to a man and inquire about his girlfriend while they're out together. What people are thinking sometimes is beyond me. Here we were, 3,000 miles from home, and nothing had changed. Her voice was luring 'em in again. Thankfully, everyone gave us a dab of respect once realizing that we were a couple. Every now and again, some idiot doesn't get the hint. Our night ended around 9:30pm as we climbed into the tent like two turtles in one shell.

Day 112 – February 2, 2012

Morning's warmth arrived. My thumb was looking good and feeling okay. *Good start to the day*. Brittany had survived another night in the wilderness known as KOA. This was her life's third-longest camping trip. She had been with me and the family on two of Harvey's annual excursions into the George Washington National Forest in southeastern West Virginia. Those were five-day events where the muggy summertime temps were defeated by drinking cold ones along the lake, racing around the park's fire roads, and laughing over stories around the night's campfire with a dozen family and friends. She may not know how to venture off into the bush and return home on her own, but with a guiding hand, she's always been up for anything.

We didn't know what to do with ourselves. We had a hankering for breakfast on the town. Our taste buds wanted something like a Sunday morning pancakes and eggs bonanza, but the need for Wi-Fi took us straight to McDonald's. As you probably know, the food wasn't much to talk about. The Wi-Fi, on the contrary, was superb. After eating and a post, we had no idea how to spend our day. Lunchtime wasn't too far away. Out of the blue I suggested that we swing up to Lake Elsinore to check out the motocross track. Lake Elsinore is seventy-five miles northeast of Chula Vista. She said that it was cool with her, so we left the golden arches in the dust and hopped on 15 N.

This was her first long ride on the back of the Goose. The homemade steel pannier supports hogged a bunch of space that would normally be open for a passenger's butt cheeks. Each side box was mounted further forward and inches higher than most motorcycle luggage. The setup was simply not designed for a passenger. In order to reach the rear footpegs, one needed Gumby's legs. Brittany managed on the long haul up to Lake Elsinore, though. When we stopped to get fuel, I asked her if she could have done 12,000 miles of riding on the rear seat. She laughed and said, "I wouldn't have an ass after that."

Back home, we made a deal before our relationship turned sour. I told her with all the sincerity in the world that if she bought a motorcycle and learned how to ride it then she could come along. I knew the impossibilities of this proposition. We were in a state of idle normality where we had a house, a dog, good credit, decent blue color jobs, and mediocre vehicles. I know that she didn't see me giving all of that up for this trip. I'm sure that she thought it was just a bunch of hot air and that our relationship would evolve into marriage, children, and bills.

Inside, however, I was blindly committed—fiendishly committed—and I wanted, more than that, needed to go alone to make it mentally successful. I told her that there was no way I'm doing the trip riding double. I expressed my concern with the bike's handling with two passengers and all of that gear. I told her how I alone would have to pay for everything while sacrificing a house that I built with my own hands. She tried over and over to change my mind about riding double. In the months that passed before we broke up, she made no progress on her end of the deal. She never saved money for a bike, which was the first step she needed to take in order to come along.

Sure, I was asking a lot, but I live by the same sword. I dream big, work hard, go for things even if they seem incredibly illogical, and never give up. When I was twenty-three, I tried to build the world's first successful, flapping, man-powered flying machine in my parent's backyard—an ornithopter. It never made it to its first test flight, but I was oh so close. It was fully assembled and just hours of tweaking away from being ready. A family dispute over my crazy project put my plans on hold—the sizeable wings were blocking sunshine, thus killing a large spot of grass in the yard. Since then, a Canadian team of college students has pulled it off. But that's the way it goes.

Life has always felt like an uphill battle, so I introduced her to the same uphill battle that I had to overcome to have an adventure, and she did nothing. It takes a person with a little madness to venture away from the safety of the herd. I do not hold her in low regard for her actions. She is the social norm through and through. It is me who is different, who has trouble fitting in, who becomes near fatally bored with normality, who doesn't waste time thinking outside the box because I exist outside the box and can't bleeping help it. *What does the inside of the box look like anyway?* That is not meant to sound self-righteous. I wish that I was as normal as Brittany. Life would be so much easier, but then again, I probably would have died before I managed to see the Grand Canyon. Breathe in . . . Breathe out . . . On with the day. . . .

We pulled up to Lake Elsinore's front gate, paid $5, and parked the Goose. The track was lined by a brilliant white fence. Around us, rounded brown mountains broke up the flatness. An industrial park bordered the part of the track near its front gate, and homes were easily visible in the vicinity. Lake Elsinore Motocross Park has been around a while, but the proximity to the homes threw up a red flag. Your average Joe Blow, HOA-loving, weekend-car-washing, football-and-beer consuming homeowner does not like the noise from nearby motocross tracks. I've seen a few motocross track owners remain mired in civil disputes for years. Saying that, just being there made me want to hop on a bike and spread some noise.

One of KTM's huge orange semitrucks was parked with a cluster of motocross bikes in front of it. Lake Elsinore had only a handful of riders out practicing, so I had to go see what the occasion was. As I neared the truck, I was star struck. Sebastian Tortelli was standing under an awning with a bright green vest on beside the line of bikes. Sebastian was one of the world's great motocross racers. He's a French fella who made an unforgettable mark on motocross in the States. There are only a few humans walking the planet who can say that they've been world champion twice and could've given Ricky Carmichael a run for his money. Sebastian was one of those guys.

Usually I just leave people of notability alone when I cross them, but this time I realized the opportunity in front of me. I politely asked, "Mr. Tortelli, will you take a picture with me?" He accepted my request with a smile. Brittany whipped out her cell phone for the quick moment of awesomeness and snapped the picture. Of course, like every picture I take with people, I wasn't looking at the camera when the shutter moved. *Damn!* I'll have to live on with that ridiculous picture and remember the good part of the moment.

I told Sebastian that I've always enjoyed watching him race, and that I was glad to meet him. He was a racer not afraid to take his motorcycle to the edge. On the track he handled obstacles at one hundred percent of his ability. From one racer to another, I knew that he always pushed. A slight mistake or a quick washout would often land him on the ground unharmed, proving that he was giving it his all. He rode like a hard worker, like a man not trying to get by on talent alone, as with some of today's racers. There was no conserving energy, or riding cautiously to protect the lead. Sebastian let it hang out wide-open all the time. He suffered more than his share of injuries for his riding style; however, it also made him one of the best to ever twist a throttle.

We let Sebastian get back to his business of hosting a riding school and headed off for a walk around the really neat and organized facility. A few of the riders were moving at an exceptionally high pace around the track. I didn't recognize any of them until I reviewed the pictures later and could read their jerseys. One fella that was riding was pro rider Mike Sleeter. He had been living my dream for a while as a professional racer and as KTM North America's number one test rider, which may be the best job in the universe. It was good to see him healthy and out there still putting in the work needed to remain fast. His speed, although superb, was just a tick off the heavily sponsored Pro Circuit riders of a few days ago. Overall, I was really impressed with Lake Elsinore's multiple tracks. I silently wished that I had one of my motocross bikes strapped to the back of the Goose.

Our trip to Lake Elsinore ended as soon as it began. The sun was getting low, and I wanted to beat rush hour in San Diego. We piled on the Goose and took off south, back to Chula Vista. Brittany and I agreed to just hang around KOA for the evening and soak up another peaceful night of fireside entertainment. The dinner menu included a few delectable hot dogs, some savory salsa, and totally tasty tortilla chips. We called it a night when the last piece of splintery wood ran out of enough carbon to keep a flame.

Day 113 – February 3, 2012

KOA and my cramped Kelty tent had been home for the past three days. Brittany and I didn't need to head back to San Diego yet, but three nights of lying on the ground with no room to stretch out was good enough for us. Transporting our things back to San Diego required the same maneuvers made days before when we moved to Chula Vista. She was scheduled to leave on Tuesday of the following week, and I wanted to be close to the airport again when her day of departure arrived.

She and I mounted my trusty two-wheeled truck and headed north to San Diego in search of a cheap room that she claimed to have noticed advertised on the day of her arrival. Unfortunately, her lack of time in San Diego and vague memory of the motel's sign left us on a wild goose chase. I gave it a go at seeking out this mystery room, but that left us riding double around a tight city with confusing one way streets and cars zipping around everywhere. Checkout time at KOA was noon. Pressure was rising to find a place quickly, so that I could ride back to Chula Vista for the tent and remaining gear.

Once it became blatantly obvious that we weren't going to find the room she noticed on her first day, I decided to rely on good ol' Motel 6 again. This time it was a Motel 6 that was within easy walking distance of the Gaslamp District and a few blocks up the hill from the one we stayed at previously. She and I checked in, and I was off to KOA to grab the rest of our things.

I packed up and checked out of KOA with minutes to spare, saying farewell to the farthest south that I'd go in California. Back at the room we decided to head downtown for lunch. In the Gaslamp District, the House of Blues looked inviting enough. We took a seat inside along a bar in a large darkened room. We were the only paying customers. On the menu was a list of lunch specials going from top to bottom in the center of one of the pages. I ordered the street tacos with a house salad, not exactly knowing what street tacos meant. Brittany went after something with a slab of chicken between two slices of bread and fries on the side. The price for lunch was what one would expect for an area like that, so let me tell you about my bit of lunch, and I mean bit.

My imagination led me to expect three or four normal tacos and a salad disproportionately dominated by the cardboard of plants, lettuce. I was right about the salad, but horribly wrong about the tacos. What came out of that kitchen looked like a joke. Brittany and I looked at each other in shock once the two tacos arrived. Without exaggeration, these "things" looked like what would happen if a taco could take a number two. They weren't even as long as my pointer finger and less than halfway filled. At any 7-eleven you can buy four of these packed with beef for a dollar.

Let's make something clear. I've always been a country boy from the Appalachians and a lot more rough around the edges than any city-slicking, metrosexual, white-collar type. I've never had a manicure or pedicure, and never will. I don't wear anything pink or purple unless it's purple primer that has stained my hands from installing PVC pipe. It takes me less than ten minutes to suit up for any occasion, including weddings and funerals. I turn holey shirts into shop rags, and I wear shoes until they fall apart before I buy another pair. I'm like seventy percent John Wayne. So I don't know how folks around San Diego feel about dearly overpaying for food, but when I pay to eat, I expect a portion of food in front of me that matches the price requested.

To say that I'd been had was correct. I was another victim of an unrighteous rip-off. Normally I tip, and tip well, but in this case I felt as if I paid for two of those tiny meals and felt completely justified as I walked away without tipping. I know there are different cultures and different ways of doing things, which I embrace, but man, this lunch was crossing a line. I expect to at least have enough food on the plate to produce an aroma. A squirrel could have eaten those things and had room to spare. Now all of this complaining would not be appropriate if the price of the tacos was $2.50, but for the going rate of $12 for a salad made of lettuce and two micro tacos, I have the right to complain and will recommend from the saddle of my high horse that you avoid ordering the street tacos for lunch like they're the plague! Breathe in . . . Breathe out . . . You know the deal. . . .

We continued strolling around the Gaslamp District until dusk, taking in the sights—an old man pedaling a child-sized bicycle covered in party beads, American flags, images of Elvis, and wearing a white lab coat and huge sunglasses. We saw a sign arching over the street that read "Gaslamp Quarter Historic Heart of San Diego." It was, by now, no surprise.

We casually meandered back to the room. We were two blocks from the motel and about to cross an intersection. We had been following two men who stopped to speak with a lady friend; she may have been in her late forties. One of the men was an ancient fella, every bit of eighty-five years old, and the other man was in his fifties and probably the son of the older gentleman. The old man spoke respectfully to the woman in a gravelly wheeze that only a man his age can produce. He was wearing hiked up khakis, a button-down shirt, and suspenders. His body, from his mid-spine to his white head of hair, hinted that he may have been a heavy reader throughout life, always looking down at the newspaper in front of him. His upper back arched like a turtle shell, and his neck held his head out a foot farther than his best forward step.

Brittany and I were passing them on foot right as they were walking away from the polite chat with the nice lady. No more than five paces away, the ancient man strained his head up to look at his mid-fifties compadre and said, "She wants my body," with a shit-eating grin. *That son of a gun!* Brittany and I lost it. We laughed aloud. The old man looked at us and laughed too, knowing that he's still got it. He was a wiry old creature.

At the room, Brittany freshened up, I dropped the kids off at the pool, and we headed back out to McFadden's to relax over a couple drinks. Everything on the road and in life is not all rosy folks, as you are well aware. Brittany and I were enjoying each other's company until the conversation led to a disagreement and a little spat. It was one of those arguments where hours later you don't even remember what it was about. Being incredibly hardheaded, I lost my desire to be social, so as quickly as we got there we left and went back to the room for a much too early night.

Day 114 – February 4, 2012
Mission of the day—Find Anaheim. Watch Supercross. Return to San Diego.

Getting to Anaheim couldn't be simpler. Freeway 5 will take you from downtown San Diego practically to the stadium's entrance. We had all day to get there, so I decided to put some curves in the ride.

We gathered our things for the first leg of the trip. This part would take us from San Diego to Camp Pendleton in San Clemente. My new friends Bob and John, whom I met in Luckenbach, recommended a visit to the base. Sticking with their suggestion meant that I could share a picture of Camp Pendleton with them via the web. These two fellas had been in contact with me almost daily via email or my blog since I left Texas. Both went to school together, they became Marines together, were stationed at Camp Pendleton together, served in Vietnam together, and at sixty-five years of age, were still best friends, still having lunch together, and still sharing life's ups and downs.

Our visit to Camp Pendleton was short, sweet, and highly interesting. I'm not fully aware of proper on-base etiquette, so as I neared the entrance gate, I veered right into the visitor center parking lot at the last moment. I had not wanted to penetrate Camp Pendleton, only stop for a few pictures of the gate for the guys. As far as I knew, nothing inside was of any attraction to me like the Naval Air Museum had been in Pensacola. I parked the Goose between two white parking lot lines. Brittany hopped off. I whipped out the camera and began snapping a few pictures of the Camp Pendleton sign. Two serious-looking fellas approached us from the visitor center. One was a police officer, judging by his uniform, and the other was a soldier in full camouflage. They were not amused. Nervously, I handed over my ID. They questioned me up and down, and after feeling satisfied with my story, they lightened up.

The soldier soon returned to the visitor center, seeing that we were no sort of threat. Brittany and I were left standing by the Goose with the federal police officer, Officer Santos. He was in his forties, of Hispanic descent, and quick to smile. Our attention turned to talking about traveling through California. He spoke of how he loved to drive along California's scenic Route 395 with his family. I told him about wanting to ride it near Mt. Whitney a couple of weeks back, and he recommended that I should. Officer Santos mentioned that he could hook us up with his RV for a few days if we needed a place to stay. He turned out to be a great guy, and I didn't blame him at all for finding us suspicious. After all, it's not every day that a fella like me, with a wacky story, shows up and starts taking pictures like he owns the place. Next time I'll ask permission first.

From Camp Pendleton we veered off Freeway 5 for another sidetrack ride. It was barely past noon. The first qualifying races weren't scheduled to start until 7:00pm. I wanted to take Brittany along the coast to see the same perfect California shoreline towns that I'd seen on my way to San Diego. We headed for Laguna Beach via a maze of endless subdivision roads, always keeping the Pacific to the left of us. Bicyclists roamed these side streets like packs of Speedo-sportin' coyotes. They hindered traffic's progress with faces always stuck in serious workout mode. Nothing was gonna keep them from owning the right of way.

We found an overlook at the end of a cul-de-sac that displayed one of Laguna Beach's stretches of sand. Down below we saw a man walking into the ocean fiddling with his scuba mask, a huge rock formation holding a group of sea lions, energetic dolphins breaking the surface, and pristine homes sticking to the sides of steep cliffs. Behind us, the hills were speckled with homes of the lightest shades of color. Brittany said, "This is just like paradise." That was the reaction that I was looking for. It was genuinely nice to share some of this hard to describe beauty with someone. We could've gazed into the blue Pacific at that overlook all day, but we had to move on. Next stop, Anaheim.

In Anaheim we were after a late lunch and looking for something near the stadium. Unbelievably, Brittany mentioned Hooter's as we passed it. I did not hesitate to second that motion with, "Good choice Brittany!" Hooter's was located right behind Angel Stadium. This was my second time eating there and her first. She took my rubbernecking well, and for the most part it was a decent lunch. My Philly cheesesteak erased the memory of yesterday's tiny tacos. Brittany's order was a bit fudged up by our top-heavy waitress, but she survived. What else can you say about a lunch at Hooter's? For me, it was awesome. For Brittany, it was lunch.

Anaheim's Angel Stadium and its giant *A* in the parking lot are features in an urban landscape that I never thought I'd actually see. Being in their presence was no less than being in a dream world. We were about to witness Supercross at the tour's most famous stop. This is our sport's apex. Unlike the Los Angeles round at Dodger Stadium, the place was packed from the trackside to the bird's-eye view seats at the tippy top. I did not notice one empty seat all night. The series was shaping up to be yet another battle to the finish. Even the heavy favorites weren't a sure thing.

We found the lucky seats that would be holding our hind ends for the duration of the show. The track was covered in the stadium walls' shadow. A blue sky looked down on us, topping off the moment of perfection.

The track was moist and tacky. A few riders were wrapping up their practice sessions. They were all pushing hard for a fast lap time that would help them with qualifying later. When the sun moved on to shed light on another part of the world, Brittany and I glazed over in the pre-race laser light show. Music boomed from giant speakers. My heart turned into a piston, pumping adrenalized blood at 10,000 rpms. It felt as though we were at the world's largest pep rally. Stadium lights flicked on, and the track took the familiar evening look that is always seen on TV. We were ready.

On this night, the same young man who stood apart at Dodger Stadium took the win again in the 250cc class. He earned it without having to pull off a jump that no one else could do. He earned it the old-fashioned way, by getting a good start and putting his nose to the grindstone for fifteen solid laps. In the premier class, one of my two favorite riders took the win. He repeated a performance much like the one in the 250cc class, where from start to finish he stayed focused in first place. He was a fellow ginger, which made the night that much sweeter.

James Stewart, the rider from Haines City, Florida, took second. He was my favorite that night. In an earlier qualifying race, he went head over heels in the whoop section, causing him to lay motionless for twenty seconds. Sixty thousand people gasped in unison. Over the past couple of years, this has become a frequent occurrence in his racing career. He's a man like Sebastian Tortelli, who knows only one speed—fast. For riders like that, a career full of injuries is inescapable. Brittany thoroughly enjoyed her first Supercross, and I was again happy to see her reaction.

Then came the tough part. In front of us were 100 miles of freeway at night in consistently dropping temperatures. Neither one of us had prepared for it. We left that morning with thin jackets on but forgot to stock up on an extra set of pants. Brittany had on stretchy Capri pants with the insulating power of a birthday suit. I'd ridden hundreds and hundreds of miles in below-freezing temperatures to get to California and was never as cold as I was that night. With fair-weather jackets on, one layer of thin pants, chilly ocean breezes, and seventy-mph winds from the saddle of the Goose, we were punished by the cold.

We completed the trip in three sections. First, while we were still warm, we slammed out sixty miles. We stopped at a fuel station for ten minutes. Our knee caps and fingers could have been cut off and put in a cocktail as ice cubes. When the heat raised our core temperature enough, we took off again for two twenty-mile runs. Each one felt longer than the first sixty miles. Her legs and fingers were purple by the time we arrived at the glorious warmth of Motel 6 in San Diego. *Next time I'll know better.*

Day 115 – February 5, 2012

Superbowl Sunday began with a morning so uneventful that it's not worth wasting the energy needed for a set of eyes to move across a sheet of paper. An odd feeling that I'd left my life in West Virginia behind for a permanent stay at Motel 6 lingered for the briefest of moments. The feeling vanished quickly.

Our day really began as we headed to the Gaslamp District, again. After a late lunch at TGI Fridays, we strolled around until we found a suitable watering hole to watch the big game. Patrick's II was the name of the place. It had a dark, fine-wood-trimmed, decorative-tin-ceiling, with giant-mirror-behind-terraced-layers-of-liquor-bottles barmosphere. Only a few tables were open. Brittany and I planted roots at one that shared a long, padded bench along the back wall. If we'd known that Patrick's II would be serving free food throughout the game then Brittany could've saved the $20 she just spent on lunch.

Most folks, stateside, watched the Superbowl, so there is absolutely no need for a recap from a motorhead, but I do have a few comments. I'm just going to add that I was rooting for the Patriots, and I'm sure that's why the Giants won. Sorry to all of the Patriots fans. The commercials were funny again, and anytime Clint Eastwood is thrown in the mix, serious commercial or not, I'm happy.

Patrick's II's restroom featured a chalkboard above the urinal with an abundance of little pieces of broken chalk. My first visit to the pisser that day introduced me to said chalkboard. In a state brought on by a pitcher and a half of beer, I sloppily drew the outline of West Virginia. It kind of looked like a turkey with no legs and an arrow sticking out of its back, but it had the general shape. That was it. I felt no need to label it. Upon returning to relieve the pressure later on, my drawing was modified, not disrespectfully, but amusingly. One of the other gentlemen who visited that urinal had a stroke of genius when he recognized the shape of the state, became briefly inspired, and labeled it Hawaii! I laughed so hard I almost couldn't pee. I corrected my confused contributor's error by putting a big *WV* right in the middle of the drawing. By the time I reached California I was no longer surprised by what little knowledge my fellow Americans had about my home state. By the time we left, my drawing of West Virginia had grown a pair of tits and a furburger (not by the hand of me).

The game ended along with our fourth pitcher of beer. From Patrick's II, we roamed the happy streets from bar to bar. We happened to meet a fellow West Virginian, my first of the trip. His last name was the same as Brittany's. We mentioned the joke about the family tree with no branches. He smiled a knowing smile. West Virginia may bear the burden of more inbreeding jokes than any other state in the country. His hometown was in the south central part of our state in Kanawha County. That area of the state is quite a different world from the yuppy-ized Eastern Panhandle that I'm from. He was in San Diego serving our country via the Navy. We shared a drink and wished him luck.

Then it was off to another place, where a fella tried to trick me into buying him a drink. I laughed in his face and told him that I'm homeless. He didn't pester me anymore after that, and I didn't lie. The bartender there hooked Brittany and me up with a couple of free shots of whiskey with a strong cinnamon flavor (dangerous stuff). I'd love to tell you where we were and back it up with intricate details, but by golly, I don't remember.

Finally, like two heat-seeking hillbillies, we found the only country bar in the Gaslamp District. There was plenty of twangy music, a mechanical bull, and a decent atmosphere; it was almost like home. Our time there was short and sweet, at least I think. A few guys tried to wrangle in Brittany but backed off. It didn't ruin the night, though. We had fun, and that capped off another successful Superbowl Sunday.

Day 116 – February 6, 2012

Did anyone keep track of the drink count on day 115? If you did, then you know I was in for a world of trouble. When I awoke, a splinter under the fingernail would have felt wonderful. This one, folks, could have been the mother of all hangovers, the hangover that all the others evolved from.

I was wearing the crown of pain, the cape of queasy, the noose of nausea, the snare of sickness, the vomit helmet, the nightcap bile sack. I was riding the swelled-brain puke train, swimming in the poisoned-liver liquor river, kickin' the kidneys in the kisser, dancing with the Duchess of Dizzyville, fighting the 'itis, watching the room spin around and around again, moaning, groaning, green around the gills, taking a ride on the helpless side, begging for mercy, begging for forgiveness, begging for answers, and begging for a cure. The Hangover Fairy had punched me in the face with brass knuckles. *That bitch!*

All of it was topped off by feeling like a hypocrite. I had binged again. *When will I ever learn?* On the bright side, when someone else foots the bill for the beverages, I don't let 'em go to waste. It's a respect thing, ya know?

The whole day was completely unproductive. Somewhere around two in the afternoon, Brittany and I rode eight grueling miles to Lolita's Taco Shop. Lolita's came to me as a recommendation from the young bartender I met in Williams, Arizona, at Twister's. She said that while in San Diego I *had* to eat a California burrito at Lolita's. Since this was our last day in the area, I wanted to follow through with my promise. Brittany and I found the place in Kearney Mesa, ordered a couple of California burritos and obliterated each one.

Our guts were primed and ready for sustenance that contained carbohydrates and lacked alcohol. The only thing worse than being hungover is being hungover with an empty stomach; the intense urge to vomit increases. I'm not sure if it was an off day at Lolita's or not, but our burritos were loaded with way too many French fries, making them really dry on the palate. Meat and sour cream was also scarce for that matter. Perhaps they were making them differently, or perhaps the bartender who recommended them was tipsy when she ate one, giving her a better impression of the burrito. We left there fighting off a serious food coma. The burritos were massive but plainly lacked flavor.

A few hours later, Brittany suggested we try Ghirardelli's Chocolate Shop one last time before leaving San Diego. A few days before, we were blown away by their awesome ice cream. She ordered another huge chocolate cone, and I busted out a banana split. Amid a sugar rush, we headed back to the room for an early night and some much-needed rest. I couldn't take anymore.

Day 117 – February 7, 2012

Time for Brittany to leave San Diego came after nine pleasant days. We had plenty of fun on her dime, and I was thankful for it. My dimes, on the other hand, were running out fast. My total monetary worth had sunk below $1,000. Two bills were scheduled to be automatically withdrawn from my checking account in a few days. When that happened, I'd be down another $308.49. Not counting each month's automatically withdrawn bills, I had managed to spend over $9,000 on the road.

During our stay in San Diego, I searched the classifieds and gained a small feel for the area. Even though I found a dream job listing from Alpinestars Motorcycle Gear—and was in Southern California, the mecca of motocross—I didn't want to take another random job to get by. The dream job at Alpinestars would've been perfect for me, and I would've been perfect for it. They were looking for a rider rep who loved the sport of motocross, was knowledgeable, and could travel to the races on their own to make sure that the professional riders sponsored under their brand were supplied properly with Alpinestars gear and all other needs filled. There may have been more to it, but that's how I interpreted the information on the job listing.

Now if, and this is a big if, my family lived in Southern California, I would've gone for it lock, stock, and barrel. However, I saw no point in taking a position that would keep me away from them for years, no matter what the perks were. Family is the number one *perk* in life.

Other thoughts had been on my mind. I knew that I could pull off a minimum wage job to get by and make the trip last a year or more, if I remained in one place for a while, but that wouldn't be any fun. Saving money for travel while paying for a place to live in Southern California wouldn't be fruitful enough to continue another half or quarter year of travel later in 2012. In my heart, I just wanted to travel nonstop until the cash flow dripped dry. I unquestionably loved what I was doing.

Then there was the third option. I could have just given up hope for any foreseeable travel or employment and joined the homeless guys hanging around the outskirts of Motel 6's parking lot, or pitched my tent under a nearby overpass with the dozen other folks living in tents and calling it home. I could have panhandled when times were really bad. On days that I was clean enough, I could've sat for hours in a library or McDonald's searching for an open couch on Couchsurfing.com. This option entered my mind long enough to weigh. I had a tent, clothes, and basic supplies. In the end, that just isn't the way I am.

So, what comes next? There was one thing, one glorious thing that I needed to see before returning home, the one thing that I'd always declared to anyone who asked as the thing I looked forward to seeing the most on my journey—the redwoods! I told Mom before leaving, "No matter what, I won't return home before I see the redwoods." I found myself hovering at just enough money to make it to Northern California, where the ancient giants live, and back home. I became incredibly excited that it was finally time to see those awesome trees!

All I had to do was ride up there. That gets me back to the morning when Brittany was scheduled to take off. We started the day like any other. We packed for her departure at 12:41pm, and I finished up a bit of writing. Knowing where I was headed, without her, had me full of mixed emotions. Brittany and I agreed to find her a cab to get her and her things to the airport, since I had an extremely long day of riding planned.

A yellow taxi pulled to the curb as we stood outside. A slight drizzle accompanied the mood. The time was just past 11:00am. She was already tearing up. I hugged her and gave her a kiss to try to comfort her. I helped her lift her things into the taxi—the heavy bag of clothes, her girly tool bag full of blow dryers and makeup and personal items, and finally, the helmet that she had borrowed from a friend to bring to California because she wanted to see me and ride on the Goose. She stepped off the curb and into the car. I closed the door and reached in for one last hug and another kiss. She was crying. I told her that I'd be home in a couple of weeks, but knew that there was little comfort in my words. She and the cab driver rolled out of sight.

I stood there silently for a second. My rain gear was keeping me dry, and the excitement for the day's adventure kept my eyes dry. I knew that we would be a couple again when I got home. I threw a leg over the Goose and studied the map in my tank bag. It displayed a long, northwesterly path to the redwoods that I wanted to see, 848 miles north, near Crescent City, California. This time, unlike the first time we parted ways in Lexington, Virginia, I didn't feel fear for the uncertain road ahead. I didn't feel alone. This time I was ready to go. Nine days of being stationary in a city proved to be more than I needed to get motivated to leave the concrete behind. I had told Brittany that that I would try to do all 848 miles in one day. My motto is "set very high goals and reach high results."

I stayed on Freeway 5 for most of the trip, passing through the San Joaquin Valley. It's the giant agricultural hub of California located north of Los Angeles and east of San Francisco. Completely flat farmland lined either side of the freeway. When I gazed farther in the distance, along some sections in the great valley, I noticed mountain ranges paralleling the road. A big mixed up sky loomed overhead. Dark clouds mixed with peaceful puffy ones. Some points during the ride through the valley reminded me of rural farmland that I rode through in Mississippi. It was strange to see folks working the fields and planting in February. Honeybee hives were strategically stationed at orchards' edges. Fruit trees were in bloom, massive fields of sprouts were poking through the rich soil, and thousands of acres of grapevines kept me entertained.

The few Californians I met through here were incredibly friendly. If not for the nice change from the concrete of the city, the ride through the valley would have been mind-numbing. It was, after all, dead straight. The only turns I made for a couple hundred miles were the ones I made to exit for fuel, which I did four times throughout the day. I'm sure the Goose's gas mileage would've been stronger if I kept it at a lower speed, but I was trying to make as many miles as possible before dark. Rain came and went like turning a light on and off. I got wet, dried, got wet again, and kept riding. The wind and the four-cylinder hum combined to make a sublime rhythm.

The race with the sun was an inevitable loss, given such a lofty goal. I had never tried for that many miles before. By the time I made it through San Francisco, I had consumed three Monster Energy drinks. It was well after 8:00pm. The caffeine kick wore off, leaving me crashing hard. I yawned in my helmet repeatedly, each time making tears blur my already bad night vision. Focus on the task at hand dissipated. I pointed at the town of Santa Rosa, thirty something miles north of San Fran on my map, and made that the new goal. The night was as dark as a closet, but the rain had stopped. After 9:00pm I found another Motel 6 in Santa Rosa. I had learned not to even look for a campground in California because it wasn't going to save me any money. I hit the sack exhausted, yet happy. Over five hundred miles of road had passed beneath the Goose since San Diego.

Day 118 – February 8, 2012

Throughout the night I had the kid-waiting-for-Christmas-morning syndrome. I studied the unadorned flatness of the ceiling for hours in the dark, waiting for morning to come. Knowing that the coming day's ride would take me to the giant redwoods of Northern California—coupled with three energy drinks engulfed while pounding out the miles from San Diego—made it nearly impossible to sleep. Unless you plan to have a bloody, neck-biting night out with the vampires, don't drink energy drinks after 7:00pm. I arose both fatigued and stoked for one of the most epic days of riding ever.

In ultra-common fashion, I left my room early for breakfast, coffee, and Wi-Fi. I was way too drowsy to want to turn a search for food and Wi-Fi into a difficult task. I wound up in McDonald's with a 1350-calorie plate full of breakfast delight, a large coffee, and an open laptop in front of me. Old folks, out for their morning coffee and gossip, kept one eye on me as I typed away. When we made eye contact, I smiled. Some of them just held a suspicious stare. For an hour I forced words together to tell yesterday's story then hit the publish button. The day was really about to begin.

The stroke of 10:00am saw me packed up and heading through the most wonderful wine country toward Jenner, California. Yellow wildflowers grew beautifully among rows of last year's fruitful grapevines. The morning sun in a blue sky shone brightly against the bald, dewy vines, making them shimmer back into the sky. I was stopped abruptly three times crossing places like this. Like California's incomparable coast, I had found wine country to match.

Before long, that region gave way to larger hills full of conifers. Among them, I gained my first taste of redwood forests. I was taken aback at how dense and dark they were. Even the trees with rather thin diameters were incredibly tall. Small homes were enchantingly tucked off the road. Everything was damp—the pavement, the forest floor, the air. I liked where this was going. I twisted and turned further and further toward the ultimate boundary.

Then, my quick taste of the redwood forests took a break as the Pacific's rugged coastline burst onto the scene. I pulled rapidly to the shoulder. Right where I had popped out of the woods, the Russian River was emptying into the mighty Pacific, and the waves were so aggressive that they seemed to push the freshwater back upstream, almost angrily rejecting it. Sea lions rested on a sandbar, outwardly oblivious to the colossal waves pounding the rocky shore nearby. I wasn't oblivious to any of it. These were the tallest waves that I'd ever seen. When they broke they thundered. Whitewater defied gravity. I was scared of them from the road surface, a hundred feet up. The Pacific was alive here, like an animal backed into a corner, ready for a fight. The coastline was wild, jagged, and perfect. A captivating, foggy, wet paradise, it was. I was destined to hug the coast for 150 miles north.

The next five miles were spent stopping repeatedly to snap pictures. It was all so new. Breaths of ocean air filled my lungs to capacity with excitement. Ultimately, I had to force myself to just get on with it. I set a goal of making it to Fort Bragg before I allowed myself to stop for photos again. I broke that rule once or twice where sections of terrain seemed unreal, but I made decent progress. I stopped for lunch in Fort Bragg at Jenny's Giant Burgers. It was a small burger stand facing the Pacific with a semi-blocked view. This gave my aching back a break and let me fuel up for the next hundred miles. Fort Bragg was perhaps the least pretty town along that part of California's coast, but that came with being the largest as well. Smaller, more storybook-like towns sparked my imagination. Fort Bragg was more normal. To its credit, I can only think of one town prettier than it in my whole state.

The next forty miles displayed stunning, grassy mountains trapped against an unending assault from the Pacific's arsenal of waves. Beauty aside, those hills were also home to the most fortunate cattle on the planet. Every so often, I would round a corner and find a stocky black cow grazing right above my head in a steep rolling pasture. I was fully aware that the cattle never sat around and pondered their existence along that remarkable stretch of road, but a part of me hoped that they would take a second once in a while to lift their heads and look around at their majestic surroundings. Unlike the cattle that I saw yesterday in the San Joaquin Valley, cruelly crammed together on a muddy farm, these cattle had it made.

After Westport, Route 1 took a hard right and left the Pacific Coast for dense forests. Again, like earlier in the day, I was surrounded by tall redwoods but not massive ones. The road twisted and turned through the mountain for twenty-two miles. I stopped in a sharp corner for a perfect 180-degree, wide-angle picture. Across the road and to my right, a large boulder sat close to the shoulder and was surrounded by thin redwoods. It may have been eight or nine feet in diameter and equally as tall. I really paid it no mind, but later upon re-viewing the picture I realized that it was no boulder at all. It was the stump of a giant redwood, decayed and covered in ferns. Having no experience around trees that size made me blind to even thinking about the possibility that it used to be an enormous redwood. My first piece of a giant redwood was right in front of me and I had completely missed it. To spot it in the photo was quite a revelation.

On I went through damp forest roads until the tiny village of Leggett advertised something that brought the Goose to a screeching halt. It was a sign: "Drive-thru Redwood 1/4 mile away." How the hell could I resist? I veered off my intended route to seek out the giant. That quarter mile was one of the most exciting of my life.

A gravel road led me to a ticket booth surrounded by a grove of redwoods larger than any I'd seen yet. They were as fat as the oldest sycamores growing along the Shenandoah, but a hundred feet taller, and there were lots of them. I paid the happy lady working the booth $3 to continue on.

The gravel road dead ended at something that looked more fairy tale than real. It was the biggest tree I'd ever seen, by three or four times. It was glorious. I couldn't take my eyes off it. The top was clean out of sight, but the first 280 feet or so were clearly visible. It was everything that I hoped it would be and more. Fascination overwhelmed me. *How can something like this exist?* It was as otherworldly as if I had walked into a room where Bigfoot was shaking hands with an alien. I was speechless. The moment was spiritual. The tree dwarfed everything around it. High in its branches, I imagined an unknown world existing. "What's up there?" I whispered. I wanted to go for a look.

They called this wonder of nature Chandelier Tree. It was 315 feet tall, twenty-one feet thick, and 2,400 years old. It had stood strong for about thirty-one human lifetimes before some folks in the thirties decided to hack out a tunnel to make it a drive-thru tree. I would've paid more than $3 to see the tree without the tunnel. Now it has stood for another human lifetime with a 6' x 6' hole at the base of its trunk. There's no way to change what happened, and I'm happy that they didn't fell the tree for lumber, as was the fate of so many others its size.

And since the thirties, hundreds of storms have come and gone and threatened the magnificent tree without toppling it. Chandelier Tree was a prime example of redwood resilience. *How long it will stand from here on out? I hope it outlasts me.* Seeing this one tree made every single mile ridden worth it.

My stay at Chandelier Tree was bittersweet. A sinking sun forced me to make tracks. I didn't want to travel through the surprisingly remote region in the absence of light. For having the highest population of any state in the nation, I was amazed yet happy to find so much of California filled with wilderness. The goal was Humboldt Redwoods State Park, forty-five miles north. On the ride there, the sun disappeared quickly, with the help of the mountains and giant trees. I was destined to set up camp in the dark, again.

I made it to Myers Flat, California, pulled off Freeway 101, and looked for the campground. With no luck the first time, I went back to town to get directions. I learned that if I had ridden a bit farther I would've found the campground. When I finally made it to my destination, it was pitch black, and giant wooden silhouettes surrounded me. I set up my tent, crawled in, and looked forward to daybreak and another chance to see the wonderful trees.

Day 119 – February 9, 2012

Today was the day I had patiently waited for, the day where I would do nothing other than bask in one of our planet's greatest treasures, the day where I would walk hand to branch with giant redwoods. It was time to take it all in.

A dark, secluded morning greeted me at Humboldt Redwoods State Park. The forest was quiet except for a bird here and there. Drops of water fell from high above to slap the coniferous blanket that covered the campground. The black silhouettes of last night gained shades of brown and green in the early morning light. Young redwoods surrounded me, shooting needle-like and arrow-straight into puffy canopies high above. Again, I barely managed a wink of sleep.

Through tossing and turning, I just couldn't get comfortable no matter what position I tried. The outside temperature was in the upper fifties, making my sleeping bag just necessary but a little too warm. I hadn't had a pillow since leaving it behind in Corona's Motel 6. When I bought my pillow, I made the mistake of not buying a pillow case. It took no time for that thing to grow a smelly environment of its own, so I tossed it. If you've ever tried to ball up some clothes and use that as a pillow, then you'll know how firm the folded material feels and the discomfort experienced from that. My neck was cramped and contorted all night while I hunted for a soft spot, one that wouldn't smash my ear. Getting out of the tent and moving around felt great.

My body was tired, but my mind was stimulated and eager to share the Chandelier Tree experience with the folks following along. Coffee, Wi-Fi, a post, and pictures sounded like a perfect start to a perfect day. There was no doubt that somewhere in these remote hills I could find steaming water dripping over a mound of crushed coffee beans and exchange it for money, but the thought of finding Wi-Fi almost made me laugh to myself. Undeterred, I left the campground in search of both.

I traveled south on Route 101 to the town of Miranda after unsuccessfully finding neither coffee nor Wi-Fi in tiny Myers Flat. Miranda was typical for this region: small, sleepy, encased in evergreens, foggy, and beautiful. I rode into town with neutral hopes. Along the main drag, a shed had been converted into a small organic coffee stand. It was yellow, dotted with signs advertising its other goods, like pastries and smoothies, and was as convenient as can be.

While ordering the coffee, I asked the gals serving it if there was any place even remotely close to Miranda that would have Wi-Fi, expecting them to laugh and say "Are you serious?" They said the market right across the street had it. *Excellent.* I headed for the market, bought a muffin and a Slim Jim for breakfast, and inquired about the Wi-Fi. As I'd learn, Miranda had a plan where you could purchase Wi-Fi for $2 a day and use it as long as you remained close by. Miranda Market didn't have any seats, so I popped the Goose up on the center stand, whipped out the ol' laptop, put it on the tank bag, and wrote as fast as I could. I had trees to see.

From Miranda, I backtracked to Humboldt State Park's visitor center. There I asked where the biggest of the big trees were located. A nice, older lady could see that I wasn't messing around. She knew that I was here to gawk, and gawk hard. She directed me to Founder's Grove, four miles up the road. I thanked her for her time and scurried off, in search of the behemoths.

Founder's Grove is a dense cluster of gargantuan redwoods. Here at Humboldt Redwoods State Park, Founder's Grove is a portion of Rockefeller Forest, which contains more old-growth coastal redwoods than anywhere on the planet. A group of concerned folks recognized the value of this small tract of land that had escaped logging, prompting them to establish a committee based on protecting this grove of redwoods.

Their actions represent an awareness that things need to change. Stands of old-growth redwoods are incredibly rare now, thanks to logging. Like lions, giant redwoods are facing a similar degree of peril. Shamefully, we've managed to saw, chop, and hack our way through ninety-six, NINETY-SIX percent of the magnificent old-growth redwood forests, just for a quick dollar, all the while neglecting to give two shits about the thousands of years required for a redwood to grow so large. It's pitiful what we've done. I swear, we're going to going wipe out everything that's cool about this planet and replace it with everything that's corporate. Thankfully, they're not all gone. They are as hearty as a plant can be. They are fire resistant, have burls growing from their trunks to sprout new life if they should fall, and have stood the test of time.

Founder's Grove, a place full of tremendous wonder, sat before me. I could already see what was coming. Giants loomed as thick as wooden silos, so dense that sections of the forest looked walled off. I was ready for the experience. The Founder's Grove trail was an easy, mulch-covered trek not so deep into the forest. It was about a half mile and had more than enough huge trees to keep me entertained. The sign at the trailhead read "Trail .53 miles Time 30 minutes." It took me over two hours to complete.

The giants in Founder's Grove were too spectacular to pass with a mere glance. I wanted to get a feel for them, and yes, on more than one occasion, I hugged them. There was one massive specimen of a tree in Founder's Grove that dwarfed the others. The monster's name was the Dyerville Giant. It seemed otherworldly with its unimaginable circumference. Here's the kicker, though. It was lying on its side. The Dyerville Giant fell in 1991, and at that time it was the world's tallest tree at 370 feet. Imagine that! Walking the length of the Dyerville Giant was like walking beside a huge, round wall. You've got to see it to believe it, so everyone pack your things and go see the redwoods. I can only say so much about their splendor. I hope they stand forever.

My hike through Founder's Grove ended, and I headed back to camp. It was already getting dark, but I had time for another half-mile hike with a trailhead beginning across the street from the campground. Like in Founder's Grove, a ton of giants—each one with its own unique majesty—grew here. I stayed in that part of the forest until dark, soaking up as much of the redwoods as possible.

Walking the trail near the campground and through Founder's Grove opened my eyes to something I thought silly prior to stepping foot near such large trees. I don't claim to be one who believes in Sasquatches, but I may have changed my mind here in Humboldt County. As I walked quietly along wide mulch paths, the forest's wide trees jostled my imagination. I thought of how incredibly easy it would be for a Sasquatch to hide here. The undergrowth was riddled with bushy ferns, young redwoods, and fallen trees. Wandering off the path for any short amount of time could lead to quick disorientation. Looking deep into the forest was impossible. Even the broadest shouldered beast could quickly duck or side step behind a tree, going undetected. A moose could stand broad way on the opposite side of a large redwood and not be visible.

I imagined myself roaming a few yards into the forest and hiding out of sight of any roaming tourist. It would have been too easy. A Sasquatch, knowing the forests well, could laugh at a man like me who walks by clueless. Humboldt County's large size and somewhat low population density could allow a Bigfoot to roam quite freely without someone always breathing down its neck. Conversely, it's hard to imagine one hiding so well under the cover of the Appalachians' thin trees. Can you picture a Sasquatch trying to hide behind a tree that is two feet wide with both of his shoulders sticking out on each side? Whether they exist or not, I walked amazed at my surroundings, and nervously kept an eye out for a stout, hairy biped looking back at me. At sunset I was off to the nearby town of Myers Flat for some grub.

Myers Flat was even smaller than Miranda. Upon entering town, I noticed a sign that said "Myers Flat elevation 204 population 200." I couldn't put my finger on where everyone was, though. A ride through gave you a glimpse of a saloon, a general store, a drive-thru tree, and a residence or two. I grabbed some food at the market and stopped in at the saloon for just one beer. This was to be my celebratory beer for concluding the length of the journey before returning home. I had a Corona. The folks that ran the place offered me a huge bowl of beans and rice, which I accepted and thanked them for, and they even gave me a large jar for the road. The folks in Northern California were absolutely great. They acknowledged me and wanted to talk. They were extremely welcoming and looked happy in their rural setting. As a whole, California had shown me an abundance of friendly people, but without question I now had my favorite part of the state nailed. It was just like home, but with bigger trees. I liked Myers Flat. It was the middle of nowhere surrounded by somewhere special. *I wish I had the money to bunk down and find work here for a few months.*

My day ended with another cold shower from one of California's state parks. One would imagine that paying $35 to pop a tent up and a dollar for the shower itself, that the shower would at least be warm. The cold showers are tied with those tiny tacos in San Diego as the biggest rip-off known to man.

Day 120 – February 10, 2012

For the third night in a row I managed a solid three hours of sleep. This time caffeine had nothing to do with it, nor did comfort. Around eight o'clock last night, a group of happy vacationers rolled into the campground in their RV and partied it up until the wee hours of the morning. They kept the music slightly shy of the volume of their loudest talker. Belly laughs and drunken stories went on for hours. I was lying on my back waiting for one of them to give. Usually when one calls it quits, in a gathering as small as theirs, some others will follow. But they kept at it. They weren't as annoying as the young couple bickering at Malibu Creek State Park, so I didn't bother to say anything. "To each their own," I thought as I patiently waited in the darkness of my tent—so little and incapable of blocking noise.

It began to rain and they were chased inside. The drops were large and consistent and pounded the top of the tent with heavy splats. This kept me awake even longer, not because of the noise, but because of the constant reminder of the long day of wet riding that was in store. Sometime barely before 4:00am, I fell asleep. My eyes reopened at 7:00am. The rain was steady. I skipped the chance to take another lovely, cold shower. Instead, I vigorously packed, then started the Goose and let that baby idle real high on choke for a bit, hoping to stir at least one of my new campground neighbors. As I rode past their RV, I blipped the throttle a couple times to let them know I was leaving and to thank them for the wonderful evening.

I was headed home. For 118 days, I crossed the southern United States, taking my time and enjoying life. Beautiful Humboldt County was the end of the line. Everything had been so perfectly unscripted, so unexpected, and so fulfilling. At home, a new life awaited me. I'd have a fresh start with a clear head. Some of the demons that had haunted me had been burnt off. I'd learned that I can survive with much less, learned that the world is dominated by good-natured people, and learned that there's no place like home, but many worth visiting. All I had to do was get there. I planned to retrace my steps at a high pace, spending more for fuel daily than anything else, hoping that I'd have enough money to make it to the East Coast.

Being on a motorcycle in February limited my options for how I'd get back. I studied the map. If it were summer, I'd do a sweeping arch through Oregon, Idaho, Montana, the Dakotas, Minnesota, Wisconsin, Michigan (by way of the upper peninsula), Ohio, and West Virginia, spending most my time on Interstate 90. That was out of the question. I had seen pictures of Igor and the crew driving the Ford Flex through Montana. Snow dominated every outdoor photo.

South of that route, I looked at a straight shot across the country with the far western portion being on Interstate 80, and picking up Interstate 70 in Utah. Again, I thought it better to look for an alternate. Like the northern route, to get home I would have to cross the ultimate speed bump, the Rocky Mountains.

I'm not the best decision maker, but February didn't feel like the right month for that. If I had made it over them, the flatness of eastern Colorado and Kansas, combined with the steady, cold wind, probably would have driven me nuts. So, it looked obvious. I'd head south, swoop under the southern tail of the Rockies, and rely on the measurably warmer Interstate 10 for most of ride east. I looked forward to crossing the United States again.

Time to make miles had arrived. Mile one passed. It was a rainy mile. I was on the Avenue of Giants and still two miles from reaching Myers Flat. Mega redwoods grew on each side of the shoulder and disappeared into the forest. Mile ten passed. It was raining. The quaint town of Miranda was a memory. I was on beautiful Route 101, curving through endless coniferous forests. On mile eighty, I stopped for a morning snack in Willits. The dense forests— loosely dotted with enchanting homes tucked away in permanent shade—were still there on the outskirts of town, but giving way to urbanism. The vendors making a living on wooden carvings of Bigfoot, Sasquatch souvenirs, and the like were long gone. The parking lot at the fuel station in Willits was wet and shiny like it had polyurethane spilled all over it.

Many drizzly but beautiful miles followed, through and then out of redwood territory. I stopped for fuel in Cloverdale at Golden Gate Gasoline, a house converted into a fuel station. I was 128 miles closer to home. At 202 miles down the Redwood Freeway, or the 101, it was still raining and I was within spitting distance of San Francisco. The toes on my left foot were frozen, my rain gear had done a decent job, and on the horizon I could see a break in the clouds. The storybook towns of Northern California—their foggy mornings, their striking forests, and friendly country folks—were now memories. I never thought that Northern California would be so rural. Until I set foot in California, my imagination always took me straight to the heavily populated southern coast.

Passing San Francisco left me longing for more money. I enjoyed seeing its tallest buildings create a ghostly cityscape. I liked knowing that the Golden Gate Bridge was just over yonder. I promised myself that I'd visit sometime in the future. For now, I settled for being just another passerby.

The great valley, the central valley, the San Joaquin Valley was approaching fast. I didn't want to ride through it again, but it was the most direct route to Interstate 10 East. The boredom associated with its long, straight stretches had not worn off from my earlier ride through. Other than having its pretty farming sections full of various fruit and nut trees, not much happened. I was startled once while fighting off highway hypnosis.

My hand was locked steady on the right grip, the Goose was humming along around seventy mph, and the ride was easy and dry. From out of no-where, two Hells Angels, with massive circular patches on the rear of their leather jackets, flew by me with uncorked Harleys. They were easily at three-digit speeds. One of the Harleys had a rear tire that wandered back and forth rapidly like the tire had broken cords or the bike wasn't set up to handle speeds that high. Believe it or not, both guys raised an arm, waving two fingers split open in the peace sign fashion. I waved back, but they were too far gone to see it. In hindsight, I don't recall seeing any mirrors on their bikes.

Well after dark, I made 500 miles for the day as I reached the San Joaquin Valley's exit 253 and found a Motel 6 with a $35 room. I called my mom to let her know that I was on my way home.

Day 121 – February 11, 2012

Morning at Motel 6 came way too soon. For the fourth night in a row, I managed three hours of sleep. I was beyond exhausted. I knew for sure that I didn't fall asleep until after 5:30am. I woke at 8:39am. Tired, grumpy, and hungry, I began packing for another 500-miler. The goal for the day was at least the Arizona border, and at best, Phoenix.

Not much happened on the ride. I fueled up four times, pulled over when I spotted something neat enough to snap a picture of, like Pyramid Lake at the curvy southern end of the valley, or the populated fields of wind turbines east of San Bernardino, and kept pushing on. The best part of the ride happened in a fifty-mile section from Beaumont to Indio, California, when a healthy tail wind pushed the Goose along as easily as if it had two more cylinders. My gas mileage was the best it had been, and the wind buffeting was nearly silenced. That, my friends, is interstate paradise. Quiet and calm, I rode along wanting the tail wind to last forever. But it wasn't to be. My stint in the easy life ended when I neared Joshua Tree National Park and the wind started coming from the south with the same sort of force. My head went into bobblehead mode. The muscles in my neck ached from fighting constant misalignment.

The sun had given up on the day when Arizona's big blue, red, and yellow sign came into view. Phoenix was 135 miles away. The town of Quartzsite helped pass a few of those miles. Campers, buses, and trailer homes sat in the thousands, alone in the desert. I could see the ones closest to me, and the rest were strung about among a sea of lights fading into vast darkness. I rode past wondering what it must be like to live there. It was the most curious of settlements, looking nomadic like the old saying "here today gone tomorrow." I wondered if it was filled with folks stricken with poverty, or folks in retirement who like the trailer home life and remote location for its simplicity. I guess I may never know.

I made a final stop at a rest area along I-10; nothing terribly exciting happened there, but a small bit of humor lightened my mood. A trucker was hauling one of those double-stacked car trailers full of new Corvettes. I watched him walk around the truck, tug on the rigging, and stretch out a bit. Unbeknownst to him, as he took off and the truck lurched forward, the small bit of G-force created by the moving truck set an alarm off on one of the Corvettes. He rode away into the darkness unaware of the blaring alarm. I listened to the piercing noise grow softer and softer. I wondered just how long it would be before he realized what happened.

From there, I was riding solo until two fellas on motorcycles passed me. One was on a Honda Goldwing and the other a Harley. I fell into formation, and the two strangers and I rode together all the way to Phoenix. The night was dark, the air comfortable, and the pavement smooth. To either side, a black wall of desert emptiness snuffed out any view. I rode along, staring at the taillights in front of me, and listening to the wind. I wondered if the guys were riding together as buddies or had joined as a pair of motorcyclists on the highway the same way that I had joined in on their ride. I could've been the stranger in the group, or all three of us could've been strangers to one another and riding together knowing that it's safer that way.

In Phoenix, I checked into a room and prayed for a good night's sleep. In the past two days, I'd ridden 5,306,400 feet from Humboldt Redwoods State Park in Northern California to Phoenix, Arizona. That's 1,005 miles.

Day 122 – February 12, 2012

Heading home at a blistering pace set me up for a tremendously different daily schedule. I wanted to take my time, knock out a post, and do some sightseeing before nightfall like I was accustomed to, but my bank account was on E, and lurking in the near future was a real chance that I could run out of loot before returning home if I didn't crank out the miles. Still, I conquered one act of sightseeing for the day. But first. . . .

I awoke rested from a full night's sleep for the first time in five days! My mood was light. I was even feeling generous with a splash of practical. I wanted to shed some weight from my gear bundle. I made an easy decision to leave behind my comforter, camping pad, and medium-sized bottles of ketchup and mustard. The camping pad and blanket caught wind like nobody's business, and besides, I didn't foresee much camping from here to home. Total cost for both pieces was $28. Brittany could vouch for the absolute worthlessness of the camping pad. She woke up with bruises on her hips due to its poorly performing padding. The comforter was okay, just unnecessary. Losing it shed about two pounds of dead weight.

I left a note for the room service folks that said, "I no longer need this stuff. It is still in good condition, and the ketchup and mustard are practically unused. If you know of anyone in need please give it to them. Thank you." Then I was off again.

Less than a mile away, I stopped to fuel up and noticed one of Phoenix's homeless residents lurking at the fuel station. He was dirty, toting a suitcase full of God knows what, and dressed for Snowmageddon. He could have used my donation. If not for time, I would've backtracked to the motel, grabbed the stuff, and given it to the homeless chap myself. I hoped it didn't end up in the garbage.

Phoenix and Tucson were in the past. Wilcox, the place where I discovered Motel 6, was just ahead. I was back in Cochise County in southeast Arizona when a sign prompted a second chance. It was advertising *The THING*. A failed attempt on Christmas left me wondering what *The THING* looked like. I pulled off exit 322 again. This time the place was open. Just one dollar was required for access to three buildings full of bizarre exhibits, and of course, *The THING*.

I walked from one building to the next looking for it. Questionable artifacts were scattered about, as if to build up excitement. In the last building I found it, or them, or whatever it was. I looked down into a glass-topped, cinder block tomb to see two mummified individuals who had seen better days. *Are they real?* I put on my anthropologist hat. A lack of proper education in anthropology left me to guess. Each figure was dark grey in color and wrapped in highly decomposed clothing. Their eye sockets lacked any residual eye material, giving them large hollow holes in the face. The largest one—presumably the mother—was holding the other figure with one arm. She almost looked normal. The small figure was clearly more deformed facially. Its mouth was crooked and its body looked slightly out of proportion. It was about half the length of the large mummy. Both figures had quite a bit of mummified tissue left on their skeletons. Their skin was grey, coarse and tattered with the mother mummy displaying ribs through a hole in her chest. If they were real, then they were amazing. I just couldn't tell.

Visiting *The THING* was worth the price of admission. What else can you get for a dollar these days? Two other fairly interesting pieces were on display: a car said to have carried Adolph Hitler, and a carriage said to have carried Abraham Lincoln in his first inaugural parade. So there it is, *The THING*. Stop by for a visit.

On and on the miles went. Once, in a fit of frustration, I whipped the bike off an exit determined to eliminate the severe wind buffeting created by the windscreen. With no genius solution, I simply took the windscreen off. Then, I rode fifty miles hoping to realize an improvement. It surely cut back on the wind noise, but I felt like I was manning a parachute, therefore killing the fuel mileage.

I put the windscreen back on and just dealt with the constant abuse. My ears were still ringing hours after climbing off the bike. Even with earplugs in, it was punishing. The windscreen's height was perfect for creating a wicked air current that impacted my face shield. If I rose up off the seat two inches, the wind steadied and the noise decreased. Even attempting to listen to music was futile. The wind overpowered the effort of my tiny ear buds.

New Mexico came and went. A dust devil spun for an entertaining second, and crossing the state line still supplied the smallest of thrills, though I didn't know why. In Lordsburg, I stopped for a late lunch at Arby's. In Las Cruces, I veered south for a new stretch of I-10 toward Texas.

El Paso owned the horizon, and across the border from that, Juarez, Mexico. I stopped to fuel up at a BP station. A small set of bright brown eyes examined me suspiciously. They belonged to a young Latina. She may have been twelve at most. She was wearing a winter coat with white fur lining the hood. I took off my thick winter gloves and pumped the fuel, noticing in my periphery that she was sitting motionless, cross-legged, and locked in a concrete stare right at me. It was freezing out. She was alone, holding a sign that read "Please help my family. We are homeless and hungry. Anything appreciated." It tugged on me. I wanted to donate something whether the sign was a sham or not. No child should have to beg. Unfortunately, I barely had more money than a homeless person. I never know what to do in these situations, so I finished pumping and shot her a caring smile. She watched me ride away.

Interstate 10 gave a surprisingly clear view of Juarez. Its urban sprawl matched El Paso's in size. Where El Paso had nice restaurants and big hotels with bright street lights, Juarez had a mix of earth-colored buildings with thousands of dim yellow bulbs glowing in the early evening light. I collected as much detail as possible from the saddle of the Goose, knowing that I wouldn't be stopping for pictures. The border fence divided the two cities with fortress-like might. All of the negative press aimed at Juarez spurred me to wonder how long I'd last on the Goose, riding in those Mexican streets. Accounts from people I'd met along the way weighed on the opposite side of the spectrum. The construction foreman that I met in Big Bend said that it wasn't so bad there, and a white couple in their mid-twenties that I met in Big Bend had ridden through Juarez on their bicycles just weeks before. They were pedaling the entire US/Mexican border to raise awareness for the folks in need in those parts. They, too, said that Juarez wasn't as bad as the media claimed. My thoughts raced as I rode on.

Night fell quickly after leaving El Paso. I found myself again in that isolated void that is West Texas, where nothing changes from mile to mile and the landscape has all the excitement of a slab of cardboard. Interstate 10 hugs Mexico for fifty miles south of El Paso, then turns due east. I aimed for Fort Stockton, but landed in Van Horn. The rain, light snow, and freezing temperatures I experienced while crossing a steep mountain pass near the town of Sierra Blanca demotivated me to the core.

For miles, I rode with one hand on the grip and one on the engine until my fingers came back to life. My gloves and feet were wet, my vision nil, and my will gone. I was beat to a pulp and just wanted to get off the bike. The road was dangerously desolate. A crash here from an animal crossing or washout would have spelled certain doom. When Van Horn materialized, I could breathe again. Lights and civilization never looked so good. Five hundred and fifty long miles had passed since Phoenix. At 9:45pm, I checked into the most welcomed warmth of Van Horn's Motel 6.

Day 123 – February 13, 2012
Life's a funny thing. We often try to take it by the horns and force our will as intelligent beings on it. I've found that to be a waste of energy, though. The

horns of life obey fundamental rules that have been here since the universe began. Change is at the forefront of those rules. Randomness is in there somewhere as well, perhaps a close second. That's what I want to talk about. What's funny is how sometimes in the chaotic bag of life, events align perfectly as if planned without a finger on a horn.

I awoke with a very solid idea of what I was going to do all day: ride east on I-10 as far as my last bit of gas money would get me. That was it, until a random force intervened. I didn't spend much time online before checkout since I knocked out a post the night before, but before I took off, I checked my email one last time. Lo and behold, I received an email from my new good friends Don and Ginnie. They were planning to head west on I-10, and Don emailed me instantly once he realized that our paths would cross at some point during the day. I got the email just minutes before they left Sonora and I left Van Horn. We made a plan to meet in Fort Stockton, a midway point in our travels.

This is the time where I'd like to veer away from where I was going with that in order to try to confuse the pants off you while I babble on about ping-pong balls. I'll try to explain. Don, Ginnie, and I have kept in touch since camping in Big Bend, but I had no idea when or if I'd ever see them again.

Since the time we are born, our lives are ever-changing and—like a ping-pong ball that is whacked with a good solid swing—bouncing several times off whatever is in its path, our lives constantly ricochet off events or occurrences that randomly appear. Even the event of being born is not chosen. We are incapable of picking the circumstances into which we are born; from the beginning of life, randomness is in charge. After a solid impact and a few decent bounces and ricochets, we cannot predict the exact spot where a ping-pong ball will stop rolling.

Since the time I left Big Bend, and Don and Ginnie left Big Bend, we went our separate ways with plans to keep our plans. However, those plans—especially for me—changed all of the time. Life had thrown me many ricochets. The decision to not work in California and instead return home was one ricochet; going to Nor Cal to see the redwoods at the last minute was another; and receiving that email this morning was another. Interruptions to plans happen all the time. Like the ping-pong ball's final resting spot, I couldn't have predicted in a million years that I would see those wonderful people again on this trip. Change and randomness just happen, and sometimes the timing is perfect.

Back to the story. I packed my things and headed to Van Horn's nearest filling station. There, I phoned my bank's automated teller service to check my account after purchasing a Slim Jim, muffin, and soda for breakfast. The monotone female voice said, "Fifteen dollars and thirty-eight cents." I panicked. *This is it. I'm stuck.* My mind raced for a solution. The shame of knowing that I'd spent myself dry was too much for me to call my folks and ask for a handout, especially since just months before I had money like it was growing on trees. I called Brittany to see if she could run to the bank and put some money in my account. Fortunately, she had the time on her hands and gave me all that she could spare. With that, I fueled up and headed east 118 miles through Texas's empty desert to Fort Stockton. I knew that at the end of the day and after another fuel stop, I'd be flat broke.

Don and Ginnie showed up fifteen minutes after I made it to Fort Stockton. While waiting in the McDonald's parking lot, I met a fellow from Harrisburg, Pennsylvania. He had been on the road since October 31, 2011, and was doing a four corners tour of the United States on his Ural motorcycle. It was equipped with a side car and trailer full of gear. He had recently retired and had a wonderful spirit about him. He had been to a lot of the places I visited on the way west, giving us plenty of stories to share. Although he was older than I, he didn't let that hold back his enthusiasm. I mentioned the redwoods and he lit up like a kid. It was great. He positively couldn't wait to see them. He told me that he was on his adventure to see things that he'd waited a lifetime to see. I respected him immensely for going for it. He and I were living the dream in that moment. I snapped pictures of him leaving until he disappeared, wondering how it would all turn out for him.

Don and Ginnie pulled in directly after. I Goosed it over to their RV to greet them. It had been two months since I'd seen them, and this time greeting them felt like greeting family. Smiles were irremovable. Ginnie gave me a big hug, whereas in Big Bend we exchanged friendly hellos as kind strangers. Now we were friends without question. The stranger thing had vanished. Our consistent contact over the last two months paved the way for that.

They welcomed me into their RV for lunch. Ginnie whipped up some chili and stuffed pitas. The food hit the spot as a great prequel to the home cooking that I'd get once returning to West Virginia. Like with the persimmon they gave me in Big Bend, they again shared a piece of fruit with me for the road. This time it was a massive grapefruit that I saved for dinner. We spent a lot of time catching up, sharing stories, and generally enjoying the wholesome company. I was so fortunate to meet folks like them on the road and felt like I had gained family in other parts of the US.

After a bit, we moseyed outside where Don noticed the huge rip in my seat cover. He fished out a roll of black duct tape and went to work applying it without a wrinkle. It was a fix fit for a West Virginian king. Noticing that I was down to my last over stretched bungee, they replenished my supply and gave me the rest of the tape and a pair of sunglasses. The pair I was wearing had a missing right ear piece. Without asking, they went above and beyond generous by donating a gas card worth $50 and $120 in cash to help me get home on. I was speechless. It was something they had in the works. My pride would have never let me ask for such help.

They did not know that I woke up in Van Horn with a total of $15 to my name with no real idea about what to do (I'd never tell 'em). They didn't know about my panicking episode at the fuel station earlier, and they will never know how much I appreciate them. They were absolute life savers, heroes in my eyes, and friends for life. As for the timing, it was epic. Things were looking pretty hairy on the making-it-home front. Now, with their help, I could get a place to stay that night and have enough for something to eat for a couple days. I couldn't thank them enough. With daylight slipping away and many miles to go, we had to say goodbye for an uncertain amount of time. I was off again, heading east. That made my day. For the next 200 miles of high-decibel wind noise, I was smiling.

I shot for San Antonio, but settled in Kerrville, changing my mind after speaking to a friend. Tomorrow is going to be another great one!

Day 124 – February 14, 2012

Four months on the road. This rate of travel, coupled with this much sightseeing, seemed to slow life in the sense that looking back just a month or two fooled me into feeling like those experiences were years ago. An incredible amount of life had happened since Bridge Day, Oktoberfest, Key West, or Clarksdale. *A full year of this would feel like ten years of life.* Perhaps that's the key to eternal youth. Stop what you're doing, take off, experience and learn something new and exciting every day, and live for every last second.

I once heard a speech that described why time seems to speed up as we get older. The speaker described a basic rundown of an adult's day. He set aside the meaningful things that an adult would do daily, like spending time with family in the evening after work, or having lunch with an old friend. Then he focused on the other hours of the day, like the ones when you are at work plugging through the same old thing you did yesterday, or the ones when you are in traffic and wishing that you were home. He said those are the hours that the body and mind have experienced a million times. They are nothing new, and you generally learn nothing new, at least daily anyway. He called them the "autopilot" hours and unfortunately they're the ones we spend most of our days trapped in.

Autopilot hours are the reason we can look back ten years and say "Where has the time gone?" Ten years of fond memories become hard to recall when you spend most of your waking hours doing exactly what you did yesterday. (Then there are a few of us who love our jobs and have a short commute, but that's a whole other story.)

We don't come into this world knowing it all, but for survival's sake—whether it be survival in a high-tech society or a backwoods swamp town—we need to learn everything we can as quickly as we can. Therefore, as children our daily lives are packed with important moments that engage our minds, moments that often end memorably. Auto pilot can't take hold at this age because of things like school work, where there is always an increasing degree of difficulty to be overcome in each grade level and subject. We don't go to first grade and hear, "That's it. You know all you need to know. Welcome to the real world." We just keep learning. It's unavoidable.

Because we're so engaged in our school years, they seem to take forever to pass. Socially, a million things are going on as well. Situations can manifest quickly when several hundred folks share a building each day. Here, on the road, I've been living life like I was back in my school years with a stimulated brain that has been engaged in learning through navigating, feeling, sensing, social encounters, and creating new things. I especially liked the daily opportunity to be creative through photography and writing. Autopilot mode was left behind at the office on October 7. Now each one of my days felt like three. It was fantastic.

Day 124 would be another day like that, but bursting with relaxation. I was welcomed to step outside of my room at Motel 6 in Kerrville, Texas, by a warm, bright, blue-sky day. *T-shirt weather in February.* Last night I called my buddy Bob, and he arranged to pick up John in the morning at his place near Houston and meet me at Luckenbach around lunchtime. These were the fellas I met on my way west at Luckenbach. They had followed along diligently as if riding in formation with me. I'd get an email almost daily from one or the other, commenting on a place they'd like to see, or recommending something I had to see along the way. I looked forward to meeting them again. I looked forward to seeing Luckenbach again.

The distance from Kerrville to Luckenbach is thirty miles. After roughly 2,000 miles in four days, my hind end welcomed the short ride. I stopped for breakfast and fuel at one of Kerrville's service stations. Two guys, both dressed for work and sitting down on the curb, casually talked with me for a few minutes while I ate. They asked about the Goose, noticing the stickers and the oversized bundle of gear. I gave a basic rundown of the ride and told them how much I liked Texas. It was nothing more than friendly BS'ing. Then we said farewell and I headed for Luckenbach.

With time to spare, I turned a thirty-mile ride into an hour. On the broad country roads in Texas it's common practice to move to the shoulder to let someone pass if you aren't going the speed limit. I moved over for at least a dozen folks who were making their way to Fredericksburg. I'd slow, cross the white line onto the wide shoulder, they'd pass with a friendly wave, and I'd return to the lane. The speed limit on some of those back roads was seventy mph.

I slowed to a stop twice for pictures. A huge white-tailed deer sculpture welded to the top of a crushed antique car marked an entrance to a driveway. This manly man's masterpiece was nearly fifteen feet tall but looked more imposing as it stood on a concrete pedestal. The ingredients used to create this monster buck were no doubt stripped from a scrapyard. I noticed chains, wire, engine parts, tools, hubcaps, springs, pulleys, and sheet metal, all rusted to a fine reddish-brown. It was perfectly proportioned as well. A reincarnation of Michelangelo is wandering around somewhere in the body of a big Texan.

[362]

In Fredericksburg, I pulled into a Subway parking lot to tighten and lube my chain before it fell off along the road and ended up as a feature welded into the next Texan deer sculpture. It was loose and had been punishing my swingarm with heavy metal slaps. The Goose was on the center stand, and I had a few tools lying about. I was cranking on the axle nut when I heard a familiar voice from behind. It came from one of the two guys that I met earlier at the service station in Kerrville. Without knowing it, I had chosen his business's parking lot to tighten the chain. He said, "Is everything alright?" seeing that I was wrenching on something. I laughed at the coincidence and assured him that it was a minor fix. He must have been one of the folks that I pulled to the shoulder for on my way to Fredericksburg. He was on the clock, so we shook hands, I thanked him for checking on me, and he went back to work. I was off to Luckenbach to wait for the guys.

I know that I've written of Luckenbach before, but I failed to give a run-down of its daily schedule. Live acoustic music takes place seven days a week, starting around noon and wrapping up around 10:00pm. A medley of local musicians show up daily, unannounced, to fill in the evening hours. Folks come and go all day long, taking pictures, having a beer, and relaxing in its unique atmosphere. I was the first one to park and stay that morning, and still had a bit of time to waste until Bob and John arrived.

Lunchtime was upon us, and the little gravel parking lot began to fill with cars and a few other lucky guys on motorcycles out enjoying a day of perfect weather. Getting out of my normal mode, I initiated a *talk bikes* session with two of these guys. They were both motorcycle safety instructors and wearing neon-green jackets. These jackets were so bright that they could have been used as replacement lighthouse lanterns. I'm not cracking on the guys for wearing them; they were actually really great folks. They told me about the first two women to ever break the million-mile mark on street bikes. The ladies were from Texas, and during their record-breaking ride, one of them put an average of 287 miles on her bike daily for a solid year at seventy-three years of age. I thought I was hard-core when I rode nearly every day for 100 days consecutive days. I guess not. *Maybe when I grow up, I'll be as tough as a little old lady.*

We were sitting on a picnic table still talking bikes when a fella rode through on his Victory motorcycle without stopping. We watched him come and go, thinking nothing of it, but then he reappeared five minutes later looking bewildered and asked, "Is this it?" The other guys and I laughed and said, "Yep. This is it." The sign saying "Town Loop" must have got him.

While we were talking to that fella, Bob and John pulled up. When the ol' Texans stepped out of the truck, I felt like I'd known them my whole life. Bob was holding a white shipping box. They had brought a surprise. The surprise came by way of Brittany. She mailed the unknown contents to Bob's place in Crosby just in time for our meeting.

The tension was mounting as I opened it. I ripped off the tape and pulled back the packing paper. Inside were two or three of each of my favorite treats. There was beef jerky, chocolate chip cookies, cliff bars, pop tarts, and best of all, Cadbury eggs. Without hesitation, I devoured one of those little round pieces of heaven. *Thanks, Brittany. You know the way to a man's heart.*

The guys wanted to grab lunch. We backtracked to Fredericksburg with Mexican food on our minds. Luckenbach offers no more than candy bars and potato chips. As with most towns in Texas, Bob had a favorite dining establishment already figured out. It was Mamacita's Mexican Restaurant, and now after having the best quesadilla of my life there, I was a new fan. Mamacita's was full of fun earthy colors the way most authentic Mexican restaurants are. We were seated near a machine with puffy white whoopee cushions being conveyed up a ramp and dropped in a stack. Bob told me to go check it out, that it was worth a picture. The "whoopee cushions" were tortillas being shaped from dough and then set in a wacky machine that baked them on a revolving metal corkscrew and spit them out the other end. The process of heating them to proper temperature inflated them to the exact shape of a whoopee cushion, minus the flapping tongue. *Interesting.* With lunch in the past, we headed back to the place where the past never comes in last, Luckenbach.

Temperatures in the seventies kept the live music outside all day. Jimmy Lee Jones was playing, his buddy from New Jersey came to play, and about three or four other folks gave their pickin' fingers a workout. The fella from New Jersey was strumming along when some tourist's dog spooked a rooster behind the singer. Trying to escape, the rooster took flight and landed on the singer's head. *What a time to have my camera off!* The singer never missed a beat, the rooster made a clean get away, the dog came up empty-handed, and the remaining daylight hours were spent basking in the simplicity of it all.

Nightfall shuffled us inside. The music kept on going, and I met a fellow West Virginian who was playing bass on the most rudimentary piece of equipment capable of producing a vibration. It was an old galvanized washtub, flipped upside down, with a string attached to the center of it. The other end of the string was tied to a stick, kind of like a bow. He would put one end of the stick on the washtub, pull the string tight, and strum the heck out of that one thick cord. He said that he had $13 wrapped up in the whole thing. I was not surprised to learn this, coming from a fellow hillbilly. His washtub bass fit Luckenbach to a *T*. On all but the biggest occasions, you won't find any electrical instruments at Luckenbach.

Speaking of fitting Luckenbach to a *T*, here are a couple of sentences about what else fits it to a *T*. First off, country folks. If you are a man and have ever crossed an episode of *Jersey Shore* and have not frantically tried to change the channel, don't bother coming to Luckenbach. Second, good people. If you are an egotistical butt monkey, then don't come to Luckenbach; it's not for you, and they don't need the hassle. If you're an old soul trapped in a young body, Luckenbach is your place. If you're a young soul trapped in an old body, Luckenbach is your place. Most of the folks who attend a day here are nearly twice as old as me and the best people you would ever want to meet.

Our night wrapped up when Luckenbach shut down at ten o'clock. The guys and I went back to Fredericksburg to our rooms. I thanked them for helping me out with a room, food, and showing up to hang out at one of my favorite places on Earth.

Day 125 – February 15, 2012

Two things were moving at a snail's pace at the start of day 125. First, there was the actual snail. On my way to grab breakfast, I walked from the room to the lobby next door, and couldn't help noticing a snail with some weight on him. *Dang.* I was going to miss a good opportunity for a picture. I didn't have my camera in hand, and I thought that by the time I'd get breakfast, grab my camera, and return, he'd be gone.

Then the light bulb went off. *It's a SNAIL!* He wasn't going anywhere soon. Hell, I could have piled up two plates of food, downed a coffee, taken a shower, shaved, flown to the moon and back, and he would've still been on the sidewalk. Surely enough, I did get breakfast, walked it back to the room, grabbed the Canon, walked back to the sidewalk, and he was only two bricks over from where he was before. That slimy little guy wasn't shy, so I snapped a couple of pictures and let him get back to his travels. I went back to the room and couldn't help but wonder if my scrambled eggs were the same consistency as the snail.

Checkout time came and saved me from trying to destroy an intangible object. The Internet connection at our motel was moving at a snail's pace. Actually, a snail's pace would have been okay. At least I would have been able to finish what I started. The connection was not only slow but dropped signal five times every four seconds. When the guys and I headed off to begin the four-hour journey to Bob's house, I was forced to give up writing yesterday's post. We made one last, quick stop at Luckenbach to say so long and were on our way.

The Goose and I were to fall in line with Bob's big blue Chevy truck. Crosby, Texas, was where we were headed in a path that was anything but direct. We had all day to get there. A couple of times a year, Bob and John make the pilgrimage to their deer lease, located in the hill country a half hour from Luckenbach. A long, narrow, unmarked road had me wondering where we were headed. Rocky soil, cacti, and dry creek beds appeared around every turn. As soon as I began to wonder if we were lost, they hung a right into an old farm.

Sheep with dirty, darkened wool grazed near a wiry, brown dog who wasn't sure if he wanted to be aggressive or not. The buildings looked unkempt, and a relic of an old truck had been taken over by a clan of cacti. The pushy plants were sprouting from wheel wells and windows, making it more a part of the landscape than a mere machine. Their deer lease was a shed-like cabin on the property similar to the cabins at Armadillo Farm Campground with bunks, supplies for a few days of hunting, and photos from years past tacked to the walls. They had been coming here to hunt for twenty years.

We left and headed for Bergheim's General Store. It was a small time place with big character. Perfectly worn, wooden floors guided you around racks with denim jeans, cowboy hats, and everything else that the local country folk needed. The tiniest of post offices was attached to the building. We grabbed a few cream sodas and snacks and kept moving.

We passed through New Braunfels. On my way west, I spent three days hanging around New Braunfels and Greune, Texas, like a drifter due to the rain. It was odd seeing the area again. I wasn't sure that I'd ever return when I left it over two months before. As I rode through again, it almost felt like the first pass through was an incredibly long time ago on a completely separate trip, twilight zone-ish perhaps.

Next stop: Clear Spring Restaurant. We went there for a lunch of seafood, but I was enticed by the river food. The menu's catfish sounded too tasty to pass up. Bob's a huge seafood fan, often saying, "I'll die happy as long as I got a fried shrimp hangin' out of my mouth." Bob ordered an appetizer fit for a king. It was a mountain of onion rings. I looked at it like a game of Jenga, trying to pry an onion ring out of the stack without it toppling over. We all picked at the plate wisely and snatched onion rings with no mess.

Red and white checkered tablecloths covered the wooden dining tables. Decorations like an antique red wagon and old Coke signs hung from the walls and ceiling. This was a down-home restaurant. I liked it, and again, Bob had picked a good food joint. We ate our entrees, picked at the plate of onion rings until we couldn't take it anymore, and continued our journey east.

Our trip through the pretty hill country ended but not before seeing a turtle the size of a dinner plate go flying through the air. The turtle was large and flat, like an aquatic species. It had started to cross a four-lane highway only to clam up and retreat to its shell directly in the kill zone of the first lane. I thought it was lucky to get that far. The traffic was fast and consistent. The cars' black, round wheels whooshing by were probably no less foreign to the turtle than an extraterrestrial aircraft speeding past your front lawn. To his credit, the driver of an eighteen wheeler swerved to miss the turtle, yet still managed to clip the front of the turtle's shell with a rear tire. The turtle flew through the air like a tossed coin right into the path of five oncoming cars. I looked back to see if it had made it through the line. I usually rescue turtles from the road; however, here I didn't have the time. The first car missed him with an evasive maneuver, but the other four surely flattened him as they drove straight ahead.

I felt bad for the helpless animal, almost wishing that I had not looked. We are turning the world into something more synthetic every day. Some species will adapt, but others, like the slow and gentle turtle, will always find themselves in the path of our forward progress, outright incapable of understanding what's going on. I was sick to my stomach for the next half hour.

The monotonous monster of I-10 came into view. From there it was 153 miles east to Houston. We stopped at an Exxon to fill up. Bob had the gas pump hanging from the tank when an ancient-looking cowboy came hobbling out of the store, bowlegged, and wearing the appropriate hat and denim jeans. He walked past a green Honda Civic and nearly jumped out of his britches. A spunky Jack Russell terrier sitting in the car charged the driver side window, near the old man, and let him have it with a yappy warning shot. The cowboy sidestepped with snail-like reflexes. The dog's protest likely jump-started parts of that old feller that hadn't moved in twenty years. Before he stepped back in his truck at the adjacent gas pump, he looked at us and said, "I damn near shit on myself," with words sounding light and raspy as if they were coming from a strong wind. We chuckled in amusement.

Sensing that we might run into rain, I put my wet weather gear on even though it was still hot and sunny. My intuition proved accurate when we reached Houston's city limits at sunset and the rain began to fall. The gear did its job, and for a half hour or so traffic was tight, visibility sucked, and I just did my best to not lose sight of Bob's truck. With Houston behind us, we hit the countryside and soon arrived at Bob's house.

Bob told to me park the Goose in the garage and took me inside to meet his wife, Wilma. I followed him in, unsure of what to expect, feeling like something the cat dragged in, again. Their home was a cozy brick Cape Cod, clean and open, with no solid walls separating the kitchen from the dining room or dining room from the living room. A neat country charm permeated throughout. Wilma greeted me with a smile that said, "Hey, I haven't seen you in a while" instead of one that said, "Bob, who is this stranger you're bringing home?" She displayed the purest example of welcoming hospitality. Those folks did nothing short of being themselves and had no idea how wonderful they looked in my eyes.

We spent the night looking at some of Bob's pictures, getting to know one another, and eating the kolaches that Bob had been telling me about. They are pastries stuffed with a fruit filling—delicious when heated up, great for the morning. John stuck around for a bit before heading back to his place. Bob, Wilma, and I made it past the midnight hour. It was another great day and one I was very thankful for.

Day 126 – February 16, 2012

Crosby, Texas, the all-American town northeast of Houston, welcomed me with a peaceful morning at Bob and Wilma's. Wilma had already left for work, and Bob picked up John and headed to the local VA center for an appointment. I had the quiet house to myself as I walked downstairs. Without question, it was odd, but I got over it quickly. After all, these folks weren't exactly strangers anymore. They had read my thoughts transferred to the web for months. They had seen my weaknesses play out in real time in unfamiliar territory, and they still made a conscious choice to stay in touch. These were folks with trusting values and deep roots in their neighborhood.

Last night they made sure to tell me, "Make yourself at home." In an effort to do so, I went for the laundry room. *What could feel more at home than doing laundry?* My clothes were swishing and tumbling away when I heard a knock at the front door. A neighbor had come over to ask to borrow something from "Asa Bob," as they called him around Crosby. I told him who I was and what I was doing there, and I told him that Bob would be out until late morning. He looked halfway suspicious and halfway satisfied with my answer. I smiled, trying to lighten the meeting. He returned to his house across the way.

I'd find out from Bob later that the neighbor was just coming by to make sure everything was alright. Bob said, "We've lived beside one another forever, and he's never needed to borrow anything before." Bob told me that the neighbor must have seen me walk to the garage to get my laundry and knew that Bob had left early that morning. I liked the strong sense of community shown in this case, even though I was the one in question. Meanwhile, Bob was wrapping up his business, and the guys were headed back home to pick me up for lunch.

We busted our seams at one of Houston's buffets and trucked it to Bob's oldest son's house. Blane was a large fella, taller than me by two or three inches with a build like a pro baseball player. He had a firm handshake and a life that I was on the road looking for. He was in his mid to late thirties, had two great parents behind him, and an energetic and youthful family full of hobbies. He was his own boss via his taxidermist shop. He was busy with work that day and I was a stranger, so we didn't talk much. If I'd known him better and the timing was right, I would've asked him a million questions about being your own boss.

A goal that I've always kept is to be in control of my day. In his case, he seemed to be doing well as a business owner, and it was great to see a small business running like a well-oiled machine. Bob gave me a tour of Blane's other shop, the one he used for restoring hot rods. Along with the business side of things going on, there was also a focus on community.

A batting cage sat in the yard. A local youth league team and coaches were there using it for practice. I liked seeing the unselfish sharing of resources to help out your neighbors. That builds better communities, and a better community than Crosby, Texas, would be hard to find. I stepped in the batting cage and aimed an aluminum bat at some eighty-mph baseballs for a while. At first I was horrible, swinging way too late, missing almost every ball with horrible form. I told one of the coaches to film me as an example of what not to do. Then I started to get it. I began to swing earlier and became the foul ball hitter of the century. At my best point, I was making contact with the ball every time, often making them deflect straight up or straight down. I didn't care. I was happy to give it a good ol' West Virginian go. I had a ton of fun. It was the first time that I'd had the chance to swing against baseballs coming that fast.

We traded our time in the not so big leagues for a stint in the Goode life. Bob, John, and I headed back to Bob's house to prepare for an evening dinner at Goode Company Texas BBQ. Wilma soon arrived home from work. We piled into their Tahoe and headed for Goode Company BBQ in Houston. Goode Company was one of those places that, if you walk into it hungry, the smell will make you feel as though you're starving while waiting in line. Hands down, it was one of the tastier places I'd smelled. Patrons of the restaurant had a choice between sitting in the dining room and taking their food outside to sit at picnic tables beneath a canopy. We chose outside. Bob and Wilma's brother-in-law, Dick, planned to meet us there.

Dick was a motorcycle rider through and through. Even at seventy-nine, he still rode like the world depended on it. He was spit off his bike and suffered a broken leg a year before and even that didn't stop him. He had followed my adventure since hearing about it from Bob and wanted to meet me. His travels had taken him to places that I can't even imagine yet. I knew we'd get along. He had a few questions about the Goose and its setup; we talked bikes, shared road trip stories, and great food. We all took turns taking pictures and once again, I was living in one of life's perfect moments. It got a bit sweeter when supper was topped with pecan pie.

We put Goode Company BBQ in the rear view and headed back to Crosby for a relaxing evening of socializing while watching slide shows and old videos. Again we made it to the midnight hour before calling it a day. Does it get better than that?

Day 127 – February 17, 2012

Morning number two at Bob and Wilma's began with a few cups of coffee and a plum-filled kolache. Wilma had already left for work, and Bob was still sleeping. I quietly updated the blog until Bob woke. We didn't have much planned. I was along for the ride, experiencing another day in Bob's life. He made a call to his long-time buddy Klaus. Lunchtime was approaching, and a decision was made to ride a couple of miles across town to the San Jacinto River and an all-you-can-eat catfish joint. Bob spoke of these lunchtime gatherings as daily occasions and a perk of retired life.

The place was rather unassuming. It was nothing more than a metal pole building with a covered front entry and a covered rear patio. Picnic tables were the seats of choice both inside and out. I noticed this as a trend in the Texas dining world. Folks preferred the option of dining outside if it was available. Here, not only was it available, but the building was so basic that dining inside felt like dining outside. A family cookout vibe defined the restaurant.

Bob and I were joined by Klaus, his son Nathan, and a fella named Glen. Klaus and Nathan normally would have been working, if not for the recent heavy rains, and Glen, I'm not sure what he did, but I did note that he looked incredibly similar to the controversial movie producer, Michael Moore. Last year, Texas suffered from a severe drought. Rain was absent for roughly nine months. My brother told me before I left that when I got to Texas, I'd bring the rain. That son of a gun was right. Texas had been a wet ride for me. I was glad that Texas wasn't in a drought anymore, but sorry to see the guys missing work.

So there we were, sitting on a picnic table in the outside dining area, looking at a gradual curve in the San Jacinto River to our right and unlimited catfish on the plate in front of us. When we would get low on the tasty strips of fried fish, a young lady would come around with a box of battered fish and some tongs to refill our plates. We ate to our heart's desire.

Bob's handiwork

Bob and I—full of fish, fries, and hushpuppies—continued touring Crosby with a stop at Lambert's Auto Parts. The store was owned by Bob's friend, Ellard. It had been the only auto parts store in Crosby for many years until a recent O'Reilly's Auto Parts was erected. We weren't there looking for parts, though. Bob took me there to witness Ellard's outstanding collection of perfectly restored antique cars. Bob understood well that I was a guy out to see and do new things.

So Ellard had been hard at work squirreling away his pristine classic car collection and creating a mock-up fifties diner full of that generation's memorabilia in a building adjacent to his parts store. When the door swung open, the first words to come out of my mouth were "holy shit." Right before my eyes were five incredibly clean hot rods, looking like they were time warped from the past. The one that held my eye longest was Ellard's pink and white 55 Ford Crown Victoria. Of course the other cars were just as clean, but that one made me question whether I was born in the right decade. I couldn't imagine seeing cars with that type of elegance and style cruising around everywhere.

Bob and I continued on, thanking Ellard's son for showing off the collection. Ellard was out of town. Next, we were off to Coy's house, Bob's youngest son. Not one to miss an opportunity, Bob made a pit stop along the way at a roadside stand for cracklin's. For those who've not experienced their glory, cracklin's are hunks of fried pig skin and fat and about as good for you as a smashed windpipe. The only thing remotely close to them that I'd tried is bacon, of course, and pork rinds sold at any convenience store, but pork rinds fall quite short of cracklin's.

We were sold a baggy full like they were an outlawed substance. Each one was an inch thick—half crunchy, bubbled skin and half soft, fried fat. I chewed through a few, never telling Bob that they were hard to eat. Don't get me wrong, they were terribly delicious. Not many things in the world can provide that bacony, greasy, salty blast like cracklin's. In fact, I don't know of anything. They were simply so bad for you that I imagined my heart trying to wrap an artery around my neck and strangle me to death for even popping one down the gullet. I did finish the baggy days later, however, one at a time, hours apart.

At Coy's we arrived to an empty house. Bob showed me around and let me snap some shots of Coy's awesome backyard, tiki-themed pool, and an old barn dilapidated to perfection. We hung around for about fifteen minutes and were

132 DAYS

heading out of the driveway when Coy pulled up. Coy, like his older brother Blane, was into restoring hot rods. Blane and Coy went to an auction earlier that day to get parts for the truck that Coy was building. Bob and I stuck around for a bit, watching the guys work on the hot rod in the garage. Plans were made to get the whole family together for supper later that night. I was in tag-along mode and happy to join them.

Back at Bob's, Wilma arrived home from work. Supper was scheduled for 6:30. We loaded up in their Tahoe and ventured out, across town, to Straight Off the Road BBQ. Somewhat unsurprisingly, Straight Off the Road BBQ was owned by another one of Bob's good friends. As we were seated, the plates started coming. When mine arrived, and I saw the size of the enormous slab of chicken fried steak, I knew that I'd been beat before I took a bite. There was no way I could finish this slab of battered meat. I had to throw in the white napkin with a few hunks left. But oh my, was it tasty.

Even better than the food was the chance to sit down and have dinner with Bob and his entire family, the sons, the wives, and the grandkids. I was in the midst of a family, an idea in motion where you stick out the hard times, live well in the good times, never give up on one another, and love one another to the end of time. These folks were the perfect example of how good life can be.

Supper concluded. Bob, Wilma, and I stayed up late once more, mostly talking and telling stories. We had a night where folks genuinely wanted to be in one another's company. It was a special night for me since it was my last night with them.

Day 128 – February 18, 2012

I didn't sleep well for the thought of leaving my newfound family and the nonstop rain drumming their metal roof. When morning came, Bob and Wilma were already awake. I walked downstairs and greeted them. They made it very clear that I could stay another day and wait out the storm, or even stay another couple days. Mentally, I was ready to travel even though it was nasty outside.

The past few days with them were indeed great. *If I didn't have strong ties to West Virginia, it wouldn't be a problem to relocate to Crosby, Texas.* I soon started to gear up. We walked outside to say goodbye. I kept a smile on my face and focused on the ride through the thunderstorm to hide my sadness. We stood in the garage with the door open. The things around us, like Bob's black hot rod truck and his decal painting area, were small pieces of an experience I wanted to lock solid in my memory. Bob handed me $200 for the road. He wanted to make sure I got home to my family without any hiccups. He didn't know that I woke up in Van Horn a few days ago with $15, but I think he could sense it. I thanked him for the help.

The Goose was also ready to go after a few days off. Bob gave me a sincere handshake, and Wilma gave me a big ol' hug. They told me that they loved me and wished me the best. I started the bike and knew that it was time to go. As I pulled out of their drive and rounded the corner, I looked back, waving until I could no longer see them. I missed them already.

They were folks who made my life better simply because we met. I had spent my whole existence over a thousand miles from them, but found them nonetheless, or maybe we found each other. I don't know. It's all randomness and perfect timing, I guess. I'll always be thankful that they were part of my journey. Like traveling all those miles to see that first colossal redwood and feeling that it was all worth it, Wilma and Bob made every inch of pavement covered worth it. They were keepers.

The first few miles in the rain were short. Rain clouds painted water all over me and the bike. Visibility was poor, even at low speeds. I was still in Crosby and following a car too closely in the center of my lane when the Goose barreled right over something. I bounced up off the seat momentarily. I turned to look behind me. It was an animal of some sort, black and wet, lying still like a pile of soggy laundry, probably a cat or raccoon. I don't think I killed it, but it was a great reminder to slow the pace and keep a good following distance. Five miles from Bob's place, I met my friend Adam at Cracker Barrel. I last saw him through an 8" x 8" window in Houston's city jail, after Thanksgiving.

I had been in touch with him since deciding to leave California and take the southern route home. There's no telling when I'd see him again if I didn't stop on the way through this time. More importantly, he became a first-time father since then when his son was born in late December.

Seeing my friend as a dad, and seeing the pride in his eyes as he held back a tear describing the moment his son came into his world, was humbling. I felt happy for him. His little boy, still so young, sat there oblivious to our encounter and oblivious to his father's love for him. He was a little ball of a guy, with tiny hands and feet. He'd open his eyes from time to time to see two smiling giants looking back at him. Adam was immensely proud. My friend had entered the realm of parenthood, a place that I haven't found the desire to visit.

Even though he was getting along just fine, I still couldn't imagine the immense responsibility that comes with parenting. If my upbringing has taught me anything, it's that raising a family is anything but an easy task. School obligations, baby sitters, doctors, diapers, and silly cartoons don't turn me on. I've always been the type to up-and-go when the slightest urge arises. There's a planet out there to see, and I've only begun. The load of stopping to raise a child is best left to folks like Adam. He was a guy who had found his way and had found happiness. I wished him the best. Our visit at Cracker Barrel was short and sweet, lasting barely longer than it took to eat breakfast. Adam and I kept in touch pretty regularly, and once in a while I'd see him when he made it up to West Virginia to visit his mom. I had to get moving if I were to beat the sunset to New Orleans, so we shook hands and parted in the heavy rain.

There I was in Cracker Barrel's parking lot, half man, half Goose, and half platypus. I was ready for the day's aquatic, 300-mile manimal ride. I took off with trash bags around my boots and rain gear covering the rest. By the first fuel stop, one trash bag had started taking on water leaving my left foot soaked. I took it off and kept riding. The rain was evil with force. Lightning thrashed all around. Next fuel stop, I was well into Louisiana on Interstate 10, almost to

Baton Rouge. The other bag failed and the rain gear started seeping. I had two wet feet, wet gloves, and now wet undershirts. Unbeaten, I rode on like a motorcyclist possessed.

On my last stop, seventy miles north of New Orleans, I was soaked from head to toe. One of the front pockets in my rain jacket, where the cell phone was riding, took on water and ruined the phone. *What's the point of designing rain gear that doesn't fucking work?* Frustrated and tired, I made it to New Orleans at dusk, one hundred percent soaked to the bone and freezing to death. Drowned rats have seen better days.

So why leave a warm home and wonderful people behind in Crosby? And why go back to the unruly city where a misguided youth stuck a gun to my neck? The reason came from an invitation from an old friend of mine, Sherman. He had left Pennsylvania behind for a few days in New Orleans to partake in everything Mardi Gras. He was on his annual walkabout. It had been a couple years since he and I talked. We became friends years ago through shared weekends at the motocross track. He raced, his son raced, and they gelled perfectly into our group of friends. He and his family were living in West Virginia at the time. Since moving back to Pennsylvania, we've lost touch a bit. I thought that meeting him here in New Orleans would be a perfect way to catch up and kick start our friendly connection again.

I found his hotel room and pulled in. He answered the door smiling and raring to go. I walked into his room as the utter definition of the word wet. My boots were holding water better than a mason jar. The raingear was now a rubberized cloak holding the water from escaping. I shed it slowly, trying not to flood the room. From undershirts to underwear, it all stuck to me like cold vacuum-sealed plastic. Puddles formed with every move. My fingers and toes were purple, but that's an easy color to reach when you're this pale. He gave me a few minutes to recover with a warm shower before we got on with the evening.

I came out of the bathroom with questions. I wanted to know more about his walkabout. I never knew of him taking a walkabout before. He told me that a few years back he beat cancer and now carried with him a new lease on life. That was a quick answer that silenced my curiosity. To me, it made our time in the Big Easy that much better. Cancer is a hell of an opponent. I'm glad that Sherman came out on top, and that he chose travel as a way to enrich his life.

Our plan was to go downtown and experience the craziness. I must admit that after the last bout with New Orleans, I was apprehensive about returning to the French Quarter. I decided to leave the camera behind for fear of damage. Bourbon Street is no place to bring anything larger than a cell phone. In years past at Mardi Gras, I've been pushed with the crowd so tightly that the thought of being trampled crossed my mind, and who hasn't experienced dropping a phone after tying one on good and getting the ol' loose grip? With that, Sherman called a taxi and we headed for Bourbon Street. The rain had finally passed.

The last night of Mardi Gras 2012 was upon us, but first there is a disclaimer, or spot of fine print, worth mentioning. Folks had helped me financially to get as far as I had since Van Horn. To be clear, I didn't use any of that unselfishly donated money on drinking. Sherman generously handed me a $100 to spend on my drinks and paid for anything else we found of interest, most notably a costume. I left the room with nothing other than my ID in my pocket and a shitty smile. I appreciated everyone's help to the fullest and would've done nothing to tarnish that.

With that, we had an absolute blast at Mardi Gras. The wild streets entertained us immensely. One of us had to have a costume. I quickly volunteered. There's something about being under the cover of mask that brings out the exhibitionist in me. We found a wild-looking, red-feathered mask with a long beak, and a set of rubber breasts. Perfect, perfect! And so, hilarity to the point of absurdity ensued.

Bourbon Street was filled with heavy droves of partiers. We waddled shoulder to shoulder. We were all victims of a good time, and a lot of them were victims of a nipple rub courtesy of yours truly. Sherman was in tow, cell phone camera in hand. I was on the prowl for an unsuspecting drunken humanoid standing distracted by a nearby set of breasts flopping wonderfully over a balcony (which I was also keeping one eye on), or looking in any direction as to not see me coming. In my head the music from *Jaws* played as I approached "duuuun duuun -- duuuun duuun -- duun dun -- dun dun -- dundundundundun" then WHAM, I'd strike 'em with a double-breasted nipple scrape. The intoxicated victim would turn to see what just grazed them and see my blue eyes staring intensely at them through the bright red mask. The looks were priceless and always sparked laughter. Women, men, young, old, black, white, and religious protesters, it didn't matter. They were all struck by the nipple scrape at one time or another. Sherman laughed so hard that I thought he was gonna keel over.

Every once in a while someone would retaliate by latching an air-breathing, open mouth on one of my costume's perky nipples. I'd react with an awkward laugh; more times than not, it was some college age dude instead of a hot young female. They always came out of nowhere and probably wouldn't have gone for it if they saw the last person who latched on. It was all in the name of fun. Sherman and I had a time to remember. I ended up with a neck-aching amount of beads and Sherman, a bellyaching pile of laughs. All the while, I kept an eye open for that Lisa girl that got me robbed. I was gonna have my revenge. I was gonna poke her in the eye with my beak.

When the taxi arrived to shuttle Sherman off to the airport for his 5:00am flight back to Pennsylvania, we had reached his goal of pulling an all-nighter. Not two minutes after that I was out like a light after a long and complex day and a half.

Day 129 – February 19, 2012

Two and a half hours after Sherman left, I was awake. That was way too early, so I remained in bed waiting to fall asleep. It didn't happen, and at 9:30am I got up and began packing. The plan for the day was to make as many miles through Louisi-ala-sippy as possible. A 500-mile ride seemed out of the question. I packed my wet gear on the bike and took off for I-10 East. The day was bright, the air warm, and the traffic light.

At the first fuel stop, I was standing beside the Goose and drinking coffee when a rather rough-looking character approached me. His skin was tan and leathery. His long brown hair had streaks of grey. Scuff marks adorned his shirt and blue jeans. The truck that he had walked from was an early-nineties, Chevrolet half-ton sporting a dented tailgate. He could've been a late-forties-something or a late-thirties fella who had seen a hard life, I couldn't tell. *Here we go.* He began talking in a friendly tone. I listened as I fiddled with my coffee cup, half suspicious. He wanted money. There was no doubt in my mind, but he wanted to tell his story first.

It began on Bourbon Street last night. He said that he was robbed. He had no money, wallet, or ID. I couldn't validate any of this, but could relate. The guy's appearance and ratty truck surely didn't help his chances. In fact, he looked like the sort that would perform the stick ups. His story led to asking for gas money so that he could make it the final thirty miles home to Mississippi. I turned him down at first, trying to make a wise choice, but then I thought, *Shame on you Mike. Look at how everyone has just pitched in to help you out.*

His story seemed legit enough, and he didn't want cash in hand, so I had him pull his truck to the pump. I told him that I would put $10 in his tank. When I went inside to pay the attendant, I changed my mind and gave her $15 for the stranger's gas. I wasn't traveling with a ton of loot and had to watch what I spent. Ultimately, it felt good to be on the opposite side of the helping spectrum. This time I was giving instead of receiving, and I liked it. If I learned anything on the journey, it was to give, every chance you have. The guy thanked me over and over, and I felt better for having the chance to help. The world was not all about me.

I made only one other stop. It was in Biloxi, Mississippi, at a Home Depot. Bob and I had been talking about making forward pegs for the Goose. As I was riding I thought of a way to make some without breaking the bank. I bought a thirty-six-inch piece of all-thread, two nuts, two washers, and two crush washers for $6. I slapped it all together in the parking lot. The all-thread was fished through a hollow tube in the Goose's forward engine mount. Ten inches stuck out on either side. I tightened it down with the washers and nuts. Back on the road, I propped my feet up to see if the modification made the miles any better; wow, what a relief. The seat felt more comfortable, the pain in my rear went away, and my knees could rest. It only took four months to figure that out. I haven't always been the cleverest of fellers, ya know?

From Biloxi, I forced another hundred miles in against the wind and settled in Greenville, Alabama, around 4:30pm. Like a shadow, I couldn't outride the two and a half hours of sleep from this morning. Fluffy motel pillows hardly ever felt so good. Within a half hour I was out like a light.

It had been a few days without a post. I was nearing home and had it in mind to keep up to date for the folks following along. At 11:00pm, I stirred to life minus any sign of a hangover and feeling rather spry. I ventured to the lobby to use the hotel's computer. The rainy ride to New Orleans damaged my laptop's built-in touch sensor, giving me no control over pointing and clicking anything on the screen.

From 11:30 to 3:00am I typed with vigor, all the while uploading a ton of pictures. Twenty-six hundred words were organized into a story about the last three days with photos to match. Somewhere around midnight, the autosave feature from Wordpress stopped working. This, I'd learned, happens when you borrow a Wi-Fi connection with a time limit built-in requiring you to re-up every half hour or hour. No message pops up on the screen telling you that you are about to lose connection. So you continue on, on a roll, unaware that you are about to erase all of your work when you hit the publish button and the computer directs you to the screen that tells you to login again. (In hindsight, I've learned to copy and paste the work to Notepad before hitting publish.)

If you're more tech-savvy than say, a hillbilly, then this probably isn't a problem for you, but if you look at a computer and are afraid to touch the wrong button because it may explode, then you could run into this problem now and then. Thus, one cannot imagine the pain I felt as I tried to publish the post and found that only the first 500 words were saved. Pissed, I was! I wanted to blow that sum bitch to smithereens, whoop its ass, and melt it into a pile of low-tech, plastic shit. I wanted to kill it, and kill it good! Mentally exhausted and frustrated to the tenth power, I returned to my room in total defeat.

Day 130 – February 20, 2012

A weird night of sectional sleep was no match for my biological clock. You would think that a guy with just a few hours of sleep could at least make it to the crack of 9:30 once in a while. It was 8:05 when I headed to the lobby for breakfast and another shot at posting the last three days of travel. This time I was bringing my groggy game face. The Internet connection had better watch out. I rushed through breakfast so that I could secure the only seat at the hotel's community computer. No food or drinks were allowed near it. Two hours later, in finger cramp city, I completed that damn post. Relief washed over me when it transitioned to the web without a problem. With that nightmare out of the way, it was time to get rolling. I had states to cross and time zones to change.

Interstate 85 N was on the menu for the whole day, and I had a craving for pavement and petrol stew. I ceremoniously decorated the Goose with Mardi Gras beads and left at 11:00am on the dot. Driving along 85 N in Alabama was fantastically, incredibly, extraordinarily, unbelievably, amazingly uninteresting. For most of the ride, four flat lanes of highway pushed through pine forests and were divided by a median filled with pines. Exit ramps yielded the same old fuel stations and fast-food eateries that all of America's exit ramp towns enjoy. If not for a few brief spots with just enough country flare to remind me of home, riding through Alabama would have been enough to put me asleep behind the handlebars.

But one thing stuck out, literally. There were thousands of foot-high dirt mounds. I rode and rode and those things dotted the landscape like freckles. Curiosity grew strong enough to pull to the shoulder. I had to see what sort of creature was building them. I entertained three guesses after seeing enough of them to know they weren't cow patties. My first guess was ants, second guess was termites, and my distant third guess was some sort of rodent, prairie dog in nature, but smaller. When I kicked the top off of one of them, an explosion of ants was revealed.

Ah ha! I watched to see how they would react. Amazingly, they instantly went for the larvae and took them deeper inside the mound. Within seconds, the eggs were out of sight. I was shocked by how quickly they reacted to saving the baby ants. It's like they had a plan *B* for when the day came that a giant would come and kick the top off their mound. They moved with such precision that I imagined a leader ant on a micro bullhorn shouting orders, "The prophecy was true! The giant has arrived! Save the larvae! Save the larvae!" Okay, so I had been on the road a long time. My six-legged adventure ended and north I went, still on 85. I'm afraid Alabama lent me no better story.

Everything was dandy as I passed through Atlanta. I expected it to be a headache, but the traffic was at a minimum. The headache came about fifteen miles later when I noticed that my right footpeg was getting awfully slippery, like covered in ice. I thought that I got something on the bottom of my boot, so

I dragged it along the pavement as I rode. *The friction will surely take care of it.* When I put it back on the peg, I still felt the slickness. My eyes looked down to discover oil everywhere. *Oh boy, what the hell is wrong with the Goose?* I jerked the bike to the shoulder and cut it off.

A quick inspection revealed a missing oil fill cap. The problem had been found in seconds and it was minor. I knew exactly why it was missing. Sometimes when it was really cold, I'd put my foot on that part of the engine until my toes warmed up. The last time my foot was on the engine was the night that I crossed the mountain pass in Texas near Van Horn. I must have knocked it loose and it finally vibrated out.

Instead of panic, I decided to see what the roadside could provide as a plug. I knew that there would be enough metal and plastic tidbits of trash lying along the highway to find something useful. Shamefully, this is the same for every ocean shore across the planet as well. There are no walls in the ocean stopping plastic junk from being carried by the currents to every continent, thus making beaches rich with buoyant garbage.

So, I set out like a search party of one, scouring the ground, confident that I'd find something to fill the hole. Folks who knew me really well back home were aware that I could rival MacGyver at *fixing* things, like the time when my ski binding broke and I used the strap tied to the binding to tie my boot to the ski. It worked all day. Or the time when I had to use a spark plug to hold my brother's handlebars onto his triple clamps so that he could finish the race (no one that we knew at the track had a bolt that wide with such fine threads). Here was another chance to prove it.

I collected a plastic bottle with lid and a rubber plug. Back at the Goose, I tried the rubber plug first. The damn thing fit perfectly! I couldn't have been luckier if a lonely swimsuit model had pulled over to help in her birthday suit, slipped in the oil, and landed right on me ol' baby maker—boyoyoing! That plug was a gift from above. After verifying through the sight glass that enough oil was still in the bike, I headed for the nearest fuel station to replace the amount lost (about three-quarters of a quart). I poured the new oil in and continued on. My goal of North Carolina was still feasible.

I kept riding until the South Carolina sign welcomed me. At the welcoming station, I stretched out the stompers and took some time to appreciate some things I hadn't seen in a while, like a Sycamore tree and a dandelion. The terrain was starting to resemble home, and I felt good inside. Before I left in October, South Carolina used to feel so far away; now it felt like just a stone's throw away from West Virginia. The vastness of the western states was now gone and had been replaced by the rolling green hills and tree-lined highways of the East Coast, and I was back to my original time zone. Crossing into Georgia from Alabama marked the change.

In South Carolina I stopped riding when I noticed a Motel 6 in Spartanburg advertising rooms for $29.99. That was enough to yank me right off the road, and cheaper than popping a tent up almost anywhere in California.

Day 131 – February 21, 2012
The last full day of travel on this wonderful road trip is here, and tomorrow will take me home, but the journey is not over yet. There are 450 miles of life wedged between me and West Virginia. I had just enough money to break those miles up into two days of riding, leaving a little extra time for taking it all in.

Amazingly, my mind let me sleep in to 9:20am. I wanted to pull my brain out of my head and kiss it. Sleeping has always been a problem brought about by my overactive thinker. Sometimes it feels like my body is hosting a separate entity, one that I have no control over.

Each night, while trying to fall asleep, the gears turn in my mind, but I can't find the off button to slow them down. The darkness, quiet, and relative comfort in sleeping position only speeds them up. My body will be dog tired, but my brain will say, *now is the time to take on all of life's issues. Now is the time to reflect on every conversation you've ever had, and if given a chance, find what you'd say differently. Now is the time to figure out your finances for the next eighty years. Now is the time to figure out what you're going to eat for lunch for the next week and a half. Now is the time to explore the meaning of life.*

Equally as harsh, in the morning my mind generally has me up and alert when the first rooster crows. It's always too overjoyed to be sleeping in with all of the things it's going to make my body do each day while it drives me to exhaustion like a squishy little grey drill sergeant. At any rate, it was a welcome change when I woke to see that I had over eight hours of sleep.

I set my sights on southern Virginia by day's end, and by way of back roads. Igor strongly suggested avoiding the interstate on those final days. I took his advice and planned a longer route that would avoid I-85 N after the first twenty-four miles. I packed my things and took off. At the exit where I began riding side roads, I was surprised to find Iron City Motocross Park. *I'm starting to like these side roads already.* I pulled up to the empty track to scope it out for future riding potential. With it being so close to home, the guys and I could drive down there to ride or race if the track looked fun.

It did, and Iron City's facilities were clean and well maintained, like a seasoned track where the owners cared about spectators and efficiency. Bleachers were installed on hillsides; stadium lights and sturdy scoring and restroom facilities had been built. The track itself had not seen any riding in a while. Rain ruts had it looking fairly rough, and any fresh tire tracks had certainly washed away. Finding a random track in the morning was a great way to start the day.

I was off in search of North Carolina's border via South Carolina's back roads. All was going well as I passed little farms, old, slanting barns, and dewy green pastures, all under a perfectly blue sky. My tank bag held the directions that I wrote down right before leaving the room. Twenty miles into the side roads, I hit a snag. MapQuest mentioned nothing about Route 5 and Route 161 splitting. I had copied the directions verbatim. This left me in a bind. Follow Route 5 to see if I could come across 77, or take Route 161? I didn't have a clue. To figure it out, I relied on an old wise man trick. It went something like this: "Eeny meeny miney…" you know the rest. Route 5 won that. I planned to ride ten miles on Route 5, and if I didn't find Cherry Road, the next road in the directions, then I'd turn back and take 161. Well, I had to turn back, and while traveling on 161, I came across 77. That's ultimately where I was going, anyway. I never found Cherry Road. *Should have stayed on the interstate.*

On the road again and no longer confused, I was only a handful of miles from Mecklenburg County and North Carolina. At 1:00pm, I crossed the border and aimed directly for Albemarle. There were some folks there deserving of a surprise visit and a million thanks. I couldn't wait to visit my Crossroads Yamaha pals again.

On day eleven, I stopped by looking for a single tire iron and came away with five or six new friends. They treated me like family, taking the time to talk with me, while generously donating stickers, a blue hoodie, T-shirt, and a free bike wash. Not to mention how they teamed up with Chaparral Motorsports in San Bernardino, California, to get the Goose a rear tire. We kept in touch throughout the whole ride via the blog. They were wonderful people, and I was proud to sport their logo all the way across our country. This time I just wanted to stop in and say thanks for everything along the way. They deserved that, and I wish I had more to give. They didn't owe me a single thing, and I didn't expect a single thing from them, but I should have known better. While driving there, my stomach had butterflies. I was excited!

I pulled in the parking lot not knowing if they could see me from inside. Their big storefront windows reflected the day's light back at me. Sure enough, they could see me. Jason jumped on the intercom and told everyone to come up front. When I walked in, I was greeted warmly; Carmen ran over and gave me a huge hug. I snapped a bad picture (camera was on the wrong setting) and we began to catch up on things. Carmen said, "We were following along and were wondering if you'd come by." I told her, "There's no way I'd miss it." To see them again made me happier than a man who's won the lottery twice.

Soon we walked outside to check out the Goose. Jason noticed my rear brake line rubbing the rear rim. He then said, "Pull it around back." That was a deja vu moment. When the Goose went 'round back, the Goose got a checkup. I tried to tell them not to worry about it. Besides, Jason had already pried the line away from the rim with his hands. I just wanted to visit with them and tell them thanks, but they weren't having it, so I caved.

Jeff and Jason began their assault on my bike. Jeff went to cleaning the chain with a wire brush and parts cleaner, and Jason, like a ninja with a wrench, stealthily snuck in an oil change mid-conversation. They removed an oil plug from one of the shop's bikes and screwed it on the Goose, replacing the plug I found along the road. They replaced my old blue Crossroads hoodie that was now stained and faded with a new, bright blue one. Jeff cut a few inches off my homemade forward pegs at request, and after that, they pushed the Goose outside and whipped it into shape with scrubbing brushes, engine cleaner, and a hose. We joked that there was so much road grime on the bike that I'd owe them a new set of brushes. I told them that they'd be in the mail. Again, they wouldn't let me help with the scrubbing.

Whenever Jed would get a free second from the parts counter, he would come in the back to talk motocross with me. He had been training diligently since I left there in October. I was proud to have shared a connection with the young man and to see that he was giving it his all. Carmen came back while the guys were washing the bike and said that she had to leave to take care of something. She gave me another big hug, but her leaving happened so quickly that I lost the opportunity to get a group picture.

Jeff and Jason finished what they were doing and helped me out with directions to 29 N by way of back roads. The guys were quite a bit busier with the regular duties of the shop than on my first visit, so I told them all a sincere thank you and took off, north, for the Virginia border. Riding away, I thought about the part they played in my journey. Our first meeting transformed what was a fun but long week and a half motorcycle ride into a priceless adventure, one where I'd encounter the feelings of nirvana from time to time. It was also the first day when I felt that I was meant to be on the road. My adventure rocketed to another level, and it wasn't because of an event. It was because of people, these people. When I left Crossroads then my chest felt so open, so light, like I could breathe as never before. I remember exiting the parking lot and going the wrong way. I was cloaked in and dumbfounded by one of life's greatest highs.

I knew that they met folks every day who walked through their front door with motorcycling stories, opinions about the latest bikes, or with issues with a broken part, who wanted to talk their ears off (happens in every bike shop). But I just wanted them to know that I was there to see them and hear how life had been in North Carolina. Having the privilege to do that left me fulfilled.

Jason and Jeff's directions were spot on, but my interpretation wasn't. Dusk was approaching. Tightly packed hills the size of which I hadn't seen since the Californian coast started coming into the picture, and I was riding happily along. The evening light was great, and the weather was brisk. Everything was fine until I came across 85 N. My directions said to take 85 N via exit 79A. Well, I got to exit 78A and noticed that it was I-85 N, so I took it. What I couldn't tell from the handwritten directions was that if I'd gone one more mile on Route 220 then I would have seen exit 79A, which was *Route* 85 and 29 N. I ended up riding on I-85 N for thirteen miles, looking for 29 N. Soon I realized that something was wrong, so I stopped at a McDonald's to check out the directions online. I found my mistake and backtracked thirteen miles to Route 220, followed it to exit 79A, and then took Route 85/29 N.

I stopped for a snack fifty miles south of Virginia's state line. A chunky teenager working the register spoke of snow falling to the north. I told him that I was headed for Danville. He said that I should wait it out. In the parking lot, I decided to go for it, second guessing my forecasting friend. It didn't feel like snow to me. This wasn't home, but I knew these parts well enough to know that snow wasn't coming. Nothing was coming, except plummeting temperatures.

I followed my instincts and headlights fifty miles to Danville, Virginia. The cold night wind and narrow black roads were no match for my drill sergeant brain barking orders to my body: *Watch for deer! Tuck a little further behind the windscreen! High beams on! High beams off!* I arrived at the Virginia line just after 8:00pm. Danville's appropriately named Travel Inn lured me in for a stay.

Day 132: Home will never be the same
February 22nd, 2012

I described day one as mighty. Day 132, the final day, could be summed up as peculiar. The day began similar to every other day. I was at a random motel, knocking out a post, packing my things, and loading the Goose up for a precious day of travel. The West Virginia state line loomed like a ribbon waiting to be snapped by the winner of a marathon 250 miles north of Danville. Factoring in a few fuel stops and lunch, I reckoned it would take five and a half hours to make it there. Like the day before, I stuck with Igor's advice and planned a rural route home that would parallel Interstate 81 and avoid the eighteen-wheeler-saturated highway.

Once packed, I returned the room key to the final random Indian motel owner that I'd meet. He and his wife were nice folks, young, humble, quiet, and welcoming. Their motel was an older building, one-story, and shaped like a squared-off horseshoe with a pool centered between. I could see his wife working hard to keep the rooms clean for appreciative travelers like me. It was early and she was already out pushing a cart full of towels and mini shampoo bottles from room to room. However they found themselves in the self-employed position that they were in is irrelevant. They were living more of an American dream than I ever had. They worked hard for it and had a good thing going.

A thought emerged before leaving: *I may have met more Indian folks along the way than any other group of people*. Vivek started the tally and will no doubt remain a cherished friend, but there were many more than he that I met for the quickest of moments. I learned that motel and hotel owners and employees are overwhelmingly Indian from coast to coast. All were easy to get along with, quick to smile, and not one of them gave me a hard time.

Some went the extra mile like the fella in Clarksdale, Mississippi, who took it upon himself to welcome me to his town that he was so proud of. He loved Clarksdale. Some of them just sat patiently, ready for the next person to walk through the door in need of lodging, unaware of the sense of security found in their building's lights. Those lights always assured me that I had survived another day. These folks quietly entered my day, or maybe I quietly entered theirs, but no matter how you look at it, they are just as American as you and I. We are all part of a country that is more of an idea than a rigid system. We are the world's melting pot, the place where everyone has and deserves a chance. These guys were proving that it works if you try.

I left Travel Inn aware that when I lay my head down tonight, it won't be at a motel or in a tent. It will be at home. Silently, I thanked them for a job well done and took off for 58 W and the first stop of the day. I wasn't going to miss an opportunity to experience a point of interest.

A few miles outside of Danville, I stopped to top off the tank. A man pumping gas on the opposite side of my pump stopped what he was doing to come over for a quick chat. His name was Steve. He may have been in his late forties, had long salt-and-pepper-colored hair, and was a fellow motorcyclist. He asked a familiar question when he approached, "Are you traveling?" I responded with, "Yep. Been on the road for four and a half months and I'm finally headin' home." He asked, "Where's home?" I replied, "West Virginia," saying it slowly like I'd been out to sea for three years.

He took interest, and we conversed for a bit about what it was like to do multiple-thousand-mile rides. He had ridden one thousand miles from home and back on a Harley but had yet to cross the full United States. I sincerely recommended that he give it a shot someday, telling him about how great the country is out West and such. That recommendation came with a side note, though. I told him that like a crazy person, I gave up everything to take the trip: a house, a stable job, and a relationship. Steve probably had thoughts bouncing around in his head about me escaping the loony bin, but he held them in. Inside, I could feel all of the experiences building into one final memory and just wanted to be encouraging without seeming too excited. He and I finished pumping fuel and I was off again, on 58 W in search of Lake Sugar Tree Motocross Park.

Lake Sugar Tree was the home of the famous retired motocross racer, now motocross school trainer and teacher, Gary Bailey. My directions said to turn onto Lake Sugar Tree Drive. I popped over a hill and noticed a Lake Sugar Tree Lane. I second guessed my handwritten directions. I pulled into a crossover to think about turning around to take Lake Sugar Tree Lane. About a minute later, Steve, who had left in the same direction, noticed me and pulled into that crossover. He asked if I knew where I was going. I told him about my confusion. He said that I still had a couple of miles to go. He had me follow him to Lake Sugar Tree Drive where he planned to put his right turn signal on to mark the road I was looking for. When we made it to Lake Sugar Tree Drive, his signal came on, and I threw my hand in the air as a big thank you. He spotted it in his rear view mirror and waved goodbye. Steve was a hell of a nice guy. I hoped that someday he'd get a coast-to-coast ride in.

Gary Bailey's track at Lake Sugar Tree came as a recommendation from Jed at Crossroads Yamaha yesterday. I had known about it for years but never made the ride south to race there. Jed told me not to ride by it without a look. He said that it was "sweet." That was enough for me. "Sweet" in moto terms usually means that the track has great, tacky soil, perfectly shaped jumps (and lots of them), corners that allow you to lean the bike to the ground, and wide lines good for passing.

Unfortunately, it was not so sweetly off-limits. I was met by a metal gate. Practice wasn't scheduled for that day, and I guessed that no motocross schools were being hosted either. *No worries.* I whipped out the camera for a couple of pictures with the sign; after all, this was sacred motocross ground whether I was standing right on the track or not. Gary's son David reached the penultimate level of motocross in the eighties. For a few years he was champion and unstoppable, until a nasty crash left him paralyzed. Even so, David went on to become a champion in wheelchair triathlons and had been a regular television commentator at professional level motocross races. I loved his undying spirit and respected his accomplishments. Soon after arriving at the Bailey compound, I left for roads that would take me north and a little closer to West Virginia.

The weather was beautiful, the skies were clear, and there were a million old cabins in different states of dilapidation along southern Virginia's twisty rural roads. Like times before, I had to force myself to stop pulling over to take photos. They were great opportunities for halting forward motorcycling momentum. I told my family that I'd be arriving home around four in the afternoon and planned to stick to it.

Southern Virginia's roads reminded me of earlier days on the Blue Ridge Parkway where nearly every bend in the road unwraps another piece of country treasure unique to these mountains. Out West, the landscapes dominate a motorcyclist's senses. Here, the landscapes may be more difficult to take in beyond the tree-lined roads, but that doesn't hinder the motorcycling. Cruising the curves in these eastern mountains provided plenty of stimulation.

As I rode, I thought of the guy I met in St. George, Utah, who told me about his father who said, "Nothing is worth seeing east of Colorado." Now that I was back, I wholeheartedly disagreed with that man's father. We may not have peaks over 10,000 feet here, but boy do we have bucket loads of century-old farms sitting on grassy foothills under perfect Appalachian backdrops. I find that the simplicity of it all works together to create a nearly flawless landscape. Add a trickling stream to the base of those foothills and, oh my, you've found heaven. I found heaven over and over and over in rural Virginia.

A few hours into the ride, I got hungry and had to find a place to grab a bite and disobey Mom's strict orders to not eat anything. She was preparing a feast full of my favorites. I was in the mood for home cooking, anticipating the evening's supper. Just outside of Lynchburg, Virginia, I found Jumbo's Family Restaurant. It was a small eatery of the mom-and-pop variety, a place where the waitresses know the locals by name, and the locals know too much about the other locals.

The atmosphere inside was just right. I grabbed an open stool at the front counter and placed an order. While waiting on the food, a *real* hillbilly from Lewisburg, West Virginia, came over to meet me, or look at me, or perhaps eat me for lunch. This guy was the epitome of a backwoods southern West Virginian. If you ever meet one you'll know it.

He moseyed up to my right side, propped his right forearm on the counter, and leaned hard on it. He stared at me for ten seconds, not blinking, not making a sound. This stare couldn't have been blanker if both of his eyes were made of glass. All the while, his big, blue, blank eyeballs practically rolled circles around the right side of my face. *I hope that's not the way he greets everyone.* I put my drink down and looked back at him. His mouth spit out a series of noises similar to human language. He spoke with a drawl that I couldn't fully decipher. Fifty percent of what he said might as well have been white noise. What I did make out was that he had noticed my West Virginia license plate and that he was from Lewisburg, or "Loosbur," as he pronounced it.

I attempted to keep the encounter rolling to be polite, but the guy wasn't much for talking. He just wanted to scope me out and meet a fellow West Virginian. He hadn't seen one in a while since his big move, or voyage from Loosbur to Lynchburg, 110 miles away. When he said, "Yer frum up north da state," I felt like I was from *WAY* up north, and possibly from another planet; nonetheless, I agreed with him. My fellow state dweller then went back to his table and I received my order. In a bit of a hurry, I wolfed it down and got back on the road.

I was traveling on 29 N. In Charlottesville, Virginia, I stopped at a Kroger grocery store for my last fuel stop of the trip. Being the last one, it was worth a picture and not much more. There's only so much fun to be had at a fuel pump when you don't have a lighter handy.

I continued north on 29 to Madison, Virginia, where I picked up Route 231. It parallels Skyline Drive via the low country to the east. Again, I was engulfed in the perfect rolling hills and farmland of central Virginia. Twenty-two blissful miles passed to Route 522. Now I was getting real close to familiar roads. In fact, familiarity was only twenty-five miles away in Front Royal, Virginia, the little town that unofficially kicked off this whole shebang when Igor and Vivek met me there 132 days ago.

Arriving in Front Royal was odd. While riding through the town and into the country roads north of it, I kept glancing down at the map of Virginia displayed in my tank bag, but there was no need to do that anymore. *I knew where I was going!* That was such an amazing and unexpected moment. It was a moment as powerful as one where you discover that you can fly. For months, I lived by those little folded maps, resting under their clear tank bag protector. They guided me from the Atlantic to the Pacific, through the Florida Keys to the Grand Canyon, through ghost towns and big cities, around Lake Okeechobee and to the Hoover Dam, through the desert, day and night, along the Blue Ridge Parkway and the Pacific Coast Highway. They had done their job near flawlessly. Now I had a solid habit of checking my location every couple of minutes via the maps.

I stopped looking down at the map about ten miles from the West Virginia state line, long after I was back in my stomping grounds. That was also the spot where I noticed my first West Virginia license plate since leaving home. Not one single time did I see another West Virginia plated vehicle while driving on America's roads. Deep down, I wasn't surprised.

Truly back in familiar territory, I was near the town of Berryville, Virginia, and decided to stop and pay a visit to my great-grandparents' headstones at the cemetery where they are resting. The trip taught me to love my family more, and my appreciation for where I'm from grew the entire time (albeit the encounter with the feller at Jumbo's Restaurant didn't help). If not for the decisions made by my great-grandparents years and years ago, I wouldn't have had this awesome opportunity. I told them a silent, "Thank you."

The mileage countdown to the state line entered the single digits. Each mile was familiar, and each mile flew by. Then, there it was, West Virginia, home. On the right, the same green grassy pasture was still growing strong, and on the left, Rainbow Roads, the same bar that Patsy Cline used to frequent, was still standing along Route 340. Right about there was the time when everything I had seen and done felt dreamlike. Sort of like when Dorothy went to Oz and then woke up to realize that she never left Kansas. Had I just traveled that far? Were all of those characters that I met, real? Those exotic landscapes, do they exist? The answer is, of course, yes. Was I happy to be back? The answer to that may be forever ongoing.

No matter what thoughts crossed my mind, they had to take a temporary back seat to the darkening storm clouds lingering in the direction I was heading. They were thick and purple and almost enough to make me turn for the West

Coast. I didn't know if it would start pouring before I arrived at Mom's, but I did know that I didn't feel like throwing the rain gear on, so I put the hammer down and got there quickly.

Seeing my county again felt like seeing it through an outsider's eyes. The land seemed much more rural than I pictured while on the road. I realized that I was no longer used to the area. By far and away, when I left here in October, I knew no other home; I was used to Jefferson County and one could say in tune with the place. Now it almost seemed like another random spot on the trip. My eyes were hunting down things that would make a good picture, things that never caught my eye before.

When I pulled into Mom's driveway, Igor was there with his camera out, ready to capture true-to-life reactions from my folks. Mom darted out the door with tears in her eyes. She shrieked in excited relief, snatched me up and held on for dear life. She had taken my absence hard. Her reaction was a one way trip straight from the heart and enough to make me shed a few tears in my helmet. Like those cliché coffee mugs which boast things like "world's best mom," my mom lives up to the hype and more. I knew this all along and didn't want to put her through that sort of heartache, but by golly there are just some things that one has to do to get sorted out in life.

Brittany hugged me next. She had been there all day waiting for my arrival. When I left in October we were on the outs, but now we were going to give it another go. My stepdad, Tommy, was right there as well. He is a man I respect immensely and to see him again was good. He has been nothing but a positive addition to our family. Soon Shane pulled up. Since Las Vegas was still fresh in our minds, our reunion was fairly neutral, yet full of smiles.

We were ushered inside for a feast. Igor stayed to join us, and Kayla arrived a bit later. Mom, as promised, had everything that I liked to eat, down to dessert. We spent a few hours catching up, telling jokes, and looking at pictures and videos from the trip. Mom mentioned that Monster Energy came through with the swag that they promised to send after they turned down my request for sponsorship. The package included a page full of stickers, two posters, a pin, and a keychain strap. It was nice to see that they were at least sincere.

Being home and around family was refreshing, but in the back of my mind images of long lonely roads and the people I'd met along the way played like a movie. A few hours passed, we said our goodnights to one another, and Brittany and I headed five miles away to my new home in Shepherdstown, West Virginia.

When we pulled up, I recognized the place. It was a red brick apartment building with seven units in it, two-story and long, probably built in the seventies. My first thought was *I don't want to settle here, or settle yet, for that matter. I'm not done yet and I won't give up.*

I walked in. Although it was a tiny apartment, only 20' x 20' with a combined kitchen/living area, bedroom and bathroom, it was much bigger than the back of a motorcycle and more private than a motel room. *This will take some getting used to.* Brittany gave me the grand tour, I grabbed a quick shower, and we rode into town to meet another friend of mine, Jay. He is Igor's cousin. He wanted to see me and celebrate; however, I'm not sure if it was the excitement that the day brought or the long day on the Goose, but I was wiped out. Brittany and I didn't visit long before heading back to the apartment for an early night.

I was in a state that I'd always considered home, in a town that I'd known since childhood, but something didn't feel right. I lay down for sleep thinking about what was next, feeling like I finally was able to be myself for the past four and a half months, and knowing that I didn't want to change that. That lifestyle fit me well.

Miles 17,437

Part 3

That was one hell of a ride. Life was diverse and at its best. I was engaged and interested. Happier people than me would have been hard to find. Never was I so quick to smile or so dang friendly to strangers. I developed family-like ties with folks I'd never met before. Not a soul was expecting me, yet almost everyone welcomed me. It was a powerful time when being alive really meant something. I can think of only one other moment in life as grand as these past four and a half months, but I can't remember what it was like. Hell, none of us can remember that day. It's the day we are born.

Our accounts of day one come from our parents. Their reactions tell us that it was indeed a fine day. Their smiling faces and caring words are bright windows that transport us back to the time when we were new here, when we were our smallest and when life's possibilities were their greatest. I set out to get some of those possibilities back knowing that thirty years had been checked off where I coasted along out of balance. Those years are gone now.

I thought, and more so hoped, that some magic would come from the road in the form of a rigid answer to all of my problems. I've been naive before, and likely will be naive again. One hundred and thirty-two days was certainly long enough to reset, though. Boundaries that I'd built and obeyed through years of plugging away were burnt off. I will move forward more inspired from my time on the road, but what comes next is impossible to know. Predicting the course of life and events that we all have to ricochet off of can not be done successfully. A plan of action and a simple guess is the best we can do.

I want to share a few thoughts on the most fantastic state of being. It's the state of being free. I found it out there. It was powerful. In its unmistakable form, freedom flooded me. The ride allowed me to truly know it by discarding time limits and losing track of the days of the week, to really feel it through the vibration in my palms and fingertips as I opened the throttle and rode through landscapes that I did not know, to taste it in salty Pacific breezes, and to be guided by it through chasing my relentless curiosities.

It was the ultimate blessing—the side effect of a real adventure. It was the purest of feelings. It was raw. It was life where obligations to the world I'd known had been left behind. It was freedom felt on a passionate level. It was liberating. If I wanted to drift off some road in the desert and not see a human for a month based on nothing more than a whim, I could. If I wanted to drink hard for a week straight and not see the light of day for the duration, I could. If I wanted to settle in the Florida Keys for the winter, the option was there. I simply was able to do as I pleased. With this freedom, my heart decided to keep on the move, to keep riding, to keep learning, to keep exploring America—the greatest host for one who's guided by freedom. Of course the pace was high, but freedom masked any difficulty.

Denis Diderot, a French writer and philosopher whose window of life came in the seventeen hundreds, wrote: "Man will never be free until the last king is strangled with the entrails of the last priest." That still holds true and I want to liken that quote to how we remark about The Man. The quote is relevant to my motorcycle trip in that it recognizes the struggle that the common man faces to feel free. It will be an ongoing struggle, but as my ride has shown me, there are ways to escape The Man's grasp, at least for a little while. Throughout the ride, I never felt held back and was never bothered by the reach of The Man's hand. For a few months, I was free of The Man.

No longer was I controlled by debt and unfruitful obligations. Those were replaced by the weather. That was what kept me stalled or moving forward. Those beautiful sunrises and sunsets joined the rain, snow, and wind to reconnect me to the ground. I felt lost in the world—a peaceful observer of her wonder.

Coming in contact with such a positive force has changed me, although not profoundly. It may be impossible to become someone totally new. And if it weren't, doing so would be a tragic waste of the precious time spent before. We all carry a bucket full of time, and each day it gets a little lighter. It's best not to regret how you spent the past.

The idea to take off, and my willingness to do so, played an important part in the ride, yet there's a key element demanding proper recognition for its part—it is money. Without it, an epic motorcycle adventure across America and all of the experiences attached wouldn't have been possible. It was the foundation of my freedom, and to deny that would be like denying that the world is round. To fail to acknowlege money's role in a great adventure is to invent a fairy tale.

You must eat and find shelter while traveling. You must fuel up if your mode of transportation involves an engine. Sometimes your needs will be met in the form of gifts from friendly strangers, but that is not to be relied on soley. Accidents happen and supplies run low. Even without cash or an account full of money, you can still get by on the road through relying on an old skill, a nice piece of gear that's tradable, or a tire repair kit that could be of real value in another's eyes. Whatever you bring to the table, it is a form of currency. If it's valued by someone and tradable, you might as well call it money. It's the key to traveling.

This was my first sniff of an account filled with it. I paid for things without a second thought. I ate well, ate often, and ate what I wanted. I tipped well to share my fortunate circumstances. I had lost my poor-guy virginity. I see now that there's a world that I've trudged through without money and there's a world with it with bonuses like the incomparable feeling of freedom. As I start from the bottom once more, I recognize that a lot is to be owed to the stuff.

My future is uncertain, my assests are low, but still I've grown. I've been given a gift. The gift is a tool. It has no handle and its uses aren't limited to a specific task. Its weight is not measured in metal pounds, but mental grit. Through practice and patience one can become a skilled craftsmen of the trade it is designed for. It can be used to strategically engage in any subject that humans have ever known. It came to me as a direct result of this experience and was forged through freedom—the freedom to explore the country and openly express the journey through writing.

Passion was felt in that freedom. Focus came from the passion. Writing came from being focused. Never had I felt so clear in thought with so little effort. Beautiful days passed as pieces of a puzzle linking together to create a story. Words poured out of me with the greatest of ease. My mind had found writing's endless horizon, and at its aid was plenty of experience living life as a shy observer, one who stops to listen when folks speak and holds value in the de tails when they are discovered.

I look forward to the balance that lies ahead, but I'll never forget the 132 wild and wonderful days when I dared to get more out of life with the help of a motorcycle named the Goose.

73553812R00223

Made in the USA
Columbia, SC
13 July 2017